To those who, seeing the vice and misery that spring from the unequal distribution of wealth and privilege, feel the possibility of a higher social state and would strive for its attainment

San Francisco   March, 1879

progress
and poverty

Henry George

progress
and poverty

*An inquiry
into the cause
of industrial depressions
and of increase of want
with increase of wealth
... The Remedy*

Henry George

ROBERT SCHALKENBACH FOUNDATION

50 East 69th Street, New York

1979

George, Henry, 1839-1897.
  Progress and poverty.

  Includes index.
  1. Economics. 2. Single tax. I. Title.
HB171.G27   1979   330   79-12191
ISBN 0-914016-60-1

Printed in the United States of America by Courier Printing Company
Binding by New Hampshire Bindery
Design by A.L. Morris

To those who, seeing the vice and misery that spring from the unequal distribution of wealth and privilege, feel the possibility of a higher social state and would strive for its attainment

San Francisco, March, 1879.

CONTENTS

Make for thyself a definition or description of the thing which is presented to thee, so as to see distinctly what kind of a thing it is, in its substance, in its nudity, in its complete entirety, and tell thyself its proper name, and the names of the things of which it has been compounded, and into which it will be resolved. For nothing is so productive of elevation of mind as to be able to examine methodically and truly every object which is presented to thee in life, and always to look at things so as to see at the same time what kind of universe this is, and what kind of use everything performs in it, and what value everything has with reference to the whole, and what with reference to man, who is a citizen of the highest city, of which all other cities are like families; what each thing is, and of what it is composed, and how long it is the nature of this thing to endure.

MARCUS AURELIUS ANTONINUS

PREFACE

to the

CENTENARY EDITION / 1979

A HUNDRED YEARS AGO a young unknown printer in San Francisco wrote a book he called PROGRESS AND POVERTY. He wrote after his daily working hours, in the only leisure open to him for writing. He had no real training in political economy. Indeed he had stopped schooling in the seventh grade in his native Philadelphia, and shipped before the mast as a cabin boy, making a complete voyage around the world. Three years later, he was halfway through a second voyage as able seaman when he left the ship in San Francisco and went to work as a journeyman printer. After that he took whatever honest job came to hand. All he knew of economics were the basic rules of Adam Smith, David Ricardo, and other economists, and the new philosophies of Herbert Spencer and John Stuart Mill, much of which he gleaned from reading in public libraries and from his own painstakingly amassed library. Marx was yet to be translated into English.

George was endowed for his job. He was curious and he was alertly attentive to all that went on around him. He had that rarest of all attributes in the scholar and historian — that gift without which all education is useless. He had mother wit. He read what he needed to read, and he understood what he read. What is more, he saw what was before his eyes, exactly, with the clear vision of an artist and the appraisal of a scientist. And he was fortunate. He lived and worked in a rapidly developing society in which his environment changed daily. George had the unique opportunity of studying the formation of a civilization—the change of an encampment into a thriving metropolis. He saw a city of tents and mud change into a fine town of paved streets and decent housing, with tramways and buses. And as he saw the beginning of wealth, he noted the first appearance of pauperism. He saw the coming of the first beggars the West had ever known in its entire history. He saw degradation forming as he saw the advent of leisure and affluence. It was his personal characteristic that he felt compelled to discover why they arose concurrently.

The result of his inquiry, PROGRESS AND POVERTY, is written simply, but so beautifully that it has been compared to the very greatest works of the English language. Indeed, there are pages that cannot be bettered for eloquence, for sparkling imagery, and for sound — that lovely poetic sound of the English language beautifully spoken. He always had this superb gift. His sea-log at fourteen compares with the style of Joseph Conrad.

Because he was totally unknown, no one would print his book. And so he and his friends, also printers, set the type themselves and ran off an author's edition which eventually found its way into the hands of a New York publisher, D. Appleton & Co. An English edition soon followed which aroused enormous interest. Alfred Russel Wallace, the English scientist and writer, pronounced it "the most remarkable and important book of the present century." It was not long before George was known internationally.

During his lifetime, he became the third most famous man in the United States, only surpassed in public acclaim by Thomas Edison and Mark Twain. George was translated into almost every language that knew print, and some of the greatest, most influential thinkers of his time paid tribute. Leo Tolstoy's appreciation stressed the logic of George's exposition: "The chief weapon against the teaching of Henry George was that which is always used against irrefutable and self-evident truths. This method, which is still being applied in relation to George, was that of hushing up . . . . People do not argue with the teaching of George, they simply do not know it. . . ." John Dewey fervently stressed the originality of George's system of ideas, stating that, "Henry George is one of a small number of definitely original social philosophers that the world has produced." In another appreciation Dewey said that "It would require less than the fingers of the two hands to enumerate those who, from Plato down, rank with Henry George among the world's social philosophers." And Bernard Shaw, in a letter to my mother, Anna George, years later wrote, "Your father found me a literary dilettante and militant rationalist in religion, and a barren rascal at that. By turning my mind to economics he made a man of me...."

Inevitably he was reviled as well as idolized. The men who believed in what he advocated called themselves disciples, and they were in fact nothing less: working to the death, proclaiming, advocating, haranguing, and proselytizing the idea, and even, when lacking inspired leadership, becoming fanatically foolish so that the movement which touched greatness began to founder. It was not implemented by blood, as was communism, and so was not forced on people's attention. Shortly after George's death, it dropped out of the political field. Once a badge of honor, the title, "Single Taxer," came into general disuse. Except in Alberta (the richest and most prosperous province of Canada) and in Australia and New Zealand, his plan of social action has been neglected while those of Marx, Keynes, Galbraith and Friedman have won great attention, and Marx's has been given partial implementation, for a time, at least, in large areas of the globe.

But nothing that has been tried satisfies. We, the people, the whole people, are locked in a death grapple and nothing our leaders offer, or are willing to offer, mitigates our troubles. George said, "The people must think because the people alone can act."

We have reached the deplorable circumstance where in large measure a very powerful few are in possession of the earth's resources, the land and its riches and all the franchises and other privileges that yield a return. These monopolistic positions are kept by a handful of men who are maintained virtually without taxation; they are immune to the demands made on others. The very poor, who have nothing, are the object of compulsory charity. And the rest — the workers, the middle-class, the backbone of the country — are made to support the lot by their labor. They are made to pay for the men in possession who are, in effect, their rulers, and for the paupers who are denied the opportunity and dignity of earning their own living. Forcing one group to pay for all amounts to tyranny.

We are taxed at every point of our lives, on everything we earn, on everything we save, on much that we inherit, on much that we buy at every stage of the manufacture and on the final purchase. The taxes are punishing, crippling, demoralizing. Also they are, to a great extent, unnecessary.

It was rage at unjust and proliferating taxation that drove the people of California to revolt. In June, 1978, they voted overwhelmingly to adopt Proposition 13, an amendment to the state constitution which would greatly diminish all taxes on real property — on land, houses, gardens, farms, buildings. This was neither a thoughtful nor a searching reform since the improvements and the site and all natural resources were lumped together, and income and sales tax rates were not separated. Under the so-called reform, the great landholdings remained intact and therefore the great profiteering untouched.

The voters believed that there was too much wastage in government, too much public welfare, and that they could do very well with a great deal less of both. The results so far have not been what was intended. State funds will undoubtedly be commandeered to bail out local treasuries and probably the state funding of schools, universities, libraries, symphony orchestras, museums and archives will be drastically reduced while the bureaucracy and welfare remain relatively untouched. But there has been an amount of serious thinking and if this change does not work the miracles that people hope (and it won't) at least it will cause them to study the problems thoughtfully. The electorate is, at long last, beginning to ask questions. In this sense, the adventure has been of value.

But our system, in which state and federal taxes are interlocked, is deeply intrenched and hard to correct. Moreover, it survives because it is based on bewilderment; it is maintained in a manner so bizarre and intricate that it is impossible for the ordinary citizen to know what he owes his government except with highly paid help. Contrary to basic American law which presupposes innocence until guilt is proven, the government now takes for granted that every American citizen is lying and cheating at every turn and he must pay an advocate to persuade the duly elected authority that he is neither a liar nor cheat. It comes to this: we support a large section of our government (the Internal Revenue Service) to prove that we are breaking our own laws. And we support a large profession (tax lawyers) to protect us from our own employees. College courses are given to explain the tax forms which would otherwise be quite unintelligible.

All this is galling and destructive, but it is still, in a measure, superficial. The great sinister fact, the one that we must live with, is that we are yielding up sovereignty. The nation is no longer comprised of the thirteen original states, nor of the thirty-seven younger sister states, but of the real powers: the cartels, the corporations. Owning the bulk of our productive resources, they are the issue of that concentration of ownership that George saw evolving, and warned against.

These multinationals are not American any more. Transcending nations, they serve not their country's interests, but their own. They manipulate our tax policies to help themselves. They determine our statecraft. They are autonomous. They do not need to coin money or raise armies. They use ours.

And in opposition rise up the great labor unions. It is war. In the meantime, the bureaucracy, both federal and local, supported by the deadly opposing factions, legislate themselves mounting power never originally intended for our government and exert a ubiquitous influence which can be, and often is, corrupt.

I do not wish to be misunderstood as falling into the trap of the socialists and communists who condemn all privately owned business, all factories, all machinery and organizations for producing wealth. There is nothing wrong with private corporations owning the means of producing wealth, with, as the socialists would say, Capitalism. All Georgists believe in private enterprise, and in its virtues and incentives to produce at maximum efficiency. It is the insidious linking together of special privilege, the unjust outright private ownership of natural or public resources, monopolies, franchises, that produce unfair domination and autocracy. The means of producing wealth differ at the root, some is thieved from the people and some is honestly earned. George differentiated; Marx did not. The consequences of our failure to discern lie at the heart of our trouble.

This clown civilization is ours. We have achieved it out of the hopeful agrarian society that flourished in the eighteenth century, out of a new government we had every right to believe was founded on reasonableness, wisdom and justice. We were not compelled to come to this. We knew neither king nor conqueror. We chose this of our own free

will, in our own free democracy, with all the means to
legislate intelligently readily at hand. We chose this because
we insisted on following the worn-out European grooves,
because it suited a few people to have us do so. They
counted on our mental indolence and we freely and obe-
diently conformed. We chose not to think.

Our government, alas, was predicated for its effectiveness
in expansion on free land. Now there is no more free land,
and the flaw in the great plan grows evident. We have
reached the boundaries and we turn back on ourselves and
devour.

Henry George was a lucid voice, direct and bold, that
pointed out basic truths, that cut through the confusion
which developed like rot. Each age has known such diseases
and each age has gone down for lack of understanding. It is
not valid to say that our times are more complex than ages
past and therefore the solution must be more complex. The
problems are, on the whole, the same. The fact that we now
have electricity and computers does not in any way con-
trovert the fact that we can succumb to the injustices that
toppled Rome.

To avert such a calamity, to eliminate involuntary poverty
and unemployment, and to enable each individual to attain
his maximum potential, George wrote this extraordinary
treatise a hundred years ago. His ideas stand: he who makes
should have; he who saves should enjoy; what the community produces belongs to the community for communal uses;
and God's earth, all of it, is the right of the people who
inhabit the earth. In the words of Thomas Jefferson, "The
earth belongs in usufruct to the living."

This is simple and this is unanswerable. The ramifications
may not be simple but they do not alter the fundamental
logic.

There never has been a time in our history when we have
needed so sorely to hear good sense, to learn to define terms
exactly, to draw reasonable conclusions. We needs must, or

perish. As George said, "The truth that I have tried to make clear will not find easy acceptance. If that could be, it would have been accepted long ago. If that could be, it would never have been obscured."

We are on the brink. It is possible to have another Dark Ages. But in George there is a voice of hope.

Agnes George de Mille

New York, January, 1979

Agnes George de Mille is the granddaughter of Henry George. She is famous in her own right as a choreographer and the founder of the Agnes de Mille Heritage Dance Theater, and she is a recipient of the Handel Medallion, New York's highest award for achievement in the arts. She is the author of eight books.

There must be refuge! Men
Perished in winter winds till one smote fire
From flint stones coldly hiding what they held,
The red spark treasured from the kindling sun;
They gorged on flesh like wolves, till one sowed corn,
Which grew a weed, yet makes the life of man;
They mowed and babbled till some tongue struck speech,
And patient fingers framed the lettered sound.
What good gift have my brothers, but it came
From search and strife and loving sacrifice?

—EDWIN ARNOLD

Never yet
Share of Truth was vainly set
In the world's wide fallow;
After hands shall sow the seed,
After hands, from hill and mead,
Reap the harvests yellow.

—WHITTIER

Excerpts from the
INTRODUCTION
to the
TWENTY-FIFTH ANNIVERSARY
EDITION / 1905

T HE MAN WAS HENRY GEORGE and the time was 1869 . . . . (Out of his struggles with powerful press and telegraph monopolies in New York City in which he failed came) a thing that was to grow and grow until it should fill the minds and hearts of multitudes and be as "an army with banners."

For in the intervals of rest from his newspaper struggle in this city the young correspondent had musingly walked the streets. As he walked he was filled with wonder at the manifestations of vast wealth. Here, as nowhere that he had dreamed of, were private fortunes that rivaled the riches of the fabled Monte Cristo. But here, also, side by side with the palaces of the princely rich, was to be seen a poverty and degradation, a want and shame, such as made the young man from the open West sick at heart.

Why in a land so bountifully blest, with enough and more than enough for all, should there be such inequality of conditions? Such heaped wealth interlocked with such deep and debasing want? Why, amid such superabundance, should strong men vainly look for work? Why should women faint with hunger, and little children spend the morning of life in the treadmill of toil?

Was this intended in the order of things? No, he could not believe it. And suddenly there came to him—there in day-

light, in the city street—a burning thought, a call, a vision.
Every nerve quivered. And he made a vow that he would
never rest until he had found the cause of, and if he could,
the remedy for this deepening poverty amid advancing
wealth.

Returning to San Francisco soon after his telegraphic
news failure, and keeping his vow nurtured in his heart,
Henry George perceived that land speculation locked up
vast territories against labor. Everywhere he perceived an
effort to "corner" land; an effort to get it and to hold it, not
for use, but for a "rise." Everywhere he perceived that this
caused all who wished to use it to compete with each other
for it; and he foresaw that as population grew the keener
that competition would become. Those who had a
monopoly of the land would practically own those who had
to use the land.

Filled with these ideas, Henry George in 1871 sat down
and in the course of four months wrote a little book under
title of "Our Land and Land Policy." In that small volume of
forty-eight pages he advocated the destruction of land
monopoly by shifting all taxes from labor and the products
of labor and concentrating them in one tax on the value of
land, regardless of improvements. A thousand copies of this
small book were printed, but the author quickly perceived
that really to command attention, the work would have to
be done more thoroughly.

That more thorough work came something more than six
years later. In August, 1877, the writing of "Progress and
Poverty" was begun. It was the oak that grew out of the
acorn of "Our Land and Land Policy." The larger book
became "an inquiry into industrial depressions and of increase of want with increase of wealth," and pointed out the
remedy.

The book was finished after a year and seven months of
intense labor, and the undergoing of privations that caused
the family to do without a parlor carpet, and which fre-

quently forced the author to pawn his personal effects.

And when the last page was written, in the dead of night, when he was entirely alone, Henry George flung himself upon his knees and wept like a child. He had kept his vow. The rest was in the Master's hands.

Then the manuscript was sent to New York to find a publisher. Some of the publishers there thought it visionary; some, revolutionary. Most of them thought it unsafe, and all thought that it would not sell, or at least sufficiently to repay the outlay. Works on political economy even by men of renown were notoriously not money-makers. What hope then for a work of this nature from an obscure man— unknown, and without prestige of any kind? At length, however, D. Appleton & Co. said they would publish it if the author would bear the main cost, that of making the plates. There was nothing else for it, and so in order that the platemaking should be done under his own direction Henry George had the type set in a friend's printing office in San Francisco, the author of the book setting the first two stickfuls himself.

Before the plates, made from this type, were shipped East, they were put upon a printing press and an "Author's Proof Edition" of five hundred copies was struck off. One of these copies Henry George sent to his venerable father in Philadelphia, eighty-one years old. At the same time the son wrote:

"It is with deep feeling of gratitude to Our Father in Heaven that I send you a printed copy of this book. I am grateful that I have been enabled to live to write it, and that you have been enabled to live to see it. It represents a great deal of work and a good deal of sacrifice, but now it is done. It will not be recognized at first—maybe not for some time—but it will ultimately be considered a great book, will be published in both hemispheres, and be translated into different languages. This I know, though neither of us may ever see it here. But the belief that I have expressed in this book—the belief that there is yet another life for us—makes that of little moment."

The prophecy of recognition of the book's greatness was fulfilled very quickly. The Appletons in New York brought out the first regular market edition in January, 1880, just twenty-five years ago. Certain of the San Francisco newspapers derided book and author as the "hobby" of "little Harry George," and predicted that the work would never be heard of. But the press elsewhere in the country and abroad, from the old "Thunderer" in London down, and the great periodical publications, headed by the "Edinburgh Review," hailed it as a remarkable book that could not be lightly brushed aside. In the United States and England it was put into cheap paper editions, and in that form outsold the most popular novels of the day. In both countries, too, it ran serially in the columns of newspapers. Into all the chief tongues of Europe it was translated, there being three translations into German. Probably no exact statement of the book's extent of publication can be made; but a conservative estimate is that, embracing all forms and languages, more than two million copies of "Progress and Poverty" have been printed to date; and that including with these the other books that have followed from Henry George's pen, and which might be called "The Progress and Poverty Literature," perhaps five million copies have been given to the world.

Henry George, Jr.

New York, January 24, 1905.

PREFACE
to the
FOURTH EDITION / 1880

THE VIEWS HEREIN SET FORTH were in the main briefly stated in a pamphlet entitled "Our Land and Land Policy," published in San Francisco in 1871. I then intended, as soon as I could, to present them more fully, but the opportunity did not for a long time occur. In the meanwhile I became even more firmly convinced of their truth, and saw more completely and clearly their relations; and I also saw how many false ideas and erroneous habits of thought stood in the way of their recognition, and how necessary it was to go over the whole ground.

This I have here tried to do, as thoroughly as space would permit. It has been necessary for me to clear away before I could build up, and to write at once for those who have made no previous study of such subjects, and for those who are familiar with economic reasonings; and, so great is the scope of the argument that it has been impossible to treat with the fullness they deserve many of the questions raised. What I have most endeavored to do is to establish general principles, trusting to my readers to carry further their applications where this is needed.

In certain respects this book will be best appreciated by those who have some knowledge of economic literature; but no previous reading is necessary to the understanding of the argument or the passing of judgment upon its conclusions. The facts upon which I have relied are not facts which can be verified only by a search through libraries. They are facts of common observation and common knowledge, which every reader can verify for himself, just as he can decide whether the reasoning from them is or is not valid.

Beginning with a brief statement of facts which suggest this inquiry, I proceed to examine the explanation currently given in the name of political economy of the reason why, in spite of the increase of productive power, wages tend to the minimum of a bare living. This examination shows that the current doctrine of wages is founded upon a misconception; that, in truth, wages are produced by the labor for which they are paid, and should, other things being equal, increase with the number of laborers. Here the inquiry meets a doctrine which is the foundation and center of most important economic theories, and which has powerfully influenced thought in all directions—the Malthusian doctrine, that population tends to increase faster than subsistence. Examination, however, shows that this doctrine has no real support either in fact or in analogy, and that when brought to a decisive test it is utterly disproved.

Thus far the results of the inquiry, though extremely important, are mainly negative. They show that current theories do not satisfactorily explain the connection of poverty with material progress, but throw no light upon the problem itself, beyond showing that its solution must be sought in the laws which govern the distribution of wealth. It therefore becomes necessary to carry the inquiry into this field. A preliminary review shows that the three laws of distribution must necessarily correlate with each other, which as laid down by the current political economy they fail to do, and an examination of the terminology in use reveals the confusion of thought by which this discrepancy has been slurred over. Proceeding then to work out the laws of distribution, I first take up the law of rent. This, it is readily seen, is correctly apprehended by the current political economy. But it is also seen that the full scope of this law has not been appreciated, and that it involves as corollaries the laws of wages and interest—the cause which determines what part of the produce shall go to the landowner necessarily determining what part shall be left for labor and capital. Without resting here, I proceed to an independent deduction of the laws of interest and wages. I have stopped to determine the real cause and justification of interest, and to point out a source of much misconception—the confounding of what are really the profits of monopoly with the legitimate earnings of capital. Then returning to the main inquiry, investigation shows that interest must rise and fall with wages, and depends ultimately upon the same thing as rent—the margin of cultivation or point in production where rent begins. A similar but independent investigation of the law of wages yields similar harmonious results. Thus the three laws of distribution are brought into mutual support and harmony, and the fact that with material progress rent everywhere advances is seen to explain the fact that wages and interest do not advance.

What causes this advance of rent is the next question that arises, and it necessitates an examination of the effect of material progress upon the distribution of wealth. Separating the factors of material progress into increase of population and improvements in the arts, it is first seen that increase in population tends constantly, not merely by reducing the margin of cultivation, but by localizing the economies and powers which come with increased population, to increase the proportion of the aggregate produce which is taken in rent, and to reduce that which goes as wages and interest. Then eliminating increase of population, it is seen that improvement in the methods and powers of production tends in the same direction, and, land being held as private property, would produce in a stationary population all the effects attributed by the Malthusian doc-

trine to pressure of population. And then a consideration of
the effects of the continuous increase in land values which
thus spring from material progress reveals in the speculative advance inevitably begotten when land is private property a derivative but most powerful cause of the increase of
rent and the crowding down of wages. Deduction shows that
this cause must necessarily produce periodical industrial
depressions, and induction proves the conclusion; while
from the analysis which has thus been made it is seen that
the necessary result of material progress, land being private
property, is, no matter what the increase in population, to
force laborers to wages which give but a bare living.

This identification of the cause that associates poverty
with progress points to the remedy, but it is to so radical a
remedy that I have next deemed it necessary to inquire
whether there is any other remedy. Beginning the investigation again from another starting point, I have passed in
examination the measures and tendencies currently advocated or trusted in for the improvement of the condition of
the laboring masses. The result of this investigation is to
prove the preceding one, as it shows that nothing short of
making land common property can permanently relieve
poverty and check the tendency of wages to the starvation
point.

The question of justice now naturally arises, and the inquiry passes into the field of ethics. An investigation of the
nature and basis of property shows that there is a fundamental and irreconcilable difference between property in
things which are the product of labor and property in land;
that the one has a natural basis and sanction while the other
has none, and that the recognition of exclusive property in
land is necessarily a denial of the right of property in the
products of labor. Further investigation shows that private
property in land always has, and always must, as development proceeds, lead to the enslavement of the laboring
class; that landowners can make no just claim to compensa-

tion if society choose to resume its right; that so far from
private property in land being in accordance with the
natural perceptions of men the very reverse is true, and that
in the United States we are already beginning to feel the
effects of having admitted this erroneous and destructive
principle.

The inquiry then passes to the field of practical statesmanship. It is seen that private property in land, instead of
being necessary to its improvement and use, stands in the
way of improvement and use, and entails an enormous
waste of productive forces; that the recognition of the common right to land involves no shock or dispossession, but is
to be reached by the simple and easy method of abolishing
all taxation save that upon land values. And this an inquiry
into the principles of taxation shows to be, in all respects, the
best subject of taxation.

A consideration of the effects of the change proposed
then shows that it would enormously increase production;
would secure justice in distribution; would benefit all classes; and would make possible an advance to a higher and
nobler civilization.

The inquiry now rises to a wider field, and recommences
from another starting point. For not only do the hopes
which have been raised come into collision with the widespread idea that social progress is possible only by slow race
improvement, but the conclusions we have arrived at assert
certain laws which, if they are really natural laws, must be
manifest in universal history. As a final test, it therefore
becomes necessary to work out the law of human progress,
for certain great facts which force themselves on our attention, as soon as we begin to consider this subject, seem
utterly inconsistent with what is now the current theory.
This inquiry shows that differences in civilization are not
due to differences in individuals, but rather to differences
in social organization; that progress, always kindled by association, always passes into retrogression as inequality is

developed; and that even now, in modern civilization, the causes which have destroyed all previous civilizations are beginning to manifest themselves, and that mere political democracy is running its course toward anarchy and despotism. But it also identifies the law of social life with the great moral law of justice, and, proving previous conclusions, shows how retrogression may be prevented and a grander advance begun. This ends the inquiry. The final chapter will explain itself.

The great importance of this inquiry will be obvious. If it has been carefully and logically pursued, its conclusions completely change the character of political economy, give it the coherence and certitude of a true science, and bring it into full sympathy with the aspirations of the masses of men, from which it has long been estranged. What I have done in this book, if I have correctly solved the great problem I have sought to investigate, is to unite the truth perceived by the school of Smith and Ricardo to the truth perceived by the schools of Proudhon and Lassalle; to show that *laissez faire* (in its full true meaning) opens the way to a realization of the noble dreams of socialism; to identify social law with moral law, and to disprove ideas which in the minds of many cloud grand and elevating perceptions.

This work was written between August, 1877, and March, 1879, and the plates finished by September of that year. Since that time new illustrations have been given of the correctness of the views herein advanced, and the march of events—and especially that great movement which has begun in Great Britain in the Irish land agitation—shows still more clearly the pressing nature of the problem I have endeavored to solve. But there has been nothing in the criticisms they have received to induce the change or modification of these views—in fact, I have yet to see an objection not answered in advance in the book itself. And except that some verbal errors have been corrected and a preface added, this edition is the same as previous ones.

Henry George.

New York, November, 1880.

progress
and poverty

INTRODUCTORY *THE*
PROBLEM

Ye build! ye build! but ye enter not in,
Like the tribes whom the desert devoured in their sin;
From the land of promise ye fade and die,
Ere its verdure gleams forth on your wearied eye.

MRS. SIGOURNEY

THE
INTRODUCTORY *PROBLEM*

The present century has been marked by a prodigious increase in wealth-producing power. The utilization of steam and electricity, the introduction of improved processes and laborsaving machinery, the greater subdivision and grander scale of production, the wonderful facilitation of exchanges, have multiplied enormously the effectiveness of labor.

At the beginning of this marvelous era it was natural to expect, and it was expected, that laborsaving inventions would lighten the toil and improve the condition of the laborer; that the enormous increase in the power of producing wealth would make real poverty a thing of the past. Could a man of the last century—a Franklin or a Priestley—have seen, in a vision of the future, the steamship taking the place of the sailing vessel, the railroad train of the wagon, the reaping machine of the scythe, the threshing machine of the flail; could he have heard the throb of the engines that in obedience to human will, and for the satisfaction of human desire, exert a power greater than that of all the men and all the beasts of burden of the earth combined; could he have seen the forest tree transformed into finished lumber—into doors, sashes, blinds, boxes or barrels, with hardly the touch of a human hand; the great workshops where boots and shoes are turned out by the case with less labor than the old-fashioned cobbler

3

could have put on a sole; the factories where, under the eye
of a girl, cotton becomes cloth faster than hundreds of stal-
wart weavers could have turned it out with their hand looms;
could he have seen steam hammers shaping mammoth shafts
and mighty anchors, and delicate machinery making tiny
watches; the diamond drill cutting through the heart of the
rocks, and coal oil sparing the whale; could he have realized
the enormous saving of labor resulting from improved facilities of exchange and communication—sheep killed in Australia eaten fresh in England, and the order given by the
London banker in the afternoon executed in San Francisco
in the morning of the same day; could he have conceived of
the hundred thousand improvements which these only suggest, what would he have inferred as to the social condition
of mankind?

It would not have seemed like an inference; further than
the vision went it would have seemed as though he saw; and
his heart would have leaped and his nerves would have
thrilled, as one who from a height beholds just ahead of the
thirst-stricken caravan the living gleam of rustling woods and
the glint of laughing waters. Plainly, in the sight of the imagination, he would have beheld these new forces elevating
society from its very foundations, lifting the very poorest
above the possibility of want, exempting the very lowest from
anxiety for the material needs of life; he would have seen
these slaves of the lamp of knowledge taking on themselves
the traditional curse, these muscles of iron and sinews of
steel making the poorest laborer's life a holiday, in which
every high quality and noble impulse could have scope to
grow.

And out of these bounteous material conditions he would
have seen arising, as necessary sequences, moral conditions
realizing the golden age of which mankind have always

dreamed. Youth no longer stunted and starved; age no longer harried by avarice; the child at play with the tiger; the man with the muck rake drinking in the glory of the stars. Foul things fled, fierce things tame; discord turned to harmony! For how could there be greed where all had enough? How could the vice, the crime, the ignorance, the brutality, that spring from poverty and the fear of poverty, exist where poverty had vanished? Who should crouch where all were freemen; who oppress where all were peers?

More or less vague or clear, these have been the hopes, these the dreams born of the improvements which give this wonderful century its preëminence. They have sunk so deeply into the popular mind as radically to change the currents of thought, to recast creeds and displace the most fundamental conceptions. The haunting visions of higher possibilities have not merely gathered splendor and vividness, but their direction has changed—instead of seeing behind the faint tinges of an expiring sunset, all the glory of the daybreak has decked the skies before.

It is true that disappointment has followed disappointment, and that discovery upon discovery, and invention after invention, have neither lessened the toil of those who most need respite, nor brought plenty to the poor. But there have been so many things to which it seemed this failure could be laid, that up to our time the new faith has hardly weakened. We have better appreciated the difficulties to be overcome; but not the less trusted that the tendency of the times was to overcome them.

Now, however, we are coming into collision with facts which there can be no mistaking. From all parts of the civilized world come complaints of industrial depression; of labor condemned to involuntary idleness; of capital massed and wasting; of pecuniary distress among businessmen; of want and suffering and anxiety among the working classes. All the dull, deadening pain, all the keen, maddening anguish, that to great masses of men are involved in the words "hard times," afflict the world today. This state of things, common to communities differing so widely in situation, in political institutions, in fiscal and financial systems, in density of population and in social organization, can hardly be accounted for by local causes. There is distress where large standing armies are maintained, but there is also distress where the standing armies are nominal; there is distress where protective tariffs stupidly and wastefully hamper trade, but there is also distress where trade is nearly free; there is distress where autocratic government yet prevails, but there is also distress where political power is wholly in the hands of the people; in countries where paper is money, and in countries where gold and silver are the only currency. Evidently, beneath all such things as these, we must infer a common cause.

That there is a common cause, and that it is either what we call material progress or something closely connected with material progress, becomes more than an inference when it is noted that the phenomena we class together and speak of as industrial depression are but intensifications of phenomena which always accompany material progress, and which show themselves more clearly and strongly as material progress goes on. Where the conditions to which material progress everywhere tends are most fully realized—that is to say, where population is densest, wealth greatest, and the machinery of production and exchange most highly developed—we find the deepest poverty, the sharpest struggle for existence, and the most of enforced idleness.

It is to the newer countries—that is, to the countries where material progress is yet in its earlier stages—that laborers emigrate in search of higher wages, and capital flows in search of higher interest. It is in the older countries—that is to say, the countries where material progress has reached later stages —that widespread destitution is found in the midst of the greatest abundance. Go into one of the new communities where Anglo-Saxon vigor is just beginning the race of progress; where the machinery of production and exchange is yet rude and inefficient; where the increment of wealth is not yet great enough to enable any class to live in ease and luxury; where the best house is but a cabin of logs or a cloth and paper shanty, and the richest man is forced to daily work— and though you will find an absence of wealth and all its concomitants, you will find no beggars. There is no luxury, but there is no destitution. No one makes an easy living, nor a very good living; but every one can make a living, and no one able and willing to work is oppressed by the fear of want.

But just as such a community realizes the conditions which all civilized communities are striving for, and advances in the scale of material progress—just as closer settlement and a more intimate connection with the rest of the world, and greater utilization of laborsaving machinery, make possible greater economies in production and exchange, and wealth in consequence increases, not merely in the aggregate, but in proportion to population—so does poverty take a darker aspect. Some get an infinitely better and easier living, but others find it hard to get a living at all. The "tramp" comes with the locomotive, and almshouses and prisons are as surely the marks of "material progress" as are costly dwellings, rich warehouses, and magnificent churches. Upon streets lighted with gas and patrolled by uniformed policemen, beggars wait for the passer-by, and in the shadow of college, and library, and museum, are gathering the more hideous Huns and fiercer Vandals of whom Macaulay prophesied.

This fact—the great fact that poverty and all its concomitants show themselves in communities just as they develop into the conditions toward which material progress tends— proves that the social difficulties existing wherever a certain stage of progress has been reached, do not arise from local circumstances, but are, in some way or another, engendered by progress itself.

And, unpleasant as it may be to admit it, it is at last becoming evident that the enormous increase in productive power which has marked the present century and is still going on with accelerating ratio, has no tendency to extirpate poverty or to lighten the burdens of those compelled to toil. It simply widens the gulf between Dives and Lazarus, and makes the struggle for existence more intense. The march of invention has clothed mankind with powers of which a century ago the boldest imagination could not have dreamed. But in factories where laborsaving machinery has reached its most wonderful development, little children are at work; wherever the new forces are anything like fully utilized, large classes are maintained by charity or live on the verge of recourse to it; amid the greatest accumulations of wealth, men die of starvation, and puny infants suckle dry breasts; while everywhere the greed of gain, the worship of wealth, shows the force of the fear of want. The promised land flies before us like the mirage. The fruits of the tree of knowledge turn as we grasp them to apples of Sodom that crumble at the touch.

It is true that wealth has been greatly increased, and that the average of comfort, leisure, and refinement has been raised; but these gains are not general. In them the lowest class do not share.* I do not mean that the condition of the

---

* It is true that the poorest may now in certain ways enjoy what the richest a century ago could not have commanded, but this does not show improvement of condition so long as the ability to obtain the necessaries of life is not increased. The beggar in a great city may enjoy many things

lowest class has nowhere nor in anything been improved; but that there is nowhere any improvement which can be credited to increased productive power. I mean that the tendency of what we call material progress is in nowise to improve the condition of the lowest class in the essentials of healthy, happy human life. Nay, more, that it is still further to depress the condition of the lowest class. The new forces, elevating in their nature though they be, do not act upon the social fabric from underneath, as was for a long time hoped and believed, but strike it at a point intermediate between top and bottom. It is as though an immense wedge were being forced, not underneath society, but through society. Those who are above the point of separation are elevated, but those who are below are crushed down.

This depressing effect is not generally realized, for it is not apparent where there has long existed a class just able to live. Where the lowest class barely lives, as has been the case for a long time in many parts of Europe, it is impossible for it to get any lower, for the next lowest step is out of existence, and no tendency to further depression can readily show itself. But in the progress of new settlements to the conditions of older communities it may clearly be seen that material progress does not merely fail to relieve poverty—it actually produces it. In the United States it is clear that squalor and misery, and the vices and crimes that spring from them, everywhere increase as the village grows to the city, and the march of development brings the advantages of the improved methods of production and exchange. It is in the older and richer sections of the Union that pauperism and distress among the working classes are becoming most painfully apparent. If there is less deep poverty in San Francisco

from which the backwoods farmer is debarred, but that does not prove the condition of the city beggar better than that of the independent farmer.

than in New York, is it not because San Francisco is yet behind New York in all that both cities are striving for? When San Francisco reaches the point where New York now is, who can doubt that there will also be ragged and barefooted children on her streets?

This association of poverty with progress is the great enigma of our times. It is the central fact from which spring industrial, social, and political difficulties that perplex the world, and with which statesmanship and philanthropy and education grapple in vain. From it come the clouds that overhang the future of the most progressive and self-reliant nations. It is the riddle which the Sphinx of Fate puts to our civilization and which not to answer is to be destroyed. So long as all the increased wealth which modern progress brings goes but to build up great fortunes, to increase luxury and make sharper the contrast between the House of Have and the House of Want, progress is not real and cannot be permanent. The reaction must come. The tower leans from its foundations, and every new story but hastens the final catastrophe. To educate men who must be condemned to poverty, is but to make them restive; to base on a state of most glaring social inequality political institutions under which men are theoretically equal, is to stand a pyramid on its apex.

All-important as this question is, pressing itself from every quarter painfully upon attention, it has not yet received a solution which accounts for all the facts and points to any clear and simple remedy. This is shown by the widely varying attempts to account for the prevailing depression. They exhibit not merely a divergence between vulgar notions and scientific theories, but also show that the concurrence which should exist between those who avow the same general theories breaks up upon practical questions into an anarchy of opinion. Upon high economic authority we have been told that the prevailing depression is due to overconsumption; upon equally high authority, that it is due to overproduction; while the wastes of war, the extension of railroads, the attempts of workmen to keep up wages, the demonetization of silver, the issues of paper money, the increase of laborsaving machinery, the opening of shorter avenues to trade, etc., are separately pointed out as the cause, by writers of reputation.

And while professors thus disagree, the ideas that there is a necessary conflict between capital and labor, that machinery is an evil, that competition must be restrained and interest abolished, that wealth may be created by the issue of money, that it is the duty of government to furnish capital or to furnish work, are rapidly making way among the great body of the people, who keenly feel a hurt and are sharply conscious of a wrong. Such ideas, which bring great masses of men, the repositories of ultimate political power, under the leadership of charlatans and demagogues, are fraught with danger; but they cannot be successfully combated until political economy shall give some answer to the great question which shall be consistent with all her teachings, and which shall commend itself to the perceptions of the great masses of men.

It must be within the province of political economy to give such an answer. For political economy is not a set of dogmas. It is the explanation of a certain set of facts. It is the science which, in the sequence of certain phenomena, seeks to trace mutual relations and to identify cause and effect, just as the physical sciences seek to do in other sets of phenomena. It lays its foundations upon firm ground. The premises from which it makes its deductions are truths which have the highest sanction; axioms which we all recognize; upon which we safely base the reasoning and actions of everyday life, and which may be reduced to the metaphysical ex-

pression of the physical law that motion seeks the line of
least resistance—viz., that men seek to gratify their desires
with the least exertion. Proceeding from a basis thus assured,
its processes, which consist simply in identification and separation, have the same certainty. In this sense it is as exact a
science as geometry, which, from similar truths relative to
space, obtains its conclusions by similar means, and its conclusions when valid should be as self-apparent. And although
in the domain of political economy we cannot test our theories by artificially produced combinations or conditions, as
may be done in some of the other sciences, yet we can apply
tests no less conclusive, by comparing societies in which
different conditions exist, or by, in imagination, separating,
combining, adding or eliminating forces or factors of known
direction.

I propose in the following pages to attempt to solve by the
methods of political economy the great problem I have outlined. I propose to seek the law which associates poverty with
progress, and increases want with advancing wealth; and I
believe that in the explanation of this paradox we shall find
the explanation of those recurring seasons of industrial and
commercial paralysis which, viewed independently of their
relations to more general phenomena, seem so inexplicable.
Properly commenced and carefully pursued, such an investigation must yield a conclusion that will stand every test, and
as truth, will correlate with all other truth. For in the sequence of phenomena there is no accident. Every effect has
a cause, and every fact implies a preceding fact.

That political economy, as at present taught, does not explain the persistence of poverty amid advancing wealth in a
manner which accords with the deep-seated perceptions of
men; that the unquestionable truths which it does teach are
unrelated and disjointed; that it has failed to make the prog-

ress in popular thought that truth, even when unpleasant, must make; that, on the contrary, after a century of cultivation, during which it has engrossed the attention of some of the most subtle and powerful intellects, it should be spurned by the statesman, scouted by the masses, and relegated in the opinion of many educated and thinking men to the rank of a pseudo science in which nothing is fixed or can be fixed—must, it seems to me, be due not to any inability of the science when properly pursued, but to some false step in its premises, or overlooked factor in its estimates. And as such mistakes are generally concealed by the respect paid to authority, I propose in this inquiry to take nothing for granted, but to bring even accepted theories to the test of first principles, and should they not stand the test, freshly to interrogate facts in the endeavor to discover their law.

I propose to beg no question, to shrink from no conclusion, but to follow truth wherever it may lead. Upon us is the responsibility of seeking the law, for in the very heart of our civilization today women faint and little children moan. But what that law may prove to be is not our affair. If the conclusions that we reach run counter to our prejudices, let us not flinch; if they challenge institutions that have long been deemed wise and natural, let us not turn back.

He that is to follow philosophy must be a freeman in mind.—*Ptolemy.*

CHAPTER 1

THE CURRENT DOCTRINE OF WAGES— ITS INSUFFICIENCY

Reducing to its most compact form the problem we have set out to investigate, let us examine, step by step, the explanation which political economy, as now accepted by the best authority, gives of it.

The cause which produces poverty in the midst of advancing wealth is evidently the cause which exhibits itself in the tendency, everywhere recognized, of wages to a minimum. Let us, therefore, put our inquiry into this compact form:

Why, in spite of increase in productive power, do wages tend to a minimum which will give but a bare living?

The answer of the current political economy is, that wages are fixed by the ratio between the number of laborers and the amount of capital devoted to the employment of labor, and constantly tend to the lowest amount on which laborers will consent to live and reproduce, because the increase in the number of laborers tends naturally to follow and overtake any increase in capital. The increase of the divisor being thus held in check only by the possibilities of the quotient, the dividend may be increased to infinity without greater result.

In current thought this doctrine holds all but undisputed sway. It bears the indorsement of the very highest names among the cultivators of political economy, and though there have been attacks upon it, they are generally more formal than real.* It is assumed by Buckle as the basis of his generalizations of universal history. It is taught in all, or nearly all, the great English and American universities, and is laid down in textbooks which aim at leading the masses to reason correctly upon practical affairs, while it seems to harmonize with the new philosophy, which, having in a few years all but conquered the scientific world, is now rapidly permeating the general mind.

Thus entrenched in the upper regions of thought, it is in cruder form even more firmly rooted in what may be styled the lower. What gives to the fallacies of protection such a tenacious hold, in spite of their evident inconsistencies and absurdities, is the idea that the sum to be distributed in wages is in each community a fixed one, which the competition of "foreign labor" must still further subdivide. The same idea underlies most of the theories which aim at the abolition of interest and the restriction of competition, as the means whereby the share of the laborer in the general wealth can be increased; and it crops out in every direction among those who are not thoughtful enough to have any theories, as may be seen in the columns of newspapers and the debates of legislative bodies.

---

* This seems to me true of Mr. Thornton's objections, for while he denies the existence of a predetermined wage fund, consisting of a portion of capital set apart for the purchase of labor, he yet holds (which is the essential thing) that wages are drawn from capital, and that increase or decrease of capital is increase or decrease of the fund available for the payment of wages. The most vital attack upon the wage fund doctrine of which I know is that of Professor Francis A. Walker ("The Wages Question": New York, 1876), yet he admits that wages are in large part advanced from capital—which, so far as it goes, is all that the stanchest supporter of the wage fund theory could claim— while he fully accepts the Malthusian theory. Thus his practical conclusions in nowise differ from those reached by expounders of the current theory.

And yet, widely accepted and deeply rooted as it is, it seems to me that this theory does not tally with obvious facts. For, if wages depend upon the ratio between the amount of labor seeking employment and the amount of capital devoted to its employment, the relative scarcity or abundance of one factor must mean the relative abundance or scarcity of the other. Thus, capital must be relatively abundant where wages are high, and relatively scarce where wages are low. Now, as the capital used in paying wages must largely consist of the capital constantly seeking investment, the current rate of interest must be the measure of its relative abundance or scarcity. So, if it be true that wages depend upon the ratio between the amount of labor seeking employment and the capital devoted to its employment, then high wages, the mark of the relative scarcity of labor, must be accompanied by low interest, the mark of the relative abundance of capital, and reversely, low wages must be accompanied by high interest.

This is not the fact, but the contrary. Eliminating from interest the element of insurance, and regarding only interest proper, or the return for the use of capital, is it not a general truth that interest is high where and when wages are high, and low where and when wages are low? Both wages and interest have been higher in the United States than in England, in the Pacific than in the Atlantic States. Is it not a notorious fact that where labor flows for higher wages, capital also flows for higher interest? Is it not true that wherever there has been a general rise or fall in wages there has been at the same time a similar rise or fall in interest? In California, for instance, when wages were higher than anywhere else in the world, so also was interest higher. Wages and interest have in California gone down together. When common wages were $5 a day,

the ordinary bank rate of interest was twenty-four per
cent. per annum. Now that common wages are $2 or
$2.50 a day, the ordinary bank rate is from ten to
twelve per cent.

Now, this broad, general fact, that wages are higher
in new countries, where capital is relatively scarce,
than in old countries, where capital is relatively abundant, is too glaring to be ignored. And although very
lightly touched upon, it is noticed by the expounders
of the current political economy. The manner in which
it is noticed proves what I say, that it is utterly inconsistent with the accepted theory of wages. For in explaining it such writers as Mill, Fawcett, and Price
virtually give up the theory of wages upon which, in
the same treatises, they formally insist. Though they
declare that wages are fixed by the ratio between capital
and laborers, they explain the higher wages and interest
of new countries by the greater relative production of
wealth. I shall hereafter show that this is not the fact,
but that, on the contrary, the production of wealth is
relatively larger in old and densely populated countries
than in new and sparsely populated countries. But at
present I merely wish to point out the inconsistency.
For to say that the higher wages of new countries are
due to greater proportionate production, is clearly to
make the ratio with production, and not the ratio with
capital, the determinator of wages.

Though this inconsistency does not seem to have been
perceived by the class of writers to whom I refer, it has
been noticed by one of the most logical of the expounders of the current political economy. Professor Cairnes*
endeavors in a very ingenious way to reconcile the fact
with the theory, by assuming that in new countries,

---

* "Some Leading Principles of Political Economy Newly Expounded,"
Chap. 1, Part 2.

where industry is generally directed to the production of food and what in manufactures is called raw material, a much larger proportion of the capital used in production is devoted to the payment of wages than in older countries where a greater part must be expended in machinery and material, and thus, in the new country, though capital is scarcer, and interest is higher, the amount determined to the payment of wages is really larger, and wages are also higher. For instance, of $100,000 devoted in an old country to manufactures, $80,000 would probably be expended for buildings, machinery and the purchase of materials, leaving but $20,000 to be paid out in wages; whereas in a new country, of $30,000 devoted to agriculture, etc., not more than $5,000 would be required for tools, etc., leaving $25,000 to be distributed in wages. In this way it is explained that the wage fund may be comparatively large where capital is comparatively scarce, and high wages and high interest accompany each other.

In what follows I think I shall be able to show that this explanation is based upon a total misapprehension of the relations of labor to capital—a fundamental error as to the fund from which wages are drawn; but at present it is necessary only to point out that the connection in the fluctuation of wages and interest in the same countries and in the same branches of industry cannot thus be explained. In those alternations known as "good times" and "hard times" a brisk demand for labor and good wages is always accompanied by a brisk demand for capital and stiff rates of interest. While, when laborers cannot find employment and wages droop, there is always an accumulation of capital seeking investment at low rates.* The present depression has been no less

* Times of commercial panic are marked by high rates of discount, but this is evidently not a high rate of interest, properly so called, but a high rate of insurance against risk.

marked by want of employment and distress among
the working classes than by the accumulation of unemployed capital in all the great centers, and by nominal rates of interest on undoubted security. Thus,
under conditions which admit of no explanation consistent with the current theory, do we find high interest
coinciding with high wages, and low interest with low
wages—capital seemingly scarce when labor is scarce,
and abundant when labor is abundant.

All these well known facts, which coincide with each
other, point to a relation between wages and interest,
but it is to a relation of conjunction, not of opposition.
Evidently they are utterly inconsistent with the theory
that wages are determined by the ratio between labor
and capital, or any part of capital.

How, then, it will be asked, could such a theory arise?
How is it that it has been accepted by a succession of
economists, from the time of Adam Smith to the present
day?

If we examine the reasoning by which in current
treatises this theory of wages is supported, we see at
once that it is not an induction from observed facts,
but a deduction from a previously assumed theory—
viz., that wages are drawn from capital. It being
assumed that capital is the source of wages, it necessarily follows that the gross amount of wages must be
limited by the amount of capital devoted to the employment of labor, and hence that the amount individual
laborers can receive must be determined by the ratio
between their number and the amount of capital existing for their recompense.* This reasoning is valid, but

---

* For instance McCulloch (Note VI to "Wealth of Nations") says:
"That portion of the capital or wealth of a country which the employers
of labor intend to or are willing to pay out in the purchase of labor,
may be much larger at one time than another. But whatever may be
its absolute magnitude, it obviously forms the only source from which

the conclusion, as we have seen, does not correspond with the facts. The fault, therefore, must be in the premises. Let us see.

I am aware that the theorem that wages are drawn from capital is one of the most fundamental and apparently best settled of current political economy, and that it has been accepted as axiomatic by all the great thinkers who have devoted their powers to the elucidation of the science. Nevertheless, I think it can be demonstrated to be a fundamental error—the fruitful parent of a long series of errors, which vitiate most important practical conclusions. This demonstration I am about to attempt. It is necessary that it should be clear and conclusive, for a doctrine upon which so much important reasoning is based, which is supported by such a weight of authority, which is so plausible in itself, and is so liable to recur in different forms, cannot be safely brushed aside in a paragraph.

The proposition I shall endeavor to prove, is:

*That wages, instead of being drawn from capital, are in reality drawn from the product of the labor for which they are paid.**

Now, inasmuch as the current theory that wages are

any portion of the wages of labor can be derived. No other fund is in existence from which the laborer, as such, can draw a single shilling. And hence *it follows* that the average rate of wages, or the share of the national capital appropriated to the employment of labor falling, at an average, to each laborer, must entirely depend on its amount as compared with the number of those amongst whom it has to be divided." Similar citations might be made from all the standard economists.

* We are speaking of labor expended in production, to which it is best for the sake of simplicity to confine the inquiry. Any question which may arise in the reader's mind as to wages for unproductive services had best therefore be deferred.

drawn from capital also holds that capital is reimbursed
from production, this at first glance may seem a distinction without a difference—a mere change in terminology,
to discuss which would be but to add to those unprofitable disputes that render so much that has been written
upon politico-economic subjects as barren and worthless
as the controversies of the various learned societies
about the true reading of the inscription on the stone
that Mr. Pickwick found. But that it is much more
than a formal distinction will be apparent when it is
considered that upon the difference between the two
propositions are built up all the current theories as
to the relations of capital and labor; that from it are
deduced doctrines that, themselves regarded as axiomatic, bound, direct, and govern the ablest minds in
the discussion of the most momentous questions. For,
upon the assumption that wages are drawn directly
from capital, and not from the product of the labor, is
based, not only the doctrine that wages depend upon
the ratio between capital and labor, but the doctrine
that industry is limited by capital—that capital must
be accumulated before labor is employed, and labor
cannot be employed except as capital is accumulated;
the doctrine that every increase of capital gives or is
capable of giving additional employment to industry;
the doctrine that the conversion of circulating capital
into fixed capital lessens the fund applicable to the
maintenance of labor; the doctrine that more laborers
can be employed at low than at high wages; the doctrine
that capital applied to agriculture will maintain more
laborers than if applied to manufactures; the doctrine
that profits are high or low as wages are low or high, or
that they depend upon the cost of the subsistence of
laborers; together with such paradoxes as that a demand
for commodities is not a demand for labor, or that certain commodities may be increased in cost by a reduc-

tion in wages or diminished in cost by an increase in wages.

In short, all the teachings of the current political economy, in the widest and most important part of its domain, are based more or less directly upon the assumption that labor is maintained and paid out of existing capital before the product which constitutes the ultimate object is secured. If it be shown that this is an error, and that on the contrary the maintenance and payment of labor do not even temporarily trench on capital, but are directly drawn from the product of the labor, then all this vast superstructure is left without support and must fall. And so likewise must fall the vulgar theories which also have their base in the belief that the sum to be distributed in wages is a fixed one, the individual shares in which must necessarily be decreased by an increase in the number of laborers.

The difference between the current theory and the one I advance is, in fact, similar to that between the mercantile theory of international exchanges and that with which Adam Smith supplanted it. Between the theory that commerce is the exchange of commodities for money, and the theory that it is the exchange of commodities for commodities, there may seem no real difference when it is remembered that the adherents of the mercantile theory did not assume that money had any other use than as it could be exchanged for commodities. Yet, in the practical application of these two theories, there arises all the difference between rigid governmental protection and free trade.

If I have said enough to show the reader the ultimate importance of the reasoning through which I am about to ask him to follow me, it will not be necessary to apologize in advance either for simplicity or prolixity. In arraigning a doctrine of such importance—a doctrine supported by such a weight of authority, it is necessary to be both clear and thorough.

Were it not for this I should be tempted to dismiss with a sentence the assumption that wages are drawn from capital. For all the vast superstructure which the current political economy builds upon this doctrine is in truth based upon a foundation which has been merely taken for granted, without the slightest attempt to distinguish the apparent from the real. Because wages are generally paid in money, and in many of the operations of production are paid before the product is fully completed, or can be utilized, it is inferred that wages are drawn from pre-existing capital, and, therefore, that industry is limited by capital—that is to say that labor cannot be employed until capital has been accumulated, and can only be employed to the extent that capital has been accumulated.

Yet in the very treatises in which the limitation of industry by capital is laid down without reservation and made the basis for the most important reasonings and elaborate theories, we are told that capital is stored-up or accumulated labor—"that part of wealth which is saved to assist future production." If we substitute for the word "capital" this definition of the word, the proposition carries its own refutation, for that labor cannot be employed until the results of labor are saved becomes too absurd for discussion.

Should we, however, with this *reductio ad absurdum*, attempt to close the argument, we should probably be met with the explanation, not that the first laborers were supplied by Providence with the capital necessary to set them to work, but that the proposition merely refers to a state of society in which production has become a complex operation.

But the fundamental truth, that in all economic reasoning must be firmly grasped, and never let go, is that society in its most highly developed form is but an elaboration of society in its rudest beginnings, and that principles obvious in the simpler relations of men are merely disguised and not abrogated or reversed by the more intricate relations that result from the division of labor and the use of complex tools and methods. The steam grist mill, with its complicated machinery exhibiting every diversity of motion, is simply what the rude stone mortar dug up from an ancient river bed was in its day—an instrument for grinding corn. And every man engaged in it, whether tossing wood into the furnace, running the engine, dressing stones, printing sacks or keeping books, is really devoting his labor to the same purpose that the prehistoric savage did when he used his mortar—the preparation of grain for human food.

And so, if we reduce to their lowest terms all the complex operations of modern production, we see that each individual who takes part in this infinitely subdivided and intricate network of production and exchange is really doing what the primeval man did when he climbed the trees for fruit or followed the receding tide for shellfish—endeavoring to obtain from nature by the exertion of his powers the satisfaction of his desires. If we keep this firmly in mind, if we look upon production as a whole—as the co-operation of all embraced in any of its great groups to satisfy the various desires of each, we plainly see that the reward each obtains for his exertions comes as truly and as directly from nature as the result of that exertion, as did that of the first man.

To illustrate: In the simplest state of which we can conceive, each man digs his own bait and catches his own fish. The advantages of the division of labor soon become apparent, and one digs bait while the others fish. Yet evidently the one who digs bait is in reality

doing as much toward the catching of fish as any of
those who actually take the fish. So when the advantages of canoes are discovered, and instead of all going
a-fishing, one stays behind and makes and repairs
canoes, the canoe-maker is in reality devoting his labor
to the taking of fish as much as the actual fishermen,
and the fish which he eats at night when the fishermen
come home are as truly the product of his labor as of
theirs. And thus when the division of labor is fairly
inaugurated, and instead of each attempting to satisfy
all of his wants by direct resort to nature, one fishes,
another hunts, a third picks berries, a fourth gathers
fruit, a fifth makes tools, a sixth builds huts, and a
seventh prepares clothing—each one is to the extent he
exchanges the direct product of his own labor for the
direct product of the labor of others really applying
his own labor to the production of the things he uses
—is in effect satisfying his particular desires by the
exertion of his particular powers; that is to say, what
he receives he in reality produces. If he digs roots
and exchanges them for venison, he is in effect as truly
the procurer of the venison as though he had gone in
chase of the deer and left the huntsman to dig his own
roots. The common expression, "I made so and so,"
signifying "I earned so and so," or "I earned money
with which I purchased so and so," is, economically
speaking, not metaphorically but literally true. Earning
is making.

Now, if we follow these principles, obvious enough
in a simpler state of society, through the complexities
of the state we call civilized, we shall see clearly that
in every case in which labor is exchanged for commodities, production really precedes enjoyment; that
wages are the earnings—that is to say, the makings of
labor—not the advances of capital, and that the laborer
who receives his wages in money (coined or printed,

it may be, before his labor commenced) really receives
in return for the addition his labor has made to the
general stock of wealth, a draft upon that general stock,
which he may utilize in any particular form of wealth
that will best satisfy his desires; and that neither the
money, which is but the draft, nor the particular form
of wealth which he uses it to call for, represents advances
of capital for his maintenance, but on the contrary
represents the wealth, or a portion of the wealth, his
labor has already added to the general stock.

Keeping these principles in view we see that the
draughtsman, who, shut up in some dingy office on the
banks of the Thames, is drawing the plans for a great
marine engine, is in reality devoting his labor to the
production of bread and meat as truly as though he
were garnering the grain in California or swinging a
lariat on a La Plata pampa; that he is as truly making
his own clothing as though he were shearing sheep in
Australia or weaving cloth in Paisley, and just as effectually producing the claret he drinks at dinner as
though he gathered the grapes on the banks of the
Garonne. The miner who, two thousand feet under
ground in the heart of the Comstock, is digging out
silver ore, is, in effect, by virtue of a thousand exchanges, harvesting crops in valleys five thousand feet
nearer the earth's center; chasing the whale through
Arctic icefields; plucking tobacco leaves in Virginia;
picking coffee berries in Honduras; cutting sugar cane
on the Hawaiian Islands; gathering cotton in Georgia
or weaving it in Manchester or Lowell; making quaint
wooden toys for his children in the Hartz Mountains;
or plucking amid the green and gold of Los Angeles
orchards the oranges which, when his shift is relieved,
he will take home to his sick wife. The wages which he
receives on Saturday night at the mouth of the shaft,
what are they but the certificate to all the world that

he has done these things—the primary exchange in the long series which transmutes his labor into the things he has really been laboring for?

All this is clear when looked at in this way; but to meet this fallacy in all its strongholds and lurking places we must change our investigation from the deductive to the inductive form. Let us now see, if, beginning with facts and tracing their relations, we arrive at the same conclusions as are thus obvious when, beginning with first principles, we trace their exemplification in complex facts.

CHAPTER 2 THE MEANING OF THE TERMS

Before proceeding further in our inquiry, let us make sure of the meaning of our terms, for indistinctness in their use must inevitably produce ambiguity and indeterminateness in reasoning. Not only is it requisite in economic reasoning to give to such words as "wealth," "capital," "rent," "wages," and the like, a much more definite sense than they bear in common discourse, but, unfortunately, even in political economy there is, as to some of these terms, no certain meaning assigned by common consent, different writers giving to the same term different meanings, and the same writers often using a term in different senses. Nothing can add to the force of what has been said by so many eminent authors as to the importance of clear and precise definitions, save the example, not an infrequent one, of the same authors falling into grave errors from the very cause they warned against. And nothing so shows the importance of language in thought as the spectacle of even acute thinkers basing important conclusions upon the use of the same word in varying senses. I shall endeavor to avoid these dangers. It will be my effort throughout, as any term becomes of importance, to state clearly what I mean by it, and to use it in that sense and in no other. Let me ask the reader to note and to bear in mind the definitions thus given, as otherwise I cannot hope to make myself properly understood. I shall not attempt to attach arbitrary meanings to

31

words, or to coin terms, even when it would be convenient to do so, but shall conform to usage as closely
as is possible, only endeavoring so to fix the meaning of
words that they may clearly express thought.

What we have now on hand is to discover whether,
as a matter of fact, wages are drawn from capital. As
a preliminary, let us settle what we mean by wages and
what we mean by capital. To the former word a sufficiently definite meaning has been given by economic
writers, but the ambiguities which have attached to the
use of the latter in political economy will require a
detailed examination.

As used in common discourse "wages" means a compensation paid to a hired person for his services; and
we speak of one man "working for wages," in contradistinction to another who is "working for himself."
The use of the term is still further narrowed by the
habit of applying it solely to compensation paid for
manual labor. We do not speak of the wages of professional men, managers or clerks, but of their fees,
commissions, or salaries. Thus the common meaning
of the word wages is the compensation paid to a hired
person for manual labor. But in political economy the
word wages has a much wider meaning, and includes all
returns for exertion. For, as political economists explain,
the three agents or factors in production are land, labor,
and capital, and that part of the produce which goes to
the second of these factors is by them styled wages.

Thus the term labor includes all human exertion in
the production of wealth, and wages, being that part of
the produce which goes to labor, includes all reward
for such exertion. There is, therefore, in the politico-
economic sense of the term wages no distinction as to
the kind of labor, or as to whether its reward is received through an employer or not, but wages means the
return received for the exertion of labor, as distin-

guished from the return received for the use of capital, and the return received by the landholder for the use of land. The man who cultivates the soil for himself receives his wages in its produce, just as, if he uses his own capital and owns his own land, he may also receive interest and rent; the hunter's wages are the game he kills; the fisherman's wages are the fish he takes. The gold washed out by the self-employing gold digger is as much his wages as the money paid to the hired coal miner by the purchaser of his labor,* and, as Adam Smith shows, the high profits of retail storekeepers are in large part wages, being the recompense of their labor and not of their capital. In short, whatever is received as the result or reward of exertion is "wages."

This is all it is now necessary to note as to "wages," but it is important to keep this in mind. For in the standard economic works this sense of the term wages is recognized with greater or less clearness only to be subsequently ignored.

But it is more difficult to clear away from the idea of capital the ambiguities that beset it, and to fix the scientific use of the term. In general discourse, all sorts of things that have a value or will yield a return are vaguely spoken of as capital, while economic writers vary so widely that the term can hardly be said to have a fixed meaning. Let us compare with each other the definitions of a few representative writers:

"That part of a man's stock," says Adam Smith (Book II, Chap. I), "which he expects to afford him a revenue, is called his capital," and the capital of a country or society, he goes on to say, consists of (1) machines and instruments of trade which facilitate and

---

* This was recognized in common speech in California, where the placer miners styled their earnings their "wages," and spoke of making high wages or low wages according to the amount of gold taken out.

abridge labor; (2) buildings, not mere dwellings, but which may be considered instruments of trade—such as shops, farmhouses, etc.; (3) improvements of land which better fit it for tillage or culture; (4) the acquired and useful abilities of all the inhabitants; (5) money; (6) provisions in the hands of producers and dealers, from the sale of which they expect to derive a profit; (7) the material of, or partially completed, manufactured articles still in the hands of producers or dealers; (8) completed articles still in the hands of producers or dealers. The first four of these he styles fixed capital, and the last four circulating capital, a distinction of which it is not necessary to our purpose to take any note.

Ricardo's definition is:

"Capital is that part of the wealth of a country which is employed in production, and consists of food, clothing, tools, raw materials, machinery, etc., necessary to give effect to labor."—*Principles of Political Economy*, Chap. V.

This definition, it will be seen, is very different from that of Adam Smith, as it excludes many of the things which he includes—as acquired talents, articles of mere taste or luxury in the possession of producers or dealers; and includes some things he excludes—such as food, clothing, etc., in the possession of the consumer.

McCulloch's definition is:

"The capital of a nation really comprises all those portions of the produce of industry existing in it that may be *directly* employed either to support human existence or to facilitate production."—*Notes on Wealth of Nations*, Book II, Chap. I.

This definition follows the line of Ricardo's, but is wider. While it excludes everything that is not capable of aiding production, it includes everything that is so capable, without reference to actual use or necessity for use—the horse drawing a pleasure carriage being, according to McCulloch's view, as he expressly states, as much capital as the horse drawing a plow, because he may, if need arises, be used to draw a plow.

John Stuart Mill, following the same general line as Ricardo and McCulloch, makes neither the use nor the capability of use, but the determination to use, the test of capital. He says:

"Whatever things are destined to supply productive labor with the shelter, protection, tools and materials which the work requires, and to feed and otherwise maintain the laborer during the process, are capital." —*Principles of Political Economy, Book I, Chap. IV.*

These quotations sufficiently illustrate the divergence of the masters. Among minor authors the variance is still greater, as a few examples will suffice to show.

Professor Wayland, whose "Elements of Political Economy" has long been a favorite textbook in American educational institutions, where there has been any pretense of teaching political economy, gives this lucid definition:

"The word capital is used in two senses. In relation to product it means any substance on which industry is to be exerted. In relation to industry, the material on which industry is about to confer value, that on which it has conferred value; the instruments which are used for the conferring of value, as well as the means of sustenance by which the being is supported while he is engaged in performing the operation." —*Elements of Political Economy, Book I, Chap. I.*

Henry C. Carey, the American apostle of protectionism, defines capital as "the instrument by which man obtains mastery over nature, including in it the physical and mental powers of man himself." Professor Perry, a Massachusetts free trader, very properly objects to this that it hopelessly confuses the boundaries between capital and labor, and then himself hopelessly confuses the boundaries between capital and land by defining capital as "any valuable thing outside of man himself from whose use springs a pecuniary increase or profit." An English economic writer of high standing, Mr. Wm. Thornton, begins an elaborate examination of the relations of labor and capital ("On Labor") by stating that he will include land with capital, which is very much as if one who proposed to teach algebra should begin with the declaration that he would consider the signs plus and minus as meaning the same thing and having the same value. An American writer, also of high standing, Professor Francis A. Walker, makes the same declaration in his elaborate book on "The Wages Question." Another English writer, N. A. Nicholson ("The Science of Exchanges," London, 1873), seems to cap the climax of absurdity by declaring in one paragraph (p. 26) that "capital must of course be accumulated by saving," and in the very next paragraph stating that "the land which produces a crop, the plow which turns the soil, the labor which secures the produce, and the produce itself, if a material profit is to be derived from its employment, are all alike capital." But how land and labor are to be accumulated by saving them he nowhere condescends to explain. In the same way a standard American writer, Professor Amasa Walker (p. 66, "Science of Wealth"), first declares that capital arises from the net savings of labor and then immediately afterward declares that land is capital.

I might go on for pages, citing contradictory and self-contradictory definitions. But it would only weary the reader. It is unnecessary to multiply quotations. Those already given are sufficient to show how wide a difference exists as to the comprehension of the term capital. Any one who wants further illustration of the "confusion worse confounded" which exists on this subject among the professors of political economy may find it in any library where the works of these professors are ranged side by side.

Now, it makes little difference what name we give to things, if when we use the name we always keep in view the same things and no others. But the difficulty arising in economic reasoning from these vague and varying definitions of capital is that it is only in the premises of reasoning that the term is used in the peculiar sense assigned by the definition, while in the practical conclusions that are reached it is always used, or at least it is always understood, in one general and definite sense. When, for instance, it is said that wages are drawn from capital, the word capital is understood in the same sense as when we speak of the scarcity or abundance, the increase or decrease, the destruction or increment, of capital—a commonly understood and definite sense which separates capital from the other factors of production, land and labor, and also separates it from like things used merely for gratification. In fact, most people understand well enough what capital is until they begin to define it, and I think their works will show that the economic writers who differ so widely in their definitions use the term in this commonly understood sense in all cases except in their definitions and the reasoning based on them.

This common sense of the term is that of wealth devoted to procuring more wealth. Dr. Adam Smith correctly expresses this common idea when he says: "That part of a man's stock which he expects to afford him revenue is called his capital." And the capital of a community is evidently the sum of such individual stocks, or that part of the aggregate stock which is expected to procure more wealth. This also is the derivative sense of the term. The word capital, as philologists trace it, comes down to us from a time when wealth was estimated in cattle, and a man's income depended upon the number of head he could keep for their increase.

The difficulties which beset the use of the word capital, as an exact term, and which are even more strikingly exemplified in current political and social discussions than in the definitions of economic writers, arise from two facts—first, that certain classes of things, the possession of which to the individual is precisely equivalent to the possession of capital, are not part of the capital of the community; and, second, that things of the same kind may or may not be capital, according to the purpose to which they are devoted.

With a little care as to these points, there should be no difficulty in obtaining a sufficiently clear and fixed idea of what the term capital as generally used properly includes; such an idea as will enable us to say what things are capital and what are not, and to use the word without ambiguity or slip.

Land, labor, and capital are the three factors of production. If we remember that capital is thus a term used in contradistinction to land and labor, we at once see that nothing properly included under either one of these terms can be properly classed as capital. The term land necessarily includes, not merely the surface of the earth as distinguished from the water and the air, but the whole material universe outside of man himself, for it is only by having access to land, from which his very body is drawn, that man can come in contact with or use nature. The term land embraces, in short, all natural materials, forces, and opportunities, and, therefore, nothing that is freely supplied by nature can be properly classed as capital. A fertile field, a rich vein of ore, a falling stream which supplies power, may give to the possessor advantages equivalent to the possession of capital, but to class such things as capital would be to put an end to the distinction between land and capital, and, so far as they relate to each other, to make the two terms meaningless. The term labor, in like manner, includes all human exertion, and hence human powers whether natural or acquired can never properly be classed as capital. In common parlance we often speak of a man's knowledge, skill, or industry as constituting his capital; but this is evidently a metaphorical use of language that must be eschewed in reasoning that aims at exactness. Superiority in such qualities may augment the income of an individual just as capital would, and an increase in the knowledge, skill, or industry of a community may have the same effect in increasing its production as would an increase of capital; but this effect is due to the increased power of labor and not to capital. Increased velocity may give to the impact of a cannon ball the same effect as increased weight, yet, nevertheless, weight is one thing and velocity another.

Thus we must exclude from the category of capital everything that may be included either as land or labor. Doing so, there remain only things which are neither land nor labor, but which have resulted from the union of these two original factors of production. Nothing can be properly capital that does not consist of these—that is to say, nothing can be capital that is not wealth.

But it is from ambiguities in the use of this inclusive term wealth that many of the ambiguities which beset the term capital are derived.

As commonly used the word "wealth" is applied to anything having an exchange value. But when used as a term of political economy it must be limited to a much more definite meaning, because many things are commonly spoken of as wealth which in taking account of collective or general wealth cannot be considered as wealth at all. Such things have an exchange value, and are commonly spoken of as wealth, insomuch as they represent as between individuals, or between sets of individuals, the power of obtaining wealth; but they are not truly wealth, inasmuch as their increase or decrease does not affect the sum of wealth. Such are bonds, mortgages, promissory notes, bank bills, or other stipulations for the transfer of wealth. Such are slaves, whose value represents merely the power of one class to appropriate the earnings of another class. Such are lands, or other natural opportunities, the value of which is but the result of the acknowledgment in favor of certain persons of an exclusive right to their use, and which represents merely the power thus given to the owners to demand a share of the wealth produced by those who use them. Increase in the amount of bonds, mortgages, notes, or bank bills cannot increase the wealth of the community that includes as well those who promise to pay as those who are entitled to receive. The enslavement of a part of their number could not increase the wealth of a people, for what the enslavers gained the enslaved would lose. Increase in land values does not represent increase in the common wealth, for what landowners gain by higher prices, the tenants or purchasers who must pay them will lose. And all this relative wealth, which, in common thought and speech, in legislation and law, is undistinguished from actual wealth, could, without the destruction or consumption of anything more than a few drops of ink and a piece of paper, be utterly annihilated. By enactment of the sovereign political power debts might be canceled, slaves emancipated, and land resumed as the common property of the whole people, without the aggregate wealth being diminished by the value of a pinch of snuff, for what some would lose others would gain. There would be no more destruction of wealth than there was creation of wealth when Elizabeth Tudor enriched her favorite courtiers by the grant of monopolies, or when

Boris Godoonof made Russian peasants merchantable property.

All things which have an exchange value are, therefore, not wealth, in the only sense in which the term can be used in political economy. Only such things can be wealth the production of which increases and the destruction of which decreases the aggregate of wealth. If we consider what these things are, and what their nature is, we shall have no difficulty in defining wealth.

When we speak of a community increasing in wealth —as when we say that England has increased in wealth since the accession of Victoria, or that California is a wealthier country than when it was a Mexican territory—we do not mean to say that there is more land, or that the natural powers of the land are greater, or that there are more people, for when we wish to express that idea we speak of increase of population; or that the debts or dues owing by some of these people to others of their number have increased; but we mean that there is an increase of certain tangible things, having an actual and not merely a relative value—such as buildings, cattle, tools, machinery, agricultural and mineral products, manufactured goods, ships, wagons, furniture, and the like. The increase of such things constitutes an increase of wealth; their decrease is a lessening of wealth; and the community that, in proportion to its numbers, has most of such things is the wealthiest community. The common character of these things is that they consist of natural substances or products which have been adapted by human labor to human use or gratification, their value depending on the amount of labor which upon the average would be required to produce things of like kind.

Thus wealth, as alone the term can be used in political economy, consists of natural products that have been secured, moved, combined, separated, or in other ways modified by human exertion, so as to fit them for the gratification of human desires. It is, in other words, labor impressed upon matter in such a way as to store up, as the heat of the sun is stored up in coal, the power of human labor to minister to human desires. Wealth is not the sole object of labor, for labor is also expended in ministering directly to desire; but it is the object and result of what we call productive labor— that is, labor which gives value to material things. Nothing which nature supplies to man without his labor is wealth, nor yet does the expenditure of labor result in wealth unless there is a tangible product which has and retains the power of ministering to desire.

Now, as capital is wealth devoted to a certain purpose, nothing can be capital which does not fall within this definition of wealth. By recognizing and keeping this in mind, we get rid of misconceptions which vitiate all reasoning in which they are permitted, which befog popular thought, and have led into mazes of contradiction even acute thinkers.

But though all capital is wealth, all wealth is not capital. Capital is only a part of wealth—that part, namely, which is devoted to the aid of production. It is in drawing this line between the wealth that is and the wealth that is not capital that a second class of misconceptions are likely to occur.

The errors which I have been pointing out, and which consist in confounding with wealth and capital things essentially distinct, or which have but a relative existence, are now merely vulgar errors. They are widespread, it is true, and have a deep root, being held, not merely by the less educated classes, but seemingly by a large majority of those who in such advanced countries as England and the United States mold and guide public opinion, make the laws in parliaments, congresses and legislatures, and administer them in the courts. They crop out, moreover, in the disquisitions of many of those flabby writers who have burdened the press and darkened counsel by numerous volumes which are dubbed political economy, and which pass as text-books with the ignorant and as authority with those who do not think for themselves. Nevertheless, they are only vulgar errors, inasmuch as they receive no countenance from the best writers on political economy. By one of those lapses which flaw his great work and strikingly evince the imperfections of the highest talent, Adam Smith counts as capital certain personal qualities, an inclusion which is not consistent with his original definition of capital as stock from which revenue is expected. But this error has been avoided by his most eminent successors, and in the definitions, previously given, of Ricardo, McCulloch, and Mill, it is not involved. Neither in their definitions nor in that of Smith is involved the vulgar error which confounds as real capital things which are only relatively capital, such as evidences of debt, land values, etc. But as to things which are really wealth, their definitions differ from each other, and widely from that of Smith, as to what is and what is not to be considered as capital. The stock of a jeweler would, for instance, be included as capital by the definition of Smith, and the food or clothing in possession of a laborer would be excluded. But the definitions of Ricardo and McCulloch would exclude the stock of the jeweler, as would also that of Mill, if understood as most persons would understand the words I have quoted. But as explained by him, it is neither the nature nor the destination of the things themselves which determines whether they are or are not capital, but the intention of the owner to devote either the things or the value received from their sale to the supply of productive labor with tools, materials, and maintenance. All these definitions, however, agree in including as capital the provisions and clothing of the laborer, which Smith excludes.

Let us consider these three definitions, which represent the best teachings of current political economy:

To McCulloch's definition of capital as "all those portions of the produce of industry that may be directly employed either to support human existence or to facilitate production," there are obvious objections. One may pass along any principal street in a thriving town or city and see stores filled with all sorts of valuable things, which, though they cannot be employed either to support human existence or to facilitate production, undoubtedly constitute part of the capital of the storekeepers and part of the capital of the community. And he can also see products of industry capable of supporting human existence or facilitating production being consumed in ostentation or useless luxury. Surely these, though they might, do not constitute part of capital.

Ricardo's definition avoids including as capital things which might be but are not employed in production, by covering only such as are employed. But it is open to the first objection made to McCulloch's. If only wealth that may be, or that is, or that is destined to be, used in supporting producers, or assisting production, is capital, then the stocks of jewelers, toy dealers, tobacconists, confectioners, picture dealers, etc.—in fact, all stocks that consist of, and all stocks in so far as they consist of articles of luxury, are not capital.

If Mill, by remitting the distinction to the mind of the capitalist, avoids this difficulty (which does not seem to me clear), it is by making the distinction so vague that no power short of omniscience could tell in any given country at any given time what was and what was not capital.

But the great defect which these definitions have in

common is that they include what clearly cannot be accounted capital, if any distinction is to be made between laborer and capitalist. For they bring into the category of capital the food, clothing, etc., in the possession of the day laborer, which he will consume whether he works or not, as well as the stock in the hands of the capitalist, with which he proposes to pay the laborer for his work.

Yet, manifestly, this is not the sense in which the term capital is used by these writers when they speak of labor and capital as taking separate parts in the work of production and separate shares in the distribution of its proceeds; when they speak of wages as drawn from capital, or as depending upon the ratio between labor and capital, or in any of the ways in which the term is generally used by them. In all these cases the term capital is used in its commonly understood sense, as that portion of wealth which its owners do not propose to use directly for their own gratification, but for the purpose of obtaining more wealth. In short, by political economists, in everything except their definitions and first principles, as well as by the world at large, "that part of a man's stock," to use the words of Adam Smith, "which he expects to afford him revenue is called his capital." This is the only sense in which the term capital expresses any fixed idea—the only sense in which we can with any clearness separate it from wealth and contrast it with labor. For, if we must consider as capital everything which supplies the laborer with food, clothing, shelter, etc., then to find a laborer who is not a capitalist we shall be forced to hunt up an absolutely naked man, destitute even of a sharpened stick, or of a burrow in the ground—a situation in which, save as the result of exceptional circumstances, human beings have never yet been found.

It seems to me that the variance and inexactitude in

these definitions arise from the fact that the idea of
what capital is has been deduced from a preconceived
idea of how capital assists production. Instead of determining what capital is, and then observing what
capital does, the functions of capital have first been
assumed, and then a definition of capital made which includes all things which do or may perform those functions. Let us reverse this process, and, adopting the
natural order, ascertain what the thing is before settling
what it does. All we are trying to do, all that it is necessary to do, is to fix, as it were, the metes and bounds of
a term that in the main is well apprehended—to make
definite, that is, sharp and clear on its verges, a common idea.

If the articles of actual wealth existing at a given
time in a given community were presented *in situ* to a
dozen intelligent men who had never read a line of
political economy, it is doubtful if they would differ in
respect to a single item, as to whether it should be accounted capital or not. Money which its owner holds
for use in his business or in speculation would be accounted capital; money set aside for household or personal expenses would not. That part of a farmer's crop
held for sale or for seed, or to feed his help in part
payment of wages, would be accounted capital; that
held for the use of his own family would not be. The
horses and carriage of a hackman would be classed as
capital, but an equipage kept for the pleasure of its
owner would not. So no one would think of counting
as capital the false hair on the head of a woman, the
cigar in the mouth of a smoker, or the toy with which
a child is playing; but the stock of a hair dealer, of a
tobacconist, or of the keeper of a toy store, would be
unhesitatingly set down as capital. A coat which a
tailor had made for sale would be accounted capital,
but not the coat he had made for himself. Food in the

possession of a hotelkeeper or a restaurateur would be accounted capital, but not the food in the pantry of a housewife, or in the lunch basket of a workman. Pig iron in the hands of the smelter, or founder, or dealer, would be accounted capital, but not the pig iron used as ballast in the hold of a yacht. The bellows of a blacksmith, the looms of a factory, would be capital, but not the sewing machine of a woman who does only her own work; a building let for hire, or used for business or productive purposes, but not a homestead. In short, I think we should find that now, as when Dr. Adam Smith wrote, "that part of a man's stock which he expects to yield him a revenue is called his capital." And, omitting his unfortunate slip as to personal qualities, and qualifying somewhat his enumeration of money, it is doubtful if we could better list the different articles of capital than did Adam Smith in the passage which in the previous part of this chapter I have condensed.

Now, if, after having thus separated the wealth that is capital from the wealth that is not capital, we look for the distinction between the two classes, we shall not find it to be as to the character, capabilities, or final destination of the things themselves, as has been vainly attempted to draw it; but it seems to me that we shall find it to be as to whether they are or are not in the possession of the consumer.* Such articles of wealth as in themselves, in their uses, or in their products, are

---

* Money may be said to be in the hands of the consumer when devoted to the procurement of gratification, as, though not in itself devoted to consumption, it represents wealth which is; and thus what in the previous paragraph I have given as the common classification would be covered by this distinction, and would be substantially correct. In speaking of money in this connection, I am of course speaking of coin, for although paper money may perform all the functions of coin, it is not wealth, and cannot therefore be capital.

yet to be exchanged are capital; such articles of wealth
as are in the hands of the consumer are not capital.
Hence, if we define capital as *wealth in course of exchange*, understanding exchange to include not merely
the passing from hand to hand, but also such transmutations as occur when the reproductive or transforming
forces of nature are utilized for the increase of wealth,
we shall, I think, comprehend all the things that the
general idea of capital properly includes, and shut out
all it does not. Under this definition, it seems to me, for
instance, will fall all such tools as are really capital.
For it is as to whether its services or uses are to be
exchanged or not which makes a tool an article of capital or merely an article of wealth. Thus, the lathe of
a manufacturer used in making things which are to be
exchanged is capital, while the lathe kept by a gentleman for his own amusement is not. Thus, wealth used
in the construction of a railroad, a public telegraph line,
a stage coach, a theater, a hotel, etc., may be said to
be placed in the course of exchange. The exchange is
not effected all at once, but little by little, with an indefinite number of people. Yet there is an exchange,
and the "consumers" of the railroad, the telegraph line,
the stage coach, theater or hotel, are not the owners, but
the persons who from time to time use them.

Nor is this definition inconsistent with the idea that
capital is that part of wealth devoted to production.
It is too narrow an understanding of production which
confines it merely to the making of things. Production
includes not merely the making of things, but the bringing of them to the consumer. The merchant or
storekeeper is thus as truly a producer as is the manufacturer, or farmer, and his stock or capital is as much
devoted to production as is theirs. But it is not worth
while now to dwell upon the functions of capital, which
we shall be better able to determine hereafter. Nor is

the definition of capital I have suggested of any importance. I am not writing a textbook, but only attempting to discover the laws which control a great social
problem, and if the reader has been led to form a clear
idea of what things are meant when we speak of capital
my purpose is served.

But before closing this digression let me call attention
to what is often forgotten—namely, that the terms
"wealth," "capital," "wages," and the like, as used in
political economy are abstract terms, and that nothing
can be generally affirmed or denied of them that cannot
be affirmed or denied of the whole class of things they
represent. The failure to bear this in mind has led to
much confusion of thought, and permits fallacies, otherwise transparent, to pass for obvious truths. Wealth
being an abstract term, the idea of wealth, it must be
remembered, involves the idea of exchangeability. The
possession of wealth to a certain amount is potentially
the possession of any or all species of wealth to that
equivalent in exchange. And, consequently, so of
capital.

CHAPTER 3 — WAGES NOT DRAWN FROM CAPITAL, BUT PRODUCED BY THE LABOR

The importance of this digression will, I think, become more and more apparent as we proceed in our inquiry, but its pertinency to the branch we are now engaged in may at once be seen.

It is at first glance evident that the economic meaning of the term wages is lost sight of, and attention is concentrated upon the common and narrow meaning of the word, when it is affirmed that wages are drawn from capital. For, in all those cases in which the laborer is his own employer and takes directly the produce of his labor as its reward, it is plain enough that wages are not drawn from capital, but result directly as the product of the labor. If, for instance, I devote my labor to gathering birds' eggs or picking wild berries, the eggs or berries I thus get are my wages. Surely no one will contend that in such a case wages are drawn from capital. There is no capital in the case. An absolutely naked man, thrown on an island where no human being has before trod, may gather birds' eggs or pick berries.

Or if I take a piece of leather and work it up into a pair of shoes, the shoes are my wages—the reward of my exertion. Surely they are not drawn from capital—either my capital or any one else's capital—but are brought into existence by the labor of which they become the wages; and in obtaining this pair of shoes as the wages of my labor, capital is not even momentarily lessened one iota. For, if we call in the idea of capital, my capital at the beginning consists of the piece of leather, the thread, etc. As my labor goes on, value is steadily added, until, when my labor results in the finished shoes, I have my capital plus the difference in value between the material and the shoes. In obtaining this additional value—my wages—how is capital at any time drawn upon?

Adam Smith, who gave the direction to economic thought that has resulted in the current elaborate theories of the relation between wages and capital, recognized the fact that in such simple cases as I have instanced, wages are the produce of labor, and thus begins his chapter upon the wages of labor (Chap. VIII):

"*The produce of labor constitutes the natural recompense or wages of labor.* In that original state of things which precedes both the appropriation of land and the accumulation of stock, the whole produce of labor belongs to the laborer. He has neither landlord nor master to share with him."

Had the great Scotchman taken this as the initial point of his reasoning, and continued to regard the produce of labor as the natural wages of labor, and the landlord and master but as sharers, his conclusions would have been very different, and political economy today would not embrace such a mass of contradictions and absurdities; but instead of following the truth obvious in the simple modes of production as a clew through the perplexities of the more complicated forms, he momentarily recognizes it, only immediately to abandon it, and stating that "in every part of Europe twenty workmen serve under a master for one that is independent," he recommences the inquiry from a point of view in which the master is considered as providing from his capital the wages of his workmen.

BOOK I   CHAPTER 3

It is evident that in thus placing the proportion of self-employing workmen as but one in twenty, Adam Smith had in mind but the mechanic arts, and that, including all laborers, the proportion who take their earnings directly, without the intervention of an employer, must, even in Europe a hundred years ago, have been much greater than this. For, besides the independent laborers who in every community exist in considerable numbers, the agriculture of large districts of Europe has, since the time of the Roman Empire, been carried on by the metayer system, under which the capitalist receives his return from the laborer instead of the laborer from the capitalist. At any rate, in the United States, where any general law of wages must apply as fully as in Europe, and where in spite of the advance of manufactures a very large part of the people are yet self-employing farmers, the proportion of laborers who get their wages through an employer must be comparatively small.

But it is not necessary to discuss the ratio in which self-employing laborers anywhere stand to hired laborers, nor is it necessary to multiply illustrations of the truism that where the laborer takes directly his wages they are the product of his labor, for as soon as it is realized that the term wages includes all the earnings of labor, as well when taken directly by the laborer in the results of his labor as when received from an employer, it is evident that the assumption that wages are drawn from capital, on which as a universal truth such a vast superstructure is in standard politico-economic treatises so unhesitatingly built, is at least in large part untrue, and the utmost that can with any plausibility be affirmed is that some wages (i. e., wages received by the laborer from an employer) are drawn from capital. This restriction of the major premise at once invalidates all the deductions that are made from it; but without resting here, let us see whether even in this restricted sense it accords with the facts. Let us pick up the clew where Adam Smith dropped it, and advancing step by step, see whether the relation of facts which is obvious in the simplest forms of production does not run through the most complex.

Next in simplicity to "that original state of things," of which many examples may yet be found, where the whole produce of labor belongs to the laborer, is the arrangement in which the laborer, though working for another person, or with the capital of another person, receives his wages in kind—that is to say, in the things his labor produces. In this case it is as clear as in the case of the self-employing laborer that the wages are really drawn from the product of the labor, and not at all from capital. If I hire a man to gather eggs, to pick berries, or to make shoes, paying him from the eggs, the berries, or the shoes that his labor secures, there can be no question that the source of the wages is the labor for which they are paid. Of this form of hiring is the saer-and-daer stock tenancy, treated of with such perspicuity by Sir Henry Maine in his "Early History of Institutions," and which so clearly involved the relation of employer and employed as to render the acceptor of cattle the man or vassal of the capitalist who thus employed him. It was on such terms as these that Jacob worked for Laban, and to this day, even in civilized countries, it is not an infrequent mode of employing labor. The farming of land on shares, which prevails to a considerable extent in the southern states of the Union and in California, the metayer system of Europe, as well as the many cases in which superintendents, salesmen, etc., are paid by a percentage of profits, what are they but the employment of labor for wages which consist of part of its produce?

The next step in the advance from simplicity to com-

plexity is where the wages, though estimated in kind,
are paid in an equivalent of something else. For instance, on American whaling ships the custom is not to
pay fixed wages, but a "lay," or proportion of the catch,
which varies from a sixteenth to a twelfth to the captain
down to a three-hundredth to the cabin boy. Thus,
when a whaleship comes into New Bedford or San
Francisco after a successful cruise, she carries in her
hold the wages of her crew, as well as the profits of
her owners, and an equivalent which will reimburse
them for all the stores used up during the voyage. Can
anything be clearer than that these wages—this oil and
bone which the crew of the whaler have taken—have
not been drawn from capital, but are really a part of
the produce of their labor? Nor is this fact changed or
obscured in the slightest degree where, as a matter of
convenience, instead of dividing up between the crew
their proportion of the oil and bone, the value of each
man's share is estimated at the market price, and he
is paid for it in money. The money is but the equivalent of the real wages, the oil and bone. In no way
is there any advance of capital in this payment. The
obligation to pay wages does not accrue until the value
from which they are to be paid is brought into port.
At the moment when the owner takes from his capital
money to pay the crew he adds to his capital oil and
bone.

So far there can be no dispute. Let us now take
another step, which will bring us to the usual method of
employing labor and paying wages.

The Farallone Islands, off the Bay of San Francisco,
are a hatching ground of seafowl, and a company who
claim these islands employ men in the proper season to
collect the eggs. They might employ these men for a
proportion of the eggs they gather, as is done in the
whale fishery, and probably would do so if there were

much uncertainty attending the business; but as the fowl are plentiful and tame, and about so many eggs can be gathered by so much labor, they find it more convenient to pay their men fixed wages. The men go out and remain on the islands, gathering the eggs and bringing them to a landing, whence, at intervals of a few days, they are taken in a small vessel to San Francisco and sold. When the season is over the men return and are paid their stipulated wages in coin. Does not this transaction amount to the same thing as if, instead of being paid in coin, the stipulated wages were paid in an equivalent of the eggs gathered? Does not the coin represent the eggs, by the sale of which it was obtained, and are not these wages as much the product of the labor for which they are paid as the eggs would be in the possession of a man who gathered them for himself without the intervention of any employer?

To take another example, which shows by reversion the identity of wages in money with wages in kind. In San Buenaventura lives a man who makes an excellent living by shooting for their oil and skins the common hair seals which frequent the islands forming the Santa Barbara Channel. When on these sealing expeditions he takes two or three Chinamen along to help him, whom at first he paid wholly in coin. But it seems that the Chinese highly value some of the organs of the seal, which they dry and pulverize for medicine, as well as the long hairs in the whiskers of the male seal, which, when over a certain length, they greatly esteem for some purpose that to outside barbarians is not very clear. And this man soon found that the Chinamen were very willing to take instead of money these parts of the seals killed, so that now, in large part, he thus pays them their wages.

Now, is not what may be seen in all these cases—the identity of wages in money with wages in kind—true of all cases in which wages are paid for productive labor? Is not the fund created by the labor really the fund from which the wages are paid?

It may, perhaps, be said: "There is this difference— where a man works for himself, or where, when working for an employer, he takes his wages in kind, his wages depend upon the result of his labor. Should that, from any misadventure, prove futile, he gets nothing. When he works for an employer, however, he gets his wages anyhow—they depend upon the performance of the labor, not upon the result of the labor." But this is evidently not a real distinction. For on the average, the labor that is rendered for fixed wages not only yields the amount of the wages, but more; else employers could make no profit. When wages are fixed, the employer takes the whole risk and is compensated for this assurance, for wages when fixed are always somewhat less than wages contingent. But though when fixed wages are stipulated the laborer who has performed his part of the contract has usually a legal claim upon the employer, it is frequently, if not generally, the case that the disaster which prevents the employer from reaping benefit from the labor prevents him from paying the wages. And in one important department of industry the employer is legally exempt in case of disaster, although the contract be for wages certain and not contingent. For the maxim of admiralty law is, that "freight is the mother of wages," and though the seaman may have performed his part, the disaster which prevents the ship from earning freight deprives him of claim for his wages.

In this legal maxim is embodied the truth for which I am contending. Production is always the mother of wages. Without production, wages would not and could not be. It is from the produce of labor, not from the advances of capital that wages come.

Wherever we analyze the facts this will be found to be true. For labor always precedes wages. This is as universally true of wages received by the laborer from an employer as it is of wages taken directly by the laborer who is his own employer. In the one class of cases as in the other, reward is conditioned upon exertion. Paid sometimes by the day, oftener by the week or month, occasionally by the year, and in many branches of production by the piece, the payment of wages by an employer to an employee always implies the previous rendering of labor by the employee for the benefit of the employer, for the few cases in which advance payments are made for personal services are evidently referable either to charity or to guarantee and purchase. The name "retainer," given to advance payments to lawyers, shows the true character of the transaction, as does the name "blood money" given in 'longshore vernacular to a payment which is nominally wages advanced to sailors, but which in reality is purchase money—both English and American law considering a sailor as much a chattel as a pig.

I dwell on this obvious fact that labor always precedes wages, because it is all-important to an understanding of the more complicated phenomena of wages that it should be kept in mind. And obvious as it is, as I have put it, the plausibility of the proposition that wages are drawn from capital—a proposition that is made the basis for such important and far-reaching deductions—comes in the first instance from a statement that ignores and leads the attention away from this truth. That statement is, that labor cannot exert its productive power unless supplied by capital with maintenance.* The unwary reader at once recognizes the fact that the laborer must have food, clothing, etc., in order

---

* "Industry is limited by capital. . . . There can be no more industry than is supplied with materials to work up and food to eat. Self-evident

to enable him to perform the work, and having been
told that the food, clothing, etc., used by productive
laborers are capital, he assents to the conclusion that
the consumption of capital is necessary to the application of labor, and from this it is but an obvious deduction that industry is limited by capital—that the
demand for labor depends upon the supply of capital,
and hence that wages depend upon the ratio between
the number of laborers looking for employment and
the amount of capital devoted to hiring them.

But I think the discussion in the previous chapter
will enable any one to see wherein lies the fallacy of this
reasoning—a fallacy which has entangled some of the
most acute minds in a web of their own spinning. It is
in the use of the term capital in two senses. In the
primary proposition that capital is necessary to the
exertion of productive labor, the term "capital" is understood as including all food, clothing, shelter, etc.;
whereas, in the deductions finally drawn from it, the
term is used in its common and legitimate meaning of
wealth devoted, not to the immediate gratification of desire, but to the procurement of more wealth—of wealth
in the hands of employers as distinguished from
laborers. The conclusion is no more valid than it would
be from the acceptance of the proposition that a laborer
cannot go to work without his breakfast and some
clothes, to infer that no more laborers can go to work

as the thing is, it is often forgotten that the people of a country are
maintained and have their wants supplied not by the produce of present
labor, but of past. They consume what has been produced, not what is
about to be produced. Now, of what has been produced a part only
is allotted to the support of productive labor, and there will not and
cannot be more of that labor than the portion so allotted (which is
the capital of the country) can feed and provide with the materials and
instruments of production."—John Stuart Mill, "Principles of Political
Economy," Book I, Chap. V, Sec. I.

than employers first furnish with breakfasts and clothes. Now, the fact is that laborers generally furnish their own breakfasts and the clothes in which they go to work; and the further fact is, that capital (in the sense in which the word is used in distinction to labor) in exceptional cases sometimes may, but is never compelled to make advances to labor before the work begins. Of all the vast number of unemployed laborers in the civilized world today, there is probably not a single one willing to work who could not be employed without any advance of wages. A great proportion would doubtless gladly go to work on terms which did not require the payment of wages before the end of a month; it is doubtful if there are enough to be called a class who would not go to work and wait for their wages until the end of the week, as most laborers habitually do; while there are certainly none who would not wait for their wages until the end of the day, or if you please, until the next meal hour. The precise time of the payment of wages is immaterial; the essential point —the point I lay stress on—is that it is *after* the performance of work.

The payment of wages, therefore, always implies the previous rendering of labor. Now, what does the rendering of labor in production imply? Evidently the production of wealth, which, if it is to be exchanged or used in production, is capital. Therefore, the payment of capital in wages presupposes a production of capital by the labor for which the wages are paid. And as the employer generally makes a profit, the payment of wages is, so far as he is concerned, but the return to the laborer of a portion of the capital he has received from the labor. So far as the employee is concerned, it is but the receipt of a portion of the capital his labor has previously produced. As the value paid in the wages is thus exchanged for a value brought into being by the labor, how can it be said that wages are drawn from capital or advanced by capital? As in the exchange of labor for wages the employer always gets the capital created by the labor before he pays out capital in the wages, at what point is his capital lessened even temporarily?*

Bring the question to the test of facts. Take, for instance, an employing manufacturer who is engaged in turning raw material into finished products—cotton into cloth, iron into hardware, leather into boots, or so on, as may be, and who pays his hands, as is generally the case, once a week. Make an exact inventory of his capital on Monday morning before the beginning of work, and it will consist of his buildings, machinery, raw materials, money on hand, and finished products in stock. Suppose, for the sake of simplicity, that he neither buys nor sells during the week, and after work has stopped and he has paid his hands on Saturday night, take a new inventory of his capital. The item of money will be less, for it has been paid out in wages; there will be less raw material, less coal, etc., and a proper deduction must be made from the value of the buildings and machinery for the week's wear and tear. But if he is doing a remunerative business, which must

---

* I speak of labor producing capital for the sake of greater clearness. What labor always procures is either wealth, which may or may not be capital, or services, the cases in which nothing is obtained being merely exceptional cases of misadventure. Where the object of the labor is simply the gratification of the employer, as where I hire a man to black my boots, I do not pay the wages from capital, but from wealth which I have devoted, not to reproductive uses, but to consumption for my own satisfaction. Even if wages thus paid be considered as drawn from capital, then by that act they pass from the category of capital to that of wealth devoted to the gratification of the possessor, as when a cigar dealer takes a dozen cigars from the stock he has for sale and puts them in his pocket for his own use.

on the average be the case, the item of finished products will be so much greater as to compensate for all these deficiencies and show in the summing up an increase of capital. Manifestly, then, the value he paid his hands in wages was not drawn from his capital, or from any one else's capital. It came, not from capital, but from the value created by the labor itself. There was no more advance of capital than if he had hired his hands to dig clams, and paid them with a part of the clams they dug. Their wages were as truly the produce of their labor as were the wages of the primitive man, when, long "before the appropriation of land and the accumulation of stock," he obtained an oyster by knocking it with a stone from the rocks.

As the laborer who works for an employer does not get his wages until he has performed the work, his case is similar to that of the depositor in a bank who cannot draw money out until he has put money in. And as by drawing out what he has previously put in, the bank depositor does not lessen the capital of the bank, neither can laborers by receiving wages lessen even temporarily either the capital of the employer or the aggregate capital of the community. Their wages no more come from capital than the checks of depositors are drawn against bank capital. It is true that laborers in receiving wages do not generally receive back wealth in the same form in which they have rendered it, any more than bank depositors receive back the identical coins or bank notes they have deposited, but they receive it in equivalent form, and as we are justified in saying that the depositor receives from the bank the money he paid in, so are we justified in saying that the laborer receives in wages the wealth he has rendered in labor.

That this universal truth is so often obscured, is largely due to that fruitful source of economic obscurities, the confounding of wealth with money; and it is remarkable to see so many of those who, since Dr. Adam Smith made the egg stand on its head, have copiously demonstrated the fallacies of the mercantile system, fall into delusions of the very same kind in treating of the relations of capital and labor. Money being the general medium of exchanges, the common flux through which all transmutations of wealth from one form to another take place, whatever difficulties may exist to an exchange will generally show themselves on the side of reduction to money, and thus it is sometimes easier to exchange money for any other form of wealth than it is to exchange wealth in a particular form into money, for the reason that there are more holders of wealth who desire to make some exchange than there are who desire to make any particular exchange. And so a producing employer who has paid out his money in wages may sometimes find it difficult to turn quickly back into money the increased value for which his money has really been exchanged, and is spoken of as having exhausted or advanced his capital in the payment of wages. Yet, unless the new value created by the labor is less than the wages paid, which can be only an exceptional case, the capital which he had before in money he now has in goods—it has been changed in form, but not lessened.

There is one branch of production in regard to which the confusions of thought which arise from the habit of estimating capital in money are least likely to occur, inasmuch as its product is the general material and standard of money. And it so happens that this business furnishes us, almost side by side, with illustrations of production passing from the simplest to most complex forms.

In the early days of California, as afterward in Australia, the placer miner, who found in river bed or surface deposit the glittering particles which the slow processes of nature had for ages been accumulating, picked up or washed out his "wages" (so, too, he called them) in actual money, for coin being scarce, gold dust passed as currency by weight, and at the end of the day had his wages in money in a buckskin bag in his pocket. There can be no dispute as to whether these wages came from capital or not. They were manifestly the produce of his labor. Nor could there be any dispute when the holder of a specially rich claim hired men to work for him and paid them off in the identical money which their labor had taken from gulch or bar. As coin became more abundant, its greater convenience in saving the trouble and loss of weighing assigned gold dust to the place of a commodity, and with coin obtained by the sale of the dust their labor had procured, the employing miner paid off his hands. Where he had coin enough to do so, instead of selling his gold dust at the nearest store and paying a dealer's profit, he retained it until he got enough to take a trip, or send by express to San Francisco, where at the mint he could have it turned into coin without charge. While thus accumulating gold dust he was lessening his stock of coin; just as the manufacturer, while accumulating a stock of goods, lessens his stock of money. Yet no one would be obtuse enough to imagine that in thus taking in gold dust and paying out coin the miner was lessening his capital.

But the deposits that could be worked without preliminary labor were soon exhausted, and gold mining rapidly took a more elaborate character. Before claims could be opened so as to yield any return deep shafts had to be sunk, great dams constructed, long tunnels cut through the hardest rock, water brought for miles over mountain ridges and across deep valleys, and expensive machinery put up. These works could not be constructed without capital. Sometimes their construc-

tion required years, during which no return could be
hoped for, while the men employed had to be paid their
wages every week, or every month. Surely, it will be
said, in such cases, even if in no others, that wages do
actually come from capital; are actually advanced by
capital; and must necessarily lessen capital in their payment! Surely here, at least, industry is limited by capital, for without capital such works could not be carried
on! Let us see:

It is cases of this class that are always instanced as
showing that wages are advanced from capital. For
where wages are paid before the object of the labor is
obtained, or is finished—as in agriculture, where plowing and sowing must precede by several months the
harvesting of the crop; as in the erection of buildings,
the construction of ships, railroads, canals, etc.—it is
clear that the owners of the capital paid in wages cannot expect an immediate return, but, as the phrase is,
must "outlay it," or "lie out of it" for a time, which
sometimes amounts to many years. And hence, if first
principles are not kept in mind, it is easy to jump to
the conclusion that wages are advanced by capital.

But such cases will not embarrass the reader to whom
in what has preceded I have made myself clearly understood. An easy analysis will show that these instances
where wages are paid before the product is finished, or
even produced, do not afford any exception to the rule
apparent where the product is finished before wages are
paid.

If I go to a broker to exchange silver for gold, I lay
down my silver, which he counts and puts away, and
then hands me the equivalent in gold, minus his commission. Does the broker advance me any capital?
Manifestly not. What he had before in gold he now has
in silver, plus his profit. And as he got the silver before

he paid out the gold, there is on his part not even momentarily an advance of capital.

Now, this operation of the broker is precisely analogous to what the capitalist does, when, in such cases as we are now considering, he pays out capital in wages. As the rendering of labor precedes the payment of wages, and as the rendering of labor in production implies the creation of value, the employer receives value before he pays out value—he but exchanges capital of one form for capital of another form. For the creation of value does not depend upon the finishing of the product; it takes place at every stage of the process of production, as the immediate result of the application of labor, and hence, no matter how long the process in which it is engaged, labor always adds to capital by its exertion before it takes from capital in its wages.

Here is a blacksmith at his forge making picks. Clearly he is making capital—adding picks to his employer's capital before he draws money from it in wages. Here is a machinist or boilermaker working on the keel plates of a Great Eastern. Is not he also just as clearly creating value—making capital? The giant steamship, as the pick, is an article of wealth, an instrument of production, and though the one may not be completed for years, while the other is completed in a few minutes, each day's work, in the one case as in the other, is as clearly a production of wealth—an addition to capital. In the case of the steamship, as in the case of the pick, it is not the last blow, any more than the first blow, that creates the value of the finished product —the creation of value is continuous, it immediately results from the exertion of labor.

We see this very clearly wherever the division of labor has made it customary for different parts of the full process of production to be carried on by different sets of producers—that is to say, wherever we are in the habit of estimating the amount of value which the labor expended in any preparatory stage of production has created. And a moment's reflection will show that this is the case as to the vast majority of products. Take a ship, a building, a jackknife, a book, a lady's thimble or a loaf of bread. They are finished products. But they were not produced at one operation or by one set of producers. And this being the case, we readily distinguish different points or stages in the creation of the value which as completed articles they represent. When we do not distinguish different parts in the final process of production we do distinguish the value of the materials. The value of these materials may often be again decomposed many times, exhibiting as many clearly defined steps in the creation of the final value. At each of these steps we habitually estimate a creation of value, an addition to capital. The batch of bread which the baker is taking from the oven has a certain value. But this is composed in part of the value of the flour from which the dough was made. And this again is composed of the value of the wheat, the value given by milling, etc. Iron in the form of pigs is very far from being a completed product. It must yet pass through several, or, perhaps, through many, stages of production before it results in the finished articles that were the ultimate objects for which the iron ore was extracted from the mine. Yet, is not pig iron capital? And so the process of production is not really completed when a crop of cotton is gathered, nor yet when it is ginned and pressed; nor yet when it arrives at Lowell or Manchester; nor yet when it is converted into yarn; nor yet when it becomes cloth; but only when it is finally placed in the hands of the consumer. Yet at each step in this progress there is clearly enough a creation of value—an addition to capital. Why, therefore, although we do not so habitually distinguish and estimate it, is there not a creation of value—an addition to capital—when the ground is plowed for the crop? Is it because it may possibly be a bad season and the crop may fail? Evidently not; for a like possibility of misadventure attends every one of the many steps in the production of the finished article. On the average a crop is sure to come up, and so much plowing and sowing will on the average result in so much cotton in the boll, as surely as so much spinning of cotton yarn will result in so much cloth.

In short, as the payment of wages is always conditioned upon the rendering of labor, the payment of wages in production, no matter how long the process, never involves any advance of capital, or even temporarily lessens capital. It may take a year, or even years, to build a ship, but the creation of value of which the finished ship will be the sum goes on day by day, and hour by hour, from the time the keel is laid or even the ground is cleared. Nor by the payment of wages before the ship is completed, does the master builder lessen either his capital or the capital of the community, for the value of the partially completed ship stands in place of the value paid out in wages. There is no advance of capital in this payment of wages, for the labor of the workmen during the week or month creates and renders to the builder more capital than is paid back to them at the end of the week or month, as is shown by the fact that if the builder were at any stage of the construction asked to sell a partially completed ship he would expect a profit.

And so, when a Sutro or St. Gothard tunnel or a Suez canal is cut, there is no advance of capital. The tunnel or canal, as it is cut, becomes capital as much as the money spent in cutting it—or, if you please, the powder, drills, etc., used in the work, and the food, clothes, etc., used by the workmen—as is shown by the fact that the value of the capital stock of the company is not lessened as capital in these forms is gradually changed into capital in the form of tunnel or canal. On the contrary, it probably, and on the average, increases as the work progresses, just as the capital invested in a speedier mode of production would on the average increase.

And this is obvious in agriculture also. That the creation of value does not take place all at once when the crop is gathered, but step by step during the whole process which the gathering of the crop concludes, and that no payment of wages in the interim lessens the farmer's capital, is tangible enough when land is sold or rented during the process of production, as a plowed field will bring more than an unplowed field, or a field that has been sown more than one merely plowed. It is tangible enough when growing crops are sold, as is sometimes done, or where the farmer does not harvest himself, but lets a contract to the owner of harvesting machinery. It is tangible in the case of orchards and vineyards which, though not yet in bearing, bring prices proportionate to their age. It is tangible in the case of horses, cattle and sheep, which increase in value as they grow toward maturity. And if not always tangible between what may be called the usual exchange points in production, this increase of value as surely takes place with every exertion of labor. Hence, where labor is rendered before wages are paid, the advance of capital is really made by labor, and is from the employed to the employer, not from the employer to the employed.

"Yet," it may be said, "in such cases as we have been considering capital is required!" Certainly; I do not dispute that. But it is not required in order to make advances to labor. It is required for quite another purpose. What that purpose is we may readily see.

When wages are paid in kind—that is to say, in wealth

of the same species as the labor produces; as, for instance, if I hire men to cut wood, agreeing to give them as wages a portion of the wood they cut, a method sometimes adopted by the owners or lessees of woodland, it is evident that no capital is required for the payment of wages. Nor yet when, for the sake of mutual convenience, arising from the fact that a large quantity of wood can be more readily and more advantageously exchanged than a number of small quantities, I agree to pay wages in money, instead of wood, shall I need any capital, provided I can make the exchange of the wood for money before the wages are due. It is only when I cannot make such an exchange, or such an advantageous exchange as I desire, until I accumulate a large quantity of wood that I shall need capital. Nor even then shall I need capital if I can make a partial or tentative exchange by borrowing on my wood. If I cannot, or do not choose, either to sell the wood or to borrow upon it, and yet wish to go ahead accumulating a large stock of wood, I shall need capital. But manifestly, I need this capital, not for the payment of wages, but for the accumulation of a stock of wood. Likewise in cutting a tunnel. If the workmen were paid in tunnel (which, if convenient, might easily be done by paying them in stock of the company), no capital for the payment of wages would be required. It is only when the undertakers wish to accumulate capital in the shape of a tunnel that they will need capital. To recur to our first illustration: The broker to whom I sell my silver cannot carry on his business without capital. But he does not need this capital because he makes any advance of capital to me when he receives my silver and hands me gold. He needs it because the nature of the business requires the keeping of a certain amount of capital on hand, in order that when a customer comes he may be prepared to make the exchange the customer desires.

And so we shall find it in every branch of production. Capital has never to be set aside for the payment of wages when the produce of the labor for which the wages are paid is exchanged as soon as produced; it is only required when this produce is stored up, or what is to the individual the same thing, placed in the general current of exchanges without being at once drawn against —that is, sold on credit. But the capital thus required is not required for the payment of wages, nor for advances to labor, as it is always represented in the produce of the labor. It is never as an employer of labor that any producer needs capital; when he does need capital, it is because he is not only an employer of labor, but a merchant or speculator in, or an accumulator of, the products of labor. This is generally the case with employers.

To recapitulate: The man who works for himself gets his wages in the things he produces, as he produces them, and exchanges this value into another form whenever he sells the produce. The man who works for another for stipulated wages in money works under a contract of exchange. He also creates his wages as he renders his labor, but he does not get them except at stated times, in stated amounts, and in a different form. In performing the labor he is advancing in exchange; when he gets his wages the exchange is completed. During the time he is earning the wages he is advancing capital to his employer, but at no time, unless wages are paid before work is done, is the employer advancing capital to him. Whether the employer who receives this produce in exchange for the wages immediately re-exchanges it, or keeps it for awhile, no more alters the character of the transaction than does the final disposition of the product made by the ultimate receiver, who may, perhaps, be in another quarter of the globe and at the end of a series of exchanges numbering hundreds.

CHAPTER 4

THE MAINTENANCE OF LABORERS NOT DRAWN FROM CAPITAL

But a stumbling block may yet remain, or may recur, in the mind of the reader.

As the plowman cannot eat the furrow, nor a partially completed steam engine aid in any way in producing the clothes the machinist wears, have I not, in the words of John Stuart Mill, "forgotten that the people of a country are maintained and have their wants supplied, not by the produce of present labor, but of past"? Or, to use the language of a popular elementary work—that of Mrs. Fawcett—have I not "forgotten that many months must elapse between the sowing of the seed and the time when the produce of that seed is converted into a loaf of bread," and that "it is, therefore, evident that laborers cannot live upon that which their labor is assisting to produce, but are maintained by that wealth which their labor, or the labor of others, has previously produced, which wealth is capital"?*

The assumption made in these passages—the assumption that it is so self-evident that labor must be subsisted from capital that the proposition has but to be stated to compel recognition—runs through the whole fabric of current political economy. And so confidently is it held that the maintenance of labor is drawn from capi-

* "Political Economy for Beginners," by Millicent Garrett Fawcett, Chap. III, p. 25.

tal that the proposition that "population regulates itself by the funds which are to employ it, and, therefore, always increases or diminishes with the increase or diminution of capital,"* is regarded as equally axiomatic, and in its turn made the basis of important reasoning.

Yet being resolved, these propositions are seen to be, not self-evident, but absurd; for they involve the idea that labor cannot be exerted until the products of labor are saved—thus putting the product before the producer.

And being examined, they will be seen to derive their apparent plausibility from a confusion of thought.

I have already pointed out the fallacy, concealed by an erroneous definition, which underlies the proposition that because food, raiment and shelter are necessary to productive labor, therefore industry is limited by capital. To say that a man must have his breakfast before going to work is not to say that he cannot go to work unless a capitalist furnishes him with a breakfast, for his breakfast may, and in point of fact in any country where there is not actual famine will, come not from wealth set apart for the assistance of production, but from wealth set apart for subsistence. And, as has been previously shown, food, clothing, etc.—in short, all articles of wealth—are only capital so long as they remain in the possession of those who propose, not to consume, but to exchange them for other commodities or for productive services, and cease to be capital when they pass into the possession of those who will consume them; for in that transaction they pass from the stock of wealth held for the purpose of procuring other wealth, and pass into the stock of wealth held for purposes of gratification, irrespective of whether their consumption will aid in the production of wealth or not. Unless this distinc-

---

* The words quoted are Ricardo's (Chap. II); but the idea is common in standard works.

tion is preserved it is impossible to draw the line between the wealth that is capital and the wealth that is not capital, even by remitting the distinction to the "mind of the possessor," as does John Stuart Mill. For men do not eat or abstain, wear clothes or go naked, as they propose to engage in productive labor or not. They eat because they are hungry, and wear clothes because they would be uncomfortable without them. Take the food on the breakfast table of a laborer who will work or not that day as he gets the opportunity. If the distinction between capital and noncapital be the support of productive labor, is this food capital or not? It is as impossible for the laborer himself as for any philosopher of the Ricardo-Mill school to tell. Nor yet can it be told when it gets into his stomach; nor, supposing that he does not get work at first, but continues the search, can it be told until it has passed into the blood and tissues. Yet the man will eat his breakfast all the same.

But, though it would be logically sufficient, it is hardly safe to rest here and leave the argument to turn on the distinction between wealth and capital. Nor is it necessary. It seems to me that the proposition that present labor must be maintained by the produce of past labor will upon analysis prove to be true only in the sense that the afternoon's labor must be performed by the aid of the noonday meal, or that before you eat the hare he must be caught and cooked. And this, manifestly, is not the sense in which the proposition is used to support the important reasoning that is made to hinge upon it. That sense is, that before a work which will not immediately result in wealth available for subsistence can be carried on, there must exist such a stock of subsistence as will support the laborers during the process. Let us see if this be true:

The canoe which Robinson Crusoe made with such

infinite toil and pains was a production in which his labor could not yield an immediate return. But was it necessary that, before he commenced, he should accumulate a stock of food sufficient to maintain him while he felled the tree, hewed out the canoe, and finally launched her into the sea? Not at all. It was necessary only that he should devote part of his time to the procurement of food while he was devoting part of his time to the building and launching of the canoe. Or supposing a hundred men to be landed, without any stock of provisions, in a new country. Will it be necessary for them to accumulate a season's stock of provisions before they can begin to cultivate the soil? Not at all. It will be necessary only that fish, game, berries, etc., shall be so abundant that the labor of a part of the hundred may suffice to furnish daily enough of these for the maintenance of all, and that there shall be such a sense of mutual interest, or such a correlation of desires, as shall lead those who in the present get the food to divide (exchange) with those whose efforts are directed to future recompense.

What is true in these cases is true in all cases. It is not necessary to the production of things that cannot be used as subsistence, or cannot be immediately utilized, that there should have been a previous production of the wealth required for the maintenance of the laborers while the production is going on. It is only necessary that there should be, somewhere within the circle of exchange, a contemporaneous production of sufficient subsistence for the laborers, and a willingness to exchange this subsistence for the thing on which the labor is being bestowed.

And as a matter of fact is it not true, in any normal condition of things, that consumption is supported by contemporaneous production?

Here is a luxurious idler, who does no productive work

either with head or hand, but lives, we say, upon wealth
which his father left him securely invested in government bonds. Does his subsistence, as a matter of fact,
come from wealth accumulated in the past or from the
productive labor that is going on around him? On his
table are new-laid eggs, butter churned but a few days
before, milk which the cow gave this morning, fish which
twenty-four hours ago were swimming in the sea, meat
which the butcher boy has just brought in time to be
cooked, vegetables fresh from the garden, and fruit from
the orchard—in short, hardly anything that has not recently left the hand of the productive laborer (for in
this category must be included transporters and distribu-
tors as well as those who are engaged in the first stages
of production), and nothing that has been produced for
any considerable length of time, unless it may be some
bottles of old wine. What this man inherited from his
father, and on which we say he lives, is not actually
wealth at all, but only the power of commanding wealth
as others produce it. And it is from this contemporaneous production that his subsistence is drawn.

The fifty square miles of London undoubtedly contain
more wealth than within the same space anywhere else
exists. Yet were productive labor in London absolutely
to cease, within a few hours people would begin to die
like rotten sheep, and within a few weeks, or at most
a few months, hardly one would be left alive. For an
entire suspension of productive labor would be a disaster
more dreadful than ever yet befell a beleaguered city.
It would not be a mere external wall of circumvallation,
such as Titus drew around Jerusalem, which would prevent the constant incoming of the supplies on which a
great city lives, but it would be the drawing of a similar
wall around each household. Imagine such a suspension
of labor in any community, and you will see how true it
is that mankind really lives from hand to mouth; that

it is the daily labor of the community that supplies the community with its daily bread.

Just as the subsistence of the laborers who built the Pyramids was drawn not from a previously hoarded stock, but from the constantly recurring crops of the Nile Valley; just as a modern government when it undertakes a great work of years does not appropriate to it wealth already produced, but wealth yet to be produced, which is taken from producers in taxes as the work progresses; so it is that the subsistence of the laborers engaged in production which does not directly yield subsistence comes from the production of subsistence in which others are simultaneously engaged.

If we trace the circle of exchange by which work done in the production of a great steam engine secures to the worker bread, meat, clothes and shelter, we shall find that though between the laborer on the engine and the producers of the bread, meat, etc., there may be a thousand intermediate exchanges, the transaction, when reduced to its lowest terms, really amounts to an exchange of labor between him and them. Now the cause which induces the expenditure of the labor on the engine is evidently that some one who has power to give what is desired by the laborer on the engine wants in exchange an engine—that is to say, there exists a demand for an engine on the part of those producing bread, meat, etc., or on the part of those who are producing what the producers of the bread, meat, etc., desire. It is this demand which directs the labor of the machinist to the production of the engine, and hence, reversely, the demand of the machinist for bread, meat, etc., really directs an equivalent amount of labor to the production of these things, and thus his labor, actually exerted in the production of the engine, virtually produces the things in which he expends his wages.

Or, to formularize this principle:

The demand for consumption determines the direction in which labor will be expended in production.

This principle is so simple and obvious that it needs no further illustration, yet in its light all the complexities of our subject disappear, and we thus reach the same view of the real objects and rewards of labor in the intricacies of modern production that we gained by observing in the first beginnings of society the simpler forms of production and exchange. We see that now, as then, each laborer is endeavoring to obtain by his exertions the satisfaction of his own desires; we see that although the minute division of labor assigns to each producer the production of but a small part, or perhaps nothing at all, of the particular things he labors to get, yet, in aiding in the production of what other producers want, he is directing other labor to the production of the things he wants—in effect, producing them himself. And thus, if he make jackknives and eat wheat, the wheat is really as much the produce of his labor as if he had grown it for himself and left wheatgrowers to make their own jackknives.

We thus see how thoroughly and completely true it is, that in whatever is taken or consumed by laborers in return for labor rendered, there is no advance of capital to the laborers. If I have made jackknives, and with the wages received have bought wheat, I have simply exchanged jackknives for wheat—added jackknives to the existing stock of wealth and taken wheat from it. And as the demand for consumption determines the direction in which labor will be expended in production, it cannot even be said, so long as the limit of wheat production has not been reached, that I have lessened the stock of wheat, for, by placing jackknives in the exchangeable stock of wealth and taking wheat out, I have determined labor at the other end of a series of

exchanges to the production of wheat, just as the wheat
grower, by putting in wheat and demanding jackknives,
determined labor to the production of jackknives, as
the easiest way by which wheat could be obtained.

And so the man who is following the plow—though
the crop for which he is opening the ground is not yet
sown, and after being sown will take months to arrive at
maturity—he is yet, by the exertion of his labor in plowing, virtually producing the food he eats and the wages
he receives. For, though plowing is but a part of the
operation of producing a crop, it *is* a part, and as necessary a part as harvesting. The doing of it is a step toward procuring a crop, which, by the assurance which it
gives of the future crop, sets free from the stock constantly held the subsistence and wages of the plowman.
This is not merely theoretically true, it is practically and
literally true. At the proper time for plowing, let plowing cease. Would not the symptoms of scarcity at once
manifest themselves without waiting for the time of the
harvest? Let plowing cease, and would not the effect at
once be felt in counting room, and machine shop, and
factory? Would not loom and spindle soon stand as idle
as the plow? That this would be so, we see in the effect
which immediately follows a bad season. And if this
would be so, is not the man who plows really producing
his subsistence and wages as much as though during the
day or week his labor actually resulted in the things for
which his labor is exchanged?

As a matter of fact, where there is labor looking for
employment, the want of capital does not prevent the
owner of land which promises a crop for which there is
a demand from hiring it. Either he makes an agreement to cultivate on shares, a common method in
some parts of the United States, in which case the laborers, if they are without means of subsistence, will, on the
strength of the work they are doing, obtain credit at the

nearest store; or, if he prefers to pay wages, the farmer will himself obtain credit, and thus the work done in cultivation is immediately utilized or exchanged as it is done. If anything more will be used up than would be used up if the laborers were forced to beg instead of to work (for in any civilized country during a normal condition of things the laborers must be supported anyhow), it will be the reserve capital drawn out by the prospect of replacement, and which is in fact replaced by the work as it is done. For instance, in the purely agricultural districts of Southern California there was in 1877 a total failure of the crop, and of millions of sheep nothing remained but their bones. In the great San Joaquin Valley were many farmers without food enough to support their families until the next harvest time, let alone to support any laborers. But the rains came again in proper season, and these very farmers proceeded to hire hands to plow and to sow. For every here and there was a farmer who had been holding back part of his crop. As soon as the rains came he was anxious to sell before the next harvest brought lower prices, and the grain thus held in reserve, through the machinery of exchanges and advances, passed to the use of the cultivators—set free, in effect produced, by the work done for the next crop.

The series of exchanges which unite production and consumption may be likened to a curved pipe filled with water. If a quantity of water is poured in at one end, a like quantity is released at the other. It is not identically the same water, but is its equivalent. And so they who do the work of production put in as they take out—they receive in subsistence and wages but the produce of their labor.

CHAPTER **5** THE REAL
FUNCTIONS OF CAPITAL

It may now be asked: If capital is not required for the payment of wages or the support of labor during production, what, then, are its functions?

The previous examination has made the answer clear. Capital, as we have seen, consists of wealth used for the procurement of more wealth, as distinguished from wealth used for the direct satisfaction of desire; or, as I think it may be defined, of wealth in the course of exchange.

Capital, therefore, increases the power of labor to produce wealth: (1) By enabling labor to apply itself in more effective ways, as by digging up clams with a spade instead of the hand, or moving a vessel by shoveling coal into a furnace, instead of tugging at an oar. (2) By enabling labor to avail itself of the reproductive forces of nature, as to obtain corn by sowing it, or animals by breeding them. (3) By permitting the division of labor, and thus, on the one hand, increasing the efficiency of the human factor of wealth, by the utilization of special capabilities, the acquisition of skill, and the reduction of waste; and, on the other, calling in the powers of the natural factor at their highest, by taking advantage of the diversities of soil, climate and situation, so as to obtain each particular species of wealth where nature is most favorable to its production.

Capital does not supply the materials which labor works up into wealth, as is erroneously taught; the materials of wealth are supplied by nature. But such materials partially worked up and in the course of exchange are capital.

Capital does not supply or advance wages, as is erroneously taught. Wages are that part of the produce of his labor obtained by the laborer.

Capital does not maintain laborers during the progress of their work, as is erroneously taught. Laborers are maintained by their labor, the man who produces, in whole or in part, anything that will exchange for articles of maintenance, virtually producing that maintenance.

Capital, therefore, does not limit industry, as is erroneously taught, the only limit to industry being the access to natural material. But capital may limit the form of industry and the productiveness of industry, by limiting the use of tools and the division of labor.

That capital may limit the form of industry is clear. Without the factory, there could be no factory operatives; without the sewing machine, no machine sewing; without the plow, no plowman; and without a great capital engaged in exchange, industry could not take the many special forms which are concerned with exchanges. It is also as clear that the want of tools must greatly limit the productiveness of industry. If the farmer must use the spade because he has not capital enough for a plow, the sickle instead of the reaping machine, the flail instead of the thresher; if the machinist must rely upon the chisel for cutting iron; the weaver on the hand loom, and so on, the productiveness of industry cannot be a tithe of what it is when aided by capital in the shape of the best tools now in use. Nor could the division of labor go further than the very rudest and almost imperceptible beginnings, nor the exchanges which make it possible extend beyond the nearest neighbors, unless a portion of the things produced were constantly kept in stock or in transit. Even the pursuits of hunting, fishing, gathering nuts, and making weapons could not be specialized so that an individual could devote himself to any one, unless some part of what was procured by each was reserved from immediate consumption, so that he who devoted himself to the procurement of things of one kind could obtain the others as he wanted them, and could make the good luck of one day supply the shortcomings of the next. While to permit the minute subdivision of labor that is characteristic of, and necessary to, high civilization, a great amount of wealth of all descriptions must be constantly kept in stock or in transit. To enable the resident of a civilized community to exchange his labor at option with the labor of those around him and with the labor of men in the most remote parts of the globe, there must be stocks of goods in warehouses, in stores, in the holds of ships, and in railway cars, just as to enable the denizen of a great city to draw at will a cupful of water, there must be thousands of millions of gallons stored in reservoirs and moving through miles of pipe.

But to say that capital may limit the form of industry or the productiveness of industry is a very different thing from saying that capital limits industry. For the dictum of the current political economy that "capital limits industry," means not that capital limits the form of labor or the productiveness of labor, but that it limits the exertion of labor. This proposition derives its plausibility from the assumption that capital supplies labor with materials and maintenance—an assumption that we have seen to be unfounded, and which is indeed transparently preposterous the moment it is remembered that capital is produced by labor, and hence that there must be labor before there can be capital. Capital may limit the form of industry and the productiveness of industry; but this is not to say that there could be no industry without capital, any more than it is to say that without the power loom there could be no weaving; without the sewing machine no sewing; no cultivation without the plow; or that in a community of one, like that of Robinson Crusoe, there could be no labor because there could be no exchange.

And to say that capital may limit the form and productiveness of industry is a different thing from saying that capital does. For the cases in which it can be truly said that the form or productiveness of the industry of a community is limited by its capital, will, I think, appear upon examination to be more theoretical than real. It is evident that in such a country as Mexico or Tunis the larger and more general use of capital would greatly change the forms of industry and enormously increase its productiveness; and it is often said of such countries that they need capital for the development of their resources. But is there not something back of this—a want which includes the want of capital? Is it not the rapacity and abuses of government, the insecurity of property, the ignorance and prejudice of the people, that prevent the accumulation and use of capital? Is not the real limitation in these things, and not in the want of capital, which would not be used even if placed there? We can, of course, imagine a community in which the want of capital would be the only obstacle to an increased productiveness of labor, but it is only by imagining a conjunction of conditions that seldom, if ever, occurs, except by accident or as a passing phase. A community in which capital has been swept away by war, conflagration, or convulsion of nature, and, possibly, a community composed of civilized people just settled in a new land, seem to me to furnish the only examples. Yet how quickly the capital habitually used is reproduced in a community that has been swept by war, has long been noticed, while the rapid production of the capital it can, or is disposed to use, is equally noticeable in the case of a new community.

I am unable to think of any other than such rare and passing conditions in which the productiveness of labor is really limited by the want of capital. For, although there may be in a community individuals who from want of capital cannot apply their labor as efficiently as they would, yet so long as there is a sufficiency of capital in the community at large, the real limitation is not the want of capital, but the want of its proper distribution. If bad government rob the laborer of his capital, if unjust laws take from the producer the wealth with which he would assist production, and hand it over to those who are mere pensioners upon industry, the real limitation to the effectiveness of labor is in misgovernment, and not in want of capital. And so of ignorance, or custom, or other conditions which prevent the use of capital. It is they, not the want of capital, that really constitute the limitation. To give a circular saw to a Terra del Fuegan, a locomotive to a Bedouin Arab, or a sewing machine to a Flathead squaw, would not be to add to the efficiency of their labor. Neither does it seem possible by giving anything else to add to their capital, for any wealth beyond what they had been accustomed to use as capital would be consumed or suffered to waste. It is not the want of seeds and tools that keeps the Apache and the Sioux from cultivating the soil. If provided with seeds and tools they would not use them productively unless at the same time restrained from wandering and taught to cultivate the soil. If all the capital of a London were given them in their present condition, it would simply cease to be capital, for they would only use productively such infinitesimal part as might assist in the chase, and would not even use that until all the edible part of the stock thus showered upon them had been consumed. Yet such capital as they do want they manage to acquire, and in some forms in spite of the greatest difficulties. These wild tribes hunt and fight with the best weapons that American and English factories produce, keeping up with the latest improvements. It is only as they became civilized that they would care for such other capital as the civilized state requires, or that it would be of any use to them.

In the reign of George IV, some returning missionaries took with them to England a New Zealand chief called Hongi. His noble appearance and beautiful tattooing attracted much attention, and when about to return to his people he was presented by the monarch and some of the religious societies with a considerable stock of tools, agricultural instruments, and seeds. The grateful New Zealander did use this capital in the production of food, but it was in a manner of which his English entertainers little dreamed. In Sydney, on his way back, he exchanged it all for arms and ammunition, with which, on getting home, he began war against another tribe with such success that on the first battle field three hundred of his prisoners were cooked and eaten, Hongi having preluded the main repast by scooping out and swallowing the eyes and sucking the warm blood of his mortally wounded adversary, the opposing chief.* But now that their once constant wars have ceased, and the remnant of the Maoris have largely adopted European habits, there are among them many who have and use considerable amounts of capital.

Likewise it would be a mistake to attribute the simple modes of production and exchange which are resorted to in new communities solely to a want of capital. These modes, which require little capital, are in themselves rude and inefficient, but when the conditions of

---

* "New Zealand and its Inhabitants," Rev. Richard Taylor. London, 1855. Chap. XXI.

such communities are considered, they will be found in reality the most effective. A great factory with all the latest improvements is the most efficient instrument that has yet been devised for turning wool or cotton into cloth, but only so where large quantities are to be made. The cloth required for a little village could be made with far less labor by the spinning wheel and hand loom. A perfecting press will, for each man required, print many thousand impressions while a man and a boy would be printing a hundred with a Stanhope or Franklin press; yet to work off the small edition of a country newspaper the old-fashioned press is by far the most efficient machine. To carry occasionally two or three passengers, a canoe is a better instrument than a steamboat; a few sacks of flour can be transported with less expenditure of labor by a pack horse than by a railroad train; to put a great stock of goods into a cross-roads store in the backwoods would be but to waste capital. And, generally, it will be found that the rude devices of production and exchange which obtain among the sparse populations of new countries result not so much from the want of capital as from inability profitably to employ it.

As, no matter how much water is poured in, there can never be in a bucket more than a bucketful, so no greater amount of wealth will be used as capital than is required by the machinery of production and exchange that under all the existing conditions—intelligence, habit, security, density of population, etc.—best suit the people. And I am inclined to think that as a general rule this amount will be had—that the social organism secretes, as it were, the necessary amount of capital just as the human organism in a healthy condition secretes the requisite fat.

But whether the amount of capital ever does limit the productiveness of industry, and thus fix a maximum which wages cannot exceed, it is evident that it is not from any scarcity of capital that the poverty of the masses in civilized countries proceeds. For not only do wages nowhere reach the limit fixed by the productiveness of industry, but wages are relatively the lowest where capital is most abundant. The tools and machinery of production are in all the most progressive countries evidently in excess of the use made of them, and any prospect of remunerative employment brings out more than the capital needed. The bucket is not only full; it is overflowing. So evident is this, that not only among the ignorant, but by men of high economic reputation, is industrial depression attributed to the abundance of machinery and the accumulation of capital; and war, which is the destruction of capital, is looked upon as the cause of brisk trade and high wages—an idea strangely enough, so great is the confusion of thought on such matters, countenanced by many who hold that capital employs labor and pays wages.

Our purpose in this inquiry is to solve the problem to which so many self-contradictory answers are given. In ascertaining clearly what capital really is and what capital really does, we have made the first, and an all-important step. But it is only a first step. Let us recapitulate and proceed.

We have seen that the current theory that wages depend upon the ratio between the number of laborers and the amount of capital devoted to the employment of labor is inconsistent with the general fact that wages and interest do not rise and fall inversely, but conjointly.

This discrepancy having led us to an examination of the grounds of the theory, we have seen, further, that, contrary to the current idea, wages are not drawn from capital at all, but come directly from the produce of the labor for which they are paid. We have seen that capi-

tal does not advance wages or subsist laborers, but that
its functions are to assist labor in production with tools,
seed, etc., and with the wealth required to carry on exchanges.

We are thus irresistibly led to practical conclusions
so important as amply to justify the pains taken to
make sure of them.

For if wages are drawn, not from capital, but from
the produce of labor, the current theories as to the relations of capital and labor are invalid, and all remedies,
whether proposed by professors of political economy or
workingmen, which look to the alleviation of poverty
either by the increase of capital or the restriction of the
number of laborers or the efficiency of their work, must
be condemned.

If each laborer in performing the labor really creates
the fund from which his wages are drawn, then wages
cannot be diminished by the increase of laborers, but, on
the contrary, as the efficiency of labor manifestly increases with the number of laborers, the more laborers,
other things being equal, the higher should wages be.

But this necessary proviso, "other things being equal,"
brings us to a question which must be considered and
disposed of before we can further proceed. That question is: Do the productive powers of nature tend to
diminish with the increasing drafts made upon them by
increasing population?

Are God and Nature then at strife
  That Nature lends such evil dreams?
  So careful of the type she seems,
So careless of the single life.
               —TENNYSON.

CHAPTER 1 THE MALTHUSIAN THEORY, ITS GENESIS AND SUPPORT

Behind the theory we have been considering lies a theory we have yet to consider. The current doctrine as to the derivation and law of wages finds its strongest support in a doctrine as generally accepted—the doctrine to which Malthus has given his name—that population naturally tends to increase faster than subsistence. These two doctrines, fitting in with each other, frame the answer which the current political economy gives to the great problem we are endeavoring to solve.

In what has preceded, the current doctrine that wages are determined by the ratio between capital and laborers has, I think, been shown to be so utterly baseless as to excite surprise as to how it could so generally and so long obtain. It is not to be wondered at that such a theory should have arisen in a state of society where the great body of laborers seem to depend for employment and wages upon a separate class of capitalists, nor yet that under these conditions it should have maintained itself among the masses of men, who rarely take the trouble to separate the real from the apparent. But it is surprising that a theory which on examination appears to be so groundless could have been successively accepted by so many acute thinkers as have during the present century devoted their powers to the elucidation and development of the science of political economy.

The explanation of this otherwise unaccountable fact is to be found in the general acceptance of the Malthu-

sian theory. The current theory of wages has never
been fairly put upon its trial, because, backed by the
Malthusian theory, it has seemed in the minds of political economists a self-evident truth. These two theories
mutually blend with, strengthen, and defend each other,
while they both derive additional support from a principle brought prominently forward in the discussions of
the theory of rent—viz., that past a certain point the
application of capital and labor to land yields a diminishing return. Together they give such an explanation
of the phenomena presented in a highly organized and
advancing society as seems to fit all the facts, and which
has thus prevented closer investigation.

Which of these two theories is entitled to historical
precedence it is hard to say. The theory of population
was not formulated in such a way as to give it the standing of a scientific dogma until after that had been done
for the theory of wages. But they naturally spring up
and grow with each other, and were both held in a form
more or less crude long prior to any attempt to construct
a system of political economy. It is evident, from
several passages, that though he never fully developed
it, the Malthusian theory was in rudimentary form present in the mind of Adam Smith, and to this, it seems to
me, must be largely due the misdirection which on the
subject of wages his speculations took. But, however
this may be, so closely are the two theories connected,
so completely do they complement each other, that
Buckle, reviewing the history of the development of political economy in his "Examination of the Scotch Intellect during the Eighteenth Century," attributes mainly
to Malthus the honor of "decisively proving" the current theory of wages by advancing the current theory
of the pressure of population upon subsistence. He says
in his "History of Civilization in England," Vol. 3,
Chap. 5:

"Scarcely had the Eighteenth Century passed away when it was decisively proved that the reward of labor depends solely on two things; namely, the magnitude of that national fund out of which all labor is paid, and the number of laborers among whom the fund is to be divided. This vast step in our knowledge is due, mainly, though not entirely, to Malthus, whose work on population, besides marking an epoch in the history of speculative thought, has already produced considerable practical results, and will probably give rise to others more considerable still. It was published in 1798; so that Adam Smith, who died in 1790, missed what to him would have been the intense pleasure of seeing how, in it, his own views were expanded rather than corrected. Indeed, it is certain that without Smith there would have been no Malthus; that is, unless Smith had laid the foundation, Malthus could not have raised the superstructure."

The famous doctrine which ever since its enunciation has so powerfully influenced thought, not alone in the province of political economy, but in regions of even higher speculation, was formulated by Malthus in the proposition that, as shown by the growth of the North American colonies, the natural tendency of population is to double itself at least every twenty-five years, thus increasing in a geometrical ratio, while the subsistence that can be obtained from land "under circumstances the most favorable to human industry could not possibly be made to increase faster than in an arithmetical ratio, or by an addition every twenty-five years of a quantity equal to what it at present produces." "The necessary effects of these two different rates of increase, when brought together," Mr. Malthus naïvely goes on to say, "will be very striking." And thus (Chap. I) he brings them together:

"Let us call the population of this island eleven millions; and suppose the present produce equal to the easy support of such a number. In the first twenty-five years the population would be twenty-two millions, and the food being also doubled, the means of subsistence would be equal to this increase. In the next twenty-five years the population would be forty-four millions, and the means of subsistence only equal

to the support of thirty-three millions. In the next period the population would be equal to eighty-eight millions, and the means of subsistence just equal to the support of half that number. And at the
conclusion of the first century, the population would be a hundred
and seventy-six millions, and the means of subsistence only equal to
the support of fifty-five millions; leaving a population of a hundred
and twenty-one millions totally unprovided for.

"Taking the whole earth instead of this island, emigration would of
course be excluded; and supposing the present population equal to a
thousand millions, the human species would increase as the numbers
1, 2, 4, 8, 16, 32, 64, 128, 256, and subsistence as 1, 2, 3, 4, 5, 6,
7, 8, 9. In two centuries the population would be to the means of
subsistence as 256 to 9; in three centuries, 4,096 to 13, and in two thousand years the difference would be almost incalculable."

Such a result is of course prevented by the physical
fact that no more people can exist than can find subsistence, and hence Malthus' conclusion is, that this tendency of population to indefinite increase must be held
back either by moral restraint upon the reproductive
faculty, or by the various causes which increase mortality, which he resolves into vice and misery. Such
causes as prevent propagation he styles the preventive
check; such causes as increase mortality he styles the
positive check. This is the famous Malthusian doctrine,
as promulgated by Malthus himself in the "Essay on
Population."

It is not worth while to dwell upon the fallacy involved in the assumption of geometrical and arithmetical
rates of increase, a play upon proportions which hardly
rises to the dignity of that in the familiar puzzle of the
hare and the tortoise, in which the hare is made to
chase the tortoise through all eternity without coming
up with him. For this assumption is not necessary to
the Malthusian doctrine, or at least is expressly repudiated by some of those who fully accept that doctrine;
as, for instance, John Stuart Mill, who speaks of it as
"an unlucky attempt to give precision to things which

do not admit of it, which every person capable of reasoning must see is wholly superfluous to the argument."* The essence of the Malthusian doctrine is, that population tends to increase faster than the power of providing food, and whether this difference be stated as a geometrical ratio for population and an arithmetical ratio for subsistence, as by Malthus; or as a constant ratio for population and a diminishing ratio for subsistence, as by Mill, is only a matter of statement. The vital point, on which both agree, is, to use the words of Malthus, "that there is a natural tendency and constant effort in population to increase beyond the means of subsistence."

The Malthusian doctrine, as at present held, may be thus stated in its strongest and least objectionable form:

That population, constantly tending to increase, must, when unrestrained, ultimately press against the limits of subsistence, not as against a fixed, but as against an elastic barrier, which makes the procurement of subsistence progressively more and more difficult. And thus, wherever reproduction has had time to assert its power, and is unchecked by prudence, there must exist that degree of want which will keep population within the bounds of subsistence.

Although in reality not more repugnant to the sense of harmonious adaptation by creative beneficence and wisdom than the complacent no-theory which throws the responsibility for poverty and its concomitants upon the inscrutable decrees of Providence, without attempt-

---

* "Principles of Political Economy," Book II, Chap. IX, Sec. VI.—Yet notwithstanding what Mill says, it is clear that Malthus himself lays great stress upon his geometrical and arithmetical ratios, and it is also probable that it is to these ratios that Malthus is largely indebted for his fame, as they supplied one of those high-sounding formulas that with many people carry far more weight than the clearest reasoning.

ing to trace them, this theory, in avowedly making vice and suffering the necessary results of a natural instinct with which are linked the purest and sweetest affections, comes rudely in collision with ideas deeply rooted in the human mind, and it was, as soon as formally promulgated, fought with a bitterness in which zeal was often more manifest than logic. But it has triumphantly withstood the ordeal, and in spite of the refutations of the Godwins, the denunciations of the Cobbetts, and all the shafts that argument, sarcasm, ridicule, and sentiment could direct against it, today it stands in the world of thought as an accepted truth, which compels the recognition even of those who would fain disbelieve it.

The causes of its triumph, the sources of its strength, are not obscure. Seemingly backed by an indisputable arithmetical truth—that a continuously increasing population must eventually exceed the capacity of the earth to furnish food or even standing room, the Malthusian theory is supported by analogies in the animal and vegetable kingdoms, where life everywhere beats wastefully against the barriers that hold its different species in check—analogies to which the course of modern thought, in leveling distinctions between different forms of life, has given a greater and greater weight; and it is apparently corroborated by many obvious facts, such as the prevalence of poverty, vice, and misery amid dense populations; the general effect of material progress in increasing population without relieving pauperism; the rapid growth of numbers in newly settled countries and the evident retardation of increase in more densely settled countries by the mortality among the class condemned to want.

The Malthusian theory furnishes a general principle which accounts for these and similar facts, and accounts for them in a way which harmonizes with the doctrine that wages are drawn from capital, and with all the principles that are deduced from it. According to the current doctrine of wages, wages fall as increase in the number of laborers necessitates a more minute division of capital; according to the Malthusian theory, poverty appears as increase in population necessitates the more minute division of subsistence. It requires but the identification of capital with subsistence, and number of laborers with population, an identification made in the current treatises on political economy, where the terms are often converted, to make the two propositions as identical formally as they are substantially.* And thus it is, as stated by Buckle in the passage previously quoted, that the theory of population advanced by Malthus has appeared to prove decisively the theory of wages advanced by Smith.

Ricardo, who a few years subsequent to the publication of the "Essay on Population" corrected the mistake into which Smith had fallen as to the nature and cause of rent, furnished the Malthusian theory an additional support by calling attention to the fact that rent would increase as the necessities of increasing population forced cultivation to less and less productive lands, or to less and less productive points on the same lands, thus explaining the rise of rent. In this way was formed a triple combination, by which the Malthusian theory has been buttressed on both sides—the previously received doctrine of wages and the subsequently received doctrine of rent exhibiting in this view but special examples of the operation of the general principle to which the name of Malthus has been attached—the fall in wages and the rise in rents which come with increasing popula-

* The effect of the Malthusian doctrine upon the definitions of capital may, I think, be seen by comparing (see pp. 33, 34, 35) the definition of Smith, who wrote prior to Malthus, with the definitions of Ricardo, McCulloch and Mill, who wrote subsequently.

tion being but modes in which the pressure of population upon subsistence shows itself.

Thus taking its place in the very framework of political economy (for the science as currently accepted has undergone no material change or improvement since the time of Ricardo, though in some minor points it has been cleared and illustrated), the Malthusian theory, though repugnant to sentiments before alluded to, is not repugnant to other ideas which, in older countries at least, generally prevail among the working classes; but, on the contrary, like the theory of wages by which it is supported and in turn supports, it harmonizes with them. To the mechanic or operative the cause of low wages and of the inability to get employment is obviously the competition caused by the pressure of numbers, and in the squalid abodes of poverty what seems clearer than that there are too many people?

But the great cause of the triumph of this theory is, that, instead of menacing any vested right or antagonizing any powerful interest, it is eminently soothing and reassuring to the classes who, wielding the power of wealth, largely dominate thought. At a time when old supports were falling away, it came to the rescue of the special privileges by which a few monopolize so much of the good things of this world, proclaiming a natural cause for the want and misery which, if attributed to political institutions, must condemn every government under which they exist. The "Essay on Population" was avowedly a reply to William Godwin's "Inquiry concerning Political Justice," a work asserting the principle of human equality; and its purpose was to justify existing inequality by shifting the responsibility for it from human institutions to the laws of the Creator. There was nothing new in this, for Wallace, nearly forty years before, had brought forward the danger of excessive multiplication as the answer to the demands of justice

for an equal distribution of wealth; but the circumstances of the times were such as to make the same
idea, when brought forward by Malthus, peculiarly
grateful to a powerful class, in whom an intense fear of
any questioning of the existing state of things had been
generated by the outburst of the French Revolution.

Now, as then, the Malthusian doctrine parries the demand for reform, and shelters selfishness from question
and from conscience by the interposition of an inevitable
necessity. It furnishes a philosophy by which Dives as
he feasts can shut out the image of Lazarus who faints
with hunger at his door; by which wealth may com-
placently button up its pocket when poverty asks an
alms, and the rich Christian bend on Sundays in a nicely
upholstered pew to implore the good gifts of the All
Father without any feeling of responsibility for the
squalid misery that is festering but a square away. For
poverty, want, and starvation are by this theory not
chargeable either to individual greed or to social maladjustments; they are the inevitable results of universal
laws, with which, if it were not impious, it were as hopeless to quarrel as with the law of gravitation. In this
view, he who in the midst of want has accumulated
wealth, has but fenced in a little oasis from the driving
sand which else would have overwhelmed it. He has
gained for himself, but has hurt nobody. And even if
the rich were literally to obey the injunctions of Christ
and divide their wealth among the poor, nothing would
be gained. Population would be increased, only to press
again upon the limits of subsistence or capital, and the
equality that would be produced would be but the equality of common misery. And thus reforms which would
interfere with the interests of any powerful class are
discouraged as hopeless. As the moral law forbids any
forestalling of the methods by which the natural law
gets rid of surplus population and thus holds in check

a tendency to increase potent enough to pack the surface of the globe with human beings as sardines are packed in a box, nothing can really be done, either by individual or by combined effort, to extirpate poverty, save to trust to the efficacy of education and preach the necessity of prudence.

A theory that, falling in with the habits of thought of the poorer classes, thus justifies the greed of the rich and the selfishness of the powerful, will spread quickly and strike its roots deep. This has been the case with the theory advanced by Malthus.

And of late years the Malthusian theory has received new support in the rapid change of ideas as to the origin of man and the genesis of species. That Buckle was right in saying that the promulgation of the Malthusian theory marked an epoch in the history of speculative thought could, it seems to me, be easily shown; yet to trace its influence in the higher domains of philosophy, of which Buckle's own work is an example, would, though extremely interesting, carry us beyond the scope of this investigation. But how much be reflex and how much original, the support which is given to the Malthusian theory by the new philosophy of development, now rapidly spreading in every direction, must be noted in any estimate of the sources from which this theory derives its present strength. As in political economy, the support received from the doctrine of wages and the doctrine of rent combined to raise the Malthusian theory to the rank of a central truth, so the extension of similar ideas to the development of life in all its forms has the effect of giving it a still higher and more impregnable position. Agassiz, who, to the day of his death, was a strenuous opponent of the new philosophy, spoke of Darwinism as "Malthus all over,"* and Darwin himself

* Address before Massachusetts State Board of Agriculture, 1872. "Report U. S. Department of Agriculture, 1873."

says the struggle for existence "is the doctrine of Malthus applied with manifold force to the whole animal and vegetable kingdoms."*

It does not, however, seem to me exactly correct to say that the theory of development by natural selection or survival of the fittest is extended Malthusianism, for the doctrine of Malthus did not originally and does not necessarily involve the idea of progression. But this was soon added to it. McCulloch† attributes to the "principle of increase" social improvement and the progress of the arts, and declares that the poverty that it engenders acts as a powerful stimulus to the development of industry, the extension of science and the accumulation of wealth by the upper and middle classes, without which stimulus society would quickly sink into apathy and decay. What is this but the recognition in regard to human society of the developing effects of the "struggle for existence" and "survival of the fittest," which we are now told on the authority of natural science have been the means which Nature has employed to bring forth all the infinitely diversified and wonderfully adapted forms which the teeming life of the globe assumes? What is it but the recognition of the force, which, seemingly cruel and remorseless, has yet in the course of unnumbered ages developed the higher from the lower type, differentiated the man and the monkey, and made the Nineteenth Century succeed the age of stone?

Thus commended and seemingly proved, thus linked and buttressed, the Malthusian theory—the doctrine that poverty is due to the pressure of population against subsistence, or, to put it in its other form, the doctrine that the tendency to increase in the number of laborers must always tend to reduce wages to the minimum on

---

* "Origin of Species," Chap. III.
† Note IV to "Wealth of Nations."

which laborers can reproduce—is now generally accepted as an unquestionable truth, in the light of which social phenomena are to be explained, just as for ages the phenomena of the sidereal heavens were explained upon the supposition of the fixity of the earth, or the facts of geology upon that of the literal inspiration of the Mosaic record. If authority were alone to be considered, formally to deny this doctrine would require almost as much audacity as that of the colored preacher who recently started out on a crusade against the opinion that the earth moves around the sun, for in one form or another, the Malthusian doctrine has received in the intellectual world an almost universal indorsement, and in the best as in the most common literature of the day may be seen cropping out in every direction. It is indorsed by economists and by statesmen, by historians and by natural investigators; by social science congresses and by trade unions; by churchmen and by materialists; by conservatives of the strictest sect and by the most radical of radicals. It is held and habitually reasoned from by many who never heard of Malthus and who have not the slightest idea of what his theory is.

Nevertheless, as the grounds of the current theory of wages have vanished when subjected to a candid examination, so, do I believe, will vanish the grounds of this, its twin. In proving that wages are not drawn from capital we have raised this Antæus from the earth.

CHAPTER 2 INFERENCES FROM FACTS

The general acceptance of the Malthusian theory and the high authority by which it is indorsed have seemed to me to make it expedient to review its grounds and the causes which have conspired to give it such a dominating influence in the discussion of social questions.

But when we subject the theory itself to the test of straightforward analysis, it will, I think, be found as utterly untenable as the current theory of wages.

In the first place, the facts which are marshaled in support of this theory do not prove it, and the analogies do not countenance it.

And in the second place, there are facts which conclusively disprove it.

I go to the heart of the matter in saying that there is no warrant, either in experience or analogy, for the assumption that there is any tendency in population to increase faster than subsistence. The facts cited to show this simply show that where, owing to the sparseness of population, as in new countries, or where, owing to the unequal distribution of wealth, as among the poorer classes in old countries, human life is occupied with the physical necessities of existence, the tendency to reproduce is at a rate which would, were it to go on unchecked, some time exceed subsistence. But it is not a legitimate inference from this that the tendency to reproduce would show itself in the same force where population was sufficiently dense and wealth distributed with sufficient evenness to lift a whole community above

the necessity of devoting their energies to a struggle for
mere existence. Nor can it be assumed that the tendency to reproduce, by causing poverty, must prevent
the existence of such a community; for this, manifestly,
would be assuming the very point at issue, and reasoning in a circle. And even if it be admitted that the
tendency to multiply must ultimately produce poverty,
it cannot from this alone be predicated of existing poverty that it is due to this cause, until it be shown that
there are no other causes which can account for it—a
thing in the present state of government, laws, and
customs, manifestly impossible.

This is abundantly shown in the "Essay on Population" itself. This famous book, which is much oftener
spoken of than read, is still well worth perusal, if only
as a literary curiosity. The contrast between the merits
of the book itself and the effect it has produced, or is at
least credited with (for though Sir James Stewart, Mr.
Townsend, and others, share with Malthus the glory of
discovering "the principle of population," it was the
publication of the "Essay on Population" that brought
it prominently forward), is, it seems to me, one of the
most remarkable things in the history of literature; and
it is easy to understand how Godwin, whose "Political
Justice" provoked the "Essay on Population," should
until his old age have disdained a reply. It begins with
the assumption that population tends to increase in a
geometrical ratio, while subsistence can at best be made
to increase only in an arithmetical ratio—an assumption
just as valid, and no more so, than it would be, from the
fact that a puppy doubled the length of his tail while
he added so many pounds to his weight, to assert a geometric progression of tail and an arithmetical progression of weight. And, the inference from the assumption
is just such as Swift in satire might have credited to the
savants of a previously dogless island, who, by bringing

these two ratios together, might deduce the very "striking consequence" that by the time the dog grew to a
weight of fifty pounds his tail would be over a mile long,
and extremely difficult to wag, and hence recommend
the prudential check of a bandage as the only alternative to the positive check of constant amputations.
Commencing with such an absurdity, the essay includes
a long argument for the imposition of a duty on the importation, and the payment of a bounty for the exportation of corn, an idea that has long since been sent to the
limbo of exploded fallacies. And it is marked throughout the argumentative portions by passages which show
on the part of the reverend gentleman the most ridiculous incapacity for logical thought—as, for instance,
that if wages were to be increased from eighteen pence
or two shillings per day to five shillings, meat would
necessarily increase in price from eight or nine pence to
two or three shillings per pound, and the condition of
the laboring classes would therefore not be improved, a
statement to which I can think of no parallel so close as
a proposition I once heard a certain printer gravely advance—that because an author, whom he had known,
was forty years old when he was twenty, the author
must now be eighty years old because he (the printer)
was forty. This confusion of thought does not merely
crop out here and there; it characterizes the whole
work.* The main body of the book is taken up with
what is in reality a refutation of the theory which the

---

* Malthus' other works, though written after he became famous,
made no mark, and are treated with contempt even by those who find
in the Essay a great discovery. The Encyclopædia Britannica, for instance,
though fully accepting the Malthusian theory, says of Malthus' Political Economy: "It is very ill arranged, and is in no respect either a
practical or a scientific exposition of the subject. It is in great part
occupied with an examination of parts of Mr. Ricardo's peculiar doctrines, and with an inquiry into the nature and causes of value. Nothing,

book advances, for Malthus' review of what he calls the positive checks to population is simply the showing that the results which he attributes to overpopulation actually arise from other causes. Of all the cases cited, and pretty much the whole globe is passed over in the survey, in which vice and misery check increase by limiting marriages or shortening the term of human life, there is not a single case in which the vice and misery can be traced to an actual increase in the number of mouths over the power of the accompanying hands to feed them; but in every case the vice and misery are shown to spring either from unsocial ignorance and rapacity, or from bad government, unjust laws or destructive warfare.

Nor what Malthus failed to show has any one since him shown. The globe may be surveyed and history may be reviewed in vain for any instance of a considerable country* in which poverty and want can be fairly attributed to the pressure of an increasing population. Whatever be the possible dangers involved in the power of human increase, they have never yet appeared. Whatever may some time be, this never yet has been the evil that has afflicted mankind. Population always tending to overpass the limit of subsistence! How is it, then, that this globe of ours, after all the thousands, and it is now thought millions, of years that man has been

---

however, can be more unsatisfactory than these discussions. In truth Mr. Malthus never had any clear or accurate perception of Mr. Ricardo's theories, or of the principles which determine the value in exchange of different articles."

* I say considerable country, because there may be small islands, such as Pitcairn's Island, cut off from communication with the rest of the world and consequently from the exchanges which are necessary to the improved modes of production resorted to as population becomes dense, which may seem to offer examples in point. A moment's reflection, however, will show that these exceptional cases are not in point.

upon the earth, is yet so thinly populated? How is it, then, that so many of the hives of human life are now deserted—that once cultivated fields are rank with jungle, and the wild beast licks her cubs where once were busy haunts of men?

It is a fact, that, as we count our increasing millions, we are apt to lose sight of—nevertheless it is a fact— that in what we know of the world's history decadence of population is as common as increase. Whether the aggregate population of the earth is now greater than at any previous epoch is a speculation which can deal only with guesses. Since Montesquieu, in the early part of the last century, asserted, what was then probably the prevailing impression, that the population of the earth had, since the Christian era, greatly declined, opinion has run the other way. But the tendency of recent in-vestigation and exploration has been to give greater credit to what have been deemed the exaggerated ac-counts of ancient historians and travelers, and to reveal indications of denser populations and more advanced civilizations than had before been suspected, as well as of a higher antiquity in the human race. And in basing our estimates of population upon the development of trade, the advance of the arts, and the size of cities, we are apt to underrate the density of population which the intensive cultivations, characteristic of the earlier civili-zations, are capable of maintaining—especially where irrigation is resorted to. As we may see from the closely cultivated districts of China and Europe a very great population of simple habits can readily exist with very little commerce and a much lower stage of those arts in which modern progress has been most marked, and without that tendency to concentrate in cities which modern populations show.*

* As may be seen from the map in H. H. Bancroft's "Native Races," the State of Vera Cruz is not one of those parts of Mexico noticeable

Be this as it may, the only continent which we can be sure now contains a larger population than ever before is Europe. But this is not true of all parts of Europe. Certainly Greece, the Mediterranean Islands, and Turkey in Europe, probably Italy, and possibly Spain, have contained larger populations than now, and this may be likewise true of Northwestern and parts of Central and Eastern Europe.

America also has increased in population during the time we know of it; but this increase is not so great as is popularly supposed, some estimates giving to Peru alone at the time of the discovery a greater population than now exists on the whole continent of South America. And all the indications are that previous to the discovery the population of America had been declining. What great nations have run their course, what empires have arisen and fallen in "that new world which is the old," we can only imagine. But fragments of massive ruins yet attest a grander pre-Incan civilization; amid the tropical forests of Yucatan and Central America are the remains of great cities forgotten ere the Spanish conquest; Mexico, as Cortez found it, showed the superimposition of barbarism upon a higher social development, while through a great part of what is now the United States are scattered mounds which prove a once relatively dense population, and here and there, as in the Lake Superior copper mines, are traces of higher arts

---

for its antiquities. Yet Hugo Fink, of Cordova, writing to the Smithsonian Institution (Reports 1870), says there is hardly a foot in the whole State in which by excavation either a broken obsidian knife or a broken piece of pottery is not found; that the whole country is intersected with parallel lines of stones intended to keep the earth from washing away in the rainy season, which shows that even the very poorest land was put into requisition, and that it is impossible to resist the conclusion that the ancient population was at least as dense as it is at present in the most populous districts of Europe.

than were known to the Indians with whom the whites came in contact.

As to Africa there can be no question. Northern Africa can contain but a fraction of the population that it had in ancient times; the Nile Valley once held an enormously greater population than now, while south of the Sahara there is nothing to show increase within historic times, and widespread depopulation was certainly caused by the slave trade.

As for Asia, which even now contains more than half the human race, though it is not much more than half as densely populated as Europe, there are indications that both India and China once contained larger populations than now, while that great breeding ground of men from which issued swarms that overran both countries and sent great waves of people rolling upon Europe, must have been once far more populous. But the most marked change is in Asia Minor, Syria, Babylonia, Persia, and in short that vast district which yielded to the conquering arms of Alexander. Where were once great cities and teeming populations are now squalid villages and barren wastes.

It is somewhat strange that among all the theories that have been raised, that of a fixed quantity to human life on this earth has not been broached. It would at least better accord with historical facts than that of the constant tendency of population to outrun subsistence. It is clear that population has here ebbed and there flowed; its centers have changed; new nations have arisen and old nations declined; sparsely settled districts have become populous and populous districts have lost their population; but as far back as we can go without abandoning ourselves wholly to inference, there is nothing to show continuous increase, or even clearly to show an aggregate increase from time to time. The advance of the pioneers of peoples has, so far as we can discern, never been into uninhabited lands—their march has always been a battle with some other people previously in possession; behind dim empires vaguer ghosts of empire loom. That the population of the world must have had its small beginnings we confidently infer, for we know that there was a geologic era when human life could not have existed, and we cannot believe that men sprang up all at once, as from the dragon teeth sowed by Cadmus; yet through long vistas, where history, tradition and antiquities shed a light that is lost in faint glimmers, we may discern large populations. And during these long periods the principle of population has not been strong enough fully to settle the world, or even so far as we can clearly see materially to increase its aggregate population. Compared with its capacities to support human life the earth as a whole is yet most sparsely populated.

There is another broad, general fact which cannot fail to strike any one who, thinking of this subject, extends his view beyond modern society. Malthusianism predicates a universal law—that the natural tendency of population is to outrun subsistence. If there be such a law, it must, wherever population has attained a certain density, become as obvious as any of the great natural laws which have been everywhere recognized. How is it, then, that neither in classical creeds and codes, nor in those of the Jews, the Egyptians, the Hindoos, the Chinese, nor any of the peoples who have lived in close association and have built up creeds and codes, do we find any injunctions to the practice of the prudential restraints of Malthus; but that, on the contrary, the wisdom of the centuries, the religions of the world, have always inculcated ideas of civic and religious duty the very reverse of those which the current political economy enjoins, and which Annie Besant is now trying to popularize in England?

And it must be remembered that there have been societies in which the community guaranteed to every member employment and subsistence. John Stuart Mill says (Book II, Chap. XII, Sec. 2), that to do this without state regulation of marriages and births, would be to produce a state of general misery and degradation. "These consequences," he says, "have been so often and so clearly pointed out by authors of reputation that ignorance of them on the part of educated persons is no longer pardonable." Yet in Sparta, in Peru, in Paraguay, as in the industrial communities which appear almost everywhere to have constituted the primitive agricultural organization, there seems to have been an utter ignorance of these dire consequences of a natural tendency.

Besides the broad, general facts I have cited, there are facts of common knowledge which seem utterly inconsistent with such an overpowering tendency to multiplication. If the tendency to reproduce be so strong as Malthusianism supposes, how is it that families so often become extinct—families in which want is unknown? How is it, then, that when every premium is offered by hereditary titles and hereditary possessions, not alone to the principle of increase, but to the preservation of genealogical knowledge and the proving up of descent, that in such an aristocracy as that of England, so many peerages should lapse, and the House of Lords be kept up from century to century only by fresh creations?

For the solitary example of a family that has survived any great lapse of time, even though assured of subsistence and honor, we must go to unchangeable China. The descendants of Confucius still exist there, and enjoy peculiar privileges and consideration, forming, in fact, the only hereditary aristocracy. On the presumption that population tends to double every twenty-five years, they should, in 2,150 years after the death of Confucius, have amounted to 859,559,193,106,-709,670,198,710,528 souls. Instead of any such unimaginable number, the descendants of Confucius, 2,150 years after his death, in the reign of Kanghi numbered 11,000 males, or say 22,000 souls. This is quite a discrepancy, and is the more striking when it is remembered that the esteem in which this family is held on account of their ancestor, "the Most Holy Ancient Teacher," has prevented the operation of the positive check, while the maxims of Confucius inculcate anything but the prudential check.

Yet, it may be said, that even this increase is a great one. Twenty-two thousand persons descended from a single pair in 2,150 years is far short of the Malthusian rate. Nevertheless, it is suggestive of possible overcrowding.

But consider. Increase of descendants does not show increase of population. It could only do this when the breeding was in and in. Smith and his wife have a son and daughter, who marry respectively some one else's daughter and son, and each have two children. Smith and his wife would thus have four grandchildren; but there would be in the one generation no greater number than in the other—each child would have four grandparents. And supposing this process were to go on, the line of descent might constantly spread out into hundreds, thousands and millions; but in each generation of descendants there would be no more individuals than in any previous generation of ancestors. The web of generations is like lattice-work or the diagonal threads in cloth. Commencing at any point at the top, the eye follows lines which at the bottom widely diverge; but beginning at any point at the bottom, the lines diverge in the same way to the top. How many children a man may have is problematical. But that he had two parents is certain, and that these again had two parents each is also certain. Follow this geometrical progression through a few generations and see if it does not lead to quite as "striking consequences" as Mr. Malthus' peopling of the solar systems.

But from such considerations as these let us advance to a more definite inquiry. I assert that the cases commonly cited as instances of overpopulation will not bear investigation. India, China, and Ireland furnish the strongest of these cases. In each of these countries, large numbers have perished by starvation and large classes are reduced to abject misery or compelled to emigrate. But is this really due to over-population?

Comparing total population with total area, India and China are far from being the most densely populated countries of the world. According to the estimates of MM. Behm and Wagner, the population of India is but 132 to the square mile and that of China 119, whereas Saxony has a population of 442 to the square mile; Belgium 441; England 442; the Netherlands 291; Italy 234 and Japan 233.* There are thus in both countries large areas unused or not fully used, but even in their more densely populated districts there can be no doubt that either could maintain a much greater population in a much higher degree of comfort, for in both countries is labor applied to production in the rudest and most inefficient ways, and in both countries great natural resources are wholly neglected. This arises from no

---

* I take these figures from the Smithsonian Report for 1873, leaving out decimals. MM. Behm and Wagner put the population of China at 446,500,000, though there are some who contend that it does not exceed 150,000,000. They put the population of Hither India at 206,225,580, giving 132.29 to the square mile; of Ceylon at 2,405,287 or 97.36 to the square mile; of Further India at 21,018,062, or 27.94 to the square mile. They estimate the population of the world at 1,377,000,000, an average of 26.64 to the square mile.

innate deficiency in the people, for the Hindoo, as comparative philology has shown, is of our own blood, and China possessed a high degree of civilization and the rudiments of the most important modern inventions when our ancestors were wandering savages. It arises from the form which the social organization has in both countries taken, which has shackled productive power and robbed industry of its reward.

In India from time immemorial, the working classes have been ground down by exactions and oppressions into a condition of helpless and hopeless degradation. For ages and ages the cultivator of the soil has esteemed himself happy if, of his produce, the extortion of the strong hand left him enough to support life and furnish seed; capital could nowhere be safely accumulated or to any considerable extent be used to assist production; all wealth that could be wrung from the people was in the possession of princes who were little better than robber chiefs quartered on the country, or in that of their farmers or favorites, and was wasted in useless or worse than useless luxury, while religion, sunken into an elaborate and terrible superstition, tyrannized over the mind as physical force did over the bodies of men. Under these conditions, the only arts that could advance were those that ministered to the ostentation and luxury of the great. The elephants of the rajah blazed with gold of exquisite workmanship, and the umbrellas that symbolized his regal power glittered with gems; but the plow of the ryot was only a sharpened stick. The ladies of the rajah's harem wrapped themselves in muslins so fine as to take the name of woven wind, but the tools of the artisan were of the poorest and rudest description and commerce could only be carried on, as it were, by stealth.

Is it not clear that this tyranny and insecurity have produced the want and starvation of India; and not, as according to Buckle, the pressure of population upon subsistence that has produced the want, and the want the tyranny.* Says the Rev. William Tennant, a chaplain in the service of the East India Company, writing in 1796, two years before the publication of the "Essay on Population":

"When we reflect upon the great fertility of Hindostan, it is amazing to consider the frequency of famine. It is evidently not owing to any sterility of soil or climate; the evil must be traced to some political cause, and it requires but little penetration to discover it in the avarice and extortion of the various governments. The great spur to industry, that of security, is taken away. Hence no man raises more grain than is barely sufficient for himself, and the first unfavorable season produces a famine.

"The Mogul government at no period offered full security to the prince, still less to his vassals; and to peasants the most scanty protection of all. It was a continued tissue of violence and insurrection, treachery and punishment, under which neither commerce nor the arts could prosper, nor agriculture assume the appearance of a system. Its downfall gave rise to a state still more afflictive, since anarchy is worse than misrule. The Mohammedan government, wretched as it was, the European nations have not the merit of overturning. It fell beneath the weight of its own corruption, and had already been succeeded by the multifarious tyranny of petty chiefs, whose right to govern consisted in their treason to the state, and whose exactions on the peasants were as boundless as their avarice. The rents to government were, and, where natives rule, still are, levied twice a year by a merciless banditti, under the semblance of an army, who wantonly destroy or carry off whatever part of the produce may satisfy their caprice or satiate their avidity, after having hunted the ill-fated peasants from the villages to the woods. Any attempt of the peasants to defend their persons or property within the mud walls of their villages only calls for the more signal vengeance on those useful, but ill-fated mortals.

* "History of Civilization," Vol. I, Chap. 2. In this chapter Buckle has collected a great deal of evidence of the oppression and degradation of the people of India from the most remote times, a condition which, blinded by the Malthusian doctrine he has accepted and made the cornerstone of his theory of the development of civilization, he attributes to the ease with which food can there be produced.

They are then surrounded and attacked with musketry and field pieces till resistance ceases, when the survivors are sold, and their habitations burned and leveled with the ground. Hence you will frequently meet with the ryots gathering up the scattered remnants of what had yesterday been their habitation, if fear has permitted them to return; but oftener the ruins are seen smoking, after a second visitation of this kind, without the appearance of a human being to interrupt the awful silence of destruction. This description does not apply to the Mohammedan chieftains alone; it is equally applicable to the Rajahs in the districts governed by Hindoos."*

To this merciless rapacity, which would have produced want and famine were the population but one to a square mile and the land a Garden of Eden, succeeded, in the first era of British rule in India, as merciless a rapacity, backed by a far more irresistible power. Says Macaulay, in his essay on Lord Clive:

"Enormous fortunes were rapidly accumulated at Calcutta, while millions of human beings were reduced to the extremity of wretchedness. They had been accustomed to live under tyranny, but never under tyranny like this. They found the little finger of the Company thicker than the loins of Surajah Dowlah. * * * It resembled the government of evil genii, rather than the government of human tyrants. Sometimes they submitted in patient misery. Sometimes they fled from the white man as their fathers had been used to fly from the Maharatta, and the palanquin of the English traveler was often carried through silent villages and towns that the report of his approach had made desolate."

Upon horrors that Macaulay thus but touches, the vivid eloquence of Burke throws a stronger light—whole districts surrendered to the unrestrained cupidity of the worst of human kind, poverty-stricken peasants fiendishly tortured to compel them to give up their little hoards, and once populous tracts turned into deserts.

* "India Recreations," by Rev. Wm. Tennant. London, 1804, Vol. I, Sec. XXXIX.

But the lawless license of early English rule has been long restrained. To all that vast population the strong hand of England has given a more than Roman peace; the just principles of English law have been extended by an elaborate system of codes and law officers designed to secure to the humblest of these abject peoples the rights of Anglo-Saxon freemen; the whole peninsula has been intersected by railways, and great irrigation works have been constructed. Yet, with increasing frequency, famine has succeeded famine, raging with greater intensity over wider areas.

Is not this a demonstration of the Malthusian theory? Does it not show that no matter how much the possibilities of subsistence are increased, population still continues to press upon it? Does it not show, as Malthus contended, that, to shut up the sluices by which superabundant population is carried off, is but to compel nature to open new ones, and that unless the sources of human increase are .checked by prudential regulation, the alternative of war is famine? This has been the orthodox explanation. But the truth, as may be seen in the facts brought forth in recent discussions of Indian affairs in the English periodicals, is that these famines, which have been, and are now, sweeping away their millions, are no more due to the pressure of population upon the natural limits of subsistence than was the desolation of the Carnatic when Hyder Ali's horsemen burst upon it in a whirlwind of destruction.

The millions of India have bowed their necks beneath the yokes of many conquerors, but worst of all is the steady, grinding weight of English domination—a weight which is literally crushing millions out of existence, and, as shown by English writers, is inevitably tending to a most frightful and widespread catastrophe. Other conquerors have lived in the land, and, though bad and tyrannous in their rule, have understood and been understood by the people; but India now is like a great estate owned by an absentee and alien landlord. A most expensive military and civil establishment is kept up, managed and officered by Englishmen who regard India as but a place of temporary exile; and an enormous sum, estimated as at least £20,000,000 annually, raised from a population where laborers are in many places glad in good times to work for 1½d. to 4d. a day, is drained away to England in the shape of remittances, pensions, home charges of the government, etc.—a tribute for which there is no return. The immense sums lavished on railroads have, as shown by the returns, been economically unproductive; the great irrigation works are for the most part costly failures. In large parts of India the English, in their desire to create a class of landed proprietors, turned over the soil in absolute possession to hereditary taxgatherers, who rackrent the cultivators most mercilessly. In other parts, where the rent is still taken by the State in the shape of a land tax, assessments are so high, and taxes are collected so relentlessly, as to drive the ryots, who get but the most scanty living in good seasons, into the claws of money lenders, who are, if possible, even more rapacious than the zemindars. Upon salt, an article of prime necessity everywhere, and of especial necessity where food is almost exclusively vegetable, a tax of nearly twelve hundred per cent. is imposed, so that its various industrial uses are prohibited, and large bodies of the people cannot get enough to keep either themselves or their cattle in health. Below the English officials are a horde of native employees who oppress and extort. The effect of English law, with its rigid rules, and, to the native, mysterious proceedings, has been but to put a potent instrument of plunder into the hands of the native money lenders, from whom the peasants are compelled to borrow on the most extravagant terms

to meet their taxes, and to whom they are easily induced
to give obligations of which they know not the meaning.
"We do not care for the people of India," writes Florence Nightingale, with what seems like a sob. "The
saddest sight to be seen in the East—nay, probably in
the world—is the peasant of our Eastern Empire." And
she goes on to show the causes of the terrible famines,
in taxation which takes from the cultivators the very
means of cultivation, and the actual slavery to which
the ryots are reduced as "the consequences of our own
laws"; producing in "the most fertile country in the
world, a grinding, chronic semi-starvation in many places
where what is called famine does not exist."* "The
famines which have been devastating India," says H. M.
Hyndman,† "are in the main financial famines. Men
and women cannot get food, because they cannot save
the money to buy it. Yet we are driven, so we say, to
tax these people more." And he shows how, even from
famine stricken districts, food is exported in payment
of taxes, and how the whole of India is subjected to a
steady and exhausting drain, which, combined with the
enormous expenses of government, is making the population year by year poorer. The exports of India con-

* Miss Nightingale ("The People of India," in *Nineteenth Century*
for August, 1878) gives instances, which she says represent millions of
cases, of the state of peonage to which the cultivators of southern India
have been reduced through the facilities afforded by the Civil Courts
to the frauds and oppressions of money lenders and minor native officials. "Our Civil Courts are regarded as institutions for enabling the
rich to grind the faces of the poor, and many are fain to seek a refuge
from their jurisdiction within native territory," says Sir David Wed-
derburn, in an article, "Protected Princes in India," in a previous
(July) number of the same magazine, in which he also gives a native
state, where taxation is comparatively light, as an instance of the most
prosperous population of India.

† See articles in *Nineteenth Century* for October, 1878, and March,
1879.

sist almost exclusively of agricultural products. For at
least one-third of these, as Mr. Hyndman shows, no return whatever is received; they represent tribute—remittances made by Englishmen in India, or expenses
of the English branch of the Indian government.* And
for the rest, the return is for the most part government
stores, or articles of comfort and luxury used by the
English masters of India. He shows that the expenses
of government have been enormously increased under
Imperial rule; that the relentless taxation of a population so miserably poor that the masses are not more
than half fed, is robbing them of their scanty means for
cultivating the soil; that the number of bullocks (the
Indian draft animal) is decreasing, and the scanty im-
plements of culture being given up to money lenders,
from whom "we, a business people, are forcing the cultivators to borrow at 12, 24, 60 per cent.† to build and
pay the interest on the cost of vast public works, which
have never paid nearly five per cent." Says Mr. Hyndman: "The truth is that Indian society as a whole has
been frightfully impoverished under our rule, and that
the process is now going on at an exceedingly rapid
rate"—a statement which cannot be doubted, in view
of the facts presented not only by such writers as I have
referred to, but by Indian officials themselves. The very
efforts made by the government to alleviate famines
do, by the increased taxation imposed, but intensify and
extend their real cause. Although in the recent famine

---

* Prof. Fawcett, in a recent article on the proposed loans to India,
calls attention to such items as £1,200 for outfit and passage of a member of the Governor General's Council; £2,450 for outfit and passage of
bishops of Calcutta and Bombay.

† Florence Nightingale says 100 per cent. is common, and even then
the cultivator is robbed in ways which she illustrates. It is hardly necessary to say that these rates, like those of the pawnbroker, are not interest in the economic sense of the term.

in Southern India six millions of people, it is estimated, perished of actual starvation, and the great mass of those who survived were actually stripped, yet the taxes were not remitted and the salt tax, already prohibitory to the great bulk of these poverty-stricken people, was increased forty per cent., just as after the terrible Bengal famine in 1770 the revenue was actually driven up, by raising assessments upon the survivors and rigorously enforcing collection.

In India now, as in India in past times, it is only the most superficial view that can attribute want and starvation to pressure of population upon the ability of the land to produce subsistence. Could the cultivators retain their little capital—could they be released from the drain which, even in non-famine years, reduces great masses of them to a scale of living not merely below what is deemed necessary for the sepoys, but what English humanity gives to the prisoners in the jails—reviving industry, assuming more productive forms, would undoubtedly suffice to keep a much greater population. There are still in India great areas uncultivated, vast mineral resources untouched, and it is certain that the population of India does not reach, as within historical times it never has reached, the real limit of the soil to furnish subsistence, or even the point where this power begins to decline with the increasing drafts made upon it. The real cause of want in India has been, and yet is, the rapacity of man, not the niggardliness of nature.

What is true of India is true of China. Densely populated as China is in many parts, that the extreme poverty of the lower classes is to be attributed to causes similar to those which have operated in India, and not to too great population, is shown by many facts. Insecurity prevails, production goes on under the greatest disadvantages, and exchange is closely fettered. Where the government is a succession of squeezings, and security for capital of any sort must be purchased of a mandarin; where men's shoulders are the great reliance for inland transportation; where the junk is obliged to be constructed so as to unfit it for a sea boat; where piracy is a regular trade, and robbers often march in regiments, poverty would prevail and the failure of a crop result in famine, no matter how sparse the population.* That China is capable of supporting a much greater population is shown not only by the great extent of uncultivated land to which all travelers testify, but by the immense unworked mineral deposits which are there known to exist. China, for instance, is said to contain the largest and finest deposit of coal yet anywhere discovered. How much the working of these coal beds would add to the ability to support a greater population, may readily be imagined. Coal is not food, it is true; but its production is equivalent to the production of food. For, not only may coal be exchanged for food, as is done in all mining districts, but the force evolved by its consumption may be used in the production of food, or may set labor free for the production of food.

Neither in India nor China, therefore, can poverty and starvation be charged to the pressure of population against subsistence. It is not dense population, but the causes which prevent social organization from taking its natural development and labor from securing its full return, that keep millions just on the verge of starvation, and every now and again force millions beyond it. That the Hindoo laborer thinks himself fortunate to get a handful of rice, that the Chinese eat rats and puppies, is no more due to the pressure of population than it is due to the pressure of population that the Digger Indians live on grasshoppers, or the aboriginal inhabitants of Australia eat the worms found in rotten wood.

* The seat of recent famine in China was not the most thickly settled districts.

Let me be understood. I do not mean merely to say that India or China could, with a more highly developed civilization, maintain a greater population, for to this any Malthusian would agree. The Malthusian doctrine does not deny that an advance in the productive arts would permit a greater population to find subsistence. But the Malthusian theory affirms—and this is its essence—that, whatever be the capacity for production, the natural tendency of population is to come up with it, and, in the endeavor to press beyond it, to produce, to use the phrase of Malthus, that degree of vice and misery which is necessary to prevent further increase; so that as productive power is increased, population will correspondingly increase, and in a little time produce the same results as before. What I say is this: that nowhere is there any instance which will support this theory; that nowhere can want be properly attributed to the pressure of population against the power to procure subsistence in the then existing degree of human knowledge; that everywhere the vice and misery attributed to overpopulation can be traced to the warfare, tyranny, and oppression which prevent knowledge from being utilized and deny the security essential to production. The reason why the natural increase of population does not produce want, we shall come to hereafter. The fact that it has not yet anywhere done so, is what we are now concerned with. This fact is obvious with regard to India and China. It will be obvious, too, wherever we trace to their causes the results which on superficial view are often taken to proceed from overpopulation.

Ireland, of all European countries, furnishes the great stock example of overpopulation. The extreme poverty of the peasantry and the low rate of wages there prevailing, the Irish famine, and Irish emigration, are constantly referred to as a demonstration of the Malthusian theory worked out under the eyes of the civilized world. I doubt if a more striking instance can be cited of the power of a preaccepted theory to blind men as to the true relations of facts. The truth is, and it lies on the surface, that Ireland has never yet had a population which the natural powers of the country, in the existing state of the productive arts, could not have maintained in ample comfort. At the period of her greatest population (1840–45) Ireland contained something over eight millions of people. But a very large proportion of them managed merely to exist—lodging in miserable cabins, clothed with miserable rags, and with but potatoes for their staple food. When the potato blight came, they died by thousands. But was it the inability of the soil to support so large a population that compelled so many to live in this miserable way, and exposed them to starvation on the failure of a single root crop? On the contrary, it was the same remorseless rapacity that robbed the Indian ryot of the fruits of his toil and left him to starve where nature offered plenty. A merciless banditti of tax-gatherers did not march through the land plundering and torturing, but the laborer was just as effectually stripped by as merciless a horde of landlords, among whom the soil had been divided as their absolute possession, regardless of any rights of those who lived upon it.

Consider the conditions of production under which this eight million managed to live until the potato blight came. It was a condition to which the words used by Mr. Tennant in reference to India may as appropriately be applied—"the great spur to industry, that of security, was taken away." Cultivation was for the most part carried on by tenants at will, who, even if the rackrents which they were forced to pay had permitted them, did not dare to make improvements which would have been but the signal for an increase of rent. Labor was thus applied in the most inefficient and wasteful manner, and labor was dissipated in aimless idleness that, with any security for its fruits, would have been applied unremittingly. But even under these conditions, it is a matter of fact that Ireland did more than support eight millions. For when her population was at its highest, Ireland was a food exporting country. Even during the famine, grain and meat and butter and cheese were carted for exportation along roads lined with the starving and past trenches into which the dead were piled. For these exports of food, or at least for a great part of them, there was no return. So far as the people of Ireland were concerned, the food thus exported might as well have been burned up or thrown into the sea, or never produced. It went not as an exchange, but as a tribute—to pay the rent of absentee landlords; a levy wrung from producers by those who in no wise contributed to production.

Had this food been left to those who raised it; had the cultivators of the soil been permitted to retain and use the capital their labor produced; had security stimulated industry and permitted the adoption of economical methods, there would have been enough to support in bounteous comfort the largest population Ireland ever had, and the potato blight might have come and gone without stinting a single human being of a full meal. For it was not the imprudence "of Irish peasants," as English economists coldly say, which induced them to make the potato the staple of their food. Irish emigrants, when they can get other things, do not live upon the potato, and certainly in the United States the prudence of the Irish character, in endeavoring to lay by something for a rainy day, is remarkable. They lived on the potato, because rackrents stripped everything else from them. The truth is, that the poverty and misery of Ireland have never been fairly attributable to overpopulation.

BOOK II   CHAPTER 2

McCulloch, writing in 1838, says, in Note IV to
"Wealth of Nations":

"The wonderful density of population in Ireland is the immediate
cause of the abject poverty and depressed condition of the great bulk
of the people. It is not too much to say that there are at present more
than double the persons in Ireland it is, with its existing means of production, able either fully to employ or to maintain in a moderate state
of comfort."

As in 1841 the population of Ireland was given as
8,175,124, we may set it down in 1838 as about eight
millions. Thus, to change McCulloch's negative into an
affirmative, Ireland would, according to the overpopulation theory, have been able to employ fully and maintain in a moderate state of comfort something less than
four million persons. Now, in the early part of the
preceding century, when Dean Swift wrote his "Modest
Proposal," the population of Ireland was about two
millions. As neither the means nor the arts of production had perceptibly advanced in Ireland during the
interval, then—if the abject poverty and depressed condition of the Irish people in 1838 were attributable to
overpopulation—there should, upon McCulloch's own
admission, have been in Ireland in 1727 more than full
employment, and much more than a moderate state of
comfort, for the whole two millions. Yet, instead of
this being the case, the abject poverty and depressed
condition of the Irish people in 1727 were such, that,
with burning, blistering irony, Dean Swift proposed to
relieve surplus population by cultivating a taste for
roasted babies, and bringing yearly to the shambles, as
dainty food for the rich, 100,000 Irish infants!
It is difficult for one who has been looking over the
literature of Irish misery, as while writing this chapter
I have been doing, to speak in decorous terms of the
complacent attribution of Irish want and suffering to
overpopulation which is to be found even in the works

of such high-minded men as Mill and Buckle. I know
of nothing better calculated to make the blood boil
than the cold accounts of the grasping, grinding tyranny
to which the Irish people have been subjected, and to
which, and not to any inability of the land to support
its population, Irish pauperism and Irish famine are
to be attributed; and were it not for the enervating effect which the history of the world proves to be everywhere the result of abject poverty, it would be difficult
to resist something like a feeling of contempt for a race
who, stung by such wrongs, have only occasionally murdered a landlord!

Whether overpopulation ever did cause pauperism
and starvation, may be an open question; but the
pauperism and starvation of Ireland can no more be attributed to this cause than can the slave trade be attributed to the overpopulation of Africa, or the destruction
of Jerusalem to the inability of subsistence to keep pace
with reproduction. Had Ireland been by nature a grove
of bananas and bread fruit, had her coasts been lined
by the guano deposits of the Chinchas, and the sun of
lower latitudes warmed into more abundant life her
moist soil, the social conditions that have prevailed
there would still have brought forth poverty and starvation. How could there fail to be pauperism and
famine in a country where rackrents wrested from the
cultivator of the soil all the produce of his labor except
just enough to maintain life in good seasons; where
tenure at will forbade improvements and removed incentive to any but the most wasteful and poverty-
stricken culture; where the tenant dared not accumulate
capital, even if he could get it, for fear the landlord
would demand it in the rent; where in fact he was an
abject slave, who, at the nod of a human being like himself, might at any time be driven from his miserable
mud cabin, a houseless, homeless, starving wanderer,

forbidden even to pluck the spontaneous fruits of the earth, or to trap a wild hare to satisfy his hunger? No matter how sparse the population, no matter what the natural resources, are not pauperism and starvation necessary consequences in a land where the producers of wealth are compelled to work under conditions which deprive them of hope, of self-respect, of energy, of thrift; where absentee landlords drain away without return at least a fourth of the net produce of the soil, and when, besides them, a starving industry must support resident landlords, with their horses and hounds, agents, jobbers, middlemen and bailiffs, an alien state church to insult religious prejudices, and an army of policemen and soldiers to overawe and hunt down any opposition to the iniquitous system? Is it not impiety far worse than atheism to charge upon natural laws misery so caused?

What is true in these three cases will be found upon examination true of all cases. So far as our knowledge of facts goes, we may safely deny that the increase of population has ever yet pressed upon subsistence in such a way as to produce vice and misery; that increase of numbers has ever yet decreased the relative production of food. The famines of India, China, and Ireland can no more be credited to overpopulation than the famines of sparsely populated Brazil. The vice and misery that come of want can no more be attributed to the niggardliness of Nature than can the six millions slain by the sword of Genghis Khan, Tamerlane's pyramid of skulls, or the extermination of the ancient Britons or of the aboriginal inhabitants of the West Indies.

CHAPTER 3 INFERENCES FROM ANALOGY

If we turn from an examination of the facts brought forward in illustration of the Malthusian theory to consider the analogies by which it is supported, we shall find the same inconclusiveness.

The strength of the reproductive force in the animal and vegetable kingdoms—such facts as that a single pair of salmon might, if preserved from their natural enemies for a few years, fill the ocean; that a pair of rabbits would, under the same circumstances, soon overrun a continent; that many plants scatter their seeds by the hundred fold, and some insects deposit thousands of eggs; and that everywhere through these kingdoms each species constantly tends to press, and when not limited by the number of its enemies, evidently does press, against the limits of subsistence—is constantly cited, from Malthus down to the textbooks of the present day, as showing that population likewise tends to press against subsistence, and, when unrestrained by other means, its natural increase must necessarily result in such low wages and want, or, if that will not suffice, and the increase still goes on, in such actual starvation, as will keep it within the limits of subsistence.

But is this analogy valid? It is from the vegetable and animal kingdoms that man's food is drawn, and hence the greater strength of the reproductive force in the vegetable and animal kingdoms than in man simply proves the power of subsistence to increase faster than population. Does not the fact that all of the things which furnish man's subsistence have the power to multiply many fold—some of them many thousand fold, and some of them many million or even billion fold—while he is only doubling his numbers, show that, let human beings increase to the full extent of their reproductive power, the increase of population can never exceed subsistence? This is clear when it is remembered that though in the vegetable and animal kingdoms each species, by virtue of its reproductive power, naturally and necessarily presses against the conditions which limit its further increase, yet these conditions are nowhere fixed and final. No species reaches the ultimate limit of soil, water, air, and sunshine; but the actual limit of each is in the existence of other species, its rivals, its enemies, or its food. Thus the conditions which limit the existence of such of these species as afford him subsistence man can extend (in some cases his mere appearance will extend them), and thus the reproductive forces of the species which supply his wants, instead of wasting themselves against their former limit, start forward in his service at a pace which his powers of increase cannot rival. If he but shoot hawks, food-birds will increase; if he but trap foxes the wild rabbits will multiply; the honey bee moves with the pioneer, and on the organic matter with which man's presence fills the rivers, fishes feed.

Even if any consideration of final causes be excluded; even if it be not permitted to suggest that the high and constant reproductive force in vegetables and animals has been ordered to enable them to subserve the uses of man, and that therefore the pressure of the lower forms of life against subsistence does not tend to show that it must likewise be so with man, "the roof and crown of things"; yet there still remains a distinction between man and all other forms of life that destroys the analogy. Of all living things, man is the only one who can give play to the reproductive forces, more powerful than his own, which supply him with food. Beast, insect, bird, and fish take only what they find. Their increase is at the expense of their food, and when they have reached the existing limits of food, their food must increase before they can increase. But unlike that of any other living thing, the increase of man involves the increase of his food. If bears instead of men had been shipped from Europe to the North American continent, there would now be no more bears than in the time of Columbus, and possibly fewer, for bear food would not have been increased nor the conditions of bear life extended, by the bear immigration, but probably the reverse. But within the limits of the United States alone, there are now forty-five millions of men where then there were only a few hundred thousand, and yet there is now within that territory much more food per capita for the forty-five millions than there was then for the few hundred thousand. It is not the increase of food that has caused this increase of men; but the increase of men that has brought about the increase of food. There is more food, simply because there are more men.

Here is a difference between the animal and the man. Both the jayhawk and the man eat chickens, but the more jayhawks the fewer chickens, while the more men the more chickens. Both the seal and the man eat salmon, but when a seal takes a salmon there is a salmon the less, and were seals to increase past a certain point salmon must diminish; while by placing the spawn of the salmon under favorable conditions man can so increase the number of salmon as more than to make up for all he may take, and thus, no matter how much men may increase, their increase need never outrun the supply of salmon.

BOOK II CHAPTER 3

In short, while all through the vegetable and animal kingdoms the limit of subsistence is independent of the thing subsisted, with man the limit of subsistence is, within the final limits of earth, air, water, and sunshine, dependent upon man himself. And this being the case, the analogy which it is sought to draw between the lower forms of life and man manifestly fails. While vegetables and animals do press against the limits of subsistence, man cannot press against the limits of his subsistence until the limits of the globe are reached. Observe, this is not merely true of the whole, but of all the parts. As we cannot reduce the level of the smallest bay or harbor without reducing the level not merely of the ocean with which it communicates, but of all the seas and oceans of the world, so the limit of subsistence in any particular place is not the physical limit of that place, but the physical limit of the globe. Fifty square miles of soil will in the present state of the productive arts yield subsistence for only some thousands of people, but on the fifty square miles which comprise the city of London some three and a half millions of people are maintained, and subsistence increases as population increases. So far as the limit of subsistence is concerned, London may grow to a population of a hundred millions, or five hundred millions, or a thousand millions, for she draws for subsistence upon the whole globe, and the limit which subsistence sets to her growth in population is the limit of the globe to furnish food for its inhabitants.

But here will arise another idea from which the Malthusian theory derives great support—that of the diminishing productiveness of land. As conclusively proving the law of diminishing productiveness it is said in the current treatises that were it not true that beyond a certain point land yields less and less to additional applications of labor and capital, increasing population would not cause any extension of cultivation, but that all the increased supplies needed could and would be raised without taking into cultivation any fresh ground. Assent to this seems to involve assent to the doctrine that the difficulty of obtaining subsistence must increase with increasing population.

But I think the necessity is only in seeming. If the proposition be analyzed it will be seen to belong to a class that depend for validity upon an implied or suggested qualification—a truth relatively, which taken absolutely becomes a nontruth. For that man cannot exhaust or lessen the powers of nature follows from the indestructibility of matter and the persistence of force. Production and consumption are only relative terms. Speaking absolutely, man neither produces nor consumes. The whole human race, were they to labor to infinity, could not make this rolling sphere one atom heavier or one atom lighter, could not add to or diminish by one iota the sum of the forces whose everlasting circling produces all motion and sustains all life. As the water that we take from the ocean must again return to the ocean, so the food we take from the reservoirs of nature is, from the moment we take it, on its way back to those reservoirs. What we draw from a limited extent of land may temporarily reduce the productiveness of that land, because the return may be to other land, or may be divided between that land and other land, or, perhaps, all land; but this possibility lessens with increasing area, and ceases when the whole globe is considered. That the earth could maintain a thousand billions of people as easily as a thousand millions is a necessary deduction from the manifest truths that, at least so far as our agency is concerned, matter is eternal and force must forever continue to act. Life does not use up the forces that maintain life. We come into the material universe bringing nothing; we take nothing away when we depart. The human being, physically considered, is but a transient form of matter, a changing mode of motion. The matter remains and the force persists. Nothing is lessened, nothing is weakened. And from this it follows that the limit to the population of the globe can be only the limit of space.

Now this limitation of space—this danger that the human race may increase beyond the possibility of finding elbow room—is so far off as to have for us no more practical interest than the recurrence of the glacial period or the final extinguishment of the sun. Yet remote and shadowy as it is, it is this possibility which gives to the Malthusian theory its apparently self-evident character. But if we follow it, even this shadow will disappear. It, also, springs from a false analogy. That vegetable and animal life tend to press against the limits of space does not prove the same tendency in human life.

Granted that man is only a more highly developed animal; that the ring-tailed monkey is a distant relative who has gradually developed acrobatic tendencies, and the humpbacked whale a far-off connection who in early life took to the sea—granted that back of these he is kin to the vegetable, and is still subject to the same laws as plants, fishes, birds, and beasts. Yet there is still this difference between man and all other animals —he is the only animal whose desires increase as they are fed; the only animal that is never satisfied. The wants of every other living thing are uniform and fixed. The ox of to-day aspires to no more than did the ox when man first yoked him. The sea gull of the English Channel, who poises himself above the swift steamer, wants no better food or lodging than the gulls who circled round as the keels of Cæsar's galleys first grated on a British beach. Of all that nature offers them, be it ever so abundant, all living things save man can take, and care for, only enough to supply wants which are definite and fixed. The only use they can make of additional supplies or additional opportunities is to multiply.

But not so with man. No sooner are his animal wants satisfied than new wants arise. Food he wants first, as does the beast; shelter next, as does the beast; and these given, his reproductive instincts assert their sway, as do those of the beast. But here man and beast part company. The beast never goes further; the man has but set his feet on the first step of an infinite progression—a progression upon which the beast never enters; a progression away from and above the beast.

The demand for quantity once satisfied, he seeks quality. The very desires that he has in common with the beast become extended, refined, exalted. It is not merely hunger, but taste, that seeks gratification in food; in clothes, he seeks not merely comfort, but adornment; the rude shelter becomes a house; the undiscriminating sexual attraction begins to transmute itself into subtile influences, and the hard and common stock of animal life to blossom and to bloom into shapes of delicate beauty. As power to gratify his wants increases, so does aspiration grow. Held down to lower levels of desire, Lucullus will sup with Lucullus; twelve boars turn on spits that Antony's mouthful of meat may be done to a turn; every kingdom of Nature be ransacked to add to Cleopatra's charms, and marble colonnades and hanging gardens and pyramids that rival the hills arise. Passing into higher forms of desire, that which slumbered in the plant and fitfully stirred in the beast, awakes in the man. The eyes of the mind are opened, and he longs to know. He braves the scorching heat of the desert and the icy blasts of the polar sea, but not for food; he watches all night, but it is to trace the circling of the eternal stars. He adds toil to toil, to gratify a hunger no animal has felt; to assuage a thirst no beast can know.

Out upon nature, in upon himself, back through the mists that shroud the past, forward into the darkness that overhangs the future, turns the restless desire that arises when the animal wants slumber in satisfaction. Beneath things, he seeks the law; he would know how the globe was forged and the stars were hung, and trace to their origins the springs of life. And, then, as the man develops his nobler nature, there arises the desire higher yet—the passion of passions, the hope of hopes—the desire that he, even he, may somehow aid in making life better and brighter, in destroying want and sin, sorrow and shame. He masters and curbs the animal; he turns his back upon the feast and renounces the place of power; he leaves it to others to accumulate wealth, to gratify pleasant tastes, to bask themselves in the warm sunshine of the brief day. He works for those he never saw and never can see; for a fame, or maybe but for a scant justice, that can only come long after the clods have rattled upon his coffin lid. He toils in the advance, where it is cold, and there is little cheer from men, and the stones are sharp and the brambles thick. Amid the scoffs of the present and the sneers that stab like knives, he builds for the future; he cuts the trail that progressive humanity may hereafter broaden into a highroad. Into higher, grander spheres desire mounts and beckons, and a star that rises in the east leads him on. Lo! the pulses of the man throb with the yearnings of the god—he would aid in the process of the suns!

Is not the gulf too wide for the analogy to span? Give more food, open fuller conditions of life, and the vegetable or animal can but multiply; the man will develop. In the one the expansive force can but extend existence in new numbers; in the other, it will inevitably tend to extend existence in higher forms and wider powers. Man is an animal; but he is an animal plus something else. He is the mythic earth tree, whose roots are in the ground, but whose topmost branches may blossom in the heavens!

Whichever way it be turned, the reasoning by which this theory of the constant tendency of population to press against the limits of subsistence is supported shows an unwarranted assumption, an undistributed middle, as the logicians would say. Facts do not warrant it, analogy does not countenance it. It is a pure chimera of the imagination, such as those that for a long time prevented men from recognizing the rotundity and motion of the earth. It is just such a theory as that underneath us everything not fastened to the earth must fall off; as that a ball dropped from the mast of a ship in motion must fall behind the mast; as that a live fish placed in a vessel full of water will displace no water. It is as unfounded, if not as grotesque, as an assumption we can imagine Adam might have made had he been of an arithmetical turn of mind and figured on the growth of his first baby from the rate of its early months. From the fact that at birth it weighed ten pounds and in eight months thereafter twenty pounds, he might, with the arithmetical knowledge which some sages have supposed him to possess, have ciphered out a result quite as striking as that of Mr. Malthus; namely, that by the time it got to be ten years old it would be as heavy as an ox, at twelve as heavy as an elephant, and at thirty would weigh no less than 175,716,339,548 tons.

The fact is, there is no more reason for us to trouble ourselves about the pressure of population upon subsistence than there was for Adam to worry himself about the rapid growth of his baby. So far as an inference is really warranted by facts and suggested by analogy, it is that the law of population includes such beautiful adaptations as investigation has already shown in other natural laws, and that we are no more warranted in assuming that the instinct of reproduction, in the natural development of society, tends to produce misery and vice, than we should be in assuming that the force of gravitation must hurl the moon to the earth and the earth to the sun, or than in assuming from the contraction of water with reductions of temperature down to thirty-two degrees that rivers and lakes must freeze to the bottom with every frost, and the temperate regions of earth be thus rendered uninhabitable by even moderate winters. That, besides the positive and prudential checks of Malthus, there is a third check which comes into play with the elevation of the standard of comfort and the development of the intellect, is pointed to by many well-known facts. The proportion of births is notoriously greater in new settlements, where the struggle with nature leaves little opportunity for intellectual life, and among the poverty-bound classes of older countries, who in the midst of wealth are deprived of all its advantages and reduced to all but an animal existence, than it is among the classes to whom the increase of wealth has brought independence, leisure, comfort, and a fuller and more varied life. This fact, long ago recognized in the homely adage, "a rich man for luck, and a poor man for children," was noted by Adam Smith, who says it is not uncommon to find a poor half-starved Highland woman has been the mother of twenty-three or twenty-four children, and is everywhere so clearly perceptible that it is only necessary to allude to it.

If the real law of population is thus indicated, as I think it must be, then the tendency to increase, instead of being always uniform, is strong where a greater population would give increased comfort, and where the perpetuity of the race is threatened by the mortality induced by adverse conditions; but weakens just as the higher development of the individual becomes possible and the perpetuity of the race is assured. In other words, the law of population accords with and is subordinate to the law of intellectual development, and any danger that human beings may be brought into a world where they cannot be provided for arises not from the ordinances of nature, but from social maladjustments that in the midst of wealth condemn men to want. The truth of this will, I think, be conclusively demonstrated when, after having cleared the ground, we trace out the true laws of social growth. But it would disturb the natural order of the argument to anticipate them now. If I have succeeded in maintaining a negative—in showing that the Malthusian theory is not proved by the reasoning by which it is supported—it is enough for the present. In the next chapter I propose to take the affirmative and show that it is disproved by facts.

CHAPTER 4 — DISPROOF OF THE MALTHUSIAN THEORY

So deeply rooted and thoroughly entwined with the reasonings of the current political economy is this doctrine that increase of population tends to reduce wages and produce poverty, so completely does it harmonize with many popular notions, and so liable is it to recur in different shapes, that I have thought it necessary to meet and show in some detail the insufficiency of the arguments by which it is supported, before bringing it to the test of facts; for the general acceptance of this theory adds a most striking instance to the many which the history of thought affords of how easily men ignore facts when blindfolded by a preaccepted theory.

To the supreme and final test of facts we can easily bring this theory. Manifestly the question whether increase of population necessarily tends to reduce wages and cause want, is simply the question whether it tends to reduce the amount of wealth that can be produced by a given amount of labor.

This is what the current doctrine holds. The accepted theory is, that the more that is required from nature the less generously does she respond, so that doubling the application of labor will not double the product; and hence, increase of population must tend to reduce wages and deepen poverty, or, in the phrase of Malthus, must result in vice and misery. To quote the language of John Stuart Mill:

"A greater number of people cannot, in any given state of civilization, be collectively so well provided for as a smaller. The niggardliness of nature, not the injustice of society, is the cause of the penalty attached to over-population. An unjust distribution of wealth does not aggravate the evil, but, at most, causes it to be somewhat earlier felt. It is in vain to say that all mouths which the increase of mankind calls into existence bring with them hands. The new mouths require as much food as the old ones, and the hands do not produce as much. If all instruments of production were held in joint property by the whole people, and the produce divided with perfect equality among them, and if in a society thus constituted, industry were as energetic and the produce as ample as at the present time, there would be enough to make all the existing population extremely comfortable; but when that population had doubled itself, as, with existing habits of the people, under such an encouragement, it undoubtedly would in little more than twenty years, what would then be their condition? Unless the arts of production were in the same time improved in an almost unexampled degree, the inferior soils which must be resorted to, and the more laborious and scantily remunerative cultivation which must be employed on the superior soils, to procure food for so much larger a population, would, by an insuperable necessity, render every individual in the community poorer than before. If the population continued to increase at the same rate, a time would soon arrive when no one would have more than mere necessaries, and, soon after, a time when no one would have a sufficiency of those, and the further increase of population would be arrested by death."*

All this I deny. I assert that the very reverse of these propositions is true. I assert that in any given state of civilization a greater number of people can collectively be better provided for than a smaller. I assert that the injustice of society, not the niggardliness of nature, is the cause of the want and misery which the current theory attributes to overpopulation. I assert that the new mouths which an increasing population calls into existence require no more food than the old ones, while the hands they bring with them can in the natural order of things produce more. I assert that, other things being equal, the greater the population, the greater the comfort which an equitable distribution of wealth would give to each individual. I assert that in

---

* "Principles of Political Economy," Book I, Chap. XIII, Sec. 2.

BOOK II CHAPTER 4

a state of equality the natural increase of population would constantly tend to make every individual richer instead of poorer.

I thus distinctly join issue, and submit the question to the test of facts.

But observe (for even at the risk of repetition I wish to warn the reader against a confusion of thought that is observable even in writers of great reputation), that the question of fact into which this issue resolves itself is not in what stage of population is most subsistence produced? but in what stage of population is there exhibited the greatest power of producing wealth? For the power of producing wealth in any form is the power of producing subsistence—and the consumption of wealth in any form, or of wealth-producing power, is equivalent to the consumption of subsistence. I have, for instance, some money in my pocket. With it I may buy either food or cigars or jewelry or theater tickets, and just as I expend my money do I determine labor to the production of food, of cigars, of jewelry, or of theatrical representations. A set of diamonds has a value equal to so many barrels of flour—that is to say, it takes on the average as much labor to produce the diamonds as it would to produce so much flour. It I load my wife with diamonds, it is as much an exertion of subsistence-producing power as though I had devoted so much food to purposes of ostentation. If I keep a footman, I take a possible plowman from the plow. The breeding and maintenance of a race horse require care and labor which would suffice for the breeding and maintenance of many work horses. The destruction of wealth involved in a general illumination or the firing of a salute is equivalent to the burning up of so much food; the keeping of a regiment of soldiers, or of a warship and her crew, is the diversion to unproductive uses of labor that could produce subsistence for many thousands of people. Thus the power of any population to produce the necessaries of life is not to be measured by the necessaries of life actually produced, but by the expenditure of power in all modes.

There is no necessity for abstract reasoning. The question is one of simple fact. Does the relative power of producing wealth decrease with the increase of population?

The facts are so patent that it is only necessary to call attention to them. We have, in modern times, seen many communities advance in population. Have they not at the same time advanced even more rapidly in wealth? We see many communities still increasing in population. Are they not also increasing their wealth still faster? Is there any doubt that while England has been increasing her population at the rate of two per cent. per annum, her wealth has been growing in still greater proportion? Is it not true that while the population of the United States has been doubling every twenty-nine* years her wealth has been doubling at much shorter intervals? Is it not true that under similar conditions—that is to say, among communities of similar people in a similar stage of civilization—the most densely populated community is also the richest? Are not the more densely populated eastern states richer in proportion to population than the more sparsely populated western or southern states? Is not England, where population is even denser than in the eastern states of the Union, also richer in proportion? Where will you find wealth devoted with the most lavishness to nonproductive use—costly buildings, fine furniture, luxurious equipages, statues, pictures, pleasure gardens and yachts? Is it not where population is densest rather than where it is sparsest? Where will

* The rate up to 1860 was 35 per cent. each decade.

you find in largest proportion those whom the general production suffices to keep without productive labor on their part—men of income and of elegant leisure, thieves, policemen, menial servants, lawyers, men of letters, and the like? Is it not where population is dense rather than where it is sparse? Whence is it that capital overflows for remunerative investment? Is it not from densely populated countries to sparsely populated countries? These things conclusively show that wealth is greatest where population is densest; that the production of wealth to a given amount of labor increases as population increases. These things are apparent wherever we turn our eyes. On the same level of civilization, the same stage of the productive arts, government, etc., the most populous countries are always the most wealthy.

Let us take a particular case, and that a case which of all that can be cited seems at first blush best to support the theory we are considering—the case of a community where, while population has largely increased, wages have greatly decreased, and it is not a matter of dubious inference but of obvious fact that the generosity of nature has lessened. That community is California. When upon the discovery of gold the first wave of immigration poured into California it found a country in which nature was in the most generous mood. From the river banks and bars the glittering deposits of thousands of years could be taken by the most primitive appliances, in amounts which made an ounce ($16) per day only ordinary wages. The plains, covered with nutritious grasses, were alive with countless herds of horses and cattle, so plenty that any traveler was at liberty to shift his saddle to a fresh steed, or to kill a bullock if he needed a steak, leaving the hide, its only valuable part, for the owner. From the rich soil which came first under cultivation, the mere plowing

and sowing brought crops that in older countries, if procured at all, can only be procured by the most thorough
manuring and cultivation. In early California, amid
this profusion of nature, wages and interest were higher
than anywhere else in the world.

This virgin profusion of nature has been steadily giving way before the greater and greater demands which
an increasing population has made upon it. Poorer and
poorer diggings have been worked, until now no diggings worth speaking of can be found, and gold mining
requires much capital, large skill, and elaborate machinery, and involves great risks. "Horses cost money,"
and cattle bred on the sagebrush plains of Nevada are
brought by railroad across the mountains and killed in
San Francisco shambles, while farmers are beginning to
save their straw and look for manure, and land is in cultivation which will hardly yield a crop three years out
of four without irrigation. At the same time wages and
interest have steadily gone down. Many men are now
glad to work for a week for less than they once demanded for the day, and money is loaned by the year
for a rate which once would hardly have been thought
extortionate by the month. Is the connection between
the reduced productiveness of nature and the reduced
rate of wages that of cause and effect? Is it true that
wages are lower because labor yields less wealth? On
the contrary! Instead of the wealth-producing power
of labor being less in California in 1879 than in 1849,
I am convinced that it is greater. And, it seems to me,
that no one who considers how enormously during these
years the efficiency of labor in California has been increased by roads, wharves, flumes, railroads, steamboats,
telegraphs, and machinery of all kinds; by a closer connection with the rest of the world; and by the number-
less economies resulting from a larger population, can
doubt that the return which labor receives from nature

in California is on the whole much greater now than it was in the days of unexhausted placers and virgin soil —the increase in the power of the human factor having more than compensated for the decline in the power of the natural factor. That this conclusion is the correct one is proved by many facts which show that the consumption of wealth is now much greater, as compared with the number of laborers, than it was then. Instead of a population composed almost exclusively of men in the prime of life, a large proportion of women and children are now supported, and other nonproducers have increased in much greater ratio than the population; luxury has grown far more than wages have fallen; where the best houses were cloth and paper shanties, are now mansions whose magnificence rivals European palaces; there are liveried carriages on the streets of San Francisco and pleasure yachts on her bay; the class who can live sumptuously on their incomes has steadily grown; there are rich men beside whom the richest of the earlier years would seem little better than paupers —in short, there are on every hand the most striking and conclusive evidences that the production and consumption of wealth have increased with even greater rapidity than the increase of population, and that if any class obtains less it is solely because of the greater inequality of distribution.

What is obvious in this particular instance is obvious where the survey is extended. The richest countries are not those where nature is most prolific; but those where labor is most efficient—not Mexico, but Massachusetts; not Brazil, but England. The countries where population is densest and presses hardest upon the capabilities of nature, are, other things being equal, the countries where the largest proportion of the produce can be devoted to luxury and the support of nonproducers, the countries where capital overflows, the countries that upon exigency, such as war, can stand the greatest drain. That the production of wealth must, in proportion to the labor employed, be greater in a densely populated country like England than in new countries where wages and interest are higher, is evident from the fact that, though a much smaller proportion of the population is engaged in productive labor, a much larger surplus is available for other purposes than that of supplying physical needs. In a new country the whole available force of the community is devoted to production—there is no well man who does not do productive work of some kind, no well woman exempt from household tasks. There are no paupers or beggars, no idle rich, no class whose labor is devoted to ministering to the convenience or caprice of the rich, no purely literary or scientific class, no criminal class who live by preying upon society, no large class maintained to guard society against them. Yet with the whole force of the community thus devoted to production, no such consumption of wealth in proportion to the whole population takes place, or can be afforded, as goes on in the old country; for, though the condition of the lowest class is better, and there is no one who cannot get a living, there is no one who gets much more—few or none who can live in anything like what would be called luxury, or even comfort, in the older country. That is to say, that in the older country the consumption of wealth in proportion to population is greater, although the proportion of labor devoted to the production of wealth is less—or that fewer laborers produce more wealth; for wealth must be produced before it can be consumed.

It may, however, be said, that the superior wealth of older countries is due not to superior productive power, but to the accumulations of wealth which the new country has not yet had time to make.

It will be well for a moment to consider this idea of

accumulated wealth. The truth is, that wealth can be
accumulated but to a slight degree, and that communities really live, as the vast majority of individuals live,
from hand to mouth. Wealth will not bear much accumulation; except in a few unimportant forms it will
not keep. The matter of the universe, which, when
worked up by labor into desirable forms, constitutes
wealth, is constantly tending back to its original state.
Some forms of wealth will last for a few hours, some
for a few days, some for a few months, some for a few
years; and there are very few forms of wealth that can
be passed from one generation to another. Take wealth
in some of its most useful and permanent forms—ships,
houses, railways, machinery. Unless labor is constantly
exerted in preserving and renewing them, they will almost immediately become useless. Stop labor in any
community, and wealth would vanish almost as the jet
of a fountain vanishes when the flow of water is shut
off. Let labor again exert itself, and wealth will almost
as immediately reappear. This has been long noticed
where war or other calamity has swept away wealth,
leaving population unimpaired. There is not less wealth
in London today because of the great fire of 1666; nor
yet is there less wealth in Chicago because of the great
fire in 1870. On those fire-swept acres have arisen,
under the hand of labor, more magnificent buildings,
filled with greater stocks of goods; and the stranger
who, ignorant of the history of the city, passes along
those stately avenues would not dream that a few years
ago all lay so black and bare. The same principle—
that wealth is constantly re-created—is obvious in every
new city. Given the same population and the same
efficiency of labor, and the town of yesterday will possess and enjoy as much as the town founded by the
Romans. No one who has seen Melbourne or San
Francisco can doubt that if the population of England

were transported to New Zealand, leaving all accumulated wealth behind, New Zealand would soon be as rich as England is now; or, conversely, that if the population of England were reduced to the sparseness of the present population of New Zealand, in spite of accumulated wealth, they would soon be as poor. Accumulated wealth seems to play just about such a part in relation to the social organism as accumulated nutriment does to the physical organism. Some accumulated wealth is necessary, and to a certain extent it may be drawn upon in exigencies; but the wealth produced by past generations can no more account for the consumption of the present than the dinners he ate last year can supply a man with present strength.

But without these considerations, which I allude to more for their general than for their special bearing, it is evident that superior accumulations of wealth can account for greater consumption of wealth only in cases where accumulated wealth is decreasing, and that wherever the volume of accumulated wealth is maintained, and even more obviously where it is increasing, a greater consumption of wealth must imply a greater production of wealth. Now, whether we compare different communities with each other, or the same community at different times, it is obvious that the progressive state, which is marked by increase of population, is also marked by an increased consumption and an increased accumulation of wealth, not merely in the aggregate, but per capita. And hence, increase of population, so far as it has yet anywhere gone, does not mean a reduction, but an increase in the average production of wealth.

And the reason of this is obvious. For, even if the increase of population does reduce the power of the natural factor of wealth, by compelling a resort to poorer soils, etc., it yet so vastly increases the power of the human factor as more than to compensate. Twenty men working together will, where nature is niggardly, produce more than twenty times the wealth that one man can produce where nature is most bountiful. The denser the population the more minute becomes the subdivision of labor, the greater the economies of production and distribution, and, hence, the very reverse of the Malthusian doctrine is true; and, within the limits in which we have reason to suppose increase would still go on, in any given state of civilization a greater number of people can produce a larger proportionate amount of wealth, and more fully supply their wants, than can a smaller number.

Look simply at the facts. Can anything be clearer than that the cause of the poverty which festers in the centers of civilization is not in the weakness of the productive forces? In countries where poverty is deepest, the forces of production are evidently strong enough, if fully employed, to provide for the lowest not merely comfort but luxury. The industrial paralysis, the commercial depression which curses the civilized world today, evidently springs from no lack of productive power. Whatever be the trouble, it is clearly not in the want of ability to produce wealth.

It is this very fact—that want appears where productive power is greatest and the production of wealth is largest—that constitutes the enigma which perplexes the civilized world, and which we are trying to unravel. Evidently the Malthusian theory, which attributes want to the decrease of productive power, will not explain it. That theory is utterly inconsistent with all the facts. It is really a gratuitous attribution to the laws of God of results which, even from this examination, we may infer really spring from the maladjustments of men— an inference which, as we proceed, will become a demonstration. For we have yet to find what *does* produce poverty amid advancing wealth.

The machines that are first invented to perform any particular movement are always the most complex, and succeeding artists generally discover that with fewer wheels, with fewer principles of motion than had originally been employed, the same effects may be more easily produced. The first philosophical systems, in the same manner, are always the most complex, and a particular connecting chain, or principle, is generally thought necessary to unite every two seemingly disjointed appearances, but it often happens that one great connecting principle is afterward found to be sufficient to bind together all the discordant phenomena that occur in a whole species of things.

—ADAM SMITH,
Essay on the Principles Which Lead and Direct Philosophical Inquiries,
as Illustrated by the History of Astronomy.

1

CHAPTER

THE INQUIRY NARROWED TO THE
LAWS OF DISTRIBUTION—THE NECES-
SARY RELATION OF THESE LAWS

The preceding examination has, I think, conclusively
shown that the explanation currently given, in the name
of political economy, of the problem we are attempting
to solve, is no explanation at all.

That with material progress wages fail to increase,
but rather tend to decrease, cannot be explained by the
theory that the increase of laborers constantly tends to
divide into smaller portions the capital sum from which
wages are paid. For, as we have seen, wages do not
come from capital, but are the direct produce of labor.
Each productive laborer, as he works, creates his wages,
and with every additional laborer there is an addition
to the true wages fund—an addition to the common
stock of wealth, which, generally speaking, is considerably greater than the amount he draws in wages.

Nor, yet, can it be explained by the theory that nature
yields less to the increasing drafts which an increasing
population make upon her; for the increased efficiency
of labor makes the progressive state a state of continually increasing production per capita, and the countries
of densest population, other things being equal, are always the countries of greatest wealth.

So far, we have only increased the perplexities of the
problem. We have overthrown a theory which did, in
some sort of fashion, explain existing facts; but in doing
so have only made existing facts seem more inexplicable.

153

It is as though, while the Ptolemaic theory was yet in its strength, it had been proved simply that the sun and stars do not revolve about the earth. The phenomena of day and night, and of the apparent motion of the celestial bodies, would yet remain unexplained, inevitably to reinstate the old theory unless a better one took its place. Our reasoning has led us to the conclusion that each productive laborer produces his own wages, and that increase in the number of laborers should increase the wages of each; whereas, the apparent facts are that there are many laborers who cannot obtain remunerative employment, and that increase in the number of laborers brings diminution of wages. We have, in short, proved that wages ought to be highest where in reality they are lowest.

Nevertheless, even in doing this we have made some progress. Next to finding what we look for, is to discover where it is useless to look. We have at least narrowed the field of inquiry. For this, at least, is now clear—that the cause which, in spite of the enormous increase of productive power, confines the great body of producers to the least share of the product upon which they will consent to live, is not the limitation of capital, nor yet the limitation of the powers of nature which respond to labor. As it is not, therefore, to be found in the laws which bound the production of wealth, it must be sought in the laws which govern distribution. To them let us turn.

It will be necessary to review in its main branches the whole subject of the distribution of wealth. To discover the cause which, as population increases and the productive arts advance, deepens the poverty of the lowest class, we must find the law which determines what part of the produce is distributed to labor as wages. To find the law of wages, or at least to make sure when we have found it, we must also determine the laws which fix the part of the produce which goes to capital and the part which goes to landowners, for as land, labor, and capital join in producing wealth, it is between these three that the produce must be divided. What is meant by the produce or production of a community is the sum of the wealth produced by that community—the general fund from which, as long as previously existing stock is not lessened, all consumption must be met and all revenues drawn. As I have already explained, production does not merely mean the making of things, but includes the increase of value gained by transporting or exchanging things. There is a produce of wealth in a purely commercial community, as there is in a purely agricultural or manufacturing community; and in the one case, as in the others, some part of this produce will go to capital, some part to labor, and some part, if land have any value, to the owners of land. As a matter of fact, a portion of the wealth produced is constantly going to the replacement of capital, which is constantly consumed and constantly replaced. But it is not necessary to take this into account, as it is eliminated by considering capital as continuous, which, in speaking or thinking of it, we habitually do. When we speak of the produce, we mean, therefore, that part of the wealth produced above what is necessary to replace the capital consumed in production; and when we speak of interest, or the return to capital, we mean what goes to capital after its replacement or maintenance.

It is, further, a matter of fact, that in every community which has passed the most primitive stage some portion of the produce is taken in taxation and consumed by government. But it is not necessary, in seeking the laws of distribution, to take this into consideration. We may consider taxation either as not existing, or as by so much reducing the produce. And so, too, of what is taken from the produce by certain forms of monopoly, which will be considered in a subsequent chapter (Chap. IV), and which exercise powers analogous to taxation. After we have discovered the laws of distribution we can then see what bearing, if any, taxation has upon them.

We must discover these laws of distribution for ourselves—or, at least, two out of the three. For, that they are not, at least as a whole, correctly apprehended by the current political economy, may be seen, irrespective of our preceding examination of one of them, in any of the standard treatises.

This is evident, in the first place, from the terminology employed.

In all politico-economic works we are told that the three factors in production are land, labor, and capital, and that the whole produce is primarily distributed into three corresponding parts. Three terms, therefore, are needed, each of which shall clearly express one of these parts to the exclusion of the others. Rent, as defined, clearly enough expresses the first of these parts—that which goes to the owners of land. Wages, as defined, clearly enough expresses the second—that part which constitutes the return to labor. But as to the third term—that which should express the return to capital— there is in the standard works a most puzzling ambiguity and confusion.

Of words in common use, that which comes nearest to exclusively expressing the idea of return for the use of capital, is interest, which, as commonly used, implies the return for the use of capital, exclusive of any labor in its use or management, and exclusive of any risk, except such as may be involved in the security. The word profits, as commonly used, is almost synonymous with revenue; it means a gain, an amount received in excess of an amount expended, and frequently includes receipts that are properly rent; while it nearly always includes receipts which are properly wages, as well as compensations for the risk peculiar to the various uses of capital. Unless extreme violence is done to the meaning of the word, it cannot, therefore, be used in political economy to signify that share of the produce which goes to capital, in contradistinction to those parts which go to labor and to landowners.

Now, all this is recognized in the standard works on political economy. Adam Smith well illustrates how wages and compensation for risk largely enter into profits, pointing out how the large profits of apothecaries and small retail dealers are in reality wages for their labor, and not interest on their capital; and how the great profits sometimes made in risky businesses, such as smuggling and the lumber trade, are really but compensations for risk, which, in the long run, reduce the returns to capital so used to the ordinary, or below the ordinary, rate. Similar illustrations are given in most of the subsequent works, where profit is formally defined in its common sense, with, perhaps, the exclusion of rent. In all these works, the reader is told that profits are made up of three elements—wages of superintendence, compensation for risk, and *interest*, or the return for the use of capital.

Thus, neither in its common meaning nor in the meaning expressly assigned to it in the current political economy, can profits have any place in the discussion of the distribution of wealth between the three factors of production. Either in its common meaning or in the meaning expressly assigned to it, to talk about the distribution of wealth into rent, wages, and profits is like talking of the division of mankind into men, women, and human beings.

Yet this, to the utter bewilderment of the reader, is what is done in all the standard works. After formally decomposing profits into wages of superintendence, compensation for risk, and interest—the net return for the use of capital—they proceed to treat of the distribution of wealth between the rent of land, the wages of labor, and the PROFITS of capital.

I doubt not that there are thousands of men who have vainly puzzled their brains over this confusion of terms, and abandoned the effort in despair, thinking that as the fault could not be in such great thinkers, it must be in their own stupidity. If it is any consolation to such men they may turn to Buckle's "History of Civilization," and see how a man who certainly got a marvelously clear idea of what he read, and who had read carefully the principal economists from Smith down, was inextricably confused by this jumble of profits and interest. For Buckle (Vol. I, Chap. II, and notes) persistently speaks of the distribution of wealth into rent, wages, interest, and profits.

And this is not to be wondered at. For, after formally decomposing profits into wages of superintendence, insurance, and interest, these economists, in assigning causes which fix the general rate of profit, speak of things which evidently affect only that part of profits which they have denominated interest; and then, in speaking of the rate of interest, either give the meaningless formula of supply and demand, or speak of causes which affect the compensation for risk; evidently using the word in its common sense, and not in the economic sense they have assigned to it, from which compensation for risk is eliminated. If the reader will take up John Stuart Mill's "Principles of Political Economy," and compare the chapter on Profits (Book II, Chap. 15) with the chapter on Interest (Book III, Chap. 23), he will see the confusion thus arising exemplified in the case of the most logical of English economists, in a more striking manner than I would like to characterize.

Now, such men have not been led into such confusion
of thought without a cause. If they, one after another,
have followed Dr. Adam Smith, as boys play "follow
my leader," jumping where he jumped, and falling where
he fell, it has been that there was a fence where he
jumped and a hole where he fell.

The difficulty from which this confusion has sprung
is in the preaccepted theory of wages. For reasons
which I have before assigned, it has seemed to them a
self-evident truth that the wages of certain classes of
laborers depended upon the ratio between capital and
the number of laborers. But there are certain kinds of
reward for exertion to which this theory evidently will
not apply, so the term wages has in use been contracted
to include only wages in the narrow common sense.
This being the case, if the term interest were used, as
consistently with their definitions it should have been
used, to represent the third part of the division of the
produce, all rewards of personal exertion, save those of
what are commonly called wage-workers, would clearly
have been left out. But by treating the division of
wealth as between rent, wages, and profits, instead of
between rent, wages and interest, this difficulty is
glossed over, all wages which will not fall under the
preaccepted law of wages being vaguely grouped under
profits, as wages of superintendence.

To read carefully what economists say about the distribution of wealth is to see that, though they correctly
define it, wages, as they use it in this connection, is what
logicians would call an undistributed term—it does not
mean all wages, but only some wages—viz., the wages
of manual labor paid by an employer. So other wages
are thrown over with the return to capital, and included
under the term profits, and any clear distinction between
the returns to capital and the returns to human exertion
thus avoided. The fact is that the current political

economy fails to give any clear and consistent account of the distribution of wealth. The law of rent *is* clearly stated, but it stands unrelated. The rest is a confused and incoherent jumble.

The very arrangement of these works shows this confusion and inconclusiveness of thought. In no politico-economic treatise that I know of are these laws of distribution brought together, so that the reader can take them in at a glance and recognize their relation to each other; but what is said about each one is enveloped in a mass of political and moral reflections and dissertations. And the reason is not far to seek. To bring together the three laws of distribution as they are now taught, is to show at a glance that they lack necessary relation.

The laws of the distribution of wealth are obviously laws of proportion, and must be so related to each other that any two being given the third may be inferred. For to say that one of the three parts of a whole is increased or decreased, is to say that one or both of the other parts is, reversely, decreased or increased. If Tom, Dick, and Harry are partners in business, the agreement which fixes the share of one in the profits must at the same time fix either the separate or the joint shares of the other two. To fix Tom's share at forty per cent. is to leave but sixty per cent. to be divided between Dick and Harry. To fix Dick's share at forty per cent. and Harry's share at thirty-five per cent. is to fix Tom's share at twenty-five per cent.

But between the laws of the distribution of wealth, as laid down in the standard works, there is no such relation. If we fish them out and bring them together, we find them to be as follows:

Wages are determined by the ratio between the amount of capital devoted to the payment and subsistence of labor and the number of laborers seeking employment.

Rent is determined by the margin of cultivation; all lands yielding as rent that part of their produce which exceeds what an equal application of labor and capital could procure from the poorest land in use.

Interest is determined by the equation between the demands of borrowers and the supply of capital offered by lenders. Or, if we take what is given as the law of profits, it is determined by wages, falling as wages rise and rising as wages fall—or, to use the phrase of Mill, by the cost of labor to the capitalist.

The bringing together of these current statements of the laws of the distribution of wealth shows at a glance that they lack the relation to each other which the true laws of distribution must have. They do not correlate and co-ordinate. Hence, at least two of these three laws are either wrongly apprehended or wrongly stated. This tallies with what we have already seen, that the current apprehension of the law of wages, and, inferentially, of the law of interest, will not bear examination. Let us, then, seek the true laws of the distribution of the produce of labor into wages, rent, and interest. The proof that we have found them will be in their correlation—that they meet, and relate, and mutually bound each other.

With profits this inquiry has manifestly nothing to do. We want to find what it is that determines the division of their joint produce between land, labor, and capital; and profits is not a term that refers exclusively to any one of these three divisions. Of the three parts into which profits are divided by political economists —namely, compensation for risk, wages of superintendence, and return for the use of capital—the latter falls under the term interest, which includes all the returns for the use of capital, and excludes everything else;

wages of superintendence falls under the term wages, which includes all returns for human exertion, and excludes everything else; and compensation for risk has no place whatever, as risk is eliminated when all the transactions of a community are taken together. I shall, therefore, consistently with the definitions of political economists, use the term interest as signifying that part of the produce which goes to capital.

To recapitulate:

Land, labor, and capital are the factors of production. The term land includes all natural opportunities or forces; the term labor, all human exertion; and the term capital, all wealth used to produce more wealth. In returns to these three factors is the whole produce distributed. That part which goes to land owners as payment for the use of natural opportunities is called rent; that part which constitutes the reward of human exertion is called wages; and that part which constitutes the return for the use of capital is called interest. These terms mutually exclude each other. The income of any individual may be made up from any one, two, or all three of these sources; but in the effort to discover the laws of distribution we must keep them separate.

Let me premise the inquiry which we are about to undertake by saying that the miscarriage of political economy, which I think has now been abundantly shown, can, it seems to me, be traced to the adoption of an erroneous standpoint. Living and making their observations in a state of society in which a capitalist generally rents land and hires labor, and thus seems to be the undertaker or first mover in production, the great cultivators of the science have been led to look upon capital as the prime factor in production, land as its instrument, and labor as its agent or tool. This is apparent on every page—in the form and course of their reasoning, in the character of their illustrations, and even in their choice of terms. Everywhere capital is the starting point, the capitalist the central figure. So far does this go that both Smith and Ricardo use the term "natural wages" to express the minimum upon which laborers can live; whereas, unless injustice is natural, all that the laborer produces should rather be held as his natural wages. This habit of looking upon capital as the employer of labor has led both to the theory that wages depend upon the relative abundance of capital, and to the theory that interest varies inversely with wages, while it has led away from truths that but for this habit would have been apparent. In short, the misstep which, so far as the great laws of distribution are concerned, has led political economy into the jungles, instead of upon the mountain tops, was taken when Adam Smith, in his first book, left the standpoint indicated in the sentence, "The produce of labor constitutes the natural recompense or wages of labor," to take that in which capital is considered as employing labor and paying wages.

But when we consider the origin and natural sequence of things, this order is reversed; and capital instead of first is last; instead of being the employer of labor, it is in reality employed by labor. There must be land before labor can be exerted, and labor must be exerted before capital can be produced. Capital is a result of labor, and is used by labor to assist it in further production. Labor is the active and initial force, and labor is therefore the employer of capital. Labor can be exerted only upon land, and it is from land that the matter which it transmutes into wealth must be drawn. Land therefore is the condition precedent, the field and material of labor. The natural order is land, labor, capital; and, instead of starting from capital as our initial point, we should start from land.

There is another thing to be observed. Capital is not a necessary factor in production. Labor exerted upon land can produce wealth without the aid of capital, and in the necessary genesis of things must so produce wealth before capital can exist. Therefore the law of rent and the law of wages must correlate each other and form a perfect whole without reference to the law of capital, as otherwise these laws would not fit the cases which can readily be imagined, and which to some degree actually exist, in which capital takes no part in production. And as capital is, as is often said, but stored-up labor, it is but a form of labor, a subdivision of the general term labor; and its law must be subordinate to, and independently correlate with, the law of wages, so as to fit cases in which the whole produce is divided between labor and capital, without any deduction for rent. To resort to the illustration before used: The division of the produce between land, labor and capital must be as it would be between Tom, Dick, and Harry, if Tom and Dick were the original partners, and Harry came in but as an assistant to and sharer with Dick.

CHAPTER **2** RENT AND THE LAW OF RENT

The term rent, in its economic sense—that is, when used, as I am using it, to distinguish that part of the produce which accrues to the owners of land or other natural capabilities by virtue of their ownership—differs in meaning from the word rent as commonly used. In some respects this economic meaning is narrower than the common meaning; in other respects it is wider.

It is narrower in this: In common speech, we apply the word rent to payments for the use of buildings, machinery, fixtures, etc., as well as to payments for the use of land or other natural capabilities; and in speaking of the rent of a house or the rent of a farm, we do not separate the price for the use of the improvements from the price for the use of the bare land. But in the economic meaning of rent, payments for the use of any of the products of human exertion are excluded, and of the lumped payments for the use of houses, farms, etc., only that part is rent which constitutes the consideration for the use of the land—that part paid for the use of buildings or other improvements being properly interest, as it is a consideration for the use of capital.

It is wider in this: In common speech we speak of rent only when owner and user are distinct persons. But in the economic sense there is also rent where the same person is both owner and user. Where owner and user are thus the same person, whatever part of his income he might obtain by letting the land to another

165

is rent, while the return for his labor and capital are that part of his income which they would yield him did he hire instead of owning the land. Rent is also expressed in a selling price. When land is purchased, the payment which is made for the ownership, or right to perpetual use, is rent commuted or capitalized. If I buy land for a small price and hold it until I can sell it for a large price, I have become rich, not by wages for my labor or by interest upon my capital, but by the increase of rent. Rent, in short, is the share in the wealth produced which the exclusive right to the use of natural capabilities gives to the owner. Wherever land has an exchange value there is rent in the economic meaning of the term. Wherever land having a value is used, either by owner or hirer, there is rent actual; wherever it is not used, but still has a value, there is rent potential. It is this capacity of yielding rent which gives value to land. Until its ownership will confer some advantage, land has no value.*

Thus rent or land value does not arise from the productiveness or utility of land. It in no wise represents any help or advantage given to production, but simply the power of securing a part of the results of production. No matter what are its capabilities, land can yield no rent and have no value until some one is willing to give labor or the results of labor for the privilege of using it; and what any one will thus give depends not upon the capacity of the land, but upon its capacity as compared with that of land that can be had for nothing. I may have very rich land, but it will yield no rent and have no value so long as there is other land as good to be had without cost. But when this other land is appro-

---

* In speaking of the value of land I use and shall use the words as referring to the value of the bare land. When I wish to speak of the value of land and improvements I shall use those words.

priated, and the best land to be had for nothing is inferior, either in fertility, situation, or other quality, my land will begin to have a value and yield rent. And though the productiveness of my land may decrease, yet if the productiveness of the land to be had without charge decreases in greater proportion, the rent I can get, and consequently the value of my land, will steadily increase. Rent, in short, is the price of monopoly, arising from the reduction to individual ownership of natural elements which human exertion can neither produce nor increase.

If one man owned all the land accessible to any community, he could, of course, demand any price or condition for its use that he saw fit; and, as long as his ownership was acknowledged, the other members of the community would have but death or emigration as the alternative to submission to his terms. This has been the case in many communities; but in the modern form of society, the land, though generally reduced to individual ownership, is in the hands of too many different persons to permit the price which can be obtained for its use to be fixed by mere caprice or desire. While each individual owner tries to get all he can, there is a limit to what he can get, which constitutes the market price or market rent of the land, and which varies with different lands and at different times. The law, or relation, which, under these circumstances of free competition among all parties (the condition which in tracing out the principles of political economy is always to be assumed), determines what rent or price can be got by the owner, is styled the law of rent. This fixed with certainty, we have more than a starting point from which the laws which regulate wages and interest may be traced. For, as the distribution of wealth is a division, in ascertaining what fixes the share of the produce which goes as rent, we also ascertain what fixes the share which is left for wages, where there is no co-operation of capital; and what fixes the joint share left for wages and interest, where capital does co-operate in production.

Fortunately, as to the law of rent there is no necessity for discussion. Authority here coincides with common sense,* and the accepted dictum of the current political economy has the self-evident character of a geometric axiom. This accepted law of rent, which John Stuart Mill denominates the *pons asinorum* of political economy, is sometimes styled "Ricardo's law of rent," from the fact that, although not the first to announce it, he first brought it prominently into notice.† It is:

The rent of land is determined by the excess of its produce over that which the same application can secure from the least productive land in use.

This law, which of course applies to land used for other purposes than agriculture, and to all natural agencies, such as mines, fisheries, etc., has been exhaustively explained and illustrated by all the leading economists since Ricardo. But its mere statement has all the force of a self-evident proposition, for it is clear that the effect of competition is to make the lowest reward for

---

* I do not mean to say that the accepted law of rent has never been disputed. In all the nonsense that in the present disjointed condition of the science has been printed as political economy, it would be hard to find anything that has not been disputed. But I mean to say that it has the sanction of all economic writers who are really to be regarded as authority. As John Stuart Mill says (Book II, Chap. XVI), "there are few persons who have refused their assent to it, except from not having thoroughly understood it. The loose and inaccurate way in which it is often apprehended by those who affect to refute it is very remarkable." An observation which has received many later exemplifications.

† According to McCulloch the law of rent was first stated in a pamphlet by Dr. James Anderson of Edinburgh in 1777, and simultaneously in the beginning of this century by Sir Edward West, Mr. Malthus, and Mr. Ricardo.

which labor and capital will engage in production, the highest that they can claim; and hence to enable the owner of more productive land to appropriate in rent all the return above that required to recompense labor and capital at the ordinary rate—that is to say, what they can obtain upon the least productive land in use, or at the least productive point, where, of course, no rent is paid.

Perhaps it may conduce to a fuller understanding of the law of rent to put it in this form: The ownership of a natural agent of production will give the power of appropriating so much of the wealth produced by the exertion of labor and capital upon it as exceeds the return which the same application of labor and capital could secure in the least productive occupation in which they freely engage.

This, however, amounts to precisely the same thing, for there is no occupation in which labor and capital can engage which does not require the use of land; and, furthermore, the cultivation or other use of land will always be carried to as low a point of remuneration, all things considered, as is freely accepted in any other pursuit. Suppose, for instance, a community in which part of the labor and capital is devoted to agriculture and part to manufactures. The poorest land cultivated yields an average return which we will call 20, and 20 therefore will be the average return to labor and capital, as well in manufactures as in agriculture. Suppose that from some permanent cause the return in manufactures is now reduced to 15. Clearly, the labor and capital engaged in manufactures will turn to agriculture; and the process will not stop until, either by the extension of cultivation to inferior lands or to inferior points on the same land, or by an increase in the relative value of manufactured products, owing to the diminution of production—or, as a matter of fact, by both processes—the

yield to labor and capital in both pursuits has, all
things considered, been brought again to the same level,
so that whatever be the final point of productiveness at
which manufactures are still carried on, whether it be
18 or 17 or 16, cultivation will also be extended to that
point. And, thus, to say that rent will be the excess
in productiveness over the yield at the margin, or lowest point, of cultivation, is the same thing as to say
that it will be the excess of produce over what the
same amount of labor and capital obtains in the least
remunerative occupation.

The law of rent is, in fact, but a deduction from the
law of competition, and amounts simply to the assertion
that as wages and interest tend to a common level, all
that part of the general production of wealth which
exceeds what the labor and capital employed could
have secured for themselves, if applied to the poorest
natural agent in use, will go to landowners in the shape
of rent. It rests, in the last analysis, upon the fundamental principle, which is to political economy what the
attraction of gravitation is to physics—that men will
seek to gratify their desires with the least exertion.

This, then, is the law of rent. Although many standard treatises follow too much the example of Ricardo,
who seems to view it merely in its relation to agriculture, and in several places speaks of manufactures yielding no rent (when, in truth, manufactures and exchange
yield the highest rents, as is evinced by the greater
value of land in manufacturing and commercial cities),
thus hiding the full importance of the law, yet, ever
since the time of Ricardo, the law itself has been clearly
apprehended and fully recognized. But not so its corollaries. Plain as they are, the accepted doctrine of wages
(backed and fortified not only as has been hitherto explained, but by considerations whose enormous weight
will be seen when the logical conclusion toward which

we are tending is reached) has hitherto prevented their recognition.* Yet, is it not as plain as the simplest geometrical demonstration, that the corollary of the law of rent is the law of wages, where the division of the produce is simply between rent and wages; or the law of wages and interest taken together, where the division is into rent, wages, and interest? Stated reversely, the law of rent is necessarily the law of wages and interest taken together, for it is the assertion, that no matter what the production which results from the application of labor and capital, these two factors will receive in wages and interest only such part of the produce as they could have produced on land free to them without the payment of rent—that is, the least productive land or point in use. For, if, of the produce, all over the amount which labor and capital could secure from land for which no rent is paid must go to land owners as rent, then all that can be claimed by labor and capital as wages and interest is the amount which they could have secured from land yielding no rent.

Or to put it in algebraic form:

As Produce=Rent+Wages+Interest,

Therefore, Produce—Rent=Wages+Interest.

Thus wages and interest do not depend upon the produce of labor and capital, but upon what is left after rent is taken out; or, upon the produce which they could obtain without paying rent—that is, from the poorest land in use. And hence, no matter what be the increase in productive power, if the increase in rent keeps pace with it, neither wages nor interest can increase.

The moment this simple relation is recognized, a

---

* Buckle (Chap. II, "History of Civilization") recognizes the necessary relation between rent, interest, and wages, but evidently never worked it out.

flood of light streams in upon what was before inexplicable, and seemingly discordant facts range themselves under an obvious law. The increase of rent which goes on in progressive countries is at once seen to be the key which explains why wages and interest fail to increase with increase of productive power. For the wealth produced in every community is divided into two parts by what may be called the rent line, which is fixed by the margin of cultivation, or the return which labor and capital could obtain from such natural opportunities as are free to them without the payment of rent. From the part of the produce below this line wages and interest must be paid. All that is above goes to the owners of land. Thus, where the value of land is low, there may be a small production of wealth, and yet a high rate of wages and interest, as we see in new countries. And, where the value of land is high, there may be a very large production of wealth, and yet a low rate of wages and interest, as we see in old countries. And, where productive power increases, as it is increasing in all progressive countries, wages and interest will be affected, not by the increase, but by the manner in which rent is affected. If the value of land increases proportionately, all the increased production will be swallowed up by rent, and wages and interest will remain as before. If the value of land increases in greater ratio than productive power, rent will swallow up even more than the increase; and while the produce of labor and capital will be much larger, wages and interest will fall. It is only when the value of land fails to increase as rapidly as productive power, that wages and interest can increase with the increase of productive power. All this is exemplified in actual fact.

CHAPTER **3** OF INTEREST AND
THE CAUSE OF INTEREST

Having made sure of the law of rent, we have obtained as its necessary corollary the law of wages, where the division is between rent and wages; and the law of wages and interest taken together, where the division is between the three factors. What proportion of the produce is taken as rent must determine what proportion is left for wages, if but land and labor are concerned; or to be divided between wages and interest, if capital joins in the production.

But without reference to this deduction, let us seek each of these laws separately and independently. If, when obtained in this way, we find that they correlate, our conclusions will have the highest certainty.

And, inasmuch as the discovery of the law of wages is the ultimate purpose of our inquiry, let us take up first the subject of interest.

I have already referred to the difference in meaning between the terms profits and interest. It may be worth while, further, to say that interest, as an abstract term in the distribution of wealth, differs in meaning from the word as commonly used, in this: That it includes all returns for the use of capital, and not merely those that pass from borrower to lender; and that it excludes compensation for risk, which forms so great a part of what is commonly called interest. Compensation for risk is evidently only an equalization of return between different employments of capital. What we want to find is, what fixes the general rate of interest proper? The different rates of compensation for risk added to this will give the current rates of commercial interest.

Now, it is evident that the greatest differences in what is ordinarily called interest are due to differences in risk; but it is also evident that between different countries and different times there are also considerable variations in the rate of interest proper. In California at one time two per cent. a month would not have been considered extravagant interest on security on which loans could now be effected at seven or eight per cent. per annum, and though some part of the difference may be due to an increased sense of general stability, the greater part is evidently due to some other general cause. In the United States generally the rate of interest has been higher than in England; and in the newer States of the Union higher than in the older States; and the tendency of interest to sink as society progresses is well marked and has long been noticed. What is the law which will bind all these variations together and exhibit their cause?

It is not worth while to dwell more than has hitherto incidentally been done upon the failure of the current political economy to determine the true law of interest. Its speculations upon this subject have not the definiteness and coherency which have enabled the accepted doctrine of wages to withstand the evidence of fact, and do not require the same elaborate review. That they run counter to the facts is evident. That interest does not depend on the productiveness of labor and capital is proved by the general fact that where labor and capital are most productive interest is lowest. That it does not depend reversely upon wages (or the cost of labor), lowering as wages rise, and increasing as wages fall, is proved by the general fact that interest is high when and where wages are high, and low when and where wages are low.

Let us begin at the beginning. The nature and functions of capital have already been sufficiently shown, but even at the risk of something like a digression, let us endeavor to ascertain the cause of interest before considering its law. For in addition to aiding our inquiry by giving us a firmer and clearer grasp of the subject now in hand, it may lead to conclusions whose practical importance will be hereafter apparent.

What is the reason and justification of interest? Why should the borrower pay back to the lender more than he received? These questions are worth answering, not merely from their speculative, but from their practical importance. The feeling that interest is the robbery of industry is widespread and growing, and on both sides of the Atlantic shows itself more and more in popular literature and in popular movements. The expounders of the current political economy say that there is no conflict between labor and capital, and oppose as injurious to labor, as well as to capital, all schemes for restricting the reward which capital obtains; yet in the same works the doctrine is laid down that wages and interest bear to each other an inverse relation, and that interest will be low or high as wages are high or low.* Clearly, then, if this doctrine is correct, the only objection that from the standpoint of the laborer can be logically made to any scheme for the reduction of interest is that it will not work, which is manifestly very weak ground while ideas of the omnipotence of legislatures are yet so widespread; and though such an objection may lead to the abandonment of any one particular scheme, it will not prevent the search for another.

---

* This is really said of profits, but with the evident meaning of returns to capital.

Why should interest be? Interest, we are told, in all
the standard works, is the reward of abstinence. But,
manifestly, this does not sufficiently account for it. Abstinence is not an active, but a passive quality; it is not
a doing—it is simply a not doing. Abstinence in itself
produces nothing. Why, then, should any part of what
is produced be claimed for it? If I have a sum of
money which I lock up for a year, I have exercised as
much abstinence as though I had loaned it. Yet,
though in the latter case I will expect it to be returned
to me with an additional sum by way of interest, in
the former I will have but the same sum, and no increase. But the abstinence is the same. If it be said that
in lending it I do the borrower a service, it may be re-
plied that he also does me a service in keeping it safely
—a service that under some conditions may be very
valuable, and for which I would willingly pay, rather
than not have it; and a service which, as to some forms
of capital, may be even more obvious than as to money.
For there are many forms of capital which will not
keep, but must be constantly renewed; and many which
are onerous to maintain if one has no immediate use
for them. So, if the accumulator of capital helps the
user of capital by loaning it to him, does not the user
discharge the debt in full when he hands it back?
Is not the secure preservation, the maintenance, the
re-creation of capital, a complete offset to the use?
Accumulation is the end and aim of abstinence.
Abstinence can go no further and accomplish no more;
nor of itself can it even do this. If we were merely
to abstain from using it, how much wealth would disappear in a year! And how little would be left at the
end of two years! Hence, if more is demanded for
abstinence than the safe return of capital, is not labor
wronged? Such ideas as these underlie the widespread
opinion that interest can accrue only at the expense of

labor, and is in fact a robbery of labor which in a social condition based on justice would be abolished.

The attempts to refute these views do not appear to me always successful. For instance, as it illustrates the usual reasoning, take Bastiat's oft-quoted illustration of the plane. One carpenter, James, at the expense of ten days' labor, makes himself a plane, which will last in use for 290 of the 300 working days of the year. William, another carpenter, proposes to borrow the plane for a year, offering to give back at the end of that time, when the plane will be worn out, a new plane equally as good. James objects to lending the plane on these terms, urging that if he merely gets back a plane he will have nothing to compensate him for the loss of the advantage which the use of the plane during the year would give him. William, admitting this, agrees not merely to return a plane, but, in addition, to give James a new plank. The agreement is carried out to mutual satisfaction. The plane is used up during the year, but at the end of the year James receives as good a one, and a plank in addition. He lends the new plane again and again, until finally it passes into the hands of his son, "who still continues to lend it," receiving a plank each time. This plank, which represents interest, is said to be a natural and equitable remuneration, as by giving it in return for the use of the plane, William "obtains the power which exists in the tool to increase the productiveness of labor," and is no worse off than he would have been had he not borrowed the plane; while James obtains no more than he would have had if he had retained and used the plane instead of lending it.

Is this really so? It will be observed that it is not affirmed that James could make the plane and William could not, for that would be to make the plank the reward of superior skill. It is only that James had abstained from consuming the result of his labor until he had accumulated it in the form of a plane—which is the essential idea of capital.

Now, if James had not lent the plane he could have used it for 290 days, when it would have been worn out, and he would have been obliged to take the remaining ten days of the working year to make a new plane. If William had not borrowed the plane he would have taken ten days to make himself a plane, which he could have used for the remaining 290 days. Thus, if we take a plank to represent the fruits of a day's labor with the aid of a plane, at the end of the year, had no borrowing taken place, each would have stood with reference to the plane as he commenced, James with a plane, and William with none, and each would have had as the result of the year's work 290 planks. If the condition of the borrowing had been what William first proposed, the return of a new plane, the same relative situation would have been secured. William would have worked for 290 days, and taken the last ten days to make the new plane to return to James. James would have taken the first ten days of the year to make another plane which would have lasted for 290 days, when he would have received a new plane from William. Thus, the simple return of the plane would have put each in the same position at the end of the year as if no borrowing had taken place. James would have lost nothing to the gain of William, and William would have gained nothing to the loss of James. Each would have had the return his labor would otherwise have yielded—viz., 290 planks, and James would have had the advantage with which he started, a new plane.

But when, in addition to the return of a plane, a plank is given, James at the end of the year will be in a better position than if there had been no borrowing, and William in a worse. James will have 291 planks and a new plane, and William 289 planks and no plane. If William now borrows the plank as well as the plane on the same terms as before, he will at the end of the year have to return to James a plane, two planks and a fraction of a plank; and if this difference be again borrowed, and so on, is it not evident that the income of the one will progressively decline, and that of the other will progressively increase, until at length, if the operation be continued, the time will come when, as the result of the original lending of a plane, James will obtain the whole result of William's labor—that is to say, William will become virtually his slave?

Is interest, then, natural and equitable? There is nothing in this illustration to show it to be. Evidently what Bastiat (and many others) assigns as the basis of interest, "the power which exists in the tool to increase the productiveness of labor," is neither in justice nor in fact the basis of interest. The fallacy which makes Bastiat's illustration pass as conclusive with those who do not stop to analyze it, as we have done, is that with the loan of the plane they associate the transfer of the increased productive power which a plane gives to labor. But this is really not involved. The essential thing which James loaned to William was not the increased power which labor acquires from using planes. To suppose this, we should have to suppose that the making and using of planes was a trade secret or a patent right, when the illustration would become one of monopoly, not of capital. The essential thing which James loaned to William was not the privilege of applying his labor in a more effective way, but the use of the concrete result of ten days' labor. If "the power which exists in tools to increase the productiveness of labor" were the cause of interest, then the rate of interest would increase with the march of invention. This is not so. Nor yet will I be expected to pay more interest if I borrow

a fifty-dollar sewing machine than if I borrow fifty
dollars' worth of needles; if I borrow a steam engine
than if I borrow a pile of bricks of equal value. Capital, like wealth, is interchangeable. It is not one thing;
it is anything to that value within the circle of exchange.
Nor yet does the improvement of tools add to the reproductive power of capital; it adds to the productive power
of labor.

And I am inclined to think that if all wealth consisted of such things as planes, and all production was
such as that of carpenters—that is to say, if wealth consisted but of the inert matter of the universe, and production of working up this inert matter into different
shapes, that interest would be but the robbery of
industry, and could not long exist. This is not to say
that there would be no accumulation, for though the
hope of increase is a motive for turning wealth into
capital, it is not the motive, or, at least, not the main
motive, for accumulating. Children will save their
pennies for Christmas; pirates will add to their buried
treasure; Eastern princes will accumulate hoards of coin;
and men like Stewart or Vanderbilt, having become
once possessed of the passion of accumulating, would
continue as long as they could to add to their millions,
even though accumulation brought no increase. Nor
yet is it to say that there would be no borrowing or
lending, for this, to a large extent, would be prompted
by mutual convenience. If William had a job of work
to be immediately begun and James one that would
not commence until ten days thereafter, there might
be a mutual advantage in the loan of the plane, though
no plank should be given.

But all wealth is not of the nature of planes, or
planks, or money, which has no reproductive power;
nor is all production merely the turning into other forms
of this inert matter of the universe. It is true that

if I put away money, it will not increase. But suppose, instead, I put away wine. At the end of a year I will have an increased value, for the wine will have improved in quality. Or supposing that in a country adapted to them, I set out bees; at the end of a year I will have more swarms of bees, and the honey which they have made. Or, supposing, where there is a range, I turn out sheep, or hogs, or cattle; at the end of the year I will, upon the average, also have an increase.

Now what gives the increase in these cases is something which, though it generally requires labor to utilize it, is yet distinct and separable from labor—the active power of nature; the principle of growth, of reproduction, which everywhere characterizes all the forms of that mysterious thing or condition which we call life. And it seems to me that it is this which is the cause of interest, or the increase of capital over and above that due to labor. There are, so to speak, in the movements which make up the everlasting flux of nature, certain vital currents, which will, if we use them, aid us, with a force independent of our own efforts, in turning matter into the forms we desire—that is to say, into wealth.

While many things might be mentioned which, like money, or planes, or planks, or engines, or clothing, have no innate power of increase, yet other things are included in the terms wealth and capital which, like wine, will of themselves increase in quality up to a certain point; or, like bees or cattle, will of themselves increase in quantity; and certain other things, such as seeds, which, though the conditions which enable them to increase may not be maintained without labor, yet will, when these conditions are maintained, yield an increase, or give a return over and above that which is to be attributed to labor.

Now the interchangeability of wealth necessarily involves an average between all the species of wealth of any special advantage which accrues from the possession of any particular species, for no one would keep capital in one form when it could be changed into a more advantageous form. No one, for instance, would grind wheat into flour and keep it on hand for the convenience of those who desire from time to time to exchange wheat or its equivalent for flour, unless he could by such exchange secure an increase equal to that which, all things considered, he could secure by planting his wheat. No one, if he could keep them, would exchange a flock of sheep now for their net weight in mutton to be returned next year; for by keeping the sheep he would not only have the same amount of mutton next year, but also the lambs and the fleeces. No one would dig an irrigating ditch, unless those who by its aid are enabled to utilize the reproductive forces of nature would give him such a portion of the increase they receive as to make his capital yield him as much as theirs. And so, in any circle of exchange, the power of increase which the reproductive or vital force of nature gives to some species of capital must average with all; and he who lends, or uses in exchange, money, or planes, or bricks, or clothing, is not deprived of the power to obtain an increase, any more than if he had lent or put to a reproductive use so much capital in a form capable of increase.

There is also in the utilization of the variations in the powers of nature and of man which is effected by exchange, an increase which somewhat resembles that produced by the vital forces of nature. In one place, for instance, a given amount of labor will secure 200 in vegetable food or 100 in animal food. In another place, these conditions are reversed, and the same amount of labor will produce 100 in vegetable food or 200 in animal. In the one place, the relative value of vegetable to animal food will be as two to one, and in the other as one to two; and, supposing equal amounts of each to be required, the same amount of labor will in either place secure 150 of both. But by devoting labor in the one place to the procurement of vegetable food, and in the other, to the procurement of animal food, and exchanging to the quantity required, the people of each place will be enabled by the given amount of labor to procure 200 of both, less the losses and expenses of exchange; so that in each place the produce which is taken from use and devoted to exchange brings back an increase. Thus Whittington's cat, sent to a far country where cats are scarce and rats are plenty, returns in bales of goods and bags of gold.

Of course, labor is necessary to exchange, as it is to the utilization of the reproductive forces of nature, and the produce of exchange, as the produce of agriculture, is clearly the produce of labor; but yet, in the one case as in the other, there is a distinguishable force co-operating with that of labor, which makes it impossible to measure the result solely by the amount of labor expended, but renders the amount of capital and the time it is in use integral parts in the sum of forces. Capital aids labor in all of the different modes of production, but there is a distinction between the relations of the two in such modes of production as consist merely of changing the form or place of matter, as planing boards or mining coal; and such modes of production as avail themselves of the reproductive forces of nature, or of the power of increase arising from differences in the distribution of natural and human powers, such as the raising of grain or the exchange of ice for sugar. In production of the first kind, labor alone is the efficient cause; when labor stops, production stops. When the carpenter drops his plane as the sun sets, the increase of value, which he with his plane is producing, ceases until he begins his labor again the following morning. When the factory bell rings for closing, when the mine is shut down, production ends until work is resumed. The intervening time, so far as regards production, might as well be blotted out. The lapse of days, the change of seasons, is no element in the production that depends solely upon the amount of labor expended. But in the other modes of production to which I have referred, and in which the part of labor may be likened to the operations of lumbermen who throw their logs into the stream, leaving it to the current to carry them to the boom of the sawmill many miles below, time is an element. The seed in the ground germinates and grows while the farmer sleeps or plows new fields, and the everflowing currents of air and ocean bear Whittington's cat toward the rat-tormented ruler in the regions of romance.

To recur now to Bastiat's illustration. It is evident that if there is any reason why William at the end of the year should return to James more than an equally good plane, it does not spring, as Bastiat has it, from the increased power which the tool gives to labor, for that, as I have shown, is not an element; but it springs from the element of time—the difference of a year between the lending and return of the plane. Now, if the view is confined to the illustration, there is nothing to suggest how this element should operate, for a plane at the end of the year has no greater value than a plane at the beginning. But if we substitute for the plane a calf, it is clearly to be seen that to put James in as good a position as if he had not lent, William at the end of the year must return, not a calf, but a cow. Or, if we suppose that the ten days' labor had been devoted to planting corn, it is evident that James would not have been fully recompensed if at the end of the year he had received simply so much planted corn, for during the year the planted corn would have germinated and grown and multiplied; and so if the plane had been devoted to exchange, it might during the year have been turned over several times, each exchange yielding an increase to James. Now, therefore, as James' labor might have been applied in any of those ways—or what amounts to the same thing, some of the labor devoted to making planes might have been thus transferred—he will not make a plane for William to use for the year unless he gets back more than a plane. And William can afford to give back more than a plane, because the same general average of the advantages of labor applied in different modes will enable him to obtain from his labor an advantage from the element of time. It is this general averaging, or as we may say, "pooling" of advantages, which necessarily takes place where the exigencies of society require the simultaneous carrying on of the different modes of production, which gives to the possession of wealth incapable in itself of increase an advantage similar to that which attaches to wealth used in such a way as to gain from the element of time. And, in the last analysis, the advantage which is given by the lapse of time springs from the generative force of nature and the varying powers of nature and of man.

Were the quality and capacity of matter everywhere uniform, and all productive power in man, there would be no interest. The advantage of superior tools might at times be transferred on terms resembling the payment of interest, but such transactions would be irregular and intermittent—the exception, not the rule. For the power of obtaining such returns would not, as now, inhere in the possession of capital, and the advantage of time would operate only in peculiar circumstances. That I, having a thousand dollars, can certainly let it out at interest, does not arise from the fact that there are others, not having a thousand dollars, who will gladly pay me for the use of it, if they can get it no other way; but from the fact that the capital which my thousand dollars represents has the power of yielding an increase to whosoever has it, even though he be a millionaire. For the price which anything will bring does not depend upon what the buyer would be willing to give rather than go without it, so much as upon what the seller can otherwise get. For instance, a manufacturer who wishes to retire from business has machinery to the value of $100,000. If he cannot, should he sell, take this $100,000 and invest it so that it will yield him interest, it will be immaterial to him, risk being eliminated, whether he obtains the whole price at once or in installments, and if the purchaser has the requisite capital, which we must suppose in order that the transaction may rest on its own merits, it will be immaterial whether he pay at once or after a time. If the purchaser has not the required capital, it may be to his convenience that payments should be delayed, but it would be only in exceptional circumstances that the seller would ask, or the buyer would consent, to pay any premium on this account; nor in such cases would this premium be properly interest. For interest is not properly a payment made for the use of capital, but a return accruing from the increase of capital. If the capital did not yield an increase, the cases would be few and exceptional in which the owner would get a premium. William would soon find out if it did not pay him to give a plank for the privilege of deferring payment on James' plane.

In short, when we come to analyze production we find it to fall into three modes—viz:

ADAPTING, or changing natural products either in form or in place so as to fit them for the satisfaction of human desire.

GROWING, or utilizing the vital forces of nature, as by raising vegetables or animals.

EXCHANGING, or utilizing, so as to add to the general sum of wealth, the higher powers of those natural forces which vary with locality, or of those human forces which vary with situation, occupation, or character.

In each of these three modes of production capital may aid labor—or, to speak more precisely, in the first mode capital may aid labor, but is not absolutely necessary; in the others capital must aid labor, or is necessary.

Now, while by adapting capital in proper forms we may increase the effective power of labor to impress upon matter the character of wealth, as when we adapt wood and iron to the form and use of a plane; or iron, coal, water, and oil to the form and use of a steam engine; or stone, clay, timber, and iron to that of a building, yet the characteristic of this use of capital is, that the benefit is in the use. When, however, we employ capital in the second of these modes, as when we plant grain in the ground, or place animals on a stock farm, or put away wine to improve with age, the benefit arises, not from the use, but from the increase. And so, when we employ capital in the third of these modes, and instead of using a thing we exchange it, the benefit is in the increase or greater value of the things received in return.

Primarily, the benefits which arise from use go to labor, and the benefits which arise from increase, to capital. But, inasmuch as the division of labor and the interchangeability of wealth necessitate and imply an averaging of benefits, in so far as these different modes of production correlate with each other, the benefits that arise from one will average with the benefits that arise from the others, for neither labor nor capital will be devoted to any mode of production while any other mode which is open to them will yield a greater return. That is to say, labor expended in the first mode

of production will get, not the whole return, but the
return minus such part as is necessary to give to capital
such an increase as it could have secured in the other
modes of production, and capital engaged in the second
and third modes will obtain, not the whole increase,
but the increase minus what is sufficient to give to labor
such reward as it could have secured if expended in the
first mode.

Thus interest springs from the power of increase
which the reproductive forces of nature, and the in
effect analogous capacity for exchange, give to capital.
It is not an arbitrary, but a natural thing; it is not the
result of a particular social organization, but of laws of
the universe which underlie society. It is, therefore, just.

They who talk about abolishing interest fall into an
error similar to that previously pointed out as giving
its plausibility to the doctrine that wages are drawn
from capital. When they thus think of interest, they
think only of that which is paid by the user of capital
to the owner of capital. But, manifestly, this is not all
interest, but only some interest. Whoever uses capital
and obtains the increase it is capable of giving receives
interest. If I plant and care for a tree until it comes
to maturity, I receive, in its fruit, interest upon the
capital I have thus accumulated—that is, the labor I
have expended. If I raise a cow, the milk which she
yields me, morning and evening, is not merely the reward of the labor then exerted; but interest upon the
capital which my labor, expended in raising her, has accumulated in the cow. And so, if I use my own capital
in directly aiding production, as by machinery, or in
indirectly aiding production, in exchange, I receive a
special and distinguishable advantage from the reproductive character of capital, which is as real, though
perhaps not as clear, as though I had lent my capital
to another and he had paid me interest.

CHAPTER 4

OF SPURIOUS CAPITAL AND
OF PROFITS OFTEN MISTAKEN
FOR INTEREST

The belief that interest is the robbery of industry is, I am persuaded, in large part due to a failure to discriminate between what is really capital and what is not, and between profits which are properly interest and profits which arise from other sources than the use of capital. In the speech and literature of the day every one is styled a capitalist who possesses what, independent of his labor, will yield him a return, while whatever is thus received is spoken of as the earnings or takings of capital, and we everywhere hear of the conflict of labor and capital. Whether there is, in reality, any conflict between labor and capital, I do not yet ask the reader to make up his mind; but it will be well here to clear away some misapprehensions which confuse the judgment.

Attention has already been called to the fact that land values, which constitute such an enormous part of what is commonly called capital, are not capital at all; and that rent, which is as commonly included in the receipts of capital, and which takes an ever-increasing portion of the produce of an advancing community, is not the earnings of capital, and must be carefully separated from interest. It is not necessary now to dwell further upon this point. Attention has likewise been called to the fact that the stocks, bonds, etc., which constitute another great part of what is commonly called capital, are not capital at all; but, in some of

189

their shapes, these evidences of indebtedness so closely resemble capital and in some cases actually perform, or seem to perform, the functions of capital, while they yield a return to their owners which is not only spoken of as interest, but has every semblance of interest, that it is worth while, before attempting to clear the idea of interest from some other ambiguities that beset it, to speak again of these at greater length.

Nothing can be capital, let it always be remembered, that is not wealth—that is to say, nothing can be capital that does not consist of actual, tangible things, not the spontaneous offerings of nature, which have in themselves, and not by proxy, the power of directly or indirectly ministering to human desire.

Thus, a government bond is not capital, nor yet is it the representative of capital. The capital that was once received for it by the government has been consumed unproductively—blown away from the mouths of cannon, used up in warships, expended in keeping men marching and drilling, killing and destroying. The bond cannot represent capital that has been destroyed. It does not represent capital at all. It is simply a solemn declaration that the government will, some time or other, take by taxation from the then existing stock of the people, so much wealth, which it will turn over to the holder of the bond; and that, in the meanwhile, it will, from time to time, take, in the same way, enough to make up to the holder the increase which so much capital as it some day promises to give him would yield him were it actually in his possession. The immense sums which are thus taken from the produce of every modern country to pay interest on public debts are not the earnings or increase of capital—are not really interest in the strict sense of the term, but are taxes levied on the produce of labor and capital, leaving so much less for wages and so much less for real interest.

But, supposing the bonds have been issued for the deepening of a river bed, the construction of lighthouses, or the erection of a public market; or supposing, to embody the same idea while changing the illustration, they have been issued by a railroad company. Here they do represent capital, existing and applied to productive uses, and like stock in a dividend paying company may be considered as evidences of the ownership of capital. But they can be so considered only in so far as they actually represent capital, and not as they have been issued in excess of the capital used. Nearly all our railroad companies and other incorporations are loaded down in this way. Where one dollar's worth of capital has been really used, certificates for two, three, four, five, or even ten, have been issued, and upon this fictitious amount interest or dividends are paid with more or less regularity. Now, what, in excess of the amount due as interest to the real capital invested, is thus earned by these companies and thus paid out, as well as the large sums absorbed by managing rings and never accounted for, is evidently not taken from the aggregate produce of the community on account of the services rendered by capital—it is not interest. If we are restricted to the terminology of economic writers who decompose profits into interest, insurance, and wages of superintendence, it must fall into the category of wages of superintendence.

But while wages of superintendence clearly enough include the income derived from such personal qualities as skill, tact, enterprise, organizing ability, inventive power, character, etc., to the profits we are speaking of there is another contributing element, which can only arbitrarily be classed with these—the element of monopoly.

When James I granted to his minion the exclusive privilege of making gold and silver thread, and prohibited, under severe penalties, every one else from making such thread, the income which Buckingham enjoyed in consequence did not arise from the interest upon the capital invested in the manufacture, nor from the skill, etc., of those who really conducted the operations, but from what he got from the king—viz., the exclusive privilege—in reality the power to levy a tax for his own purposes upon all the users of such thread. From a similar source comes a large part of the profits which are commonly confounded with the earnings of capital. Receipts from the patents granted for a limited term of years for the purpose of encouraging invention are clearly attributable to this source, as are the returns derived from monopolies created by protective tariffs under the pretense of encouraging home industry. But there is another far more insidious and far more general form of monopoly. In the aggregation of large masses of capital under a common control there is developed a new and essentially different power from that power of increase which is a general characteristic of capital and which gives rise to interest. While the latter is, so to speak, constructive in its nature, the power which, as aggregation proceeds, rises upon it is destructive. It is a power of the same kind as that which James granted to Buckingham, and it is often exercised with as reckless a disregard, not only of the industrial, but of the personal rights of individuals. A railroad company approaches a small town as a highwayman approaches his victim. The threat, "If you do not accede to our terms we will leave your town two or three miles to one side!" is as efficacious as the "Stand and deliver," when backed by a cocked pistol. For the threat of the railroad company is not merely to deprive the town of the benefits which the railroad might give; it is to put it in a far worse position than if no railroad had been built. Or if, where there is water communication, an opposition boat is put on; rates are reduced until she is forced off, and then the public are compelled to pay the cost of the operation, just as the Rohillas were obliged to pay the forty lacs with which Surajah Dowlah hired of Warren Hastings an English force to assist him in desolating their country and decimating their people. And just as robbers unite to plunder in concert and divide the spoil, so do the trunk lines of railroads unite to raise rates and pool their earnings, or the Pacific roads form a combination with the Pacific Mail Steamship Company by which toll gates are virtually established on land and ocean. And just as Buckingham's creatures, under authority of the gold thread patent, searched private houses, and seized papers and persons for purposes of lust and extortion, so does the great telegraph company which, by the power of associated capital, deprives the people of the United States of the full benefits of a beneficent invention, tamper with correspondence and crush out newspapers which offend it.

It is necessary only to allude to these things, not to dwell on them. Every one knows the tyranny and rapacity with which capital when concentrated in large amounts is frequently wielded to corrupt, to rob, and to destroy. What I wish to call the reader's attention to is that profits thus derived are not to be confounded with the legitimate returns of capital as an agent of production. They are for the most part to be attributed to a maladjustment of forces in the legislative department of government and to a blind adherence to ancient barbarisms and the superstitious reverence for the technicalities of a narrow profession in the administration of law; while the general cause which in advancing communities tends, with the concentration of wealth, to the concentration of power, is the solution of the great problem we are seeking for, but have not yet found.

Any analysis will show that much of the profits which are, in common thought, confounded with interest are in reality due, not to the power of capital, but to the power of concentrated capital, or of concentrated capital acting upon bad social adjustments. And it will also show that what are clearly and properly wages of superintendence are very frequently confounded with the earnings of capital.

And, so, profits properly due to the elements of risk are frequently confounded with interest. Some people acquire wealth by taking chances which to the majority of people must necessarily bring loss. Such are many forms of speculation, and especially that mode of gambling known as stock dealing. Nerve, judgment, the possession of capital, skill in what in lower forms of gambling are known as the arts of the confidence man and blackleg, give advantage to the individual; but, just as at a gaming table, whatever one gains some one else must lose.

Now, taking the great fortunes that are so often referred to as exemplifying the accumulative power of capital—the Dukes of Westminster and Marquises of Bute, the Rothschilds, Astors, Stewarts, Vanderbilts, Goulds, Stanfords, and Floods—it is upon examination readily seen that they have been built up, in greater or less part, not by interest, but by elements such as we have been reviewing.

How necessary it is to note the distinctions to which I have been calling attention is shown in current discussions, where the shield seems alternately white or black as the standpoint is shifted from one side to the other. On the one hand we are called upon to see, in the existence of deep poverty side by side with vast accumulations of wealth, the aggressions of capital on labor, and in reply it is pointed out that capital aids labor, and hence we are asked to conclude that there is nothing unjust or unnatural in the wide gulf between rich and poor; that wealth is but the reward of industry, intelligence, and thrift; and poverty but the punishment of indolence, ignorance, and imprudence.

CHAPTER **5** THE LAW OF INTEREST

Let us turn now to the law of interest, keeping in mind two things to which attention has heretofore been called—viz:

First—That it is not capital which employs labor, but labor which employs capital.

Second—That capital is not a fixed quantity, but can always be increased or decreased, (1) by the greater or less application of labor to the production of capital, and (2) by the conversion of wealth into capital, or capital into wealth, for capital being but wealth applied in a certain way, wealth is the larger and inclusive term.

It is manifest that under conditions of freedom the maximum that can be given for the use of capital will be the increase it will bring, and the minimum or zero will be the replacement of capital; for above the one point the borrowing of capital would involve a loss, and below the other, capital could not be maintained.

Observe, again: It is not, as is carelessly stated by some writers, the increased efficiency given to labor by the adaptation of capital to any special form or use which fixes this maximum, but the average power of increase which belongs to capital generally. The power of applying itself in advantageous forms is a power of labor, which capital as capital cannot claim nor share. A bow and arrows will enable an Indian to kill, let us say, a buffalo every day, while with sticks and stones he could hardly kill one in a week; but the weapon maker of the tribe could not claim from the hunter six out of every seven buffaloes killed as a return for the use of a bow and arrows; nor will capital invested in a woolen factory yield to the capitalist the difference between the produce of the factory and what the same amount of labor could have obtained with the spinning-wheel and hand loom. William when he borrows a plane from James does not in that obtain the advantage of the increased efficiency of labor when using a plane for the smoothing of boards over what it has when smoothing them with a shell or flint. The progress of knowledge has made the advantage involved in the use of planes a common property and power of labor. What he gets from James is merely such advantage as the element of a year's time will give to the possession of so much capital as is represented by the plane.

Now, if the vital forces of nature which give an advantage to the element of time be the cause of interest, it would seem to follow that this maximum rate of interest would be determined by the strength of these forces and the extent to which they are engaged in production. But while the reproductive force of nature seems to vary enormously, as, for instance, between the salmon, which spawns thousands of eggs, and the whale, which brings forth a single calf at intervals of years; between the rabbit and the elephant, the thistle and the gigantic redwood, it appears from the way the natural balance is maintained that there is an equation between the reproductive and destructive forces of nature, which in effect brings the principle of increase to a uniform point. This natural balance man has within narrow limits the power to disturb, and by the modification of natural conditions may avail himself at will of the varying strength of the reproductive force in nature. But when he does so, there arises from the wide scope of his desires another principle which brings about in the increase of wealth a similar equation and balance to that which is effected in nature between the different forms of life. This equation exhibits itself through values. If, in a country adapted to both, I go to raising rabbits and you to raising horses, my rabbits may, until the natural limit is reached, increase faster than your horses. But my capital will not increase faster, for the effect of the varying rates of increase will be to lower the value of rabbits as compared with horses, and to increase the value of horses as compared with rabbits.

Though the varying strength of the vital forces of nature is thus brought to uniformity, there may be a difference in the different stages of social development as to the proportionate extent to which, in the aggregate production of wealth, these vital forces are enlisted. But as to this, there are two remarks to be made. In the first place, although in such a country as England the part taken by manufactures in the aggregate wealth production has very much increased as compared with the part taken by agriculture, yet it is to be noticed that to a very great extent this is true only of the political or geographical division, and not of the industrial community. For industrial communities are not limited by political divisions, or bounded by seas or mountains. They are limited only by the scope of their exchanges, and the proportion which in the industrial economy of England agriculture and stock raising bear to manufactures is averaged with Iowa and Illinois, with Texas and California, with Canada and India, with Queensland and the Baltic—in short, with every country to which the world-wide exchanges of England extend. In the next place, it is to be remarked that although in the progress of civilization the tendency is to the relative increase of manufactures, as compared with agriculture, and consequently to a proportionately less reliance upon the reproductive forces of nature, yet this is accompanied by a corresponding extension of exchanges, and hence a greater calling in of the power of increase which thus arises. So these tendencies, to a great extent, and, probably, so far as we have yet gone, completely balance each other, and preserve the equilibrium which fixes the average increase of capital, or the normal rate of interest.

Now, this normal point of interest, which lies between the necessary maximum and the necessary minimum of the return to capital, must, wherever it rests, be such that all things (such as the feeling of security, desire for accumulation, etc.) considered, the reward of capital and the reward of labor will be equal—that is to say, will give an equally attractive result for the exertion or sacrifice involved. It is impossible, perhaps, to formulate this point, as wages are habitually estimated in quantity, and interest in a ratio; but if we suppose a given quantity of wealth to be the produce of a given amount of labor, co-operating for a stated time with a certain amount of capital, the proportion in which the produce would be divided between the labor and the capital would afford a comparison. There must be such a point at, or rather, about, which the rate of interest must tend to settle; since, unless such an equilibrium were effected, labor would not accept the use of capital, or capital would not be placed at the disposal of labor. For labor and capital are but different forms of the same thing—human exertion. Capital is produced by labor; it is, in fact, but labor impressed upon matter—labor stored up in matter, to be released again as needed, as the heat of the sun stored up in coal is released in the furnace. The use of capital in production is, therefore, but a mode of labor. As capital can be used only by being consumed, its use is the expenditure of labor, and for the maintenance of capital, its production by labor must be commensurate with its consumption in aid of labor. Hence the principle that, under circumstances which permit free competition, operates to bring wages to a common standard and profits to a substantial equality—the principle that men will seek to gratify their desires with the least exertion—operates to establish and maintain this equilibrium between wages and interest.

This natural relation between interest and wages—this equilibrium at which both will represent equal returns to equal exertions—may be stated in a form which suggests a relation of opposition; but this opposition is only apparent. In a partnership between Dick and Harry, the statement that Dick receives a certain proportion of the profits implies that the portion of Harry is less or greater as Dick's is greater or less; but where, as in this case, each gets only what he adds to the common fund, the increase of the portion of the one does not decrease what the other receives.

And this relation fixed, it is evident that interest and wages must rise and fall together, and that interest cannot be increased without increasing wages; nor wages lowered without depressing interest. For if wages fall, interest must also fall in proportion, else it becomes more profitable to turn labor into capital than to apply it directly; while, if interest falls, wages must likewise proportionately fall, or else the increment of capital would be checked.

We are, of course, not speaking of particular wages and particular interest, but of the general rate of wages and the general rate of interest, meaning always by interest the return which capital can secure, less insurance and wages of superintendence. In a particular case, or a particular employment, the tendency of wages and interest to an equilibrium may be impeded; but

between the general rate of wages and the general rate
of interest, this tendency must be prompt to act. For
though in a particular branch of production the line
may be clearly drawn between those who furnish labor
and those who furnish capital, yet even in communities
where there is the sharpest distinction between the general class laborers and the general class capitalists,
these two classes shade off into each other by imperceptible gradations, and on the extremes where the two
classes meet in the same persons, the interaction which
restores equilibrium, or rather prevents its disturbance,
can go on without obstruction, whatever obstacles may
exist where the separation is complete. And, furthermore, it must be remembered, as has before been stated,
that capital is but a portion of wealth, distinguished
from wealth generally only by the purpose to which it
is applied, and, hence, the whole body of wealth has
upon the relations of capital and labor the same equaliz-
ing effect that a flywheel has upon the motion of machinery, taking up capital when it is in excess and
giving it out again when there is a deficiency, just as
a jeweler may give his wife diamonds to wear when he
has a superabundant stock, and put them in his show-
case again when his stock becomes reduced. Thus any
tendency on the part of interest to rise above the equilibrium with wages must immediately beget not only
a tendency to direct labor to the production of capital,
but also the application of wealth to the uses of capital;
while any tendency of wages to rise above the equilibrium with interest must in like manner beget not only a
tendency to turn labor from the production of capital,
but also to lessen the proportion of capital by diverting
from a productive to a nonproductive use some of the
articles of wealth of which capital is composed.

To recapitulate: There is a certain relation or ratio
between wages and interest, fixed by causes, which, if

not absolutely permanent, slowly change, at which enough labor will be turned into capital to supply the capital which, in the degree of knowledge, state of the arts, density of population, character of occupations, variety, extent and rapidity of exchanges, will be demanded for production, and this relation or ratio the interaction of labor and capital constantly maintains; hence interest must rise and fall with the rise and fall of wages.

To illustrate: The price of flour is determined by the price of wheat and cost of milling. The cost of milling varies slowly and but little, the difference being, even at long intervals, hardly perceptible; while the price of wheat varies frequently and largely. Hence we correctly say that the price of flour is governed by the price of wheat. Or, to put the proposition in the same form as the preceding: There is a certain relation or ratio between the value of wheat and the value of flour, fixed by the cost of milling, which relation or ratio the interaction between the demand for flour and the supply of wheat constantly maintains; hence the price of flour must rise and fall with the rise and fall of the price of wheat.

Or, as, leaving the connecting link, the price of wheat, to inference, we say that the price of flour depends upon the character of the seasons, wars, etc., so may we put the law of interest in a form which directly connects it with the law of rent, by saying that the general rate of interest will be determined by the return to capital upon the poorest land to which capital is freely applied —that is to say, upon the best land open to it without the payment of rent. Thus we bring the law of interest into a form which shows it to be a corollary of the law of rent.

We may prove this conclusion in another way: For that interest must decrease as rent increases, we can plainly see if we eliminate wages. To do this, we must, to be sure, imagine a universe organized on totally different principles. Nevertheless, we may imagine what Carlyle would call a fool's paradise, where the production of wealth went on without the aid of labor, and solely by the reproductive force of capital—where sheep bore ready-made clothing on their backs, cows presented butter and cheese, and oxen, when they got to the proper point of fatness, carved themselves into beefsteaks and roasting ribs; where houses grew from the seed, and a jackknife thrown upon the ground would take root and in due time bear a crop of assorted cutlery. Imagine certain capitalists transported, with their capital in appropriate forms, to such a place. Manifestly, they would get, as the return for their capital, the whole amount of wealth it produced only so long as none of its produce was demanded as rent. When rent arose, it would come out of the produce of capital, and as it increased, the return to the owners of capital must necessarily diminish. If we imagine the place where capital possessed this power of producing wealth without the aid of labor to be of limited extent, say an island, we shall see that as soon as capital had increased to the limit of the island to support it, the return to capital must fall to a trifle above its minimum of mere replacement, and the landowners would receive nearly the whole produce as rent, for the only alternative capitalists would have would be to throw their capital into the sea. Or, if we imagine such an island to be in communication with the rest of the world, the return to capital would settle at the rate of return in other places. Interest there would be neither higher nor lower than anywhere else. Rent would obtain the whole of the superior advantage, and the land of such an island would have a great value.

To sum up, the law of interest is this:

The relation between wages and interest is determined by the average power of increase which attaches to capital from its use in reproductive modes. As rent arises, interest will fall as wages fall, or will be determined by the margin of cultivation.

I have endeavored at this length to trace out and illustrate the law of interest more in deference to the existing terminology and modes of thought than from the real necessities of our inquiry, were it unembarrassed by befogging discussions. In truth, the primary division of wealth in distribution is dual, not tripartite. Capital is but a form of labor, and its distinction from labor is in reality but a subdivision, just as the division of labor into skilled and unskilled would be. In our examination we have reached the same point as would have been attained had we simply treated capital as a form of labor, and sought the law which divides the produce between rent and wages; that is to say, between the possessors of the two factors, natural substances and powers, and human exertion—which two factors by their union produce all wealth.

CHAPTER **6** WAGES AND THE LAW OF WAGES

We have by inference already obtained the law of wages. But to verify the deduction and to strip the subject of all ambiguities, let us seek the law from an independent starting point.

There is, of course, no such thing as a common rate of wages, in the sense that there is at any given time and place a common rate of interest. Wages, which include all returns received from labor, not only vary with the differing powers of individuals, but, as the organization of society becomes elaborate, vary largely as between occupations. Nevertheless, there is a certain general relation between all wages, so that we express a clear and well-understood idea when we say that wages are higher or lower in one time or place than in another. In their degrees, wages rise and fall in obedience to a common law. What is this law?

The fundamental principle of human action—the law that is to political economy what the law of gravitation is to physics—is that men seek to gratify their desires with the least exertion. Evidently, this principle must bring to an equality, through the competition it induces, the reward gained by equal exertions under similar circumstances. When men work for themselves, this equalization will be largely effected by the equation of prices; and between those who work for themselves and those who work for others, the same tendency to equalization will operate. Now, under this principle, what, in conditions of freedom, will be the terms at which one man can hire others to work for him? Evidently, they will be fixed by what the men could make if laboring for themselves. The principle which will prevent him from having to give anything above this, except what is necessary to induce the change, will also prevent them from taking less. Did they demand more, the competition of others would prevent them from getting employment. Did he offer less, none would accept the terms, as they could obtain greater results by working for themselves. Thus, although the employer wishes to pay as little as possible, and the employee to receive as much as possible, wages will be fixed by the value or produce of such labor to the laborers themselves. If wages are temporarily carried either above or below this line, a tendency to carry them back at once arises.

But the result, or the earnings of labor, as is readily seen in those primary and fundamental occupations in which labor first engages, and which, even in the most highly developed condition of society, still form the base of production, does not depend merely upon the intensity or quality of the labor itself. Wealth is the product of two factors, land and labor, and what a given amount of labor will yield will vary with the powers of the natural opportunities to which it is applied. This being the case, the principle that men seek to gratify their desires with the least exertion will fix wages at the produce of such labor at the point of highest natural productiveness open to it. Now, by virtue of the same principle, the highest point of natural productiveness open to labor under existing conditions will be the lowest point at which production continues, for men, impelled by a supreme law of the human mind to seek the satisfaction of their desires with the least exertion, will not expend labor at a lower point of productiveness while a higher is open to them. Thus the wages which an employer must pay will be measured by the lowest point of natural productiveness to which production extends, and wages will rise or fall as this point rises or falls.

To illustrate: In a simple state of society, each man, as is the primitive mode, works for himself—some in hunting, let us say, some in fishing, some in cultivating the ground. Cultivation, we will suppose, has just begun, and the land in use is all of the same quality, yielding a similar return to similar exertions. Wages, therefore—for, though there is neither employer nor employed, there are yet wages—will be the full produce of labor, and, making allowance for the difference of agreeableness, risk, etc., in the three pursuits, they will be on the average equal in each—that is to say, equal exertions will yield equal results. Now, if one of their number wishes to employ some of his fellows to work for him instead of for themselves, he must pay wages fixed by this full, average produce of labor.

Let a period of time elapse. Cultivation has extended, and, instead of land of the same quality, embraces lands of different qualities. Wages, now, will not be as before, the average produce of labor. They will be the average produce of labor at the margin of cultivation, or the point of lowest return. For, as men seek to satisfy their desires with the least possible exertion, the point of lowest return in cultivation must yield to labor a return equivalent to the average return in hunting and fishing.* Labor will no longer yield equal returns to equal exertions, but those who expend their labor on the superior land will obtain a greater produce for the same exertion than those who cultivate the inferior land. Wages, however, will still be equal, for this

---

* This equalization will be effected by the equation of prices.

excess which the cultivators of the superior land receive is in reality rent, and if land has been subjected to individual ownership will give it a value. Now, if, under these changed circumstances, one member of this community wishes to hire others to work for him, he will have to pay only what the labor yields at the lowest point of cultivation. If thereafter the margin of cultivation sinks to points of lower and lower productiveness, so must wages sink; if, on the contrary, it rises, so also must wages rise; for, just as a free body tends to take the shortest route to the earth's center, so do men seek the easiest mode to the gratification of their desires.

Here, then, we have the law of wages, as a deduction from a principle most obvious and most universal. That wages depend upon the margin of cultivation—that they will be greater or less as the produce which labor can obtain from the highest natural opportunities open to it is greater or less, flows from the principle that men will seek to satisfy their wants with the least exertion.

Now, if we turn from simple social states to the complex phenomena of highly civilized societies, we shall find upon examination that they also fall under this law.

In such societies, wages differ widely, but they still bear a more or less definite and obvious relation to each other. This relation is not invariable, as at one time a philosopher of repute may earn by his lectures many fold the wages of the best mechanic, and at another can hardly hope for the pay of a footman; as in a great city occupations may yield relatively high wages, which in a new settlement would yield relatively low wages; yet these variations between wages may, under all conditions, and in spite of arbitrary divergences caused by custom, law, etc., be traced to certain circumstances. In one of his most interesting chapters Adam Smith thus enumerates the principal circumstances which "make up for a small pecuniary gain in some employments

and counterbalance a great one in others: first, the agreeableness or disagreeableness of the employments themselves; secondly, the easiness and cheapness, or the difficulty and expense of learning them; thirdly, the constancy
or inconstancy of employment in them; fourthly, the
small or great trust which must be reposed in those who
exercise them; and fifthly, the probability or improba-
bility of success in them."* It is not necessary to dwell
in detail on these causes of variation in wages between
different employments. They have been admirably explained and illustrated by Adam Smith and the economists who have followed him, who have well worked
out the details, even if they have failed to apprehend
the main law.

The effect of all the circumstances which give rise to
the differences between wages in different occupations
may be included as supply and demand, and it is perfectly correct to say that the wages in different occupations will vary relatively according to differences in the
supply and demand of labor—meaning by demand the
call which the community as a whole makes for services
of the particular kind, and by supply the relative amount
of labor which, under the existing conditions, can be
determined to the performance of those particular services. But though this is true as to the relative differences of wages, when it is said, as is commonly said,
that the general rate of wages is determined by supply
and demand, the words are meaningless. For supply
and demand are but relative terms. The supply of labor
can only mean labor offered in exchange for labor or
the produce of labor, and the demand for labor can only
mean labor or the produce of labor offered in exchange
for labor. Supply is thus demand, and demand supply,

---

* This last, which is analogous to the element of risk in profits, accounts for the high wages of successful lawyers, physicians, contractors,
actors, etc.

and, in the whole community, one must be coextensive with the other. This is clearly apprehended by the current political economy in relation to sales, and the reasoning of Ricardo, Mill, and others, which proves that alterations in supply and demand cannot produce a general rise or fall of values, though they may cause a rise or fall in the value of a particular thing, is as applicable to labor. What conceals the absurdity of speaking generally of supply and demand in reference to labor is the habit of considering the demand for labor as springing from capital and as something distinct from labor; but the analysis to which this idea has been heretofore subjected has sufficiently shown its fallacy. It is indeed evident from the mere statement, that wages can never permanently exceed the produce of labor, and hence that there is no fund from which wages can for any time be drawn, save that which labor constantly creates.

But, though all the circumstances which produce the differences in wages between occupations may be considered as operating through supply and demand, they, or rather, their effects, for sometimes the same cause operates in both ways, may be separated into two classes, according as they tend only to raise apparent wages or as they tend to raise real wages—that is, to increase the average reward for equal exertion. The high wages of some occupations much resemble what Adam Smith compares them to, the prizes of a lottery, in which the great gain of one is made up from the losses of many others. This is not only true of the professions by means of which Dr. Smith illustrates the principle, but is largely true of the wages of superintendence in mercantile pursuits, as shown by the fact that over ninety per cent. of the mercantile firms that commence business ultimately fail. The higher wages of those occupations which can be prosecuted only in

certain states of the weather, or are otherwise intermittent and uncertain, are also of this class; while
differences that arise from hardship, discredit, unhealthiness, etc., imply differences of sacrifice, the increased
compensation for which only preserves the level of
equal returns for equal exertions. All these differences
are, in fact, equalizations, arising from circumstances
which, to use the words of Adam Smith, "make up for
a small pecuniary gain in some employments and
counterbalance a great one in others." But, besides
these merely apparent differences, there are real differences in wages between occupations, which are caused
by the greater or less rarity of the qualities required
—greater abilities or skill, whether natural or acquired,
commanding on the average greater wages. Now, these
qualities, whether natural or acquired, are essentially
analogous to differences in strength and quickness in
manual labor, and as in manual labor the higher wages
paid the man who can do more would be based upon
wages paid to those who can do only the average
amount, so wages in the occupations requiring superior
abilities and skill must depend upon the common wages
paid for ordinary abilities and skill.

It is, indeed, evident from observation, as it must be
from theory, that whatever be the circumstances which
produce the differences of wages in different occupations, and although they frequently vary in relation
to each other, producing, as between time and time,
and place and place, greater or less relative differences,
yet the rate of wages in one occupation is always dependent on the rate in another, and so on, down, until
the lowest and widest stratum of wages is reached, in
occupations where the demand is more nearly uniform
and in which there is the greatest freedom to engage.

For, although barriers of greater or less difficulty may
exist, the amount of labor which can be determined

to any particular pursuit is nowhere absolutely fixed. All mechanics could act as laborers, and many laborers could readily become mechanics; all storekeepers could act as shopmen, and many shopmen could easily become storekeepers; many farmers would, upon inducement, become hunters or miners, fishermen or sailors, and many hunters, miners, fishermen, and sailors know enough of farming to turn their hands to it on demand. In each occupation there are men who unite it with others, or who alternate between occupations, while the young men who are constantly coming in to fill up the ranks of labor are drawn in the direction of the strongest inducements and least resistances. And further than this, all the gradations of wages shade into each other by imperceptible degrees, instead of being separated by clearly defined gulfs. The wages, even of the poorer paid mechanics, are generally higher than the wages of simple laborers, but there are always some mechanics who do not, on the whole, make as much as some laborers; the best paid lawyers receive much higher wages than the best paid clerks, but the best paid clerks make more than some lawyers, and in fact the worst paid clerks make more than the worst paid lawyers. Thus, on the verge of each occupation, stand those to whom the inducements between one occupation and another are so nicely balanced that the slightest change is sufficient to determine their labor in one direction or another. Thus, any increase or decrease in the demand for labor of a certain kind cannot, except temporarily, raise wages in that occupation above, nor depress them below, the relative level with wages in other occupations, which is determined by the circumstances previously adverted to, such as relative agreeableness or continuity of employment, etc. Even, as experience shows, where artificial barriers are imposed to this interaction, such as limiting laws, guild regulations, the establishment of caste, etc., they may interfere with, but cannot prevent, the maintenance of this equilibrium. They operate only as dams, which pile up the water of a stream above its natural level, but cannot prevent its overflow.

Thus, although they may from time to time alter in relation to each other, as the circumstances which determine relative levels change, yet it is evident that wages in all strata must ultimately depend upon wages in the lowest and widest stratum—the general rate of wages rising or falling as these rise or fall.

Now, the primary and fundamental occupations, upon which, so to speak, all others are built up, are evidently those which procure wealth directly from nature; hence the law of wages in them must be the general law of wages. And, as wages in such occupations clearly depend upon what labor can produce at the lowest point of natural productiveness to which it is habitually applied; therefore, wages generally depend upon the margin of cultivation, or, to put it more exactly, upon the highest point of natural productiveness to which labor is free to apply itself without the payment of rent.

So obvious is this law that it is often apprehended without being recognized. It is frequently said of such countries as California and Nevada that cheap labor would enormously aid their development, as it would enable the working of the poorer but most extensive deposits of ore. A relation between low wages and a low point of production is perceived by those who talk in this way, but they invert cause and effect. It is not low wages which will cause the working of low grade ore, but the extension of production to the lower point which will diminish wages. If wages could be arbitrarily forced down, as has sometimes been attempted by statute, the poorer mines would not be worked so long as richer mines could be worked. But if the margin of production were arbitrarily forced down, as it might be, were the superior natural opportunities in the ownership of those who chose rather to wait for future increase of value than to permit them to be used now, wages would necessarily fall.

The demonstration is complete. The law of wages we have thus obtained is that which we previously obtained as the corollary of the law of rent, and it completely harmonizes with the law of interest. It is, that:

Wages depend upon the margin of production, or upon the produce which labor can obtain at the highest point of natural productiveness open to it without the payment of rent.

This law of wages accords with and explains universal facts that without its apprehension seem unrelated and contradictory. It shows that:

Where land is free and labor is unassisted by capital, the whole produce will go to labor as wages.

Where land is free and labor is assisted by capital, wages will consist of the whole produce, less that part necessary to induce the storing up of labor as capital.

Where land is subject to ownership and rent arises, wages will be fixed by what labor could secure from the highest natural opportunities open to it without the payment of rent.

Where natural opportunities are all monopolized, wages may be forced by the competition among laborers to the minimum at which laborers will consent to reproduce.

This necessary minimum of wages (which by Smith and Ricardo is denominated the point of "natural wages," and by Mill supposed to regulate wages, which will be higher or lower as the working classes consent to reproduce at a higher or lower standard of comfort) is, however, included in the law of wages as previously stated, as it is evident that the margin of production cannot fall below that point at which enough will be left as wages to secure the maintenance of labor.

Like Ricardo's law of rent, of which it is the corollary, this law of wages carries with it its own proof and becomes self-evident by mere statement. For it is but an application of the central truth that is the foundation of economic reasoning—that men will seek to satisfy their desires with the least exertion. The average man will not work for an employer for less, all things considered, than he can earn by working for himself; nor yet will he work for himself for less than he can earn by working for an employer, and hence the return which labor can secure from such natural opportunities as are free to it must fix the wages which labor everywhere gets. That is to say, the line of rent is the necessary measure of the line of wages. In fact, the accepted law of rent depends for its recognition upon a previous, though in many cases it seems to be an unconscious, acceptance of this law of wages. What makes it evident that land of a particular quality will yield as rent the surplus of its produce over that of the least productive land in use, is the apprehension of the fact that the owner of the higher quality of land can procure the labor to work his land by the payment of what that labor could produce if exerted upon land of the poorer quality.

In its simpler manifestations, this law of wages is recognized by people who do not trouble themselves about political economy, just as the fact that a heavy body would fall to the earth was long recognized by those who never thought of the law of gravitation. It does not require a philosopher to see that if in any country natural opportunities were thrown open which would enable laborers to make for themselves wages higher than the lowest now paid, the general rate of wages would rise; while the most ignorant and stupid of the placer miners of early California knew that as the placers gave out or were monopolized, wages must fall. It requires no finespun theory to explain why wages are so high relatively to production in new countries where land is yet unmonopolized. The cause is on the surface. One man will not work for another for less than his labor will really yield, when he can go upon the next quarter section and take up a farm for himself. It is only as land becomes monopolized and these natural opportunities are shut off from labor, that laborers are obliged to compete with each other for employment, and it becomes possible for the farmer to hire hands to do his work while he maintains himself on the difference between what their labor produces and what he pays them for it.

Adam Smith himself saw the cause of high wages where land was yet open to settlement, though he failed to appreciate the importance and connection of the fact. In treating of the Causes of the Prosperity of New Colonies (Chap. VII, Book IV, "Wealth of Nations") he says:

"Every colonist gets more land than he can possibly cultivate. He has no rent and scarce any taxes to pay. . . . He is eager, therefore, to collect laborers from every quarter and to pay them the most liberal wages. But these liberal wages, joined to the plenty and cheapness of land, soon make these laborers leave him in order to become landlords themselves, and to reward with equal liberality other laborers who soon leave them for the same reason they left their first masters."

This chapter contains numerous expressions which, like the opening sentence in the chapter on The Wages of Labor, show that Adam Smith failed to appreciate the true laws of the distribution of wealth only because he turned away from the more primitive forms of society to look for first principles amid complex social manifestations, where he was blinded by a preaccepted theory of the functions of capital, and, as it seems to me, by a vague acceptance of the doctrine which, two years after his death, was formulated by Malthus. And it is impossible to read the works of the economists who since the time of Smith have endeavored to build up and elucidate the science of political economy without seeing how, over and over again, they stumble over the law of wages without once recognizing it. Yet, "if it were a dog it would bite them!" Indeed, it is difficult to resist the impression that some of them really saw this law of wages, but, fearful of the practical conclusions to which it would lead, preferred to ignore and cover it up, rather than use it as the key to problems which without it are so perplexing. A great truth to an age which has rejected and trampled on it, is not a word of peace, but a sword!

Perhaps it may be well to remind the reader, before closing this chapter, of what has been before stated— that I am using the word wages not in the sense of a quantity, but in the sense of a proportion. When I say that wages fall as rent rises, I do not mean that the quantity of wealth obtained by laborers as wages is necessarily less, but that the proportion which it bears to the whole produce is necessarily less. The proportion may diminish while the quantity remains the same or even increases. If the margin of cultivation descends from the productive point which we will call 25, to the productive point we will call 20, the rent of all lands that before paid rent will increase by this difference, and the proportion of the whole produce which goes to laborers as wages will to the same extent diminish; but if, in the meantime, the advance of the arts or the economies that become possible with greater population have so increased the productive power of labor that at 20 the same exertion will produce as much wealth as before at 25, laborers will get as wages as great a quantity as before, and the relative fall of wages will not be noticeable in any diminution of the necessaries or comforts of the laborer, but only in the increased value of land and the greater incomes and more lavish expenditure of the rent-receiving class.

CHAPTER 7   THE CORRELATION AND CO-ORDINATION OF THESE LAWS

The conclusions we have reached as to the laws which govern the distribution of wealth recast a large and most important part of the science of political economy, as at present taught, overthrowing some of its most highly elaborated theories and shedding a new light on some of its most important problems. Yet, in doing this, no disputable ground has been occupied; not a single fundamental principle advanced that is not already recognized.

The law of interest and the law of wages which we have substituted for those now taught are necessary deductions from the great law which alone makes any science of political economy possible—the all-compelling law that is as inseparable from the human mind as attraction is inseparable from matter, and without which it would be impossible to previse or calculate upon any human action, the most trivial or the most important. This fundamental law, that men seek to gratify their desires with the least exertion, becomes, when viewed in its relation to one of the factors of production, the law of rent; in relation to another, the law of interest; and in relation to a third, the law of wages. And in accepting the law of rent, which, since the time of Ricardo, has been accepted by every economist of standing, and which, like a geometrical axiom, has but to be understood to compel assent, the law of interest and law of wages, as I have stated them, are inferentially accepted, as its necessary sequences. In fact, it

218

is only relatively that they can be called sequences, as in the recognition of the law of rent they too must be recognized. For on what depends the recognition of the law of rent? Evidently upon the recognition of the fact that the effect of competition is to prevent the return to labor and capital being anywhere greater than upon the poorest land in use. It is in seeing this that we see that the owner of land will be able to claim as rent all of its produce which exceeds what would be yielded to an equal application of labor and capital on the poorest land in use.

The harmony and correlation of the laws of distribution as we have now apprehended them are in striking contrast with the want of harmony which characterizes these laws as presented by the current political economy. Let us state them side by side:

The Current Statement	The True Statement
RENT depends on the margin of cultivation, rising as it falls and falling as it rises.	RENT depends on the margin of cultivation, rising as it falls and falling as it rises.
WAGES depend upon the ratio between the number of laborers and the amount of capital devoted to their employment.	WAGES depend on the margin of cultivation, falling as it falls and rising as it rises.
INTEREST depends upon the equation between the supply of and demand for capital; or, as is stated of profits, upon wages (or the cost of labor), rising as wages fall, and falling as wages rise.	INTEREST (its ratio with wages being fixed by the net power of increase which attaches to capital) depends on the margin of cultivation, falling as it falls and rising as it rises.

In the current statement the laws of distribution have no common center, no mutual relation; they are not the correlating divisions of a whole, but measures of different qualities. In the statement we have given, they spring from one point, support and supplement each other, and form the correlating divisions of a complete whole.

CHAPTER **8** THE STATICS OF THE PROBLEM
THUS EXPLAINED

We have now obtained a clear, simple, and consistent theory of the distribution of wealth, which accords with first principles and existing facts, and which, when understood, will commend itself as self-evident.

Before working out this theory, I have deemed it necessary to show conclusively the insufficiency of current theories; for, in thought, as in action, the majority of men do but follow their leaders, and a theory of wages which has not merely the support of the highest names, but is firmly rooted in common opinions and prejudices, will, until it has been proved untenable, prevent any other theory from being even considered, just as the theory that the earth was the center of the universe prevented any consideration of the theory that it revolves on its own axis and circles round the sun, until it was clearly shown that the apparent movements of the heavenly bodies could not be explained in accordance with the theory of the fixity of the earth.

There is in truth a marked resemblance between the science of political economy, as at present taught, and the science of astronomy, as taught previous to the recognition of the Copernican theory. The devices by which the current political economy endeavors to explain the social phenomena that are now forcing themselves upon the attention of the civilized world may well be compared to the elaborate system of cycles and epicycles constructed by the learned to explain the celestial phenomena in a manner according with the dogmas of authority and the rude impressions and prejudices of the unlearned. And, just as the observations which showed that this theory of cycles and epicycles could not explain all the phenomena of the heavens cleared the way for the consideration of the simpler theory that supplanted it, so will a recognition of the inadequacy of the current theories to account for social phenomena clear the way for the consideration of a theory that will give to political economy all the simplicity and harmony which the Copernican theory gave to the science of astronomy.

But at this point the parallel ceases. That "the fixed and steadfast earth" should be really whirling through space with inconceivable velocity is repugnant to the first apprehensions of men in every state and situation; but the truth I wish to make clear is naturally perceived, and has been recognized in the infancy of every people, being obscured only by the complexities of the civilized state, the warpings of selfish interests, and the false direction which the speculations of the learned have taken. To recognize it, we have but to come back to first principles and heed simple perceptions. Nothing can be clearer than the proposition that the failure of wages to increase with increasing productive power is due to the increase of rent.

Three things unite to production—labor, capital, and land.

Three parties divide the produce—the laborer, the capitalist, and the landowner.

If, with an increase of production the laborer gets no more and the capitalist no more, it is a necessary inference that the landowner reaps the whole gain.

And the facts agree with the inference. Though neither wages nor interest anywhere increase as material progress goes on, yet the invariable accompaniment and mark of material progress is the increase of rent—the rise of land values.

The increase of rent explains why wages and interest do not increase. The cause which gives to the land-holder is the cause which denies to the laborer and capitalist. That wages and interest are higher in new than in old countries is not, as the standard economists say, because nature makes a greater return to the application of labor and capital, but because land is cheaper, and, therefore, as a smaller proportion of the return is taken by rent, labor and capital can keep for their share a larger proportion of what nature does return. It is not the total produce, but the net produce, after rent has been taken from it, that determines what can be divided as wages and interest. Hence, the rate of wages and interest is everywhere fixed, not so much by the productiveness of labor as by the value of land. Wherever the value of land is relatively low, wages and interest are relatively high; wherever land is relatively high, wages and interest are relatively low.

If production had not passed the simple stage in which all labor is directly applied to the land and all wages are paid in its produce, the fact that when the landowner takes a larger portion the laborer must put up with a smaller portion could not be lost sight of.

But the complexities of production in the civilized state, in which so great a part is borne by exchange, and so much labor is bestowed upon materials after they have been separated from the land, though they may to the unthinking disguise, do not alter the fact that all production is still the union of the two factors, land and labor, and that rent (the share of the landholder) cannot be increased except at the expense of wages (the share of the laborer) and interest (the share of capital). Just as the portion of the crop, which in the simpler forms of industrial organization the owner of agricultural land receives at the end of the harvest as his rent, lessens the amount left to the cultivator as wages and interest, so does the rental of land on which a manufacturing or commercial city is built lessen the amount which can be divided as wages and interest between the laborer and capital there engaged in the production and exchange of wealth.

In short, the value of land depending wholly upon the power which its ownership gives of appropriating wealth created by labor, the increase of land values is always at the expense of the value of labor. And, hence, that the increase of productive power does not increase wages, is because it does increase the value of land. Rent swallows up the whole gain and pauperism accompanies progress.

It is unnecessary to refer to facts. They will suggest themselves to the reader. It is the general fact, observable everywhere, that as the value of land increases, so does the contrast between wealth and want appear. It is the universal fact, that where the value of land is highest, civilization exhibits the greatest luxury side by side with the most piteous destitution. To see human beings in the most abject, the most helpless and hopeless condition, you must go, not to the unfenced prairies and the log cabins of new clearings in the backwoods, where man singlehanded is commencing the struggle with nature, and land is yet worth nothing, but to the great cities, where the ownership of a little patch of ground is a fortune.

Hitherto, it is questionable if all the mechanical inventions yet made have lightened the day's toil of any human being.

—JOHN STUART MILL.

Do ye hear the children weeping, O my brothers,
    Ere the sorrow comes with years?
They are leaning their young heads against their mothers,
    And that cannot stop their tears.
The young lambs are bleating in the meadows;
    The young birds are chirping in the nest;
The young fawns are playing with the shadows;
    The young flowers are blowing toward the west—
But the young, young children, O, my brothers,
    They are weeping bitterly!
They are weeping in the playtime of the others,
    In the country of the free.

—MRS. BROWNING.

CHAPTER 1

THE DYNAMICS
OF THE PROBLEM
YET TO SEEK

In identifying rent as the receiver of the increased
production which material progress gives, but which
labor fails to obtain; in seeing that the antagonism of
interests is not between labor and capital, as is popularly believed, but is in reality between labor and
capital on the one side and landownership on the
other, we have reached a conclusion that has most important practical bearings. But it is not worth while
to dwell on them now, for we have not yet fully solved
the problem which was at the outset proposed. To say
that wages remain low because rent advances is like
saying that a steamboat moves because its wheels turn
around. The further question is, what causes rent to
advance? What is the force or necessity that, as productive power increases, distributes a greater and
greater proportion of the produce as rent?

The only cause pointed out by Ricardo as advancing
rent is the increase of population, which by requiring
larger supplies of food necessitates the extension of
cultivation to inferior lands, or to points of inferior production on the same lands, and in current works of
other authors attention is so exclusively directed to the
extension of production from superior to inferior lands
as the cause of advancing rents that Mr. Carey (followed by Professor Perry and others) has imagined
that he has overthrown the Ricardian theory of rent

by denying that the progress of agriculture is from better to worse lands.*

Now, while it is unquestionably true that the increasing pressure of population which compels a resort to inferior points of production will raise rents, and does raise rents, I do not think that all the deductions commonly made from this principle are valid, nor yet that it fully accounts for the increase of rent as material progress goes on. There are evidently other causes which conspire to raise rent, but which seem to have been wholly or partially hidden by the erroneous views as to the functions of capital and genesis of wages which have been current. To see what these are, and how they operate, let us trace the effect of material progress upon the distribution of wealth.

The changes which constitute or contribute to material progress are three: (1) increase in population; (2) improvements in the arts of production and exchange; and (3) improvements in knowledge, education, government, police, manners, and morals, so far as they increase the power of producing wealth. Material progress, as commonly understood, consists of these three elements or directions of progression, in all of

---

* As to this, it may be worth while to say: (1) That the general fact, as shown by the progress of agriculture in the newer states of the Union and by the character of the land left out of cultivation in the older, is that the course of cultivation *is* from the better to the worse qualities of land. (2) That, whether the course of production be from the absolutely better to the absolutely worse lands or the reverse (and there is much to indicate that better or worse in this connection merely relates to our knowledge, and that future advances may discover compensating qualities in portions of the earth now esteemed most sterile), it is always, and from the nature of the human mind, must always tend to be, from land under existing conditions deemed better, to land under existing conditions deemed worse. (3) That Ricardo's law of rent does not depend upon the direction of the extension of cultivation, but upon the proposition that if land of a certain quality will yield something, land of a better quality will yield more.

which the progressive nations have for some time past been advancing, though in different degrees. As, considered in the light of material forces or economies, the increase of knowledge, the betterment of government, etc., have the same effect as improvements in the arts, it will not be necessary in this view to consider them separately. What bearing intellectual or moral progress, merely as such, has upon our problem we may hereafter consider. We are at present dealing with material progress, to which these things contribute only as they increase wealth-producing power, and shall see their effects when we see the effect of improvements in the arts.

To ascertain the effects of material progress upon the distribution of wealth, let us, therefore, consider the effects of increase of population apart from improvement in the arts, and then the effect of improvement in the arts apart from increase of population.

CHAPTER 2

THE EFFECT OF INCREASE OF POPULATION UPON THE DISTRIBUTION OF WEALTH

The manner in which increasing population advances rent, as explained and illustrated in current treatises, is that the increased demand for subsistence forces production to inferior soil or to inferior productive points. Thus, if, with a given population, the margin of cultivation is at 30, all lands of productive power over 30 will pay rent. If the population be doubled, an additional supply is required, which cannot be obtained without an extension of cultivation that will cause lands to yield rent that before yielded none. If the extension be to 20, then all the land between 20 and 30 will yield rent and have a value, and all land over 30 will yield increased rent and have increased value.

It is here that the Malthusian doctrine receives from the current elucidations of the theory of rent the support of which I spoke when enumerating the causes that have combined to give that doctrine an almost undisputed sway in current thought. According to the Malthusian theory, the pressure of population against subsistence becomes progressively harder as population increases, and although two hands come into the world with every new mouth, it becomes, to use the language of John Stuart Mill, harder and harder for the new hands to supply the new mouths. According to Ricardo's theory of rent, rent arises from the difference in productiveness of the lands in use, and as explained by Ricardo and the economists who have followed him, the advance in rents which, experience shows, accompanies increasing population, is caused by the inability of procuring more food except at a greater cost, which thus forces the margin of population to lower and lower points of production, commensurately increasing rent. Thus the two theories, as I have before explained, are made to harmonize and blend, the law of rent becoming but a special application of the more general law propounded by Malthus, and the advance of rents with increasing population a demonstration of its resistless operation. I refer to this incidentally, because it now lies in our way to see the misapprehension which has enlisted the doctrine of rent in the support of a theory to which it in reality gives no countenance. The Malthusian theory has been already disposed of, and the cumulative disproof which will prevent the recurrence of a lingering doubt will be given when it is shown, further on, that the phenomena attributed to the pressure of population against subsistence would, under existing conditions, manifest themselves were population to remain stationary.

The misapprehension to which I now refer, and which, to a proper understanding of the effect of increase of population upon the distribution of wealth, it is necessary to clear up, is the presumption, expressed or implied in all the current reasoning upon the subject of rent in connection with population, that the recourse to lower points of production involves a smaller aggregate produce in proportion to the labor expended; though that this is not always the case is clearly recognized in connection with agricultural improvements, which, to use the words of Mill, are considered "as a partial relaxation of the bonds which confine the increase of population." But it is not involved even where there is no advance in the arts, and the recourse to lower points of production is clearly the result of the increased demand of an increased population. For increased population, of itself, and without any advance in the arts, implies an increase in the productive power of labor. The labor of 100 men, other things being equal, will produce much more than one hundred times as much as the labor of one man, and the labor of 1,000 men much more than ten times as much as the labor of 100 men; and, so, with every additional pair of hands which increasing population brings, there is a more than proportionate addition to the productive power of labor. Thus, with an increasing population, there may be a recourse to lower natural powers of production, not only without any diminution in the average production of wealth as compared to labor, but without any diminution at the lowest point. If population be doubled, land of but 20 productiveness may yield to the same amount of labor as much as land of 30 productiveness could before yield. For it must not be forgotten (what often *is* forgotten) that the productiveness either of land or labor is not to be measured in any one thing, but in all desired things. A settler and his family may raise as much corn on land a hundred miles away from the nearest habitation as they could raise were their land in the center of a populous district. But in the populous district they could obtain with the same labor as good a living from much poorer land, or from land of equal quality could make as good a living after paying a high rent, because in the midst of a large population their labor would have become more effective; not, perhaps, in the production of corn, but in the production of wealth generally—or the obtaining of all the commodities and services which are the real object of their labor.

But even where there is a diminution in the productiveness of labor at the lowest point—that is to say, where the increasing demand for wealth has driven production to a lower point of natural productiveness than the addition to the power of labor from increasing population suffices to make up for—it does not follow that the aggregate production, as compared with the aggregate labor, has been lessened.

Let us suppose land of diminishing qualities. The best would naturally be settled first, and as population increased production would take in the next lower quality, and so on. But, as the increase of population, by permitting greater economies, adds to the effectiveness of labor, the cause which brought each quality of land successively into cultivation would at the same time increase the amount of wealth that the same quantity of labor could produce from it. But it would also do more than this—it would increase the power of producing wealth on all the superior lands already in cultivation. If the relations of quantity and quality were such that increasing population added to the effectiveness of labor faster than it compelled a resort to less productive qualities of land, though the margin of cultivation would fall and rent would rise, the minimum return to labor would increase. That is to say, though wages as a proportion would fall, wages as a quantity would rise. The average production of wealth would increase. If the relations were such that the increasing effectiveness of labor just compensated for the diminishing productiveness of the land as it was called into use, the effect of increasing population would be to increase rent by lowering the margin of cultivation without reducing wages as a quantity, and to increase the average production. If we now suppose population still increasing, but, between the poorest quality of land in use and the next lower quality, to be a difference so great that the increased power of labor which comes with the increased population that brings it into cultivation cannot compensate for it—the minimum return to labor will be reduced, and with the rise of rents, wages will fall, not only as a proportion, but as a quantity But unless the descent in the quality of land is far more precipitous than we can well imagine, or than, I think, ever exists, the average production will still be increased, for the increased effectiveness which comes by reason of the increased population that compels resort to the inferior quality of land attaches to all labor, and the gain on the superior qualities of land will more than compensate for the diminished production on the quality last brought in. The aggregate wealth production, as compared with the aggregate expenditure of labor, will be greater, though its distribution will be more unequal.

Thus, increase of population, as it operates to extend production to lower natural levels, operates to increase rent and reduce wages as a proportion, and may or may not reduce wages as a quantity; while it seldom can, and probably never does, reduce the aggregate production of wealth as compared with the aggregate expenditure of labor, but on the contrary increases, and frequently largely increases it.

But while the increase of population thus increases rent by lowering the margin of cultivation, it is a mistake to look upon this as the only mode by which rent advances as population grows. Increasing population increases rent, without reducing the margin of cultivation; and notwithstanding the dicta of such writers as McCulloch, who assert that rent would not arise were there an unbounded extent of equally good land, increases it without reference to the natural qualities of land, for the increased powers of co-operation and exchange which come with increased population are equivalent to—nay, I think we can say without metaphor, that they give—an increased capacity to land.

I do not mean to say merely that, like an improvement in the methods or tools of production, the increased
power which comes with increased population gives to
the same labor an increased result, which is equivalent
to an increase in the natural powers of land; but that
it brings out a superior power in labor, which is local-
ized on land—which attaches not to labor generally, but
only to labor exerted on particular land; and which thus
inheres in the land as much as any qualities of soil,
climate, mineral deposit, or natural situation, and
passes, as they do, with the possession of the land.

An improvement in the method of cultivation which,
with the same outlay, will give two crops a year in
place of one, or an improvement in tools and machinery
which will double the result of labor, will manifestly,
on a particular piece of ground, have the same effect
on the produce as a doubling of the fertility of the land.
But the difference is in this respect—the improvement
in method or in tools can be utilized on any land; but
the improvement in fertility can be utilized only on the
particular land to which it applies. Now, in large part,
the increased productiveness of labor which arises from
increased population can be utilized only on particular
land, and on particular land in greatly varying degrees.

Here, let us imagine, is an unbounded savannah,
stretching off in unbroken sameness of grass and flower,
tree and rill, till the traveler tires of the monotony.
Along comes the wagon of the first immigrant. Where
to settle he cannot tell—every acre seems as good as
every other acre. As to wood, as to water, as to fertility, as to situation, there is absolutely no choice, and
he is perplexed by the embarrassment of richness. Tired
out with the search for one place that is better than
another, he stops—somewhere, anywhere—and starts to
make himself a home. The soil is virgin and rich, game
is abundant, the streams flash with the finest trout.

Nature is at her very best. He has what, were he in a populous district, would make him rich; but he is very poor. To say nothing of the mental craving, which would lead him to welcome the sorriest stranger, he labors under all the material disadvantages of solitude. He can get no temporary assistance for any work that requires a greater union of strength than that afforded by his own family, or by such help as he can permanently keep. Though he has cattle, he cannot often have fresh meat, for to get a beefsteak he must kill a bullock. He must be his own blacksmith, wagonmaker, carpenter, and cobbler—in short, a "jack of all trades and master of none." He cannot have his children schooled, for, to do so, he must himself pay and maintain a teacher. Such things as he cannot produce himself, he must buy in quantities and keep on hand, or else go without, for he cannot be constantly leaving his work and making a long journey to the verge of civilization; and when forced to do so, the getting of a vial of medicine or the replacement of a broken auger may cost him the labor of himself and horses for days. Under such circumstances, though nature is prolific, the man is poor. It is an easy matter for him to get enough to eat; but beyond this, his labor will suffice to satisfy only the simplest wants in the rudest way.

Soon there comes another immigrant. Although every quarter section of the boundless plain is as good as every other quarter section, he is not beset by any embarrassment as to where to settle. Though the land is the same, there is one place that is clearly better for him than any other place, and that is where there is already a settler and he may have a neighbor. He settles by the side of the first comer, whose condition is at once greatly improved, and to whom many things are now possible that were before impossible, for two men may help each other to do things that one man could never do.

Another immigrant comes, and, guided by the same
attraction, settles where there are already two. Another,
and another, until around our first comer there are a
score of neighbors. Labor has now an effectiveness
which, in the solitary state, it could not approach. If
heavy work is to be done, the settlers have a logrolling,
and together accomplish in a day what singly would
require years. When one kills a bullock, the others take
part of it, returning when they kill, and thus they have
fresh meat all the time. Together they hire a schoolmaster, and the childen of each are taught for a frac-
tional part of what similar teaching would have cost
the first settler. It becomes a comparatively easy matter to send to the nearest town, for some one is always
going. But there is less need for such journeys. A
blacksmith and a wheelwright soon set up shops, and
our settler can have his tools repaired for a small part
of the labor it formerly cost him. A store is opened
and he can get what he wants as he wants it; a post-
office, soon added, gives him regular communication
with the rest of the world. Then come a cobbler, a
carpenter, a harness maker, a doctor; and a little church
soon arises. Satisfactions become possible that in the
solitary state were impossible. There are gratifications
for the social and the intellectual nature—for that part
of the man that rises above the animal. The power of
sympathy, the sense of companionship, the emulation
of comparison and contrast, open a wider, and fuller,
and more varied life. In rejoicing, there are others to
rejoice; in sorrow, the mourners do not mourn alone.
There are husking bees, and apple parings, and quilting
parties. Though the ballroom be unplastered and the
orchestra but a fiddle, the notes of the magician are
yet in the strain, and Cupid dances with the dancers.
At the wedding, there are others to admire and enjoy;
in the house of death, there are watchers; by the open

grave, stands human sympathy to sustain the mourners. Occasionally, comes a straggling lecturer to open up glimpses of the world of science, of literature, or of art; in election times, come stump speakers, and the citizen rises to a sense of dignity and power, as the cause of empires is tried before him in the struggle of John Doe and Richard Roe for his support and vote. And, by and by, comes the circus, talked of months before, and opening to children whose horizon has been the prairie, all the realms of the imagination—princes and princesses of fairy tale, mailclad crusaders and turbaned Moors, Cinderella's fairy coach, and the giants of nursery lore; lions such as crouched before Daniel, or in circling Roman amphitheater tore the saints of God; ostriches who recall the sandy deserts; camels such as stood around when the wicked brethren raised Joseph from the well and sold him into bondage; elephants such as crossed the Alps with Hannibal, or felt the sword of the Maccabees; and glorious music that thrills and builds in the chambers of the mind as rose the sunny dome of Kubla Khan.

Go to our settler now, and say to him: "You have so many fruit trees which you planted; so much fencing, such a well, a barn, a house—in short, you have by your labor added so much value to this farm. Your land itself is not quite so good. You have been cropping it, and by and by it will need manure. I will give you the full value of all your improvements if you will give it to me, and go again with your family beyond the verge of settlement." He would laugh at you. His land yields no more wheat or potatoes than before, but it does yield far more of all the necessaries and comforts of life. His labor upon it will bring no heavier crops, and, we will suppose, no more valuable crops, but it will bring far more of all the other things for which men work. The presence of other settlers—the increase of population—has added to the productiveness, in these things, of labor bestowed upon it, and this added productiveness gives it a superiority over land of equal natural quality where there are as yet no settlers. If no land remains to be taken up, except such as is as far removed from population as was our settler's land when he first went upon it, the value or rent of this land will be measured by the whole of this added capability. If, however, as we have supposed, there is a continuous stretch of equal land, over which population is now spreading, it will not be necessary for the new settler to go into the wilderness, as did the first. He will settle just beyond the other settlers, and will get the advantage of proximity to them. The value or rent of our settler's land will thus depend on the advantage which it has, from being at the center of population, over that on the verge. In the one case, the margin of production will remain as before; in the other, the margin of production will be raised.

Population still continues to increase, and as it increases so do the economies which its increase permits, and which in effect add to the productiveness of the land. Our first settler's land, being the center of population, the store, the blacksmith's forge, the wheelwright's shop, are set up on it, or on its margin, where soon arises a village, which rapidly grows into a town, the center of exchanges for the people of the whole district. With no greater agricultural productiveness than it had at first, this land now begins to develop a productiveness of a higher kind. To labor expended in raising corn, or wheat, or potatoes, it will yield no more of those things than at first; but to labor expended in the subdivided branches of production which require proximity to other producers, and, especially, to labor expended in that final part of production, which consists in distribution, it will yield much larger returns.

The wheatgrower may go further on, and find land on which his labor will produce as much wheat, and nearly as much wealth; but the artisan, the manufacturer, the storekeeper, the professional man, find that their labor expended here, at the center of exchanges, will yield them much more than if expended even at a little distance away from it; and this excess of productiveness for such purposes the landowner can claim just as he could an excess in its wheat-producing power. And so our settler is able to sell in building lots a few of his acres for prices which it would not bring for wheatgrowing if its fertility had been multiplied many times. With the proceeds, he builds himself a fine house, and furnishes it handsomely. That is to say, to reduce the transaction to its lowest terms, the people who wish to use the land build and furnish the house for him, on condition that he will let them avail themselves of the superior productiveness which the increase of population has given the land.

Population still keeps on increasing, giving greater and greater utility to the land, and more and more wealth to its owner. The town has grown into a city— a St. Louis, a Chicago or a San Francisco—and still it grows. Production is here carried on upon a great scale, with the best machinery and the most favorable facilities; the division of labor becomes extremely minute, wonderfully multiplying efficiency; exchanges are of such volume and rapidity that they are made with the minimum of friction and loss. Here is the heart, the brain, of the vast social organism that has grown up from the germ of the first settlement; here has developed one of the great ganglia of the human world. Hither run all roads, hither set all currents, through all the vast regions round about. Here, if you have anything to sell, is the market; here, if you have anything to buy, is the largest and the choicest stock. Here intellectual activity is gathered into a focus, and here springs that stimulus which is born of the collision of mind with mind. Here are the great libraries, the storehouses and granaries of knowledge, the learned professors, the famous specialists. Here are museums and art galleries, collections of philosophical apparatus, and all things rare, and valuable, and best of their kind. Here come great actors, and orators, and singers, from all over the world. Here, in short, is a center of human life, in all its varied manifestations.

So enormous are the advantages which this land now offers for the application of labor, that instead of one man with a span of horses scratching over acres, you may count in places thousands of workers to the acre, working tier on tier, on floors raised one above the other, five, six, seven and eight stories from the ground, while underneath the surface of the earth engines are throbbing with pulsations that exert the force of thousands of horses.

All these advantages attach to the land; it is on this land and no other that they can be utilized, for here is the center of population—the focus of exchanges, the market place and workshop of the highest forms of industry. The productive powers which density of population has attached to this land are equivalent to the multiplication of its original fertility by the hundredfold and the thousandfold. And rent, which measures the difference between this added productiveness and that of the least productive land in use, has increased accordingly. Our settler, or whoever has succeeded to his right to the land, is now a millionaire. Like another Rip Van Winkle, he may have lain down and slept; still he is rich—not from anything he has done, but from the increase of population. There are lots from which for every foot of frontage the owner may draw more than an average mechanic

can earn; there are lots that will sell for more than
would suffice to pave them with gold coin. In the principal streets are towering buildings, of granite, marble,
iron, and plate glass, finished in the most expensive
style, replete with every convenience. Yet they are
not worth as much as the land upon which they rest
—the same land, in nothing changed, which when our
first settler came upon it had no value at all.

That this is the way in which the increase of population powerfully acts in increasing rent, whoever, in a
progressive country, will look around him, may see for
himself. The process is going on under his eyes. The
increasing difference in the productiveness of the land
in use, which causes an increasing rise in rent, results
not so much from the necessities of increased population compelling the resort to inferior land, as from the
increased productiveness which increased population
gives to the lands already in use. The most valuable
lands on the globe, the lands which yield the highest
rent, are not lands of surpassing natural fertility, but
lands to which a surpassing utility has been given by
the increase of population.

The increase of productiveness or utility which increase of population gives to certain lands, in the way
to which I have been calling attention, attaches, as it
were, to the mere quality of extension. The valuable
quality of land that has become a center of population
is its superficial capacity—it makes no difference
whether it is fertile, alluvial soil like that of Philadelphia; rich bottom land like that of New Orleans; a
filled-in marsh like that of St. Petersburg, or a sandy
waste like the greater part of San Francisco.

And where value seems to arise from superior natural
qualities, such as deep water and good anchorage, rich
deposits of coal and iron, or heavy timber, observation
also shows that these superior qualities are brought out,

rendered tangible, by population. The coal and iron
fields of Pennsylvania, that today are worth enormous
sums, were fifty years ago valueless. What is the
efficient cause of the difference? Simply the difference
in population. The coal and iron beds of Wyoming
and Montana, which today are valueless, will, in fifty
years from now, be worth millions on millions, simply
because, in the meantime, population will have greatly
increased.

It is a well-provisioned ship, this on which we sail
through space. If the bread and beef above decks seem
to grow scarce, we but open a hatch and there is a new
supply, of which before we never dreamed. And very
great command over the services of others comes to
those who as the hatches are opened are permitted to
say, "This is mine!"

To recapitulate: The effect of increasing population
upon the distribution of wealth is to increase rent, and
consequently to diminish the proportion of the produce
which goes to capital and labor, in two ways: First,
by lowering the margin of cultivation. Second, by bringing out in land special capabilities otherwise latent,
and by attaching special capabilities to particular lands.

I am disposed to think that the latter mode, to which
little attention has been given by political economists,
is really the more important. But this, in our inquiry,
is not a matter of moment.

3 THE EFFECT OF IMPROVEMENTS IN THE ARTS UPON THE DISTRIBUTION OF WEALTH

CHAPTER

Eliminating improvements in the arts, we have seen the effects of increase of population upon the distribution of wealth. Eliminating increase of population, let us now see what effect improvements in the arts of production have upon distribution.

We have seen that increase of population increases rent, rather by increasing the productiveness of labor than by decreasing it. If it can now be shown that, irrespective of the increase of population, the effect of improvements in methods of production and exchange is to increase rent, the disproof of the Malthusian theory —and of all the doctrines derived from or related to it —will be final and complete, for we shall have accounted for the tendency of material progress to lower wages and depress the condition of the lowest class, without recourse to the theory of increasing pressure against the means of subsistence.

That this is the case will, I think, appear on the slightest consideration.

The effect of inventions and improvements in the productive arts is to save labor—that is, to enable the same result to be secured with less labor, or a greater result with the same labor.

Now, in a state of society in which the existing power of labor served to satisfy all material desires, and there was no possibility of new desires being called forth by

the opportunity of gratifying them, the effect of laborsaving improvements would be simply to reduce the
amount of labor expended. But such a state of society,
if it can anywhere be found, which I do not believe,
exists only where the human most nearly approaches
the animal. In the state of society called civilized, and
which in this inquiry we are concerned with, the very
reverse is the case. Demand is not a fixed quantity,
that increases only as population increases. In each
individual it rises with his power of getting the things
demanded. Man is not an ox, who, when he has eaten
his fill, lies down to chew the cud; he is the daughter
of the horse leech, who constantly asks for more.
"When I get some money," said Erasmus, "I will buy
me some Greek books and afterward some clothes."
The amount of wealth produced is nowhere commensurate with the desire for wealth, and desire mounts with
every additional opportunity for gratification.

This being the case, the effect of laborsaving improvements will be to increase the production of wealth.
Now, for the production of wealth, two things are
required—labor and land. Therefore, the effect of laborsaving improvements will be to extend the demand for
land, and wherever the limit of the quality of land in
use is reached, to bring into cultivation lands of less
natural productiveness, or to extend cultivation on the
same lands to a point of lower natural productiveness.
And thus, while the primary effect of laborsaving improvements is to increase the power of labor, the secondary effect is to extend cultivation, and, where this
lowers the margin of cultivation, to increase rent. Thus,
where land is entirely appropriated, as in England, or
where it is either appropriated or is capable of appropriation as rapidly as it is needed for use, as in the
United States, the ultimate effect of laborsaving ma-

chinery or improvements is to increase rent without increasing wages or interest.

It is important that this be fully understood, for it shows that effects attributed by current theories to increase of population are really due to the progress of invention, and explains the otherwise perplexing fact that laborsaving machinery everywhere fails to benefit laborers.

Yet, fully to grasp this truth, it is necessary to keep in mind what I have already more than once adverted to—the interchangeability of wealth. I refer to this again, only because it is so persistently forgotten or ignored by writers who speak of agricultural production as though it were to be distinguished from production in general, and of food or subsistence as though it were not included in the term wealth.

Let me ask the reader to bear in mind, what has already been sufficiently illustrated, that the possession or production of any form of wealth is virtually the possession or production of any other form of wealth for which it will exchange—in order that he may clearly see that it is not merely improvements which effect a saving in labor directly applied to land that tend to increase rent, but all improvements that in any way save labor.

That the labor of any individual is applied exclusively to the production of one form of wealth is solely the result of the division of labor. The object of labor on the part of any individual is not the obtainment of wealth in one particular form, but the obtainment of wealth in all the forms that consort with his desires. And, hence, an improvement which effects a saving in the labor required to produce one of the things desired, is, in effect, an increase in the power of producing all the other things. If it take half a man's labor to keep him in food, and the other half to provide him clothing and shelter, an improvement which would increase his power of producing food would also increase his power of providing clothing and shelter. If his desires for more or better food, and for more or better clothing and shelter, were equal, an improvement in one department of labor would be precisely equivalent to a like improvement in the other. If the improvement consisted in a doubling of the power of his labor in producing food, he would give one-third less labor to the production of food, and one-third more to the providing of clothing and shelter. If the improvement doubled his power to provide clothing and shelter, he would give one-third less labor to the production of these things, and one-third more to the production of food. In either case, the result would be the same—he would be enabled with the same labor to get one-third more in quantity or quality of all the things he desired.

And, so, where production is carried on by the division of labor between individuals, an increase in the power of producing one of the things sought by production in the aggregate adds to the power of obtaining others, and will increase the production of the others, to an extent determined by the proportion which the saving of labor bears to the total amount of labor expended, and by the relative strength of desires. I am unable to think of any form of wealth, the demand for which would not be increased by a saving in the labor required to produce the others. Hearses and coffins have been selected as examples of things for which the demand is little likely to increase; but this is true only as to quantity. That increased power of supply would lead to a demand for more expensive hearses and coffins, no one can doubt who has noticed how strong is the desire to show regard for the dead by costly funerals.

Nor is the demand for food limited, as in economic reasoning is frequently, but erroneously, assumed. Subsistence is often spoken of as though it were a fixed quantity; but it is fixed only as having a definite minimum. Less than a certain amount will not keep a human being alive, and less than a somewhat larger amount will not keep a human being in good health. But, above this minimum, the subsistence which a human being can use may be increased almost indefinitely. Adam Smith says, and Ricardo indorses the statement, that the desire for food is limited in every man by the narrow capacity of the human stomach; but this, manifestly, is true only in the sense that when a man's belly is filled, hunger is satisfied. His demands for food have no such limit. The stomach of a Louis XIV, a Louis XV, or a Louis XVI, could not hold or digest more than the stomach of a French peasant of equal stature, yet, while a few rods of ground would supply the black bread and herbs which constituted the subsistence of the peasant, it took hundreds of thousands of acres to supply the demands of the king, who, besides his own wasteful use of the finest qualities of food, required immense supplies for his servants, horses and dogs. And in the common facts of daily life, in the unsatisfied, though perhaps latent, desires which each one has, we may see how every increase in the power of producing any form of wealth must result in an increased demand for land and the direct products of land. The man who now uses coarse food, and lives in a small house, will, as a rule, if his income be increased, use more costly food, and move to a larger house. If he grows richer and richer he will procure horses, servants, gardens and lawns, his demand for the use of land constantly increasing with his wealth. In the city where I write, is a man—but the type of men everywhere to be found—who used to boil his own beans and fry his own bacon, but who, now that he has got rich, maintains a town house that takes up a whole block and would answer for a first-class hotel, two or three country houses with extensive grounds, a large stud of racers, a breeding farm, private track, etc. It certainly takes at least a thousand times, it may be several thousand times, as much land to supply the demands of this man now as it did when he was poor.

And, so, every improvement or invention, no matter what it be, which gives to labor the power of producing more wealth, causes an increased demand for land and its direct products, and thus tends to force down the margin of cultivation, just as would the demand caused by an increased population. This being the case, every laborsaving invention, whether it be a steam plow, a telegraph, an improved process of smelting ores, a perfecting printing press, or a sewing machine, has a tendency to increase rent.

Or, to state this truth concisely:

Wealth in all its forms being the product of labor applied to land or the products of land, any increase in the power of labor, the demand for wealth being unsatisfied, will be utilized in procuring more wealth, and thus increase the demand for land.

To illustrate this effect of laborsaving machinery and improvements, let us suppose a country where, as in all the countries of the civilized world, the land is in the possession of but a portion of the people. Let us suppose a permanent barrier fixed to further increase of population, either by the enactment and strict enforcement of an Herodian law, or from such a change in manners and morals as might result from an extensive circulation of Annie Besant's pamphlets. Let the margin of cultivation, or production, be represented by 20. Thus land or other natural opportunities which, from the application of labor and capital, will yield a return of 20, will just give the ordinary rate of wages and interest, without yielding any rent; while all lands yielding to equal applications of labor and capital more than 20 will yield the excess as rent. Population remaining fixed, let there be made inventions and improvements which will reduce by one-tenth the expenditure of labor and capital necessary to produce the same amount of wealth. Now, either one-tenth of the labor and capital may be freed, and production remain the same as before; or the same amount of labor and capital may be employed, and production be correspondingly increased. But the industrial organization, as in all civilized countries, is such that labor and capital, and especially labor, must press for employment on any terms—the industrial organization is such that mere laborers are not in a position to demand their fair share in the new adjustment, and that any reduction in the application of labor to production will, at first, at least, take the form, not of giving each laborer the same amount of produce for less work, but of throwing some of the laborers out of work and giving them none of the produce. Now, owing to the increased efficiency of labor secured by the new improvements, as great a return can be secured at the point of natural productiveness represented by 18, as before at 20. Thus, the unsatisfied desire for wealth, the competition of labor and capital for employment, would insure the extension of the margin of production, we will say to 18, and thus rent would be increased by the difference between 18 and 20, while wages and interest, in quantity, would be no more than before, and, in proportion to the whole produce, would be less. There would be a greater production of wealth, but landowners would get the whole benefit, subject to temporary deductions, which will be hereafter stated.

If invention and improvement still go on, the efficiency of labor will be still further increased, and the amount of labor and capital necessary to produce a given result further diminished. The same causes will lead to the utilization of this new gain in productive power for the production of more wealth; the margin of cultivation will be again extended, and rent will increase, both in proportion and amount, without any increase in wages and interest. And, so, as invention and improvement go on, constantly adding to the efficiency of labor, the margin of production will be pushed lower and lower, and rent constantly increased, though population should remain stationary.

I do not mean to say that the lowering of the margin of production would always exactly correspond with the increase in productive power, any more than I mean to say that the process would be one of clearly defined steps. Whether, in any particular case, the lowering of the margin of production lags behind or exceeds the increase in productive power, will depend, I conceive, upon what may be called the area of productiveness that can be utilized before cultivation is forced to the next lowest point. For instance, if the margin of cultivation be at 20, improvements which enable the same produce to be obtained with one-tenth less capital and labor will not carry the margin to 18, if the area having a productiveness of 19 is sufficient to employ all the labor and capital displaced from the cultivation of the superior lands. In this case, the margin of cultivation would rest at 19, and rents would be increased by the difference between 19 and 20, and wages and interest by the difference between 18 and 19. But if, with the same increase in productive power the area of productiveness between 20 and 18 should not be sufficient to employ all the displaced labor and capital, the margin of cultivation must, if the same amount of labor and capital press for employment, be carried lower than 18. In this case, rent would gain more than the increase in the product, and wages and interest would be less than before the improvements which increased productive power.

Nor is it precisely true that the labor set free by each improvement will all be driven to seek employment in the production of more wealth. The increased power of satisfaction, which each fresh improvement gives to a certain portion of the community, will be utilized in demanding leisure or services, as well as in demanding wealth. Some laborers will, therefore, become idlers and some will pass from the ranks of productive to those of unproductive laborers—the proportion of which, as observation shows, tends to increase with the progress of society.

But, as I shall presently refer to a cause, as yet unconsidered, which constantly tends to lower the margin of cultivation, to steady the advance of rent, and even carry it beyond the proportion that would be fixed by the actual margin of cultivation, it is not worth while to take into account these perturbations in the downward movement of the margin of cultivation and the upward movement of rent. All I wish to make clear is that, without any increase in population, the progress of invention constantly tends to give a larger proportion of the produce to the owners of land, and a smaller and smaller proportion to labor and capital.

And, as we can assign no limits to the progress of invention, neither can we assign any limits to the increase of rent, short of the whole produce. For, if labor-saving inventions went on until perfection was attained, and the necessity of labor in the production of wealth was entirely done away with, then everything that the earth could yield could be obtained without labor, and the margin of cultivation would be extended to zero. Wages would be nothing, and interest would be nothing, while rent would take everything. For the owners of the land, being enabled without labor to obtain all the wealth that could be procured from nature, there would be no use for either labor or capital, and no possible way in which either could compel any share of the wealth produced. And no matter how small population might be, if anybody but the landowners continued to exist, it would be at the whim or by the mercy of the landowners—they would be maintained either for the amusement of the landowners, or, as paupers, by their bounty.

This point, of the absolute perfection of laborsaving inventions, may seem very remote, if not impossible of attainment; but it is a point toward which the march of invention is every day more strongly tending. And in the thinning out of population in the agricultural districts of Great Britain, where small farms are being converted into larger ones, and in the great machine-worked wheat fields of California and Dakota, where one may ride for miles and miles through waving grain without seeing a human habitation, there are already suggestions of the final goal toward which the whole civilized world is hastening. The steam plow and the reaping machine are creating in the modern world latifundia of the same kind that the influx of slaves from foreign wars created in ancient Italy. And to many a poor fellow as he is shoved out of his accustomed place and forced to move on—as the Roman farmers were forced to join the proletariat of the great city, or sell their blood for bread in the ranks of the legions—it seems as though these laborsaving inventions were in themselves a curse, and we hear men talking of work, as though the wearying strain of the muscles were, in itself, a thing to be desired.

In what has preceded, I have, of course, spoken of inventions and improvements when generally diffused. It is hardly necessary to say that as long as an invention or an improvement is used by so few that they derive a special advantage from it, it does not, to the extent of this special advantage, affect the general distribution of wealth. So, in regard to the limited monopolies created by patent laws, or by the causes which give the same character to railroad and telegraph lines, etc. Although generally mistaken for profits of capital, the special profits thus arising are really the returns of monopoly, as has been explained in a previous chapter, and, to the extent that they subtract from the benefits of an improvement, do not primarily affect general distribution. For instance, the benefits of a railroad or similar improvement in cheapening transportation are diffused or monopolized, as its charges are reduced to a rate which will yield ordinary interest on the capital invested, or kept up to a point which will yield an extraordinary return, or cover the stealing of the constructors or directors. And, as is well known, the rise in rent or land values corresponds with the reduction in the charges.

As has before been said, in the improvements which advance rent are not only to be included the improvements which directly increase productive power, but also such improvements in government, manners, and morals as indirectly increase it. Considered as material forces, the effect of all these is to increase productive power, and, like improvements in the productive arts, their benefit is ultimately monopolized by the possessors of the land. A notable instance of this is to be found in the abolition of protection by England. Free trade has enormously increased the wealth of Great Britain, without lessening pauperism. It has simply increased rent. And if the corrupt governments of our great American cities were to be made models of purity and economy, the effect would simply be to increase the value of land, not to raise either wages or interest.

4

EFFECT OF THE
EXPECTATION RAISED BY
MATERIAL PROGRESS

We have now seen that while advancing population tends to advance rent, so all the causes that in a progressive state of society operate to increase the productive power of labor tend, also, to advance rent, and not to advance wages or interest. The increased production of wealth goes ultimately to the owners of land in increased rent; and, although, as improvement goes on, advantages may accrue to individuals not landholders, which concentrate in their hands considerable portions of the increased produce, yet there is in all this improvement nothing which tends to increase the general return either to labor or to capital.

But there is a cause, not yet adverted to, which must be taken into consideration fully to explain the influence of material progress upon the distribution of wealth.

That cause is the confident expectation of the future enhancement of land values, which arises in all progressive countries from the steady increase of rent, and which leads to speculation, or the holding of land for a higher price than it would then otherwise bring.

We have hitherto assumed, as is generally assumed in elucidations of the theory of rent, that the actual margin of cultivation always coincides with what may be termed the necessary margin of cultivation—that is to say, we have assumed that cultivation extends to less productive points only as it becomes necessary from the fact that natural opportunities are at the more productive points fully utilized.

This, probably, is the case in stationary or very slowly progressing communities, but in rapidly progressing communities, where the swift and steady increase of rent gives confidence to calculations of further increase, it is not the case. In such communities, the confident expectation of increased prices produces, to a greater or less extent, the effects of a combination among landholders, and tends to the withholding of land from use, in expectation of higher prices, thus forcing the margin of cultivation farther than required by the necessities of production.

This cause must operate to some extent in all progressive communities, though in such countries as England, where the tenant system prevails in agriculture, it may be shown more in the selling price of land than in the agricultural margin of cultivation, or actual rent. But in communities like the United States, where the user of land generally prefers, if he can, to own it, and where there is a great extent of land to overrun, it operates with enormous power.

The immense area over which the population of the United States is scattered shows this. The man who sets out from the Eastern Seaboard in search of the margin of cultivation, where he may obtain land without paying rent, must, like the man who swam the river to get a drink, pass for long distances through half-tilled farms, and traverse vast areas of virgin soil, before he reaches the point where land can be had free of rent— i. e., by homestead entry or pre-emption. He (and, with him, the margin of cultivation) is forced so much farther than he otherwise need have gone, by the speculation which is holding these unused lands in expectation of increased value in the future. And when he settles, he will, in his turn, take up, if he can, more land than

he can use, in the belief that it will soon become valuable; and so those who follow him are again forced
farther on than the necessities of production require,
carrying the margin of cultivation to still less productive, because still more remote points.

The same thing may be seen in every rapidly growing
city. If the land of superior quality as to location were
always fully used before land of inferior quality were
resorted to, no vacant lots would be left as a city extended, nor would we find miserable shanties in the
midst of costly buildings. These lots, some of them
extremely valuable, are withheld from use, or from the
full use to which they might be put, because their
owners, not being able or not wishing to improve them,
prefer, in expectation of the advance of land values, to
hold them for a higher rate than could now be obtained
from those willing to improve them. And, in consequence of this land being withheld from use, or from
the full use of which it is capable, the margin of the
city is pushed away so much farther from the center.

But when we reach the limits of the growing city—
the actual margin of building, which corresponds to the
margin of cultivation in agriculture—we shall not find
the land purchasable at its value for agricultural purposes, as it would be were rent determined simply by
present requirements; but we shall find that for a long
distance beyond the city, land bears a speculative value,
based upon the belief that it will be required in the
future for urban purposes, and that to reach the point
at which land can be purchased at a price not based
upon urban rent, we must go very far beyond the actual
margin of urban use.

Or, to take another case of a different kind, instances
similar to which may doubtless be found in every locality. There is in Marin County, within easy access of
San Francisco, a fine belt of redwood timber. Nat-

urally, this would be first used, before resorting for the
supply of the San Francisco market to timber lands at
a much greater distance. But it yet remains uncut,
and lumber procured many miles beyond is daily hauled
past it on the railroad, because its owner prefers to
hold for the greater price it will bring in the future.
Thus, by the withholding from use of this body of timber, the margin of production of redwood is forced so
much farther up and down the Coast Range. That
mineral land, when reduced to private ownership, is
frequently withheld from use while poorer deposits are
worked, is well known, and in new states it is common
to find individuals who are called "land poor"—that is,
who remain poor, sometimes almost to deprivation, because they insist on holding land, which they themselves
cannot use, at prices at which no one else can profitably
use it.

To recur now to the illustration we made use of in the
preceding chapter: With the margin of cultivation
standing at 20, an increase in the power of production
takes place, which renders the same result obtainable
with one-tenth less labor. For reasons before stated,
the margin of production must now be forced down, and
if it rests at 18, the return to labor and capital will
be the same as before, when the margin stood at 20.
Whether it will be forced to 18 or be forced lower
depends upon what I have called the area of productiveness which intervenes between 20 and 18. But if the
confident expectation of a further increase of rents
leads the landowners to demand 3 rent for 20 land,
2 for 19, and 1 for 18 land, and to withhold their land
from use until these terms are complied with, the area
of productiveness may be so reduced that the margin
of cultivation must fall to 17 or even lower; and thus,
as the result of the increase in the efficiency of labor,
laborers would get less than before, while interest would

be proportionately reduced, and rent would increase in greater ratio than the increase in productive power.

Whether we formulate it as an extension of the margin of production, or as a carrying of the rent line beyond the margin of production, the influence of speculation in land in increasing rent is a great fact which cannot be ignored in any complete theory of the distribution of wealth in progressive countries. It is the force, evolved by material progress, which tends constantly to increase rent in a greater ratio than progress increases production, and thus constantly tends, as material progress goes on and productive power increases, to reduce wages, not merely relatively, but absolutely. It is this expansive force which, operating with great power in new countries, brings to them, seemingly long before their time, the social diseases of older countries; produces "tramps" on virgin acres, and breeds paupers on half-tilled soil.

In short, the general and steady advance in land values in a progressive community necessarily produces that additional tendency to advance which is seen in the case of commodities when any general and continuous cause operates to increase their price. As, during the rapid depreciation of currency which marked the latter days of the Southern Confederacy, the fact that whatever was bought one day could be sold for a higher price the next, operated to carry up the price of commodities even faster than the depreciation of the currency, so does the steady increase of land values, which material progress produces, operate still further to accelerate the increase. We see this secondary cause operating in full force in those manias of land speculation which mark the growth of new communities; but though these are the abnormal and occasional manifestations, it is undeniable that the cause steadily operates, with greater or less intensity, in all progressive societies.

The cause which limits speculation in commodities, the tendency of increasing price to draw forth additional supplies, cannot limit the speculative advance in land values, as land is a fixed quantity, which human agency can neither increase nor diminish; but there is nevertheless a limit to the price of land, in the minimum required by labor and capital as the condition of engaging in production. If it were possible continuously to reduce wages until zero were reached, it would be possible continuously to increase rent until it swallowed up the whole produce. But as wages cannot be permanently reduced below the point at which laborers will consent to work and reproduce, nor interest below the point at which capital will be devoted to production, there is a limit which restrains the speculative advance of rent. Hence speculation cannot have the same scope to advance rent in countries where wages and interest are already near the minimum, as in countries where they are considerably above it. Yet that there is in all progressive countries a constant tendency in the speculative advance of rent to overpass the limit where production would cease, is, I think, shown by recurring seasons of industrial paralysis—a matter which will be more fully examined in the next book.

To whomsoever the soil at any time belongs, to him belong the fruits of it. White parasols, and elephants mad with pride are the flowers of a grant of land.

—SIR WM. JONES' TRANSLATION OF AN INDIAN GRANT OF LAND,
FOUND AT TANNA.

The widow is gathering nettles for her children's dinner; a perfumed seigneur, delicately lounging in the Œil de Bœuf, hath an alchemy whereby he will extract from her the third nettle, and call it rent.

—CARLYLE.

CHAPTER 1 THE PRIMARY CAUSE OF RECURRING PAROXYSMS OF INDUSTRIAL DEPRESSION

Our long inquiry is ended. We may now marshal the results.

To begin with the industrial depressions, to account for which so many contradictory and self-contradictory theories are broached.

A consideration of the manner in which the speculative advance in land values cuts down the earnings of labor and capital and checks production leads, I think, irresistibly to the conclusion that this is the main cause of those periodical industrial depressions to which every civilized country, and all civilized countries together, seem increasingly liable.

I do not mean to say that there are not other proximate causes. The growing complexity and interdependence of the machinery of production, which makes each shock or stoppage propagate itself through a widening circle; the essential defect of currencies which contract when most needed, and the tremendous alternations in volume that occur in the simpler forms of commercial credit, which, to a much greater extent than currency in any form, constitute the medium or flux of exchanges; the protective tariffs which present artificial barriers to the interplay of productive forces, and other similar causes, undoubtedly bear important part in producing and continuing what are called hard times. But, both from the consideration of principles and the obser-

263

vation of phenomena, it is clear that the great initiatory cause is to be looked for in the speculative advance of land values.

In the preceding chapter I have shown that the speculative advance in land values tends to press the margin of cultivation, or production, beyond its normal limit, thus compelling labor and capital to accept of a smaller return, or (and this is the only way they can resist the tendency) to cease production. Now, it is not only natural that labor and capital should resist the crowding down of wages and interest by the speculative advance of rent, but they are driven to this in self-defense, inasmuch as there is a minimum of return below which labor cannot exist nor capital be maintained. Hence, from the fact of speculation in land, we may infer all the phenomena which mark these recurring seasons of industrial depression.

Given a progressive community, in which population is increasing and one improvement succeeds another, and land must constantly increase in value. This steady increase naturally leads to speculation in which future increase is anticipated, and land values are carried beyond the point at which, under the existing conditions of production, their accustomed returns would be left to labor and capital. Production, therefore, begins to stop. Not that there is necessarily, or even probably, an absolute diminution in production; but that there is what in a progressive community would be equivalent to an absolute diminution of production in a stationary community—a failure in production to increase proportionately, owing to the failure of new increments of labor and capital to find employment at the accustomed rates.

This stoppage of production at some points must necessarily show itself at other points of the industrial network, in a cessation of demand, which would again check production there, and thus the paralysis would communicate itself through all the interlacings of industry and commerce, producing everywhere a partial disjointing of production and exchange, and resulting in the phenomena that seem to show overproduction or overconsumption, according to the standpoint from which they are viewed.

The period of depression thus ensuing would continue until (1) the speculative advance in rents had been lost; or (2) the increase in the efficiency of labor, owing to the growth of population and the progress of improvement, had enabled the normal rent line to overtake the speculative rent line; or (3) labor and capital had become reconciled to engaging in production for smaller returns. Or, most probably, all three of these causes would co-operate to produce a new equilibrium, at which all the forces of production would again engage, and a season of activity ensue; whereupon rent would begin to advance again, a speculative advance again take place, production again be checked, and the same round be gone over.

In the elaborate and complicated system of production which is characteristic of modern civilization, where, moreover, there is no such thing as a distinct and independent industrial community, but geographically or politically separated communities blend and interlace their industrial organizations in different modes and varying measures, it is not to be expected that effect should be seen to follow cause as clearly and definitely as would be the case in a simpler development of industry, and in a community forming a complete and distinct industrial whole; but, nevertheless, the phenomena actually presented by these alternate seasons of activity and depression clearly correspond with those we have inferred from the speculative advance of rent.

Deduction thus shows the actual phenomena as resulting from the principle. If we reverse the process, it is as easy by induction to reach the principle by tracing up the phenomena.

These seasons of depression are always preceded by seasons of activity and speculation, and on all hands the connection between the two is admitted—the depression being looked upon as the reaction from the speculation, as the headache of the morning is the reaction from the debauch of the night. But as to the manner in which the depression results from the speculation, there are two classes or schools of opinion, as the attempts made on both sides of the Atlantic to account for the present industrial depression will show.

One school says that the speculation produced the depression by causing overproduction, and points to the warehouses filled with goods that cannot be sold at remunerative prices, to mills closed or working on half time, to mines shut down and steamers laid up, to money lying idly in bank vaults, and workmen compelled to idleness and privation. They point to these facts as showing that the production has exceeded the demand for consumption, and they point, moreover, to the fact that when government during war enters the field as an enormous consumer, brisk times prevail, as in the United States during the civil war and in England during the Napoleonic struggle.

The other school says that the speculation has produced the depression by leading to overconsumption, and points to full warehouses, rusting steamers, closed mills, and idle workmen as evidences of a cessation of effective demand, which, they say, evidently results from the fact that people, made extravagant by a fictitious prosperity, have lived beyond their means, and are now obliged to retrench—that is, to consume less wealth. They point, moreover, to the enormous consumption of wealth by wars, by the building of unremunerative railroads, by loans to bankrupt governments, etc., as extravagances which, though not felt at the time, just as the spendthrift does not at the moment feel the impairment of his fortune, must now be made up by a season of reduced consumption.

Now, each of these theories evidently expresses one side or phase of a general truth, but each of them evidently fails to comprehend the full truth. As an explanation of the phenomena, each is equally and utterly preposterous.

For while the great masses of men want more wealth than they can get, and while they are willing to give for it that which is the basis and raw material of wealth —their labor—how can there be overproduction? And while the machinery of production wastes and producers are condemned to unwilling idleness, how can there be overconsumption?

When, with the desire to consume more, there coexist the ability and willingness to produce more, industrial and commercial paralysis cannot be charged either to overproduction or to overconsumption. Manifestly, the trouble is that production and consumption cannot meet and satisfy each other.

How does this inability arise? It is evidently and by common consent the result of speculation. But of speculation in what?

Certainly not of speculation in things which are the products of labor—in agricultural or mineral productions, or manufactured goods, for the effect of speculation in such things, as is well shown in current treatises that spare me the necessity of illustration, is simply to equalize supply and demand, and to steady the interplay of production and consumption by an action analogous to that of a flywheel in a machine.

Therefore, if speculation be the cause of these industrial depressions, it must be speculation in things not the production of labor, but yet necessary to the exertion of labor in the production of wealth—of things of fixed quantity; that is to say, it must be speculation in land.

That land speculation is the true cause of industrial depression is, in the United States, clearly evident. In each period of industrial activity land values have steadily risen, culminating in speculation which carried them up in great jumps. This has been invariably followed by a partial cessation of production, and its correlative, a cessation of effective demand (dull trade), generally accompanied by a commercial crash; and then has succeeded a period of comparative stagnation, during which the equilibrium has been again slowly established, and the same round been run again. This relation is observable throughout the civilized world. Periods of industrial activity always culminate in a speculative advance of land values, followed by symptoms of checked production, generally shown at first by cessation of demand from the newer countries, where the advance in land values has been greatest.

That this must be the main explanation of these periods of depression, will be seen by an analysis of the facts.

All trade, let it be remembered, is the exchange of commodities for commodities, and hence the cessation of demand for some commodities, which marks the depression of trade, is really a cessation in the supply of other commodities. That dealers find their sales declining and manufacturers find orders falling off, while the things which they have to sell, or stand ready to make, are things for which there is yet a widespread desire, simply shows that the supply of other things, which in the course of trade would be given for them, has declined. In common parlance we say that "buyers have no money," or that "money is becoming scarce," but in talking in this way we ignore the fact that money is but the medium of exchange. What the would-be buyers really lack is not money, but commodities which they can turn into money—what is really becoming scarcer is produce of some sort. The diminution of the effective demand of consumers is therefore but a result of the diminution of production.

This is seen very clearly by storekeepers in a manufacturing town when the mills are shut down and operatives thrown out of work. It is the cessation of production which deprives the operatives of means to make the purchases they desire, and thus leaves the storekeeper with what, in view of the lessened demand, is a superabundant stock, and forces him to discharge some of his clerks and otherwise reduce his demands. And the cessation of demand (I am speaking, of course, of general cases and not of any alteration in relative demand from such causes as change of fashion), which has left the manufacturer with superabundant stock and compelled him to discharge his hands, must arise in the same way. Somewhere, it may be at the other end of the world, a check in production has produced a check in the demand for consumption. That demand is lessened without want being satisfied, shows that production is somewhere checked.

People want the things the manufacturer makes as much as ever, just as the operatives want the things the storekeeper has to sell. But they do not have as much to give for them. Production has somewhere been checked, and this reduction in the supply of some things has shown itself in cessation of demand for others, the check propagating itself through the whole framework of industry and exchange. Now, the industrial pyramid manifestly rests on the land. The primary and fundamental occupations, which create a demand for all others, are evidently those which extract wealth from nature, and, hence, if we trace from one exchange point to another, and from one occupation to another, this check to production, which shows itself in decreased purchasing power, we must ultimately find it in some obstacle which checks labor in expending itself on land. And that obstacle, it is clear, is the speculative advance in rent, or the value of land, which produces the same effects as (in fact, it is) a lockout of labor and capital by landowners. This check to production, beginning at the basis of interlaced industry, propagates itself from exchange point to exchange point, cessation of supply becoming failure of demand, until, so to speak, the whole machine is thrown out of gear, and the spectacle is everywhere presented of labor going to waste while laborers suffer from want.

This strange and unnatural spectacle of large numbers of willing men who cannot find employment is enough to suggest the true cause to whosoever can think consecutively. For, though custom has dulled us to it, it is a strange and unnatural thing that men who wish to labor, in order to satisfy their wants, cannot find the opportunity—as, since labor is that which produces wealth, the man who seeks to exchange labor for food, clothing, or any other form of wealth, is like one who proposes to give bullion for coin, or wheat for flour. We talk about the supply of labor and the demand for labor, but, evidently, these are only relative terms. The supply of labor is everywhere the same—two hands always come into the world with one mouth, twenty-one boys to every twenty girls; and the demand for labor must always exist as long as men want things which labor alone can procure. We talk about the "want of work," but, evidently, it is not work that is short while want continues; evidently, the supply of labor cannot be too great, nor the demand for labor too small, when people suffer for the lack of things that labor produces. The real trouble must be that supply is somehow prevented from satisfying demand, that somewhere there is an obstacle which prevents labor from producing the things that laborers want.

Take the case of any one of these vast masses of unemployed men, to whom, though he never heard of Malthus, it today seems that there are too many people in the world. In his own wants, in the needs of his anxious wife, in the demands of his half-cared-for, perhaps even hungry and shivering children, there is demand enough for labor, Heaven knows! In his own willing hands is the supply. Put him on a solitary island, and though cut off from all the enormous advantages which the co-operation, combination, and machinery of a civilized community give to the productive powers of man yet his two hands can fill the mouths and keep warm the backs that depend upon them. Yet where productive power is at its highest development they cannot. Why? Is it not because in the one case he has access to the material and forces of nature, and in the other this access is denied?

Is it not the fact that labor is thus shut off from nature which can alone explain the state of things that compels men to stand idle who would willingly supply their wants by their labor? The proximate cause of enforced idleness with one set of men may be the cessation of demand on the part of other men for the particular things they produce, but trace this cause from point to point, from occupation to occupation, and you will find that enforced idleness in one trade is caused by enforced idleness in another, and that the paralysis which produces dullness in all trades cannot be said to spring from too great a supply of labor or too small a demand for labor, but must proceed from the fact that supply cannot meet demand by producing the things which satisfy want and are the object of labor.

Now, what is necessary to enable labor to produce

these things, is land. When we speak of labor creating
wealth, we speak metaphorically. Man creates nothing.
The whole human race, were they to labor forever, could
not create the tiniest mote that floats in a sunbeam—
could not make this rolling sphere one atom heavier or
one atom lighter. In producing wealth, labor, with the
aid of natural forces, but works up, into the forms desired, pre-existing matter, and, to produce wealth, must,
therefore, have access to this matter and to these forces
—that is to say, to land. The land is the source of all
wealth. It is the mine from which must be drawn the
ore that labor fashions. It is the substance to which
labor gives the form. And, hence, when labor cannot
satisfy its wants, may we not with certainty infer that
it can be from no other cause than that labor is denied
access to land?

When in all trades there is what we call scarcity of
employment; when, everywhere, labor wastes, while desire is unsatisfied, must not the obstacle which prevents
labor from producing the wealth it needs, lie at the
foundation of the industrial structure? That foundation is land. Milliners, optical instrument makers,
gilders, and polishers, are not the pioneers of new settlements. Miners did not go to California or Australia because shoemakers, tailors, machinists, and printers were
there. But those trades followed the miners, just as
they are now following the gold diggers into the Black
Hills and the diamond diggers into South Africa. It is
not the storekeeper who is the cause of the farmer, but
the farmer who brings the storekeeper. It is not the
growth of the city that develops the country, but the
development of the country that makes the city grow.
And, hence, when, through all trades, men willing to
work cannot find opportunity to do so, the difficulty
must arise in the employment that creates a demand

for all other employments—it must be because labor is shut out from land.

In Leeds or Lowell, in Philadelphia or Manchester, in London or New York, it may require a grasp of first principles to see this; but where industrial development has not become so elaborate, nor the extreme links of the chain so widely separated, one has but to look at obvious facts. Although not yet thirty years old, the city of San Francisco, both in population and in commercial importance, ranks among the great cities of the world, and, next to New York, is the most metropolitan of American cities. Though not yet thirty years old, she has had for some years an increasing number of unemployed men. Clearly, here, it is because men cannot find employment in the country that there are so many unemployed in the city; for when the harvest opens they go trooping out, and when it is over they come trooping back to the city again. If these now unemployed men were producing wealth from the land, they would not only be employing themselves, but would be employing all the mechanics of the city, giving custom to the storekeepers, trade to the merchants, audiences to the theaters, and subscribers and advertisements to the newspapers—creating effective demand that would be felt in New England and Old England, and wherever throughout the world come the articles that, when they have the means to pay for them, such a population consumes.

Now, why is it that this unemployed labor cannot employ itself upon the land? Not that the land is all in use. Though all the symptoms that in older countries are taken as showing a redundancy of population are beginning to manifest themselves in San Francisco, it is idle to talk of redundancy of population in a State that with greater natural resources than France has not yet a million of people. Within a few miles of San

Francisco is unused land enough to give employment to every man who wants it. I do not mean to say that every unemployed man could turn farmer or build himself a house, if he had the land; but that enough could and would do so to give employment to the rest. What is it, then, that prevents labor from employing itself on this land? Simply, that it has been monopolized and is held at speculative prices, based not upon present value, but upon the added value that will come with the future growth of population.

What may thus be seen in San Francisco by whoever is willing to see, may, I doubt not, be seen as clearly in other places.

The present commercial and industrial depression, which first clearly manifested itself in the United States in 1872, and has spread with greater or less intensity over the civilized world, is largely attributed to the undue extension of the railroad system, with which there are many things that seem to show its relation. I am fully conscious that the construction of railroads before they are actually needed may divert capital and labor from more to less productive employments, and make a community poorer instead of richer; and when the railroad mania was at its highest, I pointed this out in a political tract addressed to the people of California;* but to assign to this wasting of capital such a widespread industrial deadlock seems to me like attributing an unusually low tide to the drawing of a few extra bucketfuls of water. The waste of capital and labor during the civil war was enormously greater than it could possibly be by the construction of unnecessary railroads, but without producing any such result. And, certainly, there seems to be little sense in talking of the waste of capital and labor in railroads as causing this

---

* "The Subsidy Question and the Democratic Party," 1871.

depression, when the prominent feature of the depression has been the superabundance of capital and labor seeking employment.

Yet, that there is a connection between the rapid construction of railroads and industrial depression, any one who understands what increased land values mean, and who has noticed the effect which the construction of railroads has upon land speculation, can easily see. Wherever a railroad was built or projected, lands sprang up in value under the influence of speculation, and thousands of millions of dollars were added to the nominal values which capital and labor were asked to pay outright, or to pay in installments, as the price of being allowed to go to work and produce wealth. The inevitable result was to check production, and this check to production propagated itself in a cessation of demand, which checked production to the furthest verge of the wide circle of exchanges, operating with accumulated force in the centers of the great industrial commonwealth into which commerce links the civilized world.

The primary operations of this cause can, perhaps, be nowhere more clearly traced than in California, which, from its comparative isolation, has constituted a peculiarly well-defined community.

Until almost its close, the last decade was marked in California by the same industrial activity which was shown in the Northern States, and, in fact, throughout the civilized world, when the interruption of exchanges and the disarrangement of industry caused by the war and the blockade of southern ports is considered. This activity could not be attributed to inflation of the currency or to lavish expenditures of the General Government, to which in the eastern states the comparative activity of the same period has since been attributed; for, in spite of legal tender laws, the Pacific Coast adhered to a coin currency, and the taxation of the Federal

Government took away very much more than was returned in Federal expenditures. It was attributable
solely to normal causes, for, though placer mining was
declining, the Nevada silver mines were being opened,
wheat and wool were beginning to take the place of gold
in the table of exports, and an increasing population and
the improvement in the methods of production and exchange were steadily adding to the efficiency of labor.

With this material progress went on a steady enhancement in land values—its consequence. This steady
advance engendered a speculative advance, which, with
the railroad era, ran up land values in every direction.
If the population of California had steadily grown when
the long, costly, fever-haunted Isthmus route was the
principal mode of communication with the Atlantic
States, it must, it was thought, increase enormously with
the opening of a road which would bring New York
Harbor and San Francisco Bay within seven days' easy
travel, and when in the state itself the locomotive took
the place of stage coach and freight wagon. The expected increase of land values which would thus accrue
was discounted in advance. Lots on the outskirts of
San Francisco rose hundreds and thousands per cent.,
and farming land was taken up and held for high prices,
in whichever direction an immigrant was likely to go.

But the anticipated rush of immigrants did not take
place. Labor and capital could not pay so much for
land and make fair returns. Production was checked,
if not absolutely, at least relatively. As the transcon-
tinental railroad approached completion, instead of increased activity, symptoms of depression began to
manifest themselves; and, when it was completed, to
the season of activity had succeeded a period of depression which has not since been fully recovered from, during which wages and interest have steadily fallen. What
I have called the actual rent line, or margin of cultiva-

tion, is thus (as well as by the steady march of improvement and increase of population, which, though slower than it otherwise would have been, still goes on) approaching the speculative rent line, but the tenacity with which a speculative advance in the price of land is maintained in a developing community is well known.*

Now, what thus went on in California went on in every progressive section of the Union. Everywhere that a railroad was built or projected, land was monopolized in anticipation, and the benefit of the improvement was discounted in increased land values. The speculative advance in rent thus outrunning the normal advance, production was checked, demand was decreased, and labor and capital were turned back from occupations more directly concerned with land, to glut those in which the value of land is a less perceptible element. It is thus that the rapid extension of railroads is related to the succeeding depression.

And what went on in the United States went on in a greater or less obvious degree all over the progressive world. Everywhere land values have been steadily increasing with material progress, and everywhere this increase begot a speculative advance. The impulse of the primary cause not only radiated from the newer sections of the Union to the older sections, and from the United States to Europe, but everywhere the primary cause was acting. And, hence, a world-wide depression of industry and commerce, begotten of a world-wide material progress.

---

* It is astonishing how in a new country of great expectations speculative prices of land will be kept up. It is common to hear the expression, "There is no market for real estate; you cannot sell it at any price," and yet, at the same time, if you go to buy it, unless you find somebody who is absolutely compelled to sell, you must pay the prices that prevailed when speculation ran high. For owners, believing that land values must ultimately advance, hold on as long as they can.

There is one thing which, it may seem, I have overlooked, in attributing these industrial depressions to the
speculative advance of rent or land values as a main
and primary cause. The operation of such a cause,
though it may be rapid, must be progressive—resembling a pressure, not a blow. But these industrial
depressions seem to come suddenly—they have, at their
beginning, the character of a paroxysm, followed by a
comparative lethargy, as if of exhaustion. Everything
seems to be going on as usual, commerce and industry
vigorous and expanding, when suddenly there comes a
shock, as of a thunderbolt out of a clear sky—a bank
breaks, a great manufacturer or merchant fails, and, as
if a blow had thrilled through the entire industrial organization, failure succeeds failure, and on every side
workmen are discharged from employment, and capital
shrinks into profitless security.

Let me explain what I think to be the reason of this:
To do so, we must take into account the manner in
which exchanges are made, for it is by exchanges that
all the varied forms of industry are linked together into
one mutually related and interdependent organization.
To enable exchanges to be made between producers far
removed by space and time, large stocks must be kept
in store and in transit, and this, as I have already explained, I take to be the great function of capital, in
addition to that of supplying tools and seed. These exchanges are, perhaps necessarily, largely made upon
credit—that is to say, the advance upon one side is
made before the return is received on the other.

Now, without stopping to inquire as to the causes, it
is manifest that these advances are, as a rule, from
the more highly organized and later developed industries to the more fundamental. The West Coast Afri-
can, for instance, who exchanges palm oil and cocoanuts
for gaudy calico and Birmingham idols, gets his return

immediately; the English merchant, on the contrary, has to lay out of his goods a long while before he gets his returns. The farmer can sell his crop as soon as it is harvested, and for cash; the great manufacturer must keep a large stock, send his goods long distances to agents, and, generally, sell on time. Thus, as advances and credits are generally from what we may call the secondary, to what we may call the primary industries, it follows that any check to production which proceeds from the latter will not immediately manifest itself in the former. The system of advances and credits constitutes, as it were, an elastic connection, which will give considerably before breaking, but which, when it breaks, will break with a snap.

Or, to illustrate in another way what I mean: The great pyramid of Gizeh is composed of layers of masonry, the bottom layer, of course, supporting all the rest. Could we by some means gradually contract this bottom layer, the upper part of the pyramid would for some time retain its form, and then, when gravitation at length overcame the adhesiveness of the material, would not diminish gradually and regularly, but would break off suddenly, in large pieces. Now, the industrial organization may be likened to such a pyramid. What is the proportion which in a given stage of social development the various industries bear to each other, it is difficult, and perhaps impossible, to say; but it is obvious that there is such a proportion, just as in a printer's font of type there is a certain proportion between the various letters. Each form of industry, as it is developed by division of labor, springs from and rises out of the others, and all rest ultimately upon land; for, without land, labor is as impotent as would be a man in void space. To make the illustration closer to the condition of a progressive country, imagine a pyramid composed of superimposed layers—the whole constantly growing and expanding. Imagine the growth of the layer nearest the ground to be checked. The others will for a time keep on expanding—in fact, for the moment, the tendency will be to quicker expansion, for the vital force which is refused scope on the ground layer will strive to find vent in those above—until, at length, there is a decided overbalance and a sudden crumbling along all the faces of the pyramid.

That the main cause and general course of the recurring paroxysms of industrial depression, which are becoming so marked a feature of modern social life, are thus explained, is, I think, clear. And let the reader remember that it is only the main causes and general courses of such phenomena that we are seeking to trace or that, in fact, it is possible to trace with any exactness. Political economy can deal, and has need to deal, only with general tendencies. The derivative forces are so multiform, the actions and reactions are so various, that the exact character of the phenomena cannot be predicted. We know that if a tree is cut through it will fall, but precisely in what direction will be determined by the inclination of the trunk, the spread of the branches, the impact of the blows, the quarter and force of the wind; and even a bird lighting on a twig, or a frightened squirrel leaping from bough to bough, will not be without its influence. We know that an insult will arouse a feeling of resentment in the human breast, but to say how far and in what way it will manifest itself, would require a synthesis which would build up the entire man and all his surroundings, past and present.

The manner in which the sufficient cause to which I have traced them explains the main features of these industrial depressions is in striking contrast with the contradictory and self-contradictory attempts which have been made to explain them on the current theories of the distribution of wealth. That a speculative advance in rent or land values invariably precedes each of these seasons of industrial depression is everywhere clear. That they bear to each other the relations of cause and effect, is obvious to whosoever considers the necessary relations between land and labor.

And that the present depression is running its course, and that, in the manner previously indicated, a new equilibrium is being established, which will result in another season of comparative activity, may already be seen in the United States. The normal rent line and the speculative rent line are being brought together: (1) By the fall in speculative land values, which is very evident in the reduction of rents and shrinkage of real estate values in the principal cities. (2) By the increased efficiency of labor, arising from the growth of population and the utilization of new inventions and discoveries, some of which almost as important as that of the use of steam we seem to be on the verge of grasping. (3) By the lowering of the habitual standard of interest and wages, which, as to interest, is shown by the negotiation of a government loan at four per cent., and as to wages is too generally evident for any special citation. When the equilibrium is thus re-established, a season of renewed activity, culminating in a speculative advance of land values, will set in.* But wages and interest will not recover their lost ground. The net result of all these perturbations or wave-like movements is the gradual forcing of wages and interest toward their minimum. These temporary and recurring depressions exhibit, in fact, as was noticed in the opening chapter, but intensifications of the general movement which accompanies material progress.

---

* This was written a year ago. It is now (July, 1879) evident that a new period of activity has commenced, as above predicted, and in New York and Chicago real estate prices have already begun to recover.

CHAPTER **2** THE PERSISTENCE OF POVERTY
AMID ADVANCING WEALTH

The great problem, of which these recurring seasons
of industrial depression are but peculiar manifestations,
is now, I think, fully solved, and the social phenomena
which all over the civilized world appall the philanthropist and perplex the statesman, which hang with clouds
the future of the most advanced races, and suggest
doubts of the reality and ultimate goal of what we
have fondly called progress, are now explained.

*The reason why, in spite of the increase of productive
power, wages constantly tend to a minimum which will
give but a bare living, is that, with increase in productive power, rent tends to even greater increase, thus
producing a constant tendency to the forcing down of
wages.*

In every direction, the direct tendency of advancing
civilization is to increase the power of human labor to
satisfy human desires—to extirpate poverty, and to
banish want and the fear of want. All the things in
which progress consists, all the conditions which progressive communities are striving for, have for their
direct and natural result the improvement of the material (and consequently the intellectual and moral) condition of all within their influence. The growth of
population, the increase and extension of exchanges, the
discoveries of science, the march of invention, the spread
of education, the improvement of government, and the

282

amelioration of manners, considered as material forces, have all a direct tendency to increase the productive power of labor—not of some labor, but of all labor; not in some departments of industry, but in all departments of industry; for the law of the production of wealth in society is the law of "each for all, and all for each."

But labor cannot reap the benefits which advancing civilization thus brings, because they are intercepted. Land being necessary to labor, and being reduced to private ownership, every increase in the productive power of labor but increases rent—the price that labor must pay for the opportunity to utilize its powers; and thus all the advantages gained by the march of progress go to the owners of land, and wages do not increase. Wages cannot increase; for the greater the earnings of labor the greater the price that labor must pay out of its earnings for the opportunity to make any earnings at all. The mere laborer has thus no more interest in the general advance of productive power than the Cuban slave has in advance in the price of sugar. And just as an advance in the price of sugar may make the condition of the slave worse, by inducing the master to drive him harder, so may the condition of the free laborer be positively, as well as relatively, changed for the worse by the increase in the productive power of his labor. For, begotten of the continuous advance of rents, arises a speculative tendency which discounts the effect of future improvements by a still further advance of rent, and thus tends, where this has not occurred from the normal advance of rent, to drive wages down to the slave point—the point at which the laborer can just live.

And thus robbed of all the benefits of the increase in productive power, labor is exposed to certain effects of advancing civilization which, without the advantages that naturally accompany them, are positive evils, and of themselves tend to reduce the free laborer to the helpless and degraded condition of the slave.

For all improvements which add to productive power as civilization advances consist in, or necessitate, a still further subdivision of labor, and the efficiency of the whole body of laborers is increased at the expense of the independence of the constituents. The individual laborer acquires knowledge of and skill in but an infinitesimal part of the varied processes which are required to supply even the commonest wants. The aggregate produce of the labor of a savage tribe is small, but each member is capable of an independent life. He can build his own habitation, hew out or stitch together his own canoe, make his own clothing, manufacture his own weapons, snares, tools and ornaments. He has all the knowledge of nature possessed by his tribe—knows what vegetable productions are fit for food, and where they may be found; knows the habits and resorts of beasts, birds, fishes, and insects; can pilot himself by the sun or the stars, by the turning of blossoms or the mosses on the trees; is, in short, capable of supplying all his wants. He may be cut off from his fellows and still live; and thus possesses an independent power which makes him a free contracting party in his relations to the community of which he is a member.

Compare with this savage the laborer in the lowest ranks of civilized society, whose life is spent in producing but one thing, or oftener but the infinitesimal part of one thing, out of the multiplicity of things that constitute the wealth of society and go to supply even the most primitive wants; who not only cannot make even the tools required for his work, but often works with tools that he does not own, and can never hope to own. Compelled to even closer and more continuous labor than the savage, and gaining by it no more than the savage gets—the mere necessaries of life—he loses the independence of the savage. He is not only unable to apply his own powers to the direct satisfaction of his own wants, but, without the concurrence of many others, he is unable to apply them indirectly to the satisfaction of his wants. He is a mere link in an enormous chain of producers and consumers, helpless to separate himself, and helpless to move, except as they move. The worse his position in society, the more dependent is he on society; the more utterly unable does he become to do anything for himself. The very power of exerting his labor for the satisfaction of his wants passes from his own control, and may be taken away or restored by the actions of others, or by general causes over which he has no more influence than he has over the motions of the solar system. The primeval curse comes to be looked upon as a boon, and men think, and talk, and clamor, and legislate as though monotonous manual labor in itself were a good and not an evil, an end and not a means. Under such circumstances, the man loses the essential quality of manhood—the godlike power of modifying and controlling conditions. He becomes a slave, a machine, a commodity—a thing, in some respects, lower than the animal.

I am no sentimental admirer of the savage state. I do not get my ideas of the untutored children of nature from Rousseau, or Chateaubriand, or Cooper. I am conscious of its material and mental poverty, and its low and narrow range. I believe that civilization is not only the natural destiny of man, but the enfranchisement, elevation, and refinement of all his powers, and think that it is only in such moods as may lead him to envy the cud-chewing cattle, that a man who is free to the advantages of civilization could look with regret upon the savage state. But, nevertheless, I think no one who will open his eyes to the facts can resist the conclusion that there are in the heart of our civilization large classes with whom the veriest savage could not afford to exchange. It is my deliberate opinion that if, standing on the threshold of being, one were given the choice of entering life as a Tierra del Fuegan, a black fellow of Australia, an Esquimau in the Arctic Circle, or among the lowest classes in such a highly civilized country as Great Britain, he would make infinitely the better choice in selecting the lot of the savage. For those classes who in the midst of wealth are condemned to want, suffer all the privations of the savage, without his sense of personal freedom; they are condemned to more than his narrowness and littleness, without opportunity for the growth of his rude virtues; if their horizon is wider, it is but to reveal blessings that they cannot enjoy.

There are some to whom this may seem like exaggeration, but it is only because they have never suffered themselves to realize the true condition of those classes upon whom the iron heel of modern civilization presses with full force. As De Tocqueville observes, in one of his letters to Mme. Swetchine, "we so soon become used to the thought of want that we do not feel that an evil which grows greater to the sufferer the longer it lasts becomes less to the observer by the very fact of its duration"; and perhaps the best proof of the justice of this observation is that in cities where there exists a pauper class and a criminal class, where young girls shiver as they sew for bread, and tattered and barefooted children make a home in the streets, money is regularly raised to send missionaries to the heathen! Send missionaries to the heathen! it would be laughable if it were not so sad. Baal no longer stretches forth his hideous, sloping arms; but in Christian lands mothers slay their infants for a burial fee! And I challenge the production from any authentic accounts of savage life of such descriptions of degradation as are to be found in official documents of highly civilized countries—in reports of sanitary commissioners and of inquiries into the condition of the laboring poor.

The simple theory which I have outlined (if indeed it can be called a theory which is but the recognition of the most obvious relations) explains this conjunction of poverty with wealth, of low wages with high productive power, of degradation amid enlightenment, of virtual slavery in political liberty. It harmonizes, as results flowing from a general and inexorable law, facts otherwise most perplexing, and exhibits the sequence and relation between phenomena that without reference to it are diverse and contradictory. It explains why interest and wages are higher in new than in older communities, though the average, as well as the aggregate, production of wealth is less. It explains why improvements which increase the productive power of labor and capital increase the reward of neither. It explains what is commonly called the conflict between labor and capital, while proving the real harmony of interest between them. It cuts the last inch of ground from under the fallacies of protection, while showing why free trade fails to benefit permanently the working classes. It explains why want increases with abundance, and wealth tends to greater and greater aggregations. It explains the periodically recurring depressions of industry without recourse either to the absurdity of "overproduction" or the absurdity of "overconsumption." It explains the enforced idleness of large numbers of would-be producers, which wastes the productive force of advanced communities, without the absurd assumption that there is too little work to do or that there are too many to do it. It explains the ill effects upon the laboring classes which often follow the introduction of machinery, without denying the natural advantages which the use of machinery gives. It explains the vice and misery which show themselves amid dense population, without attributing to the laws of the All-Wise and All-Beneficent defects which belong only to the short-sighted and selfish enactments of men.

This explanation is in accordance with all the facts.

Look over the world today. In countries the most widely differing—under conditions the most diverse as to government, as to industries, as to tariffs, as to currency—you will find distress among the working classes; but everywhere that you thus find distress and destitution in the midst of wealth you will find that the land is monopolized; that instead of being treated as the common property of the whole people, it is treated as the private property of individuals; that, for its use by labor, large revenues are extorted from the earnings of labor. Look over the world today, comparing different countries with each other, and you will see that it is not the abundance of capital or the productiveness of labor that makes wages high or low; but the extent to which the monopolizers of land can, in rent, levy tribute upon the earnings of labor. Is it not a notorious fact, known to the most ignorant, that new countries, where the aggregate wealth is small, but where land is cheap, are always better countries for the laboring classes than the rich countries, where land is dear? Wherever you find land relatively low, will you not find wages relatively high? And wherever land is high, will you not find wages low? As land increases in value, poverty deepens and pauperism appears. In the new settlements, where land is cheap, you will find no beggars, and the inequalities in condition are very slight. In the great cities, where land is so valuable that it is measured by the foot, you will find the extremes of poverty and of luxury. And this disparity in condition between the two extremes of the social scale may always be measured by the price of land. Land in New York is more valuable than in San Francisco; and in New York, the San Franciscan may see squalor and misery that will make him stand aghast. Land is more valuable in London than in New York; and in London, there is squalor and destitution worse than that of New York.

Compare the same country in different times, and the same relation is obvious. As the result of much investigation, Hallam says he is convinced that the wages of manual labor were greater in amount in England during the Middle Ages than they are now. Whether this is so or not, it is evident that they could not have been much, if any, less. The enormous increase in the efficiency of labor, which even in agriculture is estimated at seven or eight hundred per cent., and in many branches of industry is almost incalculable, has only added to rent. The rent of agricultural land in England is now, according to Professor Rogers, 120 times as great, measured in money, as it was 500 years ago, and 14 times as great, measured in wheat; while in the rent of building land, and mineral land, the advance has been enormously greater. According to the estimate of Professor Fawcett, the capitalized rental value of the land of England now amounts to £4,500,000,000, or $21,870,000,000—that is to say, a few thousand of the people of England hold a lien upon the labor of the rest, the capitalized value of which is more than twice as great as, at the average price of southern Negroes in 1860, would be the value of her whole population were they slaves.

In Belgium and Flanders, in France and Germany, the rent and selling price of agricultural land have doubled within the last thirty years.* In short, increased power of production has everywhere added to the value of land; nowhere has it added to the value of

---

* "Systems of Land Tenure," published by the Cobden Club.

labor; for though actual wages may in some places
have somewhat risen, the rise is clearly attributable to
other causes. In more places they have fallen—that is,
where it has been possible for them to fall—for there is
a minimum below which laborers cannot keep up their
numbers. And, everywhere, wages, as a proportion of
the produce, have decreased.

How the Black Death brought about the great rise of
wages in England in the fourteenth century is clearly
discernible, in the efforts of the landholders to regulate
wages by statute. That that awful reduction in population, instead of increasing, really reduced the effective
power of labor, there can be no doubt; but the lessening of competition for land still more greatly reduced
rent, and wages advanced so largely that force and
penal laws were called in to keep them down. The reverse effect followed the monopolization of land that
went on in England during the reign of Henry VIII, in
the inclosure of commons and the division of the church
lands between the panders and parasites who were thus
enabled to found noble families. The result was the
same as that to which a speculative increase in land
values tends. According to Malthus (who, in his "Principles of Political Economy," mentions the fact without
connecting it with land tenures), in the reign of Henry
VII, half a bushel of wheat would purchase but little
more than a day's common labor, but in the latter part
of the reign of Elizabeth, half a bushel of wheat would
purchase three days' common labor. I can hardly believe that the reduction in wages could have been so
great as this comparison would indicate; but that there
was a reduction in common wages, and great distress
among the laboring classes, is evident from the complaints of "sturdy vagrants" and the statutes made to
suppress them. The rapid monopolization of the land,
the carrying of the speculative rent line beyond the nor-

mal rent line, produced tramps and paupers, just as like effects from like causes have lately been evident in the United States.

"Land which went heretofore for twenty or forty pounds a year," said Hugh Latimer, "now is let for fifty or a hundred. My father was a yeoman, and had no lands of his own; only he had a farm at a rent of three or four pounds by the year at the uttermost, and thereupon he tilled so much as kept half a dozen men. He had walk for a hundred sheep, and my mother milked thirty kine; he was able and did find the King a harness with himself and his horse when he came to the place that he should receive the King's wages. I can remember that I buckled his harness when he went to Blackheath Field. He kept me to school; he married my sisters with five pounds apiece, so that he brought them up in godliness and fear of God. He kept hospitality for his neighbors and some alms he gave to the poor. And all this he did of the same farm, where he that now hath it payeth sixteen pounds rent or more by year, and is not able to do anything for his Prince, for himself, nor his children, nor to give a cup of drink to the poor."

"In this way," said Sir Thomas More, referring to the ejectment of small farmers which characterized this advance of rent, "it comes to pass that these poor wretches, men, women, husbands, orphans, widows, parents with little children, householders greater in number than in wealth, all of these emigrate from their native fields, without knowing where to go."

And so from the stuff of the Latimers and Mores— from the sturdy spirit that amid the flames of the Oxford stake cried, "Play the man, Master Ridley!" and the mingled strength and sweetness that neither prosperity could taint nor the ax of the executioner abash —were evolved thieves and vagrants, the mass of criminality and pauperism that still blights the innermost

petals and preys a gnawing worm at the root of England's rose.

But it were as well to cite historical illustrations of
the attraction of gravitation. The principle is as universal and as obvious. That rent *must* reduce wages, is
as clear as that the greater the subtractor the less the
remainder. That rent *does* reduce wages, any one,
wherever situated, can see by merely looking around
him.

There is no mystery as to the cause which so suddenly
and so largely raised wages in California in 1849, and
in Australia in 1852. It was the discovery of the placer
mines in unappropriated land to which labor was free
that raised the wages of cooks in San Francisco restau-
rants to $500 a month, and left ships to rot in the har-
bor without officers or crew until their owners would
consent to pay rates that in any other part of the globe
seemed fabulous. Had these mines been on appropriated land, or had they been immediately monopolized so
that rent could have arisen, it would have been land
values that would have leaped upward, not wages. The
Comstock lode has been richer than the placers, but the
Comstock lode was readily monopolized, and it is only
by virtue of the strong organization of the Miners' Association and the fears of the damage which it might
do, that enables men to get four dollars a day for par-
boiling themselves two thousand feet underground,
where the air that they breathe must be pumped down
to them. The wealth of the Comstock lode has added
to rent. The selling price of these mines runs up into
hundreds of millions, and it has produced individual
fortunes whose monthly returns can be estimated only
in hundreds of thousands, if not in millions. Nor is
there any mystery about the cause which has operated
to reduce wages in California from the maximum of the
early days to very nearly a level with wages in the

eastern states, and that is still operating to reduce them. The productiveness of labor has not decreased, on the contrary it has increased, as I have before shown; but, out of what it produces labor has now to pay rent. As the placer deposits were exhausted, labor had to resort to the deeper mines and to agricultural land, but monopolization of these being permitted, men now walk the streets of San Francisco ready to go to work for almost anything—for natural opportunities are now no longer free to labor.

The truth is self-evident. Put to any one capable of consecutive thought this question:

"Suppose there should arise from the English Channel or the German Ocean a no man's land on which common labor to an unlimited amount should be able to make ten shillings a day and which should remain unappropriated and of free access, like the commons which once comprised so large a part of English soil. What would be the effect upon wages in England?"

He would at once tell you that common wages throughout England must soon increase to ten shillings a day.

And in response to another question, "What would be the effect on rents?" he would at a moment's reflection say that rents must necessarily fall; and if he thought out the next step he would tell you that all this would happen without any very large part of English labor being diverted to the new natural opportunities, or the forms and direction of industry being much changed; only that kind of production being abandoned which now yields to labor and to landlord together less than labor could secure on the new opportunities. The great rise in wages would be at the expense of rent.

Take now the same man or another—some hard-headed business man, who has no theories, but knows how to make money. Say to him: "Here is a little

village; in ten years it will be a great city—in ten years
the railroad will have taken the place of the stage coach,
the electric light of the candle; it will abound with
all the machinery and improvements that so enormously
multiply the effective power of labor. Will, in ten
years, interest be any higher?"

He will tell you, "No!"

"Will the wages of common labor be any higher; will
it be easier for a man who has nothing but his labor to
make an independent living?"

He will tell you, "No; the wages of common labor
will not be any higher; on the contrary, all the chances
are that they will be lower; it will not be easier for the
mere laborer to make an independent living; the chances
are that it will be harder."

"What, then, will be higher?"

"Rent; the value of land. Go, get yourself a piece
of ground, and hold possession."

And if, under such circumstances, you take his ad-
vice, you need do nothing more. You may sit down and
smoke your pipe; you may lie around like the lazzaroni
of Naples or the leperos of Mexico; you may go up in
a balloon, or down a hole in the ground; and without
doing one stroke of work, without adding one iota to the
wealth of the community, in ten years you will be rich!
In the new city you may have a luxurious mansion; but
among its public buildings will be an almshouse.

In all our long investigation we have been advancing
to this simple truth: That as land is necessary to the
exertion of labor in the production of wealth, to command the land which is necessary to labor, is to command all the fruits of labor save enough to enable labor
to exist. We have been advancing as through an
enemy's country, in which every step must be secured,
every position fortified, and every bypath explored;
for this simple truth, in its application to social and

political problems, is hid from the great masses of men partly by its very simplicity, and in greater part by widespread fallacies and erroneous habits of thought which lead them to look in every direction but the right one for an explanation of the evils which oppress and threaten the civilized world. And back of these elaborate fallacies and misleading theories is an active, energetic power, a power that in every country, be its political forms what they may, writes laws and molds thought—the power of a vast and dominant pecuniary interest.

But so simple and so clear is this truth, that to see it fully once is always to recognize it. There are pictures which, though looked at again and again, present only a confused labyrinth of lines or scroll work—a landscape, trees, or something of the kind—until once the attention is called to the fact that these things make up a face or a figure. This relation once recognized, is always afterward clear. It is so in this case. In the light of this truth all social facts group themselves in an orderly relation, and the most diverse phenomena are seen to spring from one great principle. It is not in the relations of capital and labor; it is not in the pressure of population against subsistence, that an explanation of the unequal development of our civilization is to be found. The great cause of inequality in the distribution of wealth is inequality in the ownership of land. The ownership of land is the great fundamental fact which ultimately determines the social, the political, and consequently the intellectual and moral condition of a people. And it must be so. For land is the habitation of man, the storehouse upon which he must draw for all his needs, the material to which his labor must be applied for the supply of all his desires; for even the products of the sea cannot be taken, the light of the sun enjoyed, or any of the forces of nature utilized, without the use of land or its products. On the land we are born, from it we live, to it we return again—children of the soil as truly as is the blade of grass or the flower of the field. Take away from man all that belongs to land, and he is but a disembodied spirit. Material progress cannot rid us of our dependence upon land; it can but add to the power of producing wealth from land; and hence, when land is monopolized, it might go on to infinity without increasing wages or improving the condition of those who have but their labor. It can but add to the value of land and the power which its possession gives. Everywhere, in all times, among all peoples, the possession of land is the base of aristocracy, the foundation of great fortunes, the source of power. As said the Brahmins, ages ago—

"To whomsoever the soil at any time belongs, to him belong the fruits of it. White parasols and elephants mad with pride are the flowers of a grant of land."

A new and fair division of the goods and rights of this world should be the main object of those who conduct human affairs.

—DE TOCQUEVILLE.

When the object is to raise the permanent condition of a people, small means do not merely produce small effects; they produce no effect at all.

—JOHN STUART MILL.

CHAPTER 1 INSUFFICIENCY OF REMEDIES CURRENTLY ADVOCATED

In tracing to its source the cause of increasing poverty amid advancing wealth, we have discovered the remedy; but before passing to that branch of our subject it will be well to review the tendencies or remedies which are currently relied on or advocated. The remedy to which our conclusions point is at once radical and simple—so radical that, on the one side, it will not be fairly considered so long as any faith remains in the efficacy of less caustic measures; so simple that, on the other side, its real efficacy and comprehensiveness are likely to be overlooked, until the effect of more elaborate measures is estimated.

The tendencies and measures which current literature and discussions show to be more or less relied on or advocated as calculated to relieve poverty and distress among the masses, may be divided into six classes. I do not mean that there are so many distinct parties or schools of thought, but merely that, for the purpose of our inquiry, prevailing opinions and proposed measures may be so grouped for review. Remedies which for the sake of greater convenience and clearness we shall consider separately are often combined in thought.

There are many persons who still retain a comfortable belief that material progress will ultimately extirpate poverty, and there are many who look to prudential restraint upon the increase of population as the most efficacious means, but the fallacy of these views has already been sufficiently shown. Let us now consider what may be hoped for:

I. From greater economy in government.

II. From the better education of the working classes and improved habits of industry and thrift.

III. From combinations of workmen for the advance of wages.

IV. From the co-operation of labor and capital.

V. From governmental direction and interference.

VI. From a more general distribution of land.

Under these six heads I think we may in essential form review all hopes and propositions for the relief of social distress short of the simple but far-reaching measure which I shall propose.

I.—From Greater Economy in Government

Until a very few years ago it was an article of faith with Americans—a belief shared by European liberals— that the poverty of the downtrodden masses of the Old World was due to aristocratic and monarchical institutions. This belief has rapidly passed away with the appearance in the United States, under republican institutions, of social distress of the same kind, if not of the same intensity, as that prevailing in Europe. But social distress is still largely attributed to the immense burdens which existing governments impose—the great debts, the military and naval establishments, the extravagance which is characteristic as well of republican as of monarchical rulers, and especially characteristic of the administration of great cities. To these must be added, in the United States, the robbery involved in the protective tariff, which for every twenty-five cents it puts in the treasury takes a dollar and it may be four or five out of the pocket of the consumer. Now, there seems to be an evident connection between the immense sums thus taken from the people and the privations of the lower classes, and it is upon a superficial view natural to suppose that a reduction in the enormous burdens thus uselessly imposed would make it easier for the poorest to get a living. But a consideration of the matter in the light of the economic principles heretofore traced out will show that this would not be the effect. A reduction in the amount taken from the aggregate produce of a community by taxation would be simply equivalent to an increase in the power of net production. It would in effect add to the productive power of labor just as do the increasing density of population and improvement in the arts. And as the advantage in the one case goes, and must go, to the owners of land, in increased rent, so would the advantage in the other.

From the produce of the labor and capital of England are now supported the burden of an immense debt, an Established Church, an expensive royal family, a large number of sinecurists, a great army and great navy. Suppose the debt repudiated, the Church disestablished, the royal family set adrift to make a living for themselves, the sinecurists cut off, the army disbanded, the officers and men of the navy discharged and the ships sold. An enormous reduction in taxation would thus become possible. There would be a great addition to the net produce which remains to be distributed among the parties to production. But it would be only such an addition as improvement in the arts has been for a long time constantly making, and not so great an addition as steam and machinery have made within the last twenty or thirty years. And as these additions have not alleviated pauperism, but have only increased rent, so would this. English landowners would reap the whole benefit. I will not dispute that if all these things could be done suddenly, and without the destruction and expense involved in a revolution, there might be a temporary im-

provement in the condition of the lowest class; but such
a sudden and peaceable reform is manifestly impossible.
And if it were, any temporary improvement would, by
the process we now see going on in the United States,
be ultimately swallowed up by increased land values.

And, so, in the United States, if we were to reduce
public expenditures to the lowest possible point, and meet
them by revenue taxation, the benefit could certainly
not be greater than that which railroads have brought.
There would be more wealth left in the hands of the
people as a whole, just as the railroads have put more
wealth in the hands of the people as a whole, but the
same inexorable laws would operate as to its distribution. The condition of those who live by their labor
would not ultimately be improved.

A dim consciousness of this pervades—or, rather, is
beginning to pervade—the masses, and constitutes one
of the grave political difficulties that are closing in
around the American republic. Those who have nothing
but their labor, and especially the proletarians of the
cities—a growing class—care little about the prodigality
of government, and in many cases are disposed to look
upon it as a good thing—"furnishing employment," or
"putting money in circulation." Tweed, who robbed
New York as a guerrilla chief might levy upon a captured town (and who was but a type of the new banditti
who are grasping the government of all our cities), was
undoubtedly popular with a majority of the voters,
though his thieving was notorious, and his spoils were
blazoned in big diamonds and lavish personal expenditure. After his indictment, he was triumphantly elected
to the Senate; and, even when a recaptured fugitive,
was frequently cheered on his way from court to prison.
He had robbed the public treasury of many millions,
but the proletarians felt that he had not robbed them.
And the verdict of political economy is the same as
theirs.

Let me be clearly understood. I do not say that governmental economy is not desirable; but simply that reduction in the expenses of government can have no direct effect in extirpating poverty and increasing wages, so long as land is monopolized.

Although this is true, yet even with sole reference to the interests of the lowest class, no effort should be spared to keep down useless expenditures. The more complex and extravagant government becomes, the more it gets to be a power distinct from and independent of the people, and the more difficult does it become to bring questions of real public policy to a popular decision. Look at our elections in the United States—upon what do they turn? The most momentous problems are pressing upon us, yet so great is the amount of money in politics, so large are the personal interests involved, that the most important questions of government are but little considered. The average American voter has prejudices, party feelings, general notions of a certain kind, but he gives to the fundamental questions of government not much more thought than a streetcar horse does to the profits of the line. Were this not the case, so many hoary abuses could not have survived and so many new ones been added. Anything that tends to make government simple and inexpensive tends to put it under control of the people and to bring questions of real importance to the front. But no reduction in the expenses of government can of itself cure or mitigate the evils that arise from a constant tendency to the unequal distribution of wealth.

II.—From the Diffusion of Education and Improved Habits of Industry and Thrift

There is, and always has been, a widespread belief among the more comfortable classes that the poverty and suffering of the masses are due to their lack of industry, frugality, and intelligence. This belief, which at once soothes the sense of responsibility and flatters by its suggestion of superiority, is probably even more prevalent in countries like the United States, where all men are politically equal, and where, owing to the newness of society, the differentiation into classes has been of individuals rather than of families, than it is in older countries, where the lines of separation have been longer, and are more sharply, drawn. It is but natural for those who can trace their own better circumstances to the superior industry and frugality that gave them a start, and the superior intelligence that enabled them to take advantage of every opportunity,* to imagine that those who remain poor do so simply from lack of these qualities.

But whoever has grasped the laws of the distribution of wealth, as in previous chapters they have been traced out, will see the mistake in this notion. The fallacy is similar to that which would be involved in the assertion that every one of a number of competitors might win a race. That any one might is true; that every one might is impossible.

For, as soon as land acquires a value, wages, as we have seen, do not depend upon the real earnings or product of labor, but upon what is left to labor after rent is taken out; and when land is all monopolized, as it is everywhere except in the newest communities, rent must drive wages down to the point at which the poorest paid class will be just able to live and reproduce, and thus wages are forced to a minimum fixed by what is called the standard of comfort—that is, the amount of necessaries and comforts which habit leads the working classes

---

* To say nothing of superior want of conscience, which is often the determining quality which makes a millionaire out of one who otherwise might have been a poor man.

to demand as the lowest on which they will consent to maintain their numbers. This being the case, industry, skill, frugality, and intelligence can avail the individual only in so far as they are superior to the general level— just as in a race speed can avail the runner only in so far as it exceeds that of his competitors. If one man work harder, or with superior skill or intelligence than ordinary, he will get ahead; but if the average of industry, skill, or intelligence be brought up to the higher point, the increased intensity of application will secure but the old rate of wages, and he who would get ahead must work harder still.

One individual may save money from his wages by living as Dr. Franklin did when, during his apprenticeship and early journeyman days, he concluded to practice vegetarianism; and many poor families might be made more comfortable by being taught to prepare the cheap dishes to which Franklin tried to limit the appetite of his employer Keimer, as a condition to his acceptance of the position of confuter of opponents to the new religion of which Keimer wished to become the prophet,* but if the working classes generally came to live in that way, wages would ultimately fall in proportion, and whoever wished to get ahead by the practice of economy, or to mitigate poverty by teaching it, would be compelled to devise some still cheaper mode of keeping soul and body together. If, under existing conditions, American mechanics would come down to the Chinese standard of living, they would ultimately have to come down to the Chinese standard of wages; or if English laborers would content themselves with the rice diet and scanty clothing

---

* Franklin, in his inimitable way, relates how Keimer finally broke his resolution and ordering a roast pig invited two lady friends to dine with him, but the pig being brought in before the company arrived, Keimer could not resist the temptation and ate it all himself.

of the Bengalee, labor would soon be as ill paid in England as in Bengal. The introduction of the potato into Ireland was expected to improve the condition of the poorer classes, by increasing the difference between the wages they received and the cost of their living. The consequences that did ensue were a rise of rent and a lowering of wages, and, with the potato blight, the ravages of famine among a population that had already reduced its standard of comfort so low that the next step was starvation.

And, so, if one individual work more hours than the average, he will increase his wages; but the wages of all cannot be increased in this way. It is notorious that in occupations where working hours are long, wages are not higher than where working hours are shorter; generally the reverse, for the longer the working day, the more helpless does the laborer become—the less time has he to look around him and develop other powers than those called forth by his work; the less becomes his ability to change his occupation or to take advantage of circumstances. And, so, the individual workman who gets his wife and children to assist him may thus increase his income; but in occupations where it has become habitual for the wife and children of the laborer to supplement his work, it is notorious that the wages earned by the whole family do not on the average exceed those of the head of the family in occupations where it is usual for him only to work. Swiss family labor in watch making competes in cheapness with American machinery. The Bohemian cigar makers of New York, who work, men, women, and children, in their tenement-house rooms, have reduced the prices of cigar making to less than the Chinese in San Francisco were getting.

These general facts are well known. They are fully recognized in standard politico-economic works, where, however, they are explained upon the Malthusian theory of the tendency of population to multiply up to the limit of subsistence. The true explanation, as I have sufficiently shown, is in the tendency of rent to reduce wages.

As to the effects of education, it may be worth while to say a few words specially, for there is a prevailing disposition to attribute to it something like a magical influence. Now, education is only education in so far as it enables a man more effectively to use his natural powers, and this is something that what we call education in very great part fails to do. I remember a little girl, pretty well along in her school geography and astronomy, who was much astonished to find that the ground in her mother's back yard was really the surface of the earth, and, if you talk with them, you will find that a good deal of the knowledge of many college graduates is much like that of the little girl. They seldom think any better, and sometimes not so well as men who have never been to college.

A gentleman who had spent many years in Australia, and knew intimately the habits of the aborigines (Rev. Dr. Bleesdale), after giving some instances of their wonderful skill in the use of their weapons, in foretelling changes in the wind and weather and in trapping the shyest birds, once said to me: "I think it a great mistake to look on these black fellows as ignorant. Their knowledge is different from ours, but in it they are generally better educated. As soon as they begin to toddle, they are taught to play with little boomerangs and other weapons, to observe and to judge, and, when they are old enough to take care of themselves, they are fully able to do so—are, in fact, in reference to the nature of their knowledge, what I should call well-educated gentlemen; which is more than I can say for many of our young fellows who have had what we call the best advantages, but who enter upon manhood unable to do anything either for themselves or for others."

Be this as it may, it is evident that intelligence, which is or should be the aim of education, until it induces and enables the masses to discover and remove the cause of the unequal distribution of wealth, can operate upon wages only by increasing the effective power of labor. It has the same effect as increased skill or industry. And it can raise the wages of the individual only in so far as it renders him superior to others. When to read and write were rare accomplishments, a clerk commanded high respect and large wages, but now the ability to read and write has become so nearly universal as to give no advantage. Among the Chinese the ability to read and write seems absolutely universal, but wages in China touch the lowest possible point. The diffusion of intelligence, except as it may make men discontented with a state of things which condemns producers to a life of toil while nonproducers loll in luxury, cannot tend to raise wages generally, or in any way improve the condition of the lowest class—the "mudsills" of society, as a southern senator once called them—who must rest on the soil, no matter how high the superstructure may be carried. No increase of the effective power of labor can increase general wages, so long as rent swallows up all the gain. This is not merely a deduction from principles. It is the fact, proved by experience. The growth of knowledge and the progress of invention have multiplied the effective power of labor over and over again without increasing wages. In England there are over a million paupers. In the United States almshouses are increasing and wages are decreasing.

It is true that greater industry and skill, greater prudence, and a higher intelligence, are, as a rule, found associated with a better material condition of the working classes; but that this is effect, not cause, is shown by the relation of the facts. Wherever the material condition of the laboring classes has been improved, improvement in their personal qualities has followed, and wherever their material condition has been depressed, deterioration in these qualities has been the result; but nowhere can improvement in material condition be shown as the result of the increase of industry, skill, prudence, or intelligence in a class condemned to toil for a bare living, though these qualities when once attained (or, rather, their concomitant—the improvement in the standard of comfort) offer a strong, and, in many cases, a sufficient, resistance to the lowering of material condition.

The fact is, that the qualities that raise man above the animal are superimposed on those which he shares with the animal, and that it is only as he is relieved from the wants of his animal nature that his intellectual and moral nature can grow. Compel a man to drudgery for the necessities of animal existence, and he will lose the incentive to industry—the progenitor of skill—and will do only what he is forced to do. Make his condition such that it cannot be much worse, while there is little hope that anything he can do will make it much better, and he will cease to look beyond the day. Deny him leisure—and leisure does not mean the want of employment, but the absence of the need which forces to uncongenial employment—and you cannot, even by running the child through a common school and supplying the man with a newspaper, make him intelligent.

It is true that improvement in the material condition of a people or class may not show immediately in mental and moral improvement. Increased wages may at first be taken out in idleness and dissipation. But they will ultimately bring increased industry, skill, intelligence, and thrift. Comparisons between different countries; between different classes in the same country; between the same people at different periods; and between the same people when their conditions are changed by emigration, show, as an invariable result, that the personal qualities of which we are speaking appear as material conditions are improved, and disappear as material conditions are depressed. Poverty is the Slough of Despond which Bunyan saw in his dream, and into which good books may be tossed forever without result. To make people industrious, prudent, skillful, and intelligent, they must be relieved from want. If you would have the slave show the virtues of the freeman, you must first make him free.

III.—From Combinations of Workmen

It is evident from the laws of distribution, as previously traced, that combinations of workmen can advance wages, and this not at the expense of other workmen, as is sometimes said, nor yet at the expense of capital, as is generally believed; but, ultimately, at the expense of rent. That no general advance in wages can be secured by combination; that any advance in particular wages thus secured must reduce other wages or the profits of capital, or both—are ideas that spring from the erroneous notion that wages are drawn from capital. The fallacy of these ideas is demonstrated, not alone by the laws of distribution as we have worked them out, but by experience, so far as it has gone. The advance of wages in particular trades by combinations of workmen, of which there are many examples, has nowhere shown any effect in lowering wages in other trades, or in reducing the rate of profits. Except as it may affect his fixed capital or current engagements, a diminution of wages can benefit, and an increase of wages injure an employer only in so far as it gives him an advantage or puts him at a disadvantage as compared with other employers. The employer who first succeeds in reducing the wages of his hands, or is first compelled to pay an advance, gains an advantage, or is put at a disadvantage in regard to his competitors, which ceases when the movement includes them also. So far, however, as the change in wages affects his contracts or stock on hand, by changing the relative cost of production, it may be to him a real gain or loss, though this gain or loss, being purely relative, disappears when the whole community is considered. And, if the change in wages works a change in relative demand, it may render capital fixed in machinery, buildings, or otherwise, more or less profitable. But, in this, a new equilibrium is soon reached; for, especially in a progressive country, fixed capital is only somewhat less mobile than circulating capital. If there is too little in a certain form, the tendency of capital to assume that form soon brings it up to the required amount; if there is too much, the cessation of increment soon restores the level.

But, while a change in the rate of wages in any particular occupation may induce a change in the relative demand for labor, it can produce no change in the aggregate demand. For instance, let us suppose that a combination of the workmen engaged in any particular manufacture raise wages in one country, while a combination of employers reduce wages in the same manufacture in another country. If the change be great enough, the demand, or part of the demand, in the first country will now be supplied by importation of such manufactures from the second. But, evidently, this increase in importations of a particular kind must necessitate either a corresponding decrease in importations of other kinds, or a corresponding increase in exportations. For, it is only with the produce of its labor and capital that one country can demand, or can obtain, in exchange, the produce of the labor and capital of another. The idea that the lowering of wages can increase, or the increase of wages can diminish, the trade of a country, is as baseless as the idea that the prosperity of a country can be increased by taxes on imports, or diminished by the removal of restrictions on trade. If all wages in any particular country were to be doubled, that country would continue to export and import the same things, and in the same proportions; for exchange is determined not by absolute, but by relative, cost of production. But, if wages in some branches of production were doubled, and in others not increased, or not increased so much, there would be a change in the proportion of the various things imported, but no change in the proportion between exports and imports.

While most of the objections made to the combination of workmen for the advance of wages are thus baseless, while the success of such combinations cannot reduce other wages, or decrease the profits of capital, or injuriously affect national prosperity, yet so great are the difficulties in the way of the effective combinations of laborers, that the good that can be accomplished by them is extremely limited, while there are inherent disadvantages in the process.

To raise wages in a particular occupation or occupations, which is all that any combination of workmen yet made has been equal to attempting, is manifestly a task the difficulty of which progressively increases. For the higher are wages of any particular kind raised above their normal level with other wages, the stronger are the tendencies to bring them back. Thus, if a printers' union, by a successful or threatened strike, raise the wages of typesetting ten per cent. above the normal rate as compared with other wages, relative demand and supply are at once affected. On the one hand, there is a tendency to a diminution of the amount of typesetting called for; and, on the other, the higher rate of wages tends to increase the number of compositors in ways the strongest combination cannot altogether prevent. If the increase be twenty per cent., these tendencies are much stronger; if it is fifty per cent., they become stronger still, and so on. So that practically—even in countries like England, where the lines between different trades are much more distinct and difficult to pass than in countries like the United States—that which trades' unions, even when supporting each other, can do in the way of raising wages is comparatively little, and this little, moreover, is confined to their own sphere, and does not affect the lower stratum of unorganized laborers, whose condition most needs alleviation and ultimately determines that of all above them. The only way by which wages could be raised to any extent and with any permanence by this method would be by a general combination, such as was aimed at by the Internationals, which should include laborers of all kinds. But such a combination may be set down as practically impossible, for the difficulties of combination, great enough in the most highly paid and smallest trades, become greater and greater as we descend in the industrial scale.

Nor, in the struggle of endurance, which is the only method which combinations not to work for less than a certain minimum have of effecting the increase of wages, must it be forgotten who are the real parties pitted against each other. It is not labor and capital. It is laborers on the one side and the owners of land on the other. If the contest were between labor and capital, it would be on much more equal terms. For the power of capital to stand out is only some little greater than that of labor. Capital not only ceases to earn anything when not used, but it goes to waste—for in nearly all its forms it can be maintained only by constant reproduction. But land will not starve like laborers or go to waste like capital—its owners can wait. They may be inconvenienced, it is true, but what is inconvenience to them, is destruction to capital and starvation to labor.

The agricultural laborers in certain parts of England are now endeavoring to combine for the purpose of securing an increase in their miserably low wages. If it was capital that was receiving the enormous difference between the real produce of their labor and the pittance they get out of it, they would have but to make an effective combination to secure success; for the farmers, who are their direct employers, can afford to go without labor but little, if any, better than the laborers can afford to go without wages. But the farmers cannot yield much without a reduction of rent; and thus it is between the landowners and the laborers that the real struggle must come. Suppose the combination to be so thorough as to include all agricultural laborers, and to prevent from doing so all who might be tempted to take their places. The laborers refuse to work except at a considerable advance of wages; the farmers can give it only by securing a considerable reduction of rent, and have no way to back their demands except as the laborers back theirs, by refusing to go on with production. If cultivation thus come to a deadlock, the landowners would lose only their rent, while the land improved by lying fallow. But the laborers would starve. And if English laborers of all kinds were united in one grand league for a general increase of wages, the real contest would be the same, and under the same conditions. For wages could not be increased except to the decrease of rent; and in a general deadlock, landowners could live, while laborers of all sorts must starve or emigrate. The owners of the land of England are by virtue of their ownership the masters of England. So true is it that "to whomsoever the soil at any time belongs, to him belong the fruits of it." The white parasols and the elephants mad with pride passed with the grant of English land, and the people at large can never regain their power until that grant is resumed. What is true of England, is universally true.

It may be said that such a deadlock in production could never occur. This is true; but true only because no such thorough combination of labor as might produce it is possible. But the fixed and definite nature of land enables landowners to combine much more easily and efficiently than either laborers or capitalists. How easy and efficient their combination is, there are many historical examples. And the absolute necessity for the use of land, and the certainty in all progressive countries that it must increase in value, produce among landowners, without any formal combination, all the effects that could be produced by the most rigorous combination among laborers or capitalists. Deprive a laborer of opportunity of employment, and he will soon be anxious to get work on any terms, but when the receding wave of speculation leaves nominal land values clearly above real values, whoever has lived in a growing country knows with what tenacity landowners hold on.

And, besides these practical difficulties in the plan of forcing by endurance an increase of wages, there are in such methods inherent disadvantages which workingmen should not blink. I speak without prejudice, for I am still an honorary member of the union which, while working at my trade, I always loyally supported. But, see: The methods by which a trade union can alone act are necessarily destructive; its organization is necessarily tyrannical. A strike, which is the only recourse by which a trade union can enforce its demands, is a destructive contest—just such a contest as that to which an eccentric, called "The Money King," once, in the early days of San Francisco, challenged a man who had taunted him with meanness, that they should go down to the wharf and alternately toss twenty-dollar pieces into the bay until one gave in. The struggle of

endurance involved in a strike is, really, what it has
often been compared to—a war; and, like all war, it
lessens wealth. And the organization for it must, like
the organization for war, be tyrannical. As even the
man who would fight for freedom, must, when he enters
an army, give up his personal freedom and become a
mere part in a great machine, so must it be with workmen who organize for a strike. These combinations are,
therefore, necessarily destructive of the very things
which workmen seek to gain through them—wealth and
freedom.

There is an ancient Hindoo mode of compelling the
payment of a just debt, traces of something akin to
which Sir Henry Maine has found in the laws of the
Irish Brehons. It is called, sitting *dharna*—the creditor
seeking enforcement of his debt by sitting down at the
door of the debtor, and refusing to eat or drink until he
is paid.

Like this is the method of labor combinations. In
their strikes, trades' unions sit *dharna*. But, unlike the
Hindoo, they have not the power of superstition to back
them.

IV.—From Co-operation

It is now, and has been for some time, the fashion to
preach co-operation as the sovereign remedy for the
grievances of the working classes. But, unfortunately
for the efficacy of co-operation as a remedy for social
evils, these evils, as we have seen, do not arise from any
conflict between labor and capital; and if co-operation
were universal, it could not raise wages or relieve poverty. This is readily seen.

Co-operation is of two kinds—co-operation in supply
and co-operation in production. Now, co-operation in
supply, let it go as far as it may in excluding middlemen,
only reduces the cost of exchanges. It is simply a device

to save labor and eliminate risk, and its effect upon distribution can be only that of the improvements and inventions which have in modern times so wonderfully cheapened and facilitated exchanges—viz., to increase rent. And co-operation in production is simply a reversion to that form of wages which still prevails in the whaling service, and is there termed a "lay." It is the substitution of proportionate wages for fixed wages—a substitution of which there are occasional instances in almost all employments; or, if the management is left to the workmen, and the capitalist but takes his proportion of the net produce, it is simply the system that has prevailed to a large extent in European agriculture since the days of the Roman Empire—the colonial or metayer system. All that is claimed for co-operation in production is, that it makes the workman more active and industrious—in other words, that it increases the efficiency of labor. Thus its effect is in the same direction as the steam engine, the cotton gin, the reaping machine—in short, all the things in which material progress consists, and it can produce only the same result—viz., the increase of rent.

It is a striking proof of how first principles are ignored in dealing with social problems, that in current economic and semi-economic literature so much importance is attached to co-operation as a means for increasing wages and relieving poverty. That it can have no such general tendency is apparent.

Waiving all the difficulties that under present conditions beset co-operation either of supply or of production, and supposing it so extended as to supplant present methods—that co-operative stores made the connection between producer and consumer with the minimum of expense, and co-operative workshops, factories, farms, and mines, abolished the employing capitalist who pays fixed wages, and greatly increased the efficiency of labor

—what then? Why, simply that it would become possible to produce the same amount of wealth with less
labor, and consequently that the owners of land, the
source of all wealth, could command a greater amount
of wealth for the use of their land. This is not a matter
of mere theory; it is proved by experience and by existing facts. Improved methods and improved machinery
have the same effect that co-operation aims at—of reducing the cost of bringing commodities to the consumer
and increasing the efficiency of labor, and it is in these
respects that the older countries have the advantage of
new settlements. But, as experience has amply shown,
improvements in the methods and machinery of production and exchange have no tendency to improve the condition of the lowest class, and wages are lower and
poverty deeper where exchange goes on at the minimum
of cost and production has the benefit of the best machinery. The advantage but adds to rent.

But suppose co-operation between producers and landowners? That would simply amount to the payment of
rent in kind—the same system under which much land
is rented in California and the Southern States where
the landowner gets a share of the crop. Save as a matter of computation it in no wise differs from the system
which prevails in England of a fixed money rent. Call
it co-operation, if you choose, the terms of the co-
operation would still be fixed by the laws which determine rent, and wherever land was monopolized,
increase in productive power would simply give the owners of the land the power to demand a larger share.

That co-operation is by so many believed to be the
solution of the "labor question" arises from the fact that,
where it has been tried, it has in many instances improved perceptibly the condition of those immediately
engaged in it. But this is due simply to the fact that
these cases are isolated. Just as industry, economy, or

skill may improve the condition of the workmen who possess them in superior degree, but cease to have this effect when improvement in these respects becomes general, so a special advantage in procuring supplies, or a special efficiency given to some labor, may secure advantages which would be lost as soon as these improvements became so general as to affect the general relations of distribution. And the truth is, that, save possibly in educational effects, co-operation can produce no general results that competition will not produce. Just as the cheap-for-cash stores have a similar effect upon prices as the co-operative supply associations, so does competition in production lead to a similar adjustment of forces and division of proceeds as would co-operative production. That increasing productive power does not add to the reward of labor, is not because of competition, but because competition is one-sided. Land, without which there can be no production, is monopolized, and the competition of producers for its use forces wages to a minimum and gives all the advantage of increasing productive power to landowners, in higher rents and increased land values. Destroy this monopoly, and competition could exist only to accomplish the end which co-operation aims at—to give to each what he fairly earns. Destroy this monopoly, and industry must become the co-operation of equals.

V.—From Governmental Direction and Interference

The limits within which I wish to keep this book will not permit an examination in detail of the methods in which it is proposed to mitigate or extirpate poverty by governmental regulation of industry and accumulation, and which in their most thoroughgoing form are called socialistic. Nor is it necessary, for the same defects attach to them all. These are the substitution of gov-

ernmental direction for the play of individual action, and
the attempt to secure by restriction what can better be
secured by freedom. As to the truths that are involved
in socialistic ideas I shall have something to say hereafter; but it is evident that whatever savors of regulation
and restriction is in itself bad, and should not be resorted to if any other mode of accomplishing the same
end presents itself. For instance, to take one of the
simplest and mildest of the class of measures I refer to
—a graduated tax on incomes. The object at which it
aims, the reduction or prevention of immense concen-
trations of wealth, is good; but this means involves the
employment of a large number of officials clothed with
inquisitorial powers; temptations to bribery, and perjury, and all other means of evasion, which beget a
demoralization of opinion, and put a premium upon unscrupulousness and a tax upon conscience; and, finally,
just in proportion as the tax accomplishes its effect, a
lessening in the incentive to the accumulation of wealth,
which is one of the strong forces of industrial progress.
While, if the elaborate schemes for regulating everything and finding a place for everybody could be carried
out, we should have a state of society resembling that of
ancient Peru, or that which, to their eternal honor, the
Jesuits instituted and so long maintained in Paraguay.

I will not say that such a state as this is not a better
social state than that to which we now seem to be tending, for in ancient Peru, though production went on
under the greatest disadvantages, from the want of iron
and the domestic animals, yet there was no such thing as
want, and the people went to their work with songs.
But this it is unnecessary to discuss. Socialism in anything approaching such a form, modern society cannot
successfully attempt. The only force that has ever
proved competent for it—a strong and definite religious
faith—is wanting and is daily growing less. We have

passed out of the socialism of the tribal state, and cannot enter it again except by a retrogression that would involve anarchy and perhaps barbarism. Our governments, as is already plainly evident, would break down in the attempt. Instead of an intelligent award of duties and earnings, we should have a Roman distribution of Sicilian corn, and the demagogue would soon become the Imperator.

The ideal of socialism is grand and noble; and it is, I am convinced, possible of realization; but such a state of society cannot be manufactured—it must grow. Society is an organism, not a machine. It can live only by the individual life of its parts. And in the free and natural development of all the parts will be secured the harmony of the whole. All that is necessary to social regeneration is included in the motto of those Russian patriots sometimes called Nihilists—"Land and Liberty!"

VI.—From a More General Distribution of Land

There is a rapidly growing feeling that the tenure of land is in some manner connected with the social distress which manifests itself in the most progressive countries; but this feeling as yet mostly shows itself in propositions which look to the more general division of landed property—in England, free trade in land, tenant right, or the equal partition of landed estates among heirs; in the United States, restrictions upon the size of individual holdings. It has been also proposed in England that the state should buy out the landlords, and in the United States that grants of money should be made to enable the settlements of colonies upon public lands. The former proposition let us pass for the present; the latter, so far as its distinctive feature is concerned, falls into the category of the measures considered in the last section. It needs no argument to show to what abuses and demoralization grants of public money or credit would lead.

How what the English writers call "free trade in land" —the removal of duties and restrictions upon conveyances—could facilitate the division of ownership in agricultural land, I cannot see, though it might to some extent have that effect as regards town property. The removal of restrictions upon buying and selling would merely permit the ownership of land to assume more quickly the form to which it tends. Now, that the tendency in Great Britain is to concentration is shown by the fact that, in spite of the difficulties interposed by the cost of transfer, landownership has been and is steadily concentrating there, and that this tendency is a general one is shown by the fact that the same process of concentration is observable in the United States. I say this unhesitatingly in regard to the United States, although statistical tables are sometimes quoted to show a different tendency. But how, in such a country as the United States, the ownership of land may be really concentrating, while census tables show rather a diminution in the average size of holdings, is readily seen. As land is brought into use, and, with the growth of population, passes from a lower to a higher or intenser use, the size of holdings tends to diminish. A small stock range would be a large farm, a small farm would be a large orchard, vineyard, nursery, or vegetable garden, and a patch of land which would be small even for these purposes would make a very large city property. Thus, the growth of population, which puts lands to higher or intenser uses, tends naturally to reduce the size of holdings, by a process very marked in new countries; but with this may go on a tendency to the concentration of landownership, which, though not revealed by tables which show the average size of holdings, is just as clearly seen. Average holdings of one acre in a city may show a much greater concentration of landownership than average holdings of 640 acres in a newly settled township. I refer to this to show the fallacy in the deductions drawn from the tables which are frequently paraded in the United States to show that land monopoly is an evil that will cure itself. On the contrary, it is obvious that the proportion of landowners to the whole population is constantly decreasing.

And that there is in the United States, as there is in Great Britain, a strong tendency to the concentration of landownership in agriculture is clearly seen. As, in England and Ireland, small farms are being thrown into larger ones, so in New England, according to the reports of the Massachusetts Bureau of Labor Statistics, is the size of farms increasing. This tendency is even more clearly noticeable in the newer states and territories. Only a few years ago a farm of 320 acres would, under the system of agriculture prevailing in the northern parts of the Union, have anywhere been a large one, probably as much as one man could cultivate to advantage. In California now there are farms (not cattle ranges) of five, ten, twenty, forty and sixty thousand acres, while the model farm of Dakota embraces 100,000 acres. The reason is obvious. It is the application of machinery to agriculture and the general tendency to production on a large scale. The same tendency which substitutes the factory, with its army of operatives, for many independent hand-loom weavers, is beginning to exhibit itself in agriculture.

Now, the existence of this tendency shows two things: first, that any measures which merely permit or facilitate the greater subdivision of land would be inoperative; and, second, that any measures which would compel it would have a tendency to check production. If land in large bodies can be cultivated more cheaply than land in small bodies, to restrict ownership to small bodies will reduce the aggregate production of wealth, and, in so far as such restrictions are imposed and take effect, will they tend to diminish the general productiveness of labor and capital.

The effort, therefore, to secure a fairer division of wealth by such restrictions is liable to the drawback of lessening the amount to be divided. The device is like that of the monkey, who, dividing the cheese between the cats, equalized matters by taking a bite off the biggest piece.

But there is not merely this objection, which weighs against every proposition to restrict the ownership of land, with a force that increases with the efficiency of the proposed measure. There is the further and fatal objection that restriction will not secure the end which is alone worth aiming at—a fair division of the produce. It will not reduce rent, and therefore cannot increase wages. It may make the comfortable classes larger, but will not improve the condition of those in the lowest class.

If what is known as the Ulster tenant right were extended to the whole of Great Britain, it would be but to carve out of the estate of the landlord an estate for the tenant. The condition of the laborer would not be a whit improved. If landlords were prohibited from asking an increase of rent from their tenants and from ejecting a tenant so long as the fixed rent was paid, the body of the producers would gain nothing. Economic rent would still increase, and would still steadily lessen the proportion of the produce going to labor and capital. The only difference would be that the tenants of the first landlords, who would become landlords in their turn, would profit by the increase.

If by a restriction upon the amount of land any one individual might hold, by the regulation of devises and successions, or by cumulative taxation, the few thousand landholders of Great Britain should be increased by two or three million, these two or three million people would be gainers. But the rest of the population would gain nothing. They would have no more share in the advantages of landownership than before. And if, what is manifestly impossible, a fair distribution of the land were made among the whole population, giving to each his equal share, and laws enacted which would interpose a barrier to the tendency to concentration by forbidding the holding by any one of more than the fixed amount, what would become of the increase of population?

Just what may be accomplished by the greater division of land may be seen in those districts of France and Belgium where minute division prevails. That such a division of land is on the whole much better, and that it gives a far more stable basis to the state than that which prevails in England, there can be no doubt. But that it does not make wages any higher or improve the condition of the class who have only their labor, is equally clear. These French and Belgian peasants practice a rigid economy unknown to any of the English-speaking peoples. And if such striking symptoms of the poverty and distress of the lowest class are not apparent as on the other side of the channel, it must, I think, be attributed, not only to this fact, but to another fact, which accounts for the continuance of the minute division of the land—that material progress has not been so rapid.

Neither has population increased with the same rapidity (on the contrary it has been nearly stationary), nor have improvements in the modes of production been so great. Nevertheless, M. de Laveleye, all of whose prepossessions are in favor of small holdings, and whose testimony will therefore carry more weight than that of English observers, who may be supposed to harbor a prejudice for the system of their own country, states in his paper on the Land Systems of Belgium and Holland, printed by the Cobden Club, that the condition of the laborer is worse under this system of the minute division of land than it is in England; while the tenant farmers —for tenancy largely prevails even where the *morcellement* is greatest—are rack-rented with a mercilessness unknown in England, and even in Ireland, and the franchise "so far from raising them in the social scale, is but a source of mortification and humiliation to them, for they are forced to vote according to the dictates of the landlord instead of following the dictates of their own inclination and convictions."

But while the subdivision of land can thus do nothing to cure the evils of land monopoly, while it can have no effect in raising wages or in improving the condition of the lowest classes, its tendency is to prevent the adoption or even advocacy of more thoroughgoing measures, and to strengthen the existing unjust system by interesting a larger number in its maintenance. M. de Laveleye, in concluding the paper from which I have quoted, urges the greater division of land as the surest means of securing the great landowners of England from something far more radical. Although in the districts where land is so minutely divided, the condition of the laborer is, he states, the worst in Europe and the renting farmer is much more ground down by his landlord than the Irish tenant, yet "feelings hostile to social order," M. de Laveleye goes on to say, "do not manifest themselves," because—

"The tenant, although ground down by the constant rise of rents, lives among his equals, peasants like himself who have tenants whom they use just as the large landholder does his. His father, his brother, perhaps the man himself, possesses something like an acre of land, which he lets at as high a rent as he can get. In the public house peasant proprietors will boast of the high rents they get for their lands, just as they might boast of having sold their pigs or potatoes very dear. Letting at as high a rent as possible comes thus to seem to him to be quite a matter of course, and he never dreams of finding fault with either the landowners as a class or with property in land. His mind is not likely to dwell on the notion of a caste of domineering landlords, of 'bloodthirsty tyrants,' fattening on the sweat of impoverished tenants and doing no work themselves; for those who drive the hardest bargains are not the great landowners but his own fellows. Thus, the distribution of a number of small properties among the peasantry forms a kind of rampart and safeguard for the holders of large estates, and peasant property may without exaggeration be called the lightning conductor that averts from society dangers which might otherwise lead to violent catastrophes.

"The concentration of land in large estates among a small number of families is a sort of provocation of leveling legislation. The position of England, so enviable in many respects, seems to me to be in this respect full of danger for the future."

To me, for the very same reason that M. de Laveleye expresses, the position of England seems full of hope.

Let us abandon all attempt to get rid of the evils of land monopoly by restricting landownership. An equal distribution of land is impossible, and anything short of that would be only a mitigation, not a cure, and a mitigation that would prevent the adoption of a cure. Nor is any remedy worth considering that does not fall in with the natural direction of social development, and swim, so to speak, with the current of the times. That concentration is the order of development there can be no mistaking—the concentration of people in large cities, the concentration of handicrafts in large factories, the concentration of transportation by railroad and steamship lines, and of agricultural operations in large fields. The most trivial businesses are being concentrated in the same way—errands are run and carpet sacks are carried by corporations. All the currents of the time run to concentration. To resist it successfully we must throttle steam and discharge electricity from human service.

CHAPTER **2** THE TRUE REMEDY

We have traced the unequal distribution of wealth which is the curse and menace of modern civilization to the institution of private property in land. We have seen that so long as this institution exists no increase in productive power can permanently benefit the masses; but, on the contrary, must tend still further to depress their condition. We have examined all the remedies, short of the abolition of private property in land, which are currently relied on or proposed for the relief of poverty and the better distribution of wealth, and have found them all inefficacious or impracticable.

There is but one way to remove an evil—and that is, to remove its cause. Poverty deepens as wealth increases, and wages are forced down while productive power grows, because land, which is the source of all wealth and the field of all labor, is monopolized. To extirpate poverty, to make wages what justice commands they should be, the full earnings of the laborer, we must therefore substitute for the individual ownership of land a common ownership. Nothing else will go to the cause of the evil—in nothing else is there the slightest hope.

This, then, is the remedy for the unjust and unequal distribution of wealth apparent in modern civilization, and for all the evils which flow from it:

We must make land common property.

We have reached this conclusion by an examination in which every step has been proved and secured. In the

328

chain of reasoning no link is wanting and no link is weak. Deduction and induction have brought us to the same truth—that the unequal ownership of land necessitates the unequal distribution of wealth. And as in the nature of things unequal ownership of land is inseparable from the recognition of individual property in land, it necessarily follows that the only remedy for the unjust distribution of wealth is in making land common property.

But this is a truth which, in the present state of society, will arouse the most bitter antagonism, and must fight its way, inch by inch. It will be necessary, therefore, to meet the objections of those who, even when driven to admit this truth, will declare that it cannot be practically applied.

In doing this we shall bring our previous reasoning to a new and crucial test. Just as we try addition by subtraction and multiplication by division, so may we, by testing the sufficiency of the remedy, prove the correctness of our conclusions as to the cause of the evil.

The laws of the universe are harmonious. And if the remedy to which we have been led is the true one, it must be consistent with justice; it must be practicable of application; it must accord with the tendencies of social development and must harmonize with other reforms.

All this I propose to show. I propose to meet all practical objections that can be raised, and to show that this simple measure is not only easy of application; but that it is a sufficient remedy for all the evils which, as modern progress goes on, arise from the greater and greater inequality in the distribution of wealth—that it will substitute equality for inequality, plenty for want, justice for injustice, social strength for social weakness, and will open the way to grander and nobler advances of civilization.

BOOK VI   CHAPTER 2

I thus propose to show that the laws of the universe do not deny the natural aspirations of the human heart; that the progress of society might be, and, if it is to continue, must be, toward equality, not toward inequality; and that the economic harmonies prove the truth perceived by the Stoic Emperor—

"We are made for co-operation—like feet, like hands, like eyelids, like the rows of the upper and lower teeth."

Justice is a relation of congruity which really subsists between two things. This relation is always the same, whatever being considers it, whether it be God, or an angel, or lastly a man.

—MONTESQUIEU.

CHAPTER **1** THE INJUSTICE OF
PRIVATE PROPERTY
IN LAND

When it is proposed to abolish private property in land
the first question that will arise is that of justice.
Though often warped by habit, superstition, and selfishness into the most distorted forms, the sentiment of
justice is yet fundamental to the human mind, and whatever dispute arouses the passions of men, the conflict
is sure to rage, not so much as to the question "Is it
wise?" as to the question "Is it right?"

This tendency of popular discussions to take an ethical
form has a cause. It springs from a law of the human
mind; it rests upon a vague and instinctive recognition
of what is probably the deepest truth we can grasp.
That alone is wise which is just; that alone is enduring
which is right. In the narrow scale of individual actions
and individual life this truth may be often obscured, but
in the wider field of national life it everywhere stands
out.

I bow to this arbitrament, and accept this test. If
our inquiry into the cause which makes low wages and
pauperism the accompaniments of material progress has
led us to a correct conclusion, it will bear translation
from terms of political economy into terms of ethics, and
as the source of social evils show a wrong. If it will not
do this, it is disproved. If it will do this, it is proved
by the final decision. If private property in land be
just, then is the remedy I propose a false one; if, on the
contrary, private property in land be unjust, then is this
remedy the true one.

333

What constitutes the rightful basis of property? What is it that enables a man justly to say of a thing, "It is mine!" From what springs the sentiment which acknowledges his exclusive right as against all the world? Is it not, primarily, the right of a man to himself, to the use of his own powers, to the enjoyment of the fruits of his own exertions? Is it not this individual right, which springs from and is testified to by the natural facts of individual organization—the fact that each particular pair of hands obey a particular brain and are related to a particular stomach; the fact that each man is a definite, coherent, independent whole—which alone justifies individual ownership? As a man belongs to himself, so his labor when put in concrete form belongs to him.

And for this reason, that which a man makes or produces is his own, as against all the world—to enjoy or to destroy, to use, to exchange, or to give. No one else can rightfully claim it, and his exclusive right to it involves no wrong to any one else. Thus there is to everything produced by human exertion a clear and indisputable title to exclusive possession and enjoyment, which is perfectly consistent with justice, as it descends from the original producer, in whom it vested by natural law. The pen with which I am writing is justly mine. No other human being can rightfully lay claim to it, for in me is the title of the producers who made it. It has become mine, because transferred to me by the stationer, to whom it was transferred by the importer, who obtained the exclusive right to it by transfer from the manufacturer, in whom, by the same process of purchase, vested the rights of those who dug the material from the ground and shaped it into a pen. Thus, my exclusive right of ownership in the pen springs from the natural right of the individual to the use of his own faculties.

Now, this is not only the original source from which

all ideas of exclusive ownership arise—as is evident from the natural tendency of the mind to revert to it when the idea of exclusive ownership is questioned, and the manner in which social relations develop—but it is necessarily the only source. There can be to the ownership of anything no rightful title which is not derived from the title of the producer and does not rest upon the natural right of the man to himself. There can be no other rightful title, because (1st) there is no other natural right from which any other title can be derived, and (2d) because the recognition of any other title is inconsistent with and destructive of this.

For (1st) what other right exists from which the right to the exclusive possession of anything can be derived, save the right of a man to himself? With what other power is man by nature clothed, save the power of exerting his own faculties? How can he in any other way act upon or affect material things or other men? Paralyze the motor nerves, and your man has no more external influence or power than a log or stone. From what else, then, can the right of possessing and controlling things be derived? If it spring not from man himself, from what can it spring? Nature acknowledges no ownership or control in man save as the result of exertion. In no other way can her treasures be drawn forth, her powers directed, or her forces utilized or controlled. She makes no discriminations among men, but is to all absolutely impartial. She knows no distinction between master and slave, king and subject, saint and sinner. All men to her stand upon an equal footing and have equal rights. She recognizes no claim but that of labor, and recognizes that without respect to the claimant. If a pirate spread his sails, the wind will fill them as well as it will fill those of a peaceful merchantman or missionary bark; if a king and a common man be thrown overboard, neither can keep his head above water except by swim-

ming; birds will not come to be shot by the proprietor of
the soil any quicker than they will come to be shot by
the poacher; fish will bite or will not bite at a hook in
utter disregard as to whether it is offered them by a good
little boy who goes to Sunday school, or a bad little boy
who plays truant; grain will grow only as the ground is
prepared and the seed is sown; it is only at the call
of labor that ore can be raised from the mine; the sun
shines and the rain falls, alike upon just and unjust.
The laws of nature are the decrees of the Creator. There
is written in them no recognition of any right save
that of labor; and in them is written broadly and clearly
the equal right of all men to the use and enjoyment of
nature; to apply to her by their exertions, and to receive
and possess her reward. Hence, as nature gives only to
labor, the exertion of labor in production is the only
title to exclusive possession.

(2d) This right of ownership that springs from labor
excludes the possibility of any other right of ownership.
If a man be rightfully entitled to the produce of his
labor, then no one can be rightfully entitled to the ownership of anything which is not the produce of his labor,
or the labor of some one else from whom the right has
passed to him. If production give to the producer the
right to exclusive possession and enjoyment, there can
rightfully be no exclusive possession and enjoyment of
anything not the production of labor, and the recognition of private property in land is a wrong. For the
right to the produce of labor cannot be enjoyed without
the right to the free use of the opportunities offered by
nature, and to admit the right of property in these is
to deny the right of property in the produce of labor.
When nonproducers can claim as rent a portion of the
wealth created by producers, the right of the producers
to the fruits of their labor is to that extent denied.

There is no escape from this position. To affirm that

a man can rightfully claim exclusive ownership in his own labor when embodied in material things, is to deny that any one can rightfully claim exclusive ownership in land. To affirm the rightfulness of property in land, is to affirm a claim which has no warrant in nature, as against a claim founded in the organization of man and the laws of the material universe.

What most prevents the realization of the injustice of private property in land is the habit of including all the things that are made the subject of ownership in one category, as property, or, if any distinction is made, drawing the line, according to the unphilosophical distinction of the lawyers, between personal property and real estate, or things movable and things immovable. The real and natural distinction is between things which are the produce of labor and things which are the gratuitous offerings of nature; or, to adopt the terms of political economy, between wealth and land.

These two classes of things are in essence and relations widely different, and to class them together as property is to confuse all thought when we come to consider the justice or the injustice, the right or the wrong of property.

A house and the lot on which it stands are alike property, as being the subject of ownership, and are alike classed by the lawyers as real estate. Yet in nature and relations they differ widely. The one is produced by human labor, and belongs to the class in political economy styled wealth. The other is a part of nature, and belongs to the class in political economy styled land.

The essential character of the one class of things is that they embody labor, are brought into being by human exertion, their existence or nonexistence, their increase or diminution, depending on man. The essential character of the other class of things is that they do not embody labor, and exist irrespective of human exertion

and irrespective of man; they are the field or environment in which man finds himself; the storehouse from
which his needs must be supplied, the raw material upon
which and the forces with which alone his labor can act.

The moment this distinction is realized, that moment
is it seen that the sanction which natural justice gives
to one species of property is denied to the other; that
the rightfulness which attaches to individual property
in the produce of labor implies the wrongfulness of individual property in land; that, whereas the recognition
of the one places all men upon equal terms, securing to
each the due reward of his labor, the recognition of the
other is the denial of the equal rights of men, permitting
those who do not labor to take the natural reward of
those who do.

Whatever may be said for the institution of private
property in land, it is therefore plain that it cannot be
defended on the score of justice.

The equal right of all men to the use of land is as
clear as their equal right to breathe the air—it is a
right proclaimed by the fact of their existence. For we
cannot suppose that some men have a right to be in this
world and others no right.

If we are all here by the equal permission of the Creator, we are all here with an equal title to the enjoyment
of his bounty—with an equal right to the use of all that
nature so impartially offers.* This is a right which is

---

* In saying that private property in land can, in the ultimate analysis,
be justified only on the theory that some men have a better right to existence than others, I am stating only what the advocates of the existing
system have themselves perceived. What gave to Malthus his popularity
among the ruling classes—what caused his illogical book to be received
as a new revelation, induced sovereigns to send him decorations, and the
meanest rich man in England to propose to give him a living, was the
fact that he furnished a plausible reason for the assumption that some

natural and inalienable; it is a right which vests in every human being as he enters the world, and which during his continuance in the world can be limited only by the equal rights of others. There is in nature no such thing as a fee simple in land. There is on earth no power which can rightfully make a grant of exclusive ownership in land. If all existing men were to unite to grant away their equal rights, they could not grant away the right of those who follow them. For what are we but tenants for a day? Have we made the earth, that we should determine the rights of those who after us shall tenant it in their turn? The Almighty, who created the earth for man and man for the earth, has entailed it upon all the generations of the children of men by a decree written upon the constitution of all things—a decree which no human action can bar and no prescription determine. Let the parchments be ever so many, or possession ever so long, natural justice can recognize no right in one man to the possession and enjoyment of land that is not equally the right of all his fellows. Though his titles have been acquiesced in by generation after generation, to the landed estates of the Duke of Westminster the poorest child that is born in London

---

have a better right to existence than others—an assumption which is necessary for the justification of private property in land, and which Malthus clearly states in the declaration that the tendency of population is constantly to bring into the world human beings for whom nature refuses to provide, and who consequently "have not the slightest right to any share in the existing store of the necessaries of life"; whom she tells as interlopers to begone, "and does not hesitate to extort by force obedience to her mandates," employing for that purpose "hunger and pestilence, war and crime, mortality and neglect of infantine life, prostitution and syphilis." And today this Malthusian doctrine is the ultimate defense upon which those who justify private property in land fall back. In no other way can it be logically defended.

BOOK VII   CHAPTER 1

today has as much right as has his eldest son.* Though
the sovereign people of the state of New York consent
to the landed possessions of the Astors, the puniest infant that comes wailing into the world in the squalidest
room of the most miserable tenement house, becomes at
that moment seized of an equal right with the million-
aires. And it is robbed if the right is denied.

Our previous conclusions, irresistible in themselves,
thus stand approved by the highest and final test.
Translated from terms of political economy into terms of
ethics they show a wrong as the source of the evils which
increase as material progress goes on.

The masses of men, who in the midst of abundance
suffer want; who, clothed with political freedom, are
condemned to the wages of slavery; to whose toil laborsaving inventions bring no relief, but rather seem to
rob them of a privilege, instinctively feel that "there is
something wrong." And they are right.

The widespreading social evils which everywhere oppress men amid an advancing civilization spring from a
great primary wrong—the appropriation, as the exclusive
property of some men, of the land on which and from
which all must live. From this fundamental injustice
flow all the injustices which distort and endanger modern

* This natural and inalienable right to the equal use and enjoyment of
land is so apparent that it has been recognized by men wherever force or
habit has not blunted first perceptions. To give but one instance: The
white settlers of New Zealand found themselves unable to get from the
Maoris what the latter considered a complete title to land, because, although a whole tribe might have consented to a sale, they would still
claim with every new child born among them an additional payment on
the ground that they had parted with only their own rights, and could
not sell those of the unborn. The government was obliged to step in and
settle the matter by buying land for a tribal annuity, in which every child
that is born acquires a share.

development, which condemn the producer of wealth to poverty and pamper the nonproducer in luxury, which rear the tenement house with the palace, plant the brothel behind the church, and compel us to build prisons as we open new schools.

There is nothing strange or inexplicable in the phenomena that are now perplexing the world. It is not that material progress is not in itself a good; it is not that nature has called into being children for whom she has failed to provide; it is not that the Creator has left on natural laws a taint of injustice at which even the human mind revolts, that material progress brings such bitter fruits. That amid our highest civilization men faint and die with want is not due to the niggardliness of nature, but to the injustice of man. Vice and misery, poverty and pauperism, are not the legitimate results of increase of population and industrial development; they only follow increase of population and industrial development because land is treated as private property— they are the direct and necessary results of the violation of the supreme law of justice, involved in giving to some men the exclusive possession of that which nature provides for all men.

The recognition of individual proprietorship of land is the denial of the natural rights of other individuals—it is a wrong which must show itself in the inequitable division of wealth. For as labor cannot produce without the use of land, the denial of the equal right to the use of land is necessarily the denial of the right of labor to its own produce. If one man can command the land upon which others must labor, he can appropriate the produce of their labor as the price of his permission to labor. The fundamental law of nature, that her enjoyment by man shall be consequent upon his exertion, is thus violated. The one receives without producing; the others produce without receiving. The one is unjustly enriched; the others are robbed. To this fundamental wrong we have traced the unjust distribution of wealth which is separating modern society into the very rich and the very poor. It is the continuous increase of rent —the price that labor is compelled to pay for the use of land, which strips the many of the wealth they justly earn, to pile it up in the hands of the few, who do nothing to earn it.

Why should they who suffer from this injustice hesitate for one moment to sweep it away? Who are the landholders that they should thus be permitted to reap where they have not sown?

Consider for a moment the utter absurdity of the titles by which we permit to be gravely passed from John Doe to Richard Roe the right exclusively to possess the earth, giving absolute dominion as against all others. In California our land titles go back to the Supreme Government of Mexico, who took from the Spanish King, who took from the Pope, when he by a stroke of the pen divided lands yet to be discovered between the Spanish or Portuguese—or if you please they rest upon conquest. In the eastern states they go back to treaties with Indians and grants from English kings; in Louisiana to the government of France; in Florida to the government of Spain; while in England they go back to the Norman conquerors. Everywhere, not to a right which obliges, but to a force which compels. And when a title rests but on force, no complaint can be made when force annuls it. Whenever the people, having the power, choose to annul those titles, no objection can be made in the name of justice. There have existed men who had the power to hold or to give exclusive possession of portions of the earth's surface, but when and where did there exist the human being who had the right?

The right to exclusive ownership of anything of human

production is clear. No matter how many the hands through which it has passed, there was, at the beginning of the line, human labor—some one who, having procured or produced it by his exertions, had to it a clear title as against all the rest of mankind, and which could justly pass from one to another by sale or gift. But at the end of what string of conveyances or grants can be shown or supposed a like title to any part of the material universe? To improvements, such an original title can be shown; but it is a title only to the improvements, and not to the land itself. If I clear a forest, drain a swamp, or fill a morass, all I can justly claim is the value given by these exertions. They give me no right to the land itself, no claim other than to my equal share with every other member of the community in the value which is added to it by the growth of the community.

But it will be said: There are improvements which in time become indistinguishable from the land itself! Very well; then the title to the improvements becomes blended with the title to the land; the individual right is lost in the common right. It is the greater that swallows up the less, not the less that swallows up the greater. Nature does not proceed from man, but man from nature, and it is into the bosom of nature that he and all his works must return again.

Yet, it will be said: As every man has a right to the use and enjoyment of nature, the man who is using land must be permitted the exclusive right to its use in order that he may get the full benefit of his labor. But there is no difficulty in determining where the individual right ends and the common right begins. A delicate and exact test is supplied by value, and with its aid there is no difficulty, no matter how dense population may become, in determining and securing the exact rights of each, the equal rights of all. The value of land, as we have seen, is the price of monopoly. It is not the absolute, but the relative, capability of land that determines its value. No matter what may be its intrinsic qualities, land that is no better than other land which may be had for the using can have no value. And the value of land always measures the difference between it and the best land that may be had for the using. Thus, the value of land expresses in exact and tangible form the right of the community in land held by an individual; and rent expresses the exact amount which the individual should pay to the community to satisfy the equal rights of all other members of the community. Thus, if we concede to priority of possession the undisturbed use of land, confiscating rent for the benefit of the community, we reconcile the fixity of tenure which is necessary for improvement with a full and complete recognition of the equal rights of all to the use of land.

As for the deduction of a complete and exclusive individual right to land from priority of occupation, that is, if possible, the most absurd ground on which landownership can be defended. Priority of occupation give exclusive and perpetual title to the surface of a globe on which, in the order of nature, countless generations succeed each other! Had the men of the last generation any better right to the use of this world than we of this? or the men of a hundred years ago? or of a thousand years ago? Had the mound builders, or the cave dwellers, the contemporaries of the mastodon and the three-toed horse, or the generations still further back, who, in dim æons that we can think of only as geologic periods, followed each other on the earth we now tenant for our little day?

Has the first comer at a banquet the right to turn back all the chairs and claim that none of the other guests shall partake of the food provided, except as they make terms with him? Does the first man who presents a ticket at the door of a theater, and passes in, acquire by his priority the right to shut the doors and have the performance go on for him alone? Does the first passenger who enters a railroad car obtain the right to scatter his baggage over all the seats and compel the passengers who come in after him to stand up?

The cases are perfectly analogous. We arrive and we depart, guests at a banquet continually spread, spectators and participants in an entertainment where there is room for all who come; passengers from station to station, on an orb that whirls through space—our rights to take and possess cannot be exclusive; they must be bounded everywhere by the equal rights of others. Just as the passenger in a railroad car may spread himself and his baggage over as many seats as he pleases, until other passengers come in, so may a settler take and use as much land as he chooses, until it is needed by others —a fact which is shown by the land acquiring a value— when his right must be curtailed by the equal rights of the others, and no priority of appropriation can give a right which will bar these equal rights of others. If this were not the case, then by priority of appropriation one man could acquire and could transmit to whom he pleased, not merely the exclusive right to 160 acres, or to 640 acres, but to a whole township, a whole state, a whole continent.

And to this manifest absurdity does the recognition of individual right to land come when carried to its ultimate —that any one human being, could he concentrate in himself the individual rights to the land of any country, could expel therefrom all the rest of its inhabitants; and could he thus concentrate the individual rights to the whole surface of the globe, he alone of all the teeming population of the earth would have the right to live.

And what upon this supposition would occur is, upon a smaller scale, realized in actual fact. The territorial lords of Great Britain, to whom grants of land have given the "white parasols and elephants mad with pride," have over and over again expelled from large districts the native population, whose ancestors had lived on the land from immemorial times—driven them off to emigrate, to become paupers, or to starve. And on uncultivated tracts of land in the new state of California may be seen the blackened chimneys of homes from which settlers have been driven by force of laws which ignore natural right, and great stretches of land which might be populous are desolate, because the recognition of exclusive ownership has put it in the power of one human creature to forbid his fellows from using it. The comparative handful of proprietors who own the surface of the British Islands would be doing only what English law gives them full power to do, and what many of them have done on a smaller scale already, were they to exclude the millions of British people from their native islands. And such an exclusion, by which a few hundred thousand should at will banish thirty million people from their native country, while it would be more striking, would not be a whit more repugnant to natural right than the spectacle now presented, of the vast body of the British people being compelled to pay such enormous sums to a few of their number for the privilege of being permitted to live upon and use the land which they so fondly call their own; which is endeared to them by memories so tender and so glorious, and for which they are held in duty bound, if need be, to spill their blood and lay down their lives.

I refer only to the British Islands, because, landownership being more concentrated there, they afford a more striking illustration of what private property in land necessarily involves. "To whomsoever the soil at any time belongs, to him belong the fruits of it," is a truth that becomes more and more apparent as population becomes denser and invention and improvement add to productive power; but it is everywhere a truth—as much in our new States as in the British Islands or by the banks of the Indus.

CHAPTER **2** THE ENSLAVEMENT OF LABORERS
THE ULTIMATE RESULT OF
PRIVATE PROPERTY IN LAND

If chattel slavery be unjust, then is private property in land unjust.

For let the circumstances be what they may—the ownership of land will always give the ownership of men, to a degree measured by the necessity (real or artificial) for the use of land. This is but a statement in different form of the law of rent.

And when that necessity is absolute—when starvation is the alternative to the use of land, then does the ownership of men involved in the ownership of land become absolute.

Place one hundred men on an island from which there is no escape, and whether you make one of these men the absolute owner of the other ninety-nine, or the absolute owner of the soil of the island, will make no difference either to him or to them.

In the one case, as the other, the one will be the absolute master of the ninety-nine—his power extending even to life and death, for simply to refuse them permission to live upon the island would be to force them into the sea.

Upon a larger scale, and through more complex relations, the same cause must operate in the same way and to the same end—the ultimate result, the enslavement of laborers, becoming apparent just as the pressure increases which compels them to live on and from land which is treated as the exclusive property of others. Take a country in which the soil is divided among a number of proprietors, instead of being in the hands of one, and in which, as in modern production, the capitalist has been specialized from the laborer, and manufactures and exchange, in all their many branches, have been separated from agriculture. Though less direct and obvious, the relations between the owners of the soil and the laborers will, with increase of population and the improvement of the arts, tend to the same absolute mastery on the one hand and the same abject helplessness on the other, as in the case of the island we have supposed. Rent will advance, while wages will fall. Of the aggregate produce, the landowner will get a constantly increasing, the laborer a constantly diminishing share. Just as removal to cheaper land becomes difficult or impossible, laborers, no matter what they produce, will be reduced to a bare living, and the free competition among them, where land is monopolized, will force them to a condition which, though they may be mocked with the titles and insignia of freedom, will be virtually that of slavery.

There is nothing strange in the fact that, in spite of the enormous increase in productive power which this century has witnessed, and which is still going on, the wages of labor in the lower and wider strata of industry should everywhere tend to the wages of slavery—just enough to keep the laborer in working condition. For the ownership of the land on which and from which a man must live is virtually the ownership of the man himself, and in acknowledging the right of some individuals to the exclusive use and enjoyment of the earth, we condemn other individuals to slavery as fully and as completely as though we had formally made them chattels.

In a simpler form of society, where production chiefly

consists in the direct application of labor to the soil, the slavery that is the necessary result of according to some the exclusive right to the soil from which all must live, is plainly seen in helotism, in villeinage, in serfdom.

Chattel slavery originated in the capture of prisoners in war, and, though it has existed to some extent in every part of the globe, its area has been small, its effects trivial, as compared with the forms of slavery which have originated in the appropriation of land. No people as a mass have ever been reduced to chattel slavery to men of their own race, nor yet on any large scale has any people ever been reduced to slavery of this kind by conquest. The general subjection of the many to the few, which we meet with wherever society has reached a certain development, has resulted from the appropriation of land as individual property. It is the ownership of the soil that everywhere gives the ownership of the men that live upon it. It is slavery of this kind to which the enduring pyramids and the colossal monuments of Egypt yet bear witness, and of the institution of which we have, perhaps, a vague tradition in the biblical story of the famine during which the Pharaoh purchased up the lands of the people. It was slavery of this kind to which, in the twilight of history, the conquerors of Greece reduced the original inhabitants of that peninsula, transforming them into helots by making them pay rent for their lands. It was the growth of the *latifundia*, or great landed estates, which transmuted the population of ancient Italy, from a race of hardy husbandmen, whose robust virtues conquered the world, into a race of cringing bondsmen; it was the appropriation of the land as the absolute property of their chieftains which gradually turned the descendants of free and equal Gallic, Teutonic and Hunnish warriors into coloni and villeins, and which changed the independent burghers of Sclavonic village communities into the boors of Russia and the serfs of Poland; which instituted the feudalism of China and Japan, as well as that of Europe, and which made the high chiefs of Polynesia the all but absolute masters of their fellows. How it came to pass that the Aryan shepherds and warriors who, as comparative philology tells us, descended from the common birthplace of the Indo-Germanic race into the lowlands of India, were turned into the suppliant and cringing Hindoo, the Sanscrit verse which I have before quoted gives us a hint. The white parasols and the elephants mad with pride of the Indian rajah are the flowers of grants of land. And could we find the key to the records of the long-buried civilizations that lie entombed in the gigantic ruins of Yucatan and Guatemala, telling at once of the pride of a ruling class and the unrequited toil to which the masses were condemned, we should read, in all human probability, of a slavery imposed upon the great body of the people through the appropriation of the land as the property of a few—of another illustration of the universal truth that they who possess the land are masters of the men who dwell upon it.

The necessary relation between labor and land, the absolute power which the ownership of land gives over men who cannot live but by using it, explains what is otherwise inexplicable—the growth and persistence of institutions, manners, and ideas so utterly repugnant to the natural sense of liberty and equality.

When the idea of individual ownership, which so justly and naturally attaches to things of human production, is extended to land, all the rest is a mere matter of development. The strongest and most cunning easily acquire a superior share in this species of property, which is to be had, not by production, but by appropriation, and in becoming lords of the land they become necessarily lords of their fellow men. The ownership of land is the basis of aristocracy. It was not nobility that gave land, but the possession of land that gave nobility. All the enormous privileges of the nobility of medieval Europe flowed from their position as the owners of the soil. The simple principle of the ownership of the soil produced, on the one side, the lord, on the other, the vassal—the one having all rights, the other none. The right of the lord to the soil acknowledged and maintained, those who lived upon it could do so only upon his terms. The manners and conditions of the times made those terms include services and servitudes, as well as rents in produce or money, but the essential thing that compelled them was the ownership of land. This power exists wherever the ownership of land exists, and can be brought out wherever the competition for the use of land is great enough to enable the landlord to make his own terms. The English landowner of to-day has, in the law which recognizes his exclusive right to the land, essentially all the power which his predecessor the feudal baron had. He might command rent in services or servitudes. He might compel his tenants to dress themselves in a particular way, to profess a particular religion, to send their children to a particular school, to submit their differences to his decision, to fall upon their knees when he spoke to them, to follow him around dressed in his livery, or to sacrifice to him female honor, if they would prefer these things to being driven off his land. He could demand, in short, any terms on which men would still consent to live on his land, and the law could not prevent him so long as it did not qualify his ownership, for compliance with them would assume the form of a free contract or voluntary act. And English landlords do exercise such of these powers as in the manners of the times they care to. Having shaken off the obligation of providing for the defense of the country, they no longer need the military

service of their tenants, and the possession of wealth
and power being now shown in other ways than by long
trains of attendants, they no longer care for personal
service. But they habitually control the votes of their
tenants, and dictate to them in many little ways. That
"right reverend father in God," Bishop Lord Plunkett,
evicted a number of his poor Irish tenants because they
would not send their children to Protestant Sunday
schools; and to that Earl of Leitrim for whom Nemesis
tarried so long before she sped the bullet of an assassin,
even darker crimes are imputed; while, at the cold
promptings of greed, cottage after cottage has been
pulled down and family after family forced into the
roads. The principle that permits this is the same principle that in ruder times and a simpler social state en-
thralled the great masses of the common people and
placed such a wide gulf between noble and peasant.
Where the peasant was made a serf, it was simply by
forbidding him to leave the estate on which he was born,
thus artificially producing the condition we supposed on
the island. In sparsely settled countries this is necessary to produce absolute slavery, but where land is
fully occupied, competition may produce substantially
the same conditions. Between the condition of the rack-
rented Irish peasant and the Russian serf, the advantage was in many things on the side of the serf. The
serf did not starve.

Now, as I think I have conclusively proved, it is the
same cause which has in every age degraded and enslaved the laboring masses that is working in the civilized world to-day. Personal liberty—that is to say, the
liberty to move about—is everywhere conceded, while
of political and legal inequality there are in the United
States no vestiges, and in the most backward civilized
countries but few. But the great cause of inequality remains, and is manifesting itself in the unequal distribu-

tion of wealth. The essence of slavery is that it takes from the laborer all he produces save enough to support an animal existence, and to this minimum the wages of free labor, under existing conditions, unmistakably tend. Whatever be the increase of productive power, rent steadily tends to swallow up the gain, and more than the gain.

Thus the condition of the masses in every civilized country is, or is tending to become, that of virtual slavery under the forms of freedom. And it is probable that of all kinds of slavery this is the most cruel and relentless. For the laborer is robbed of the produce of his labor and compelled to toil for a mere subsistence; but his taskmasters, instead of human beings, assume the forms of imperious necessities. Those to whom his labor is rendered and from whom his wages are received are often driven in their turn—contact between the laborers and the ultimate beneficiaries of their labor is sundered, and individuality is lost. The direct responsibility of master to slave, a responsibility which exercises a softening influence upon the great majority of men, does not arise; it is not one human being who seems to drive another to unremitting and ill-requited toil, but "the inevitable laws of supply and demand," for which no one in particular is responsible. The maxims of Cato the Censor—maxims which were regarded with abhorrence even in an age of cruelty and universal slaveholding—that after as much work as possible is obtained from a slave he should be turned out to die, become the common rule; and even the selfish interest which prompts the master to look after the comfort and well-being of the slave is lost. Labor has become a commodity, and the laborer a machine. There are no masters and slaves, no owners and owned, but only buyers and sellers. The higgling of the market takes the place of every other sentiment.

When the slaveholders of the South looked upon the condition of the free laboring poor in the most advanced civilized countries, it is no wonder that they easily persuaded themselves of the divine institution of slavery. That the field hands of the South were as a class better fed, better lodged, better clothed; that they had less anxiety and more of the amusements and enjoyments of life than the agricultural laborers of England there can be no doubt; and even in the northern cities, visiting slaveholders might see and hear of things impossible under what they called their organization of labor. In the southern states, during the days of slavery, the master who would have compelled his Negroes to work and live as large classes of free white men and women are compelled in free countries to work and live, would have been deemed infamous, and if public opinion had not restrained him, his own selfish interest in the maintenance of the health and strength of his chattels would. But in London, New York, and Boston, among people who have given, and would give again, money and blood to free the slave, where no one could abuse a beast in public without arrest and punishment, barefooted and ragged children may be seen running around the streets even in the winter time, and in squalid garrets and noisome cellars women work away their lives for wages that fail to keep them in proper warmth and nourishment. Is it any wonder that to the slaveholders of the South the demand for the abolition of slavery seemed like the cant of hypocrisy?

And now that slavery has been abolished, the planters of the South find they have sustained no loss. Their ownership of the land upon which the freedmen must live gives them practically as much command of labor as before, while they are relieved of responsibility, sometimes very expensive. The Negroes as yet have the alternative of emigrating, and a great movement of that kind seems now about commencing, but as population increases and land becomes dear, the planters will get a greater proportionate share of the earnings of their laborers than they did under the system of chattel slavery, and the laborers a less share—for under the system of chattel slavery the slaves always got at least enough to keep them in good physical health, but in such countries as England there are large classes of laborers who do not get that.*

The influences which, wherever there is personal relation between master and slave, slip in to modify chattel slavery, and to prevent the master from exerting to its fullest extent his power over the slave, also showed themselves in the ruder forms of serfdom that characterized the earlier periods of European development, and aided by religion, and, perhaps, as in chattel slavery, by the more enlightened but still selfish interests of the lord, and hardening into custom, universally fixed a limit to what the owner of the land could extort from the serf or peasant, so that the competition of men without means of existence bidding against each other for access to the means of existence, was nowhere suffered to go to its full length and exert its full power of deprivation and degradation. The helots of Greece, the metayers of Italy, the serfs of Russia and Poland, the peasants of feudal Europe, rendered to their landlords a fixed proportion either of their produce or their labor, and were not generally squeezed past that point. But the influences which thus stepped in to modify the

---

* One of the antislavery agitators (Col. J. A. Collins) on a visit to England addressed a large audience in a Scotch manufacturing town, and wound up as he had been used to in the United States, by giving the ration which in the slave codes of some of the states fixed the minimum of maintenance for a slave. He quickly discovered that to many of his hearers it was an anticlimax.

extortive power of landownership, and which may still be seen on English estates where the landlord and his family deem it their duty to send medicines and comforts to the sick and infirm, and to look after the well-being of their cottagers, just as the southern planter was accustomed to look after his Negroes, are lost in the more refined and less obvious form which serfdom assumes in the more complicated processes of modern production, which separates so widely and by so many intermediate gradations the individual whose labor is appropriated from him who appropriates it, and makes the relations between the members of the two classes not direct and particular, but indirect and general. In modern society, competition has free play to force from the laborer the very utmost he can give, and with what terrific force it is acting may be seen in the condition of the lowest class in the centers of wealth and industry. That the condition of this lowest class is not yet more general, is to be attributed to the great extent of fertile land which has hitherto been open on this continent, and which has not merely afforded an escape for the increasing population of the older sections of the Union, but has greatly relieved the pressure in Europe—in one country, Ireland, the emigration having been so great as actually to reduce the population. This avenue of relief cannot last forever. It is already fast closing up, and as it closes, the pressure must become harder and harder.

It is not without reason that the wise crow in the Ramayana, the crow Bushanda, "who has lived in every part of the universe and knows all events from the beginnings of time," declares that, though contempt of worldly advantages is necessary to supreme felicity, yet the keenest pain possible is inflicted by extreme poverty. The poverty to which in advancing civilization great masses of men are condemned, is not the freedom from distraction and temptation which sages have sought and philosophers have praised; it is a degrading and embruting slavery, that cramps the higher nature, dulls the finer feelings, and drives men by its pain to acts which the brutes would refuse. It is into this helpless, hopeless poverty, that crushes manhood and destroys womanhood, that robs even childhood of its innocence and joy, that the working classes are being driven by a force which acts upon them like a resistless and unpitying machine. The Boston collar manufacturer who pays his girls two cents an hour may commiserate their condition, but he, as they, is governed by the law of competition, and cannot pay more and carry on his business, for exchange is not governed by sentiment. And so, through all intermediate gradations, up to those who receive the earnings of labor without return, in the rent of land, it is the inexorable laws of supply and demand, a power with which the individual can no more quarrel or dispute than with the winds and the tides, that seem to press down the lower classes into the slavery of want.

But in reality, the cause is that which always has and always must result in slavery—the monopolization by some of what nature has designed for all.

Our boasted freedom necessarily involves slavery, so long as we recognize private property in land. Until that is abolished, Declarations of Independence and Acts of Emancipation are in vain. So long as one man can claim the exclusive ownership of the land from which other men must live, slavery will exist, and as material progress goes on, must grow and deepen!

This—and in previous chapters of this book we have traced the process, step by step—is what is going on in the civilized world today. Private ownership of land is the nether millstone. Material progress is the upper millstone. Between them, with an increasing pressure, the working classes are being ground.

CHAPTER 3 CLAIM OF LANDOWNERS TO COMPENSATION

The truth is, and from this truth there can be no escape, that there is and can be no just title to an exclusive possession of the soil, and that private property in land is a bold, bare, enormous wrong, like that of chattel slavery.

The majority of men in civilized communities do not recognize this, simply because the majority of men do not think. With them whatever is, is right, until its wrongfulness has been frequently pointed out, and in general they are ready to crucify whoever first attempts this.

But it is impossible for any one to study political economy, even as at present taught, or to think at all upon the production and distribution of wealth, without seeing that property in land differs essentially from property in things of human production, and that it has no warrant in abstract justice.

This is admitted, either expressly or tacitly, in every standard work on political economy, but in general merely by vague admission or omission. Attention is in general called away from the truth, as a lecturer on moral philosophy in a slaveholding community might call away attention from too close a consideration of the natural rights of men, and private property in land is accepted without comment, as an existing fact, or is assumed to be necessary to the proper use of land and the existence of the civilized state.

358

The examination through which we have passed has proved conclusively that private property in land cannot be justified on the ground of utility—that, on the contrary, it is the great cause to which are to be traced the poverty, misery, and degradation, the social disease and the political weakness which are showing themselves so menacingly amid advancing civilization. Expediency, therefore, joins justice in demanding that we abolish it.

When expediency thus joins justice in demanding that we abolish an institution that has no broader base or stronger ground than a mere municipal regulation, what reason can there be for hesitation?

The consideration that seems to cause hesitation, even on the part of those who see clearly that land by right is common property, is the idea that having permitted land to be treated as private property for so long, we should in abolishing it be doing a wrong to those who have been suffered to base their calculations upon its permanence; that having permitted land to be held as rightful property, we should by the resumption of common rights be doing injustice to those who have purchased it with what was unquestionably their rightful property. Thus, it is held that if we abolish private property in land, justice requires that we should fully compensate those who now possess it, as the British Government, in abolishing the purchase and sale of military commissions, felt itself bound to compensate those who held commissions which they had purchased in the belief that they could sell them again, or as in abolishing slavery in the British West Indies $100,000,-000 was paid the slaveholders.

Even Herbert Spencer, who in his "Social Statics" has so clearly demonstrated the invalidity of every title by which the exclusive possession of land is claimed, gives countenance to this idea (though it seems to me incon-

sistently) by declaring that justly to estimate and liqui-
date the claims of the present landholders "who have
either by their own acts or by the acts of their ancestors
given for their estates equivalents of honestly earned
wealth," to be "one of the most intricate problems society will one day have to solve."

It is this idea that suggests the proposition, which
finds advocates in Great Britain, that the government
shall purchase at its market price the individual proprietorship of the land of the country, and it was this
idea which led John Stuart Mill, although clearly per-
ceiving the essential injustice of private property in
land, to advocate, not a full resumption of the land, but
only a resumption of accruing advantages in the future.
His plan was that a fair and even liberal estimate
should be made of the market value of all the land in
the kingdom, and that future additions to that value,
not due to the improvements of the proprietor, should
be taken by the state.

To say nothing of the practical difficulties which such
cumbrous plans involve, in the extension of the functions of government which they would require and the
corruption they would beget, their inherent and essential defect lies in the impossibility of bridging over by
any compromise the radical difference between wrong
and right. Just in proportion as the interests of the
landholders are conserved, just in that proportion must
general interests and general rights be disregarded, and
if landholders are to lose nothing of their special privileges, the people at large can gain nothing. To buy up
individual property rights would merely be to give the
landholders in another form a claim of the same kind
and amount that their possession of land now gives
them; it would be to raise for them by taxation the
same proportion of the earnings of labor and capital
that they are now enabled to appropriate in rent. Their

unjust advantage would be preserved and the unjust disadvantage of the non-landholders would be continued. To be sure there would be a gain to the people at large when the advance of rents had made the amount which the landholders would take under the present system greater than the interest upon the purchase price of the land at present rates, but this would be only a future gain, and in the meanwhile there would not only be no relief, but the burden imposed upon labor and capital for the benefit of the present landholders would be much increased. For one of the elements in the present market value of land is the expectation of future increase of value, and thus, to buy up the lands at market rates and pay interest upon the purchase money would be to saddle producers not only with the payment of actual rent, but with the payment in full of speculative rent. Or to put it in another way: The land would be purchased at prices calculated upon a lower than the ordinary rate of interest (for the prospective increase in land values always makes the market price of land much greater than would be the price of anything else yielding the same present return), and interest upon the purchase money would be paid at the ordinary rate. Thus, not only all that the land yields them now would have to be paid the landowners, but a considerably larger amount. It would be, virtually, the state taking a perpetual lease from the present landholders at a considerable advance in rent over what they now receive. For the present the state would merely become the agent of the landholders in the collection of their rents, and would have to pay over to them not only what they received, but considerably more.

Mr. Mill's plan for nationalizing the future "unearned increase in the value of land," by fixing the present market value of all lands and appropriating to the state future increase in value, would not add to the injustice of the present distribution of wealth, but it would not remedy it. Further speculative advance of rent would cease, and in the future the people at large would gain the difference between the increase of rent and the amount at which that increase was estimated in fixing the present value of land, in which, of course, prospective, as well as present, value is an element. But it would leave, for all the future, one class in possession of the enormous advantage over others which they now have. All that can be said of this plan is, that it might be better than nothing.

Such inefficient and impracticable schemes may do to talk about, where any proposition more efficacious would not at present be entertained, and their discussion is a hopeful sign, as it shows the entrance of the thin end of the wedge of truth. Justice in men's mouths is cringingly humble when she first begins a protest against a time-honored wrong, and we of the English-speaking nations still wear the collar of the Saxon thrall, and have been educated to look upon the "vested rights" of landowners with all the superstitious reverence that ancient Egyptians looked upon the crocodile. But when the times are ripe for them, ideas grow, even though insignificant in their first appearance. One day, the Third Estate covered their heads when the king put on his hat. A little while thereafter, and the head of a son of St. Louis rolled from the scaffold. The antislavery movement in the United States commenced with talk of compensating owners, but when four millions of slaves were emancipated, the owners got no compensation, nor did they clamor for any. And by the time the people of any such country as England or the United States are sufficiently aroused to the injustice and disadvantages of individual ownership of land to induce them to attempt its nationalization, they will be sufficiently aroused to nationalize it in a much more direct and easy way than by purchase. They will not trouble themselves about compensating the proprietors of land.

Nor is it right that there should be any concern about the proprietors of land. That such a man as John Stuart Mill should have attached so much importance to the compensation of landowners as to have urged the confiscation merely of the future increase in rent, is explainable only by his acquiescence in the current doctrines that wages are drawn from capital and that population constantly tends to press upon subsistence. These blinded him as to the full effects of the private appropriation of land. He saw that "the claim of the landholder is altogether subordinate to the general policy of the state," and that "when private property in land is not expedient, it is unjust,"* but, entangled in the toils of the Malthusian doctrine, he attributed, as he expressly states in a paragraph I have previously quoted, the want and suffering that he saw around him to "the niggardliness of nature, not to the injustice of man," and thus to him the nationalization of land seemed comparatively a little thing, that could accomplish nothing toward the eradication of pauperism and the abolition of want—ends that could be reached only as men learned to repress a natural instinct. Great as he was and pure as he was—warm heart and noble mind —he yet never saw the true harmony of economic laws, nor realized how from this one great fundamental wrong flow want and misery, and vice and shame. Else he could never have written this sentence: "The land of Ireland, the land of every country, belongs to the people of that country. The individuals called landowners have no right in morality and justice to anything but the rent, or compensation for its salable value."

In the name of the Prophet—figs! If the land of any country belong to the people of that country, what

* "Principles of Political Economy," Book I, Chap. 2, Sec. 6.

right, in morality and justice, have the individuals called landowners to the rent? If the land belong to the people, why in the name of morality and justice should the people pay its salable value for their own?

Herbert Spencer says:* "Had we to deal with the parties who originally robbed the human race of its heritage, we might make short work of the matter." Why not make short work of the matter anyhow? For this robbery is not like the robbery of a horse or a sum of money, that ceases with the act. It is a fresh and continuous robbery, that goes on every day and every hour. It is not from the produce of the past that rent is drawn; it is from the produce of the present. It is a toll levied upon labor constantly and continuously. Every blow of the hammer, every stroke of the pick, every thrust of the shuttle, every throb of the steam engine, pays it tribute. It levies upon the earnings of the men who, deep under ground, risk their lives, and of those who over white surges hang to reeling masts; it claims the just reward of the capitalist and the fruits

* "Social Statics," page 142. [It may be well to say in the new reprint of this book (1897) that this and all other references to Herbert Spencer's "Social Statics" are from the edition of that book published by D. Appleton & Co., New York, with his consent, from 1864 to 1892. At that time "Social Statics" was repudiated, and a new edition under the name of "Social Statics, abridged and revised," has taken its place. From this, all that the first "Social Statics" had said in denial of property in land has been eliminated, and it of course contains nothing here referred to. Mr. Spencer has also been driven by the persistent heckling of the English single tax men, who insisted on asking him the questions suggested in the first "Social Statics," to bring out a small volume, entitled "Mr. Herbert Spencer on the Land Question," in which are reprinted in parallel columns Chap. IX of "Social Statics" with what he considers valid answers to himself as given in "Justice," 1891. This has also been reprinted by D. Appleton & Co., and constitutes, I think, the very funniest answer to himself ever made by a man who claimed to be a philosopher.]

of the inventor's patient effort; it takes little children from play and from school, and compels them to work before their bones are hard or their muscles are firm; it robs the shivering of warmth; the hungry, of food; the sick, of medicine; the anxious, of peace. It debases, and embrutes, and embitters. It crowds families of eight and ten into a single squalid room; it herds like swine agricultural gangs of boys and girls; it fills the gin palace and groggery with those who have no comfort in their homes; it makes lads who might be useful men candidates for prisons and penitentiaries; it fills brothels with girls who might have known the pure joy of motherhood; it sends greed and all evil passions prowling through society as a hard winter drives the wolves to the abodes of men; it darkens faith in the human soul, and across the reflection of a just and merciful Creator draws the veil of a hard, and blind, and cruel fate!

It is not merely a robbery in the past; it is a robbery in the present—a robbery that deprives of their birthright the infants that are now coming into the world! Why should we hesitate about making short work of such a system? Because I was robbed yesterday, and the day before, and the day before that, is it any reason that I should suffer myself to be robbed today and tomorrow? any reason that I should conclude that the robber has acquired a vested right to rob me?

If the land belong to the people, why continue to permit landowners to take the rent, or compensate them in any manner for the loss of rent? Consider what rent is. It does not arise spontaneously from land; it is due to nothing that the landowners have done. It represents a value created by the whole community. Let the landholders have, if you please, all that the possession of the land would give them in the absence of the rest of the community. But rent, the creation of the whole community, necessarily belongs to the whole community.

Try the case of the landholders by the maxims of the common law by which the rights of man and man are determined. The common law we are told is the perfection of reason, and certainly the landowners cannot complain of its decision, for it has been built up by and for landowners. Now what does the law allow to the innocent possessor when the land for which he paid his money is adjudged rightfully to belong to another? Nothing at all. That he purchased in good faith gives him no right or claim whatever. The law does not concern itself with the "intricate question of compensation" to the innocent purchaser. The law does not say, as John Stuart Mill says: "The land belongs to A, therefore B who has thought himself the owner has no right to anything but the rent, or compensation for its salable value." For that would be indeed like a famous fugitive slave case decision in which the Court was said to have given the law to the North and the Nigger to the South. The law simply says: "The land belongs to A, let the sheriff put him in possession!" It gives the innocent purchaser of a wrongful title no claim, it allows him no compensation. And not only this, it takes from him all the improvements that he has in good faith made upon the land. You may have paid a high price for land, making every exertion to see that the title is good; you may have held it in undisturbed possession for years without thought or hint of an adverse claimant; made it fruitful by your toil or erected upon it a costly building of greater value than the land itself, or a modest home in which you hope, surrounded by the fig trees you have planted and the vines you have dressed, to pass your declining days; yet if Quirk, Gammon & Snap can mouse out a technical flaw in your parchments or hunt up some forgotten heir who never dreamed of his rights, not merely the land, but all your improvements, may be taken away from you. And not merely that. According to the common law, when you have surrendered the land and given up your improvements, you may be called upon to account for the profits you derived from the land during the time you had it.

Now if we apply to this case of The People vs. The Landowners the same maxims of justice that have been formulated by landowners into law, and are applied every day in English and American courts to disputes between man and man, we shall not only not think of giving the landholders any compensation for the land, but shall take all the improvements and whatever else they may have as well.

But I do not propose, and I do not suppose that any one else will propose, to go so far. It is sufficient if the people resume the ownership of the land. Let the landowners retain their improvements and personal property in secure possession.

And in this measure of justice would be no oppression, no injury to any class. The great cause of the present unequal distribution of wealth, with the suffering, degradation, and waste that it entails, would be swept away. Even landholders would share in the general gain. The gain of even the large landholders would be a real one. The gain of the small landholders would be enormous. For in welcoming Justice, men welcome the handmaid of Love. Peace and Plenty follow in her train, bringing their good gifts, not to some, but to all.

How true this is, we shall hereafter see.

If in this chapter I have spoken of justice and expediency as if justice were one thing and expediency another, it has been merely to meet the objections of those who so talk. In justice is the highest and truest expediency.

CHAPTER 4 PRIVATE PROPERTY IN LAND HISTORICALLY CONSIDERED

What more than anything else prevents the realization of the essential injustice of private property in land and stands in the way of a candid consideration of any proposition for abolishing it, is that mental habit which makes anything that has long existed seem natural and necessary.

We are so used to the treatment of land as individual property, it is so thoroughly recognized in our laws, manners, and customs, that the vast majority of people never think of questioning it; but look upon it as necessary to the use of land. They are unable to conceive, or at least it does not enter their heads to conceive, of society as existing or as possible without the reduction of land to private possession. The first step to the cultivation or improvement of land seems to them to get for it a particular owner, and a man's land is looked on by them as fully and as equitably his, to sell, to lease, to give, or to bequeath, as his house, his cattle, his goods, or his furniture. The "sacredness of property" has been preached so constantly and effectively, especially by those "conservators of ancient barbarism," as Voltaire styled the lawyers, that most people look upon the private ownership of land as the very foundation of civilization, and if the resumption of land as common property is suggested, think of it at first blush either as a chimerical vagary, which never has and never can be realized, or as a proposition to overturn society from its base and bring about a reversion to barbarism.

If it were true that land had always been treated as private property, that would not prove the justice or necessity of continuing so to treat it, any more than the universal existence of slavery, which might once have been safely affirmed, would prove the justice or necessity of making property of human flesh and blood.

Not long ago monarchy seemed all but universal, and not only the kings but the majority of their subjects really believed that no country could get along without a king. Yet, to say nothing of America, France now gets along without a king; the Queen of England and Empress of India has about as much to do with governing her realms as the wooden figurehead of a ship has in determining its course, and the other crowned heads of Europe sit, metaphorically speaking, upon barrels of nitroglycerine.

Something over a hundred years ago, Bishop Butler, author of the famous Analogy, declared that "a constitution of civil government without any religious establishment is a chimerical project of which there is no example." As for there being no example, he was right. No government at that time existed, nor would it have been easy to name one that ever had existed, without some sort of an established religion; yet in the United States we have since proved by the practice of a century that it is possible for a civil government to exist without a state church.

But while, were it true, that land had always and everywhere been treated as private property would not prove that it should always be so treated, this is not true. On the contrary, the common right to land has everywhere been primarily recognized, and private ownership has nowhere grown up save as the result of usurpation. The primary and persistent perceptions of mankind are that all have an equal right to land, and the opinion that private property in land is necessary to society is but an offspring of ignorance that cannot look beyond its immediate surroundings—an idea of comparatively modern growth, as artificial and as baseless as that of the right divine of kings.

The observations of travelers, the researches of the critical historians who within a recent period have done so much to reconstruct the forgotten records of the people, the investigations of such men as Sir Henry Maine, Emile de Laveleye, Professor Nasse of Bonn, and others, into the growth of institutions, prove that wherever human society has formed, the common right of men to the use of the earth has been recognized, and that nowhere has unrestricted individual ownership been freely adopted. Historically, as ethically, private property in land is robbery. It nowhere springs from contract; it can nowhere be traced to perceptions of justice or expediency; it has everywhere had its birth in war and conquest, and in the selfish use which the cunning have made of superstition and law.

Wherever we can trace the early history of society, whether in Asia, in Europe, in Africa, in America, or in Polynesia, land has been considered, as the necessary relations which human life has to it would lead to its consideration—as common property, in which the rights of all who had admitted rights were equal. That is to say, that all members of the community, all citizens, as we should say, had equal rights to the use and enjoyment of the land of the community. This recognition of the common right to land did not prevent the full recognition of the particular and exclusive right in things which are the result of labor, nor was it abandoned when the development of agriculture had imposed the necessity of recognizing exclusive possession of land in order to secure the exclusive enjoyment of the results

of the labor expended in cultivating it. The division of
land between the industrial units, whether families, joint
families, or individuals, went only as far as was necessary for that purpose, pasture and forest lands being
retained as common, and equality as to agricultural land
being secured, either by a periodical redivision, as
among the Teutonic races, or by the prohibition of
alienation, as in the law of Moses.

This primary adjustment still exists, in more or less
intact form, in the village communities of India, Russia,
and the Sclavonic countries yet, or until recently, subjected to Turkish rule; in the mountain cantons of
Switzerland; among the Kabyles in the north of Africa,
and the Kaffirs in the south; among the native population of Java, and the aborigines of New Zealand—that
is to say, wherever extraneous influences have left intact
the form of primitive social organization. That it everywhere existed has been within late years abundantly
proved by the researches of many independent students
and observers, and which are, to my knowledge, best
summarized in the "Systems of Land Tenure in Various
Countries," published under authority of the Cobden
Club, and in M. Emile de Laveleye's "Primitive Property," to which I would refer the reader who desires to
see this truth displayed in detail.

"In all primitive societies," says M. de Laveleye, as
the result of an investigation which leaves no part of
the world unexplored—"in all primitive societies, the
soil was the joint property of the tribes and was subject
to periodical distribution among all the families, so
that all might live by their labor as nature has ordained.
The comfort of each was thus proportioned to his energy
and intelligence; no one, at any rate, was destitute
of the means of subsistence, and inequality increasing
from generation to generation was provided against."

If M. de Laveleye be right in this conclusion, and

that he is right there can be no doubt, how, it will be asked, has the reduction of land to private ownership become so general?

The causes which have operated to supplant this original idea of the equal right to the use of land by the idea of exclusive and unequal rights may, I think, be everywhere vaguely but certainly traced. They are everywhere the same which have led to the denial of equal personal rights and to the establishment of privileged classes.

These causes may be summarized as the concentration of power in the hands of chieftains and the military class, consequent on a state of warfare, which enabled them to monopolize common lands; the effect of conquest, in reducing the conquered to a state of predial slavery, and dividing their lands among the conquerors, and in disproportionate share to the chiefs; the differentiation and influence of a sacerdotal class, and the differentiation and influence of a class of professional lawyers, whose interests were served by the substitution of exclusive, in place of common, property in land* —inequality once produced always tending to greater inequality, by the law of attraction.

It was the struggle between this idea of equal rights to the soil and the tendency to monopolize it in individual possession, that caused the internal conflicts of Greece and Rome; it was the check given to this tendency—in Greece by such institutions as those of Lycurgus and Solon, and in Rome by the Licinian Law and subsequent divisions of land—that gave to each their days of strength and glory; and it was the final triumph of this tendency that destroyed both. Great

---

* The influence of the lawyers has been very marked in Europe, both on the Continent and in Great Britain, in destroying all vestiges of the ancient tenure, and substituting the idea of the Roman law, exclusive ownership.

estates ruined Greece, as afterward "great estates ruined Italy,"* and as the soil, in spite of the warnings of great legislators and statesmen, passed finally into the possession of a few, population declined, art sank, the intellect became emasculate, and the race in which humanity had attained its most splendid development became a byword and reproach among men.

The idea of absolute individual property in land, which modern civilization derived from Rome, reached its full development there in historic times. When the future mistress of the world first looms up, each citizen had his little homestead plot, which was inalienable, and the general domain—"the cornland which was of public right"—was subject to common use, doubtless under regulations or customs which secured equality, as in the Teutonic mark and Swiss allmend. It was from this public domain, constantly extended by conquest, that the patrician families succeeded in carving their great estates. These great estates by the power with which the great attracts the less, in spite of temporary checks by legal limitation and recurring divisions, finally crushed out all the small proprietors, adding their little patrimonies to the *latifundia* of the enormously rich, while they themselves were forced into the slave gangs, became rent-paying coloni, or else were driven into the freshly conquered foreign provinces, where land was given to the veterans of the legions; or to the metropolis, to swell the ranks of the proletariat who had nothing to sell but their votes.

Cæsarism, soon passing into an unbridled despotism of the Eastern type, was the inevitable political result, and the empire, even while it embraced the world, became in reality a shell, kept from collapse only by the healthier life of the frontiers, where the land had been divided among military settlers or the primitive usages

* *Latifundia perdidere Italiam.*—Pliny.

longer survived. But the *latifundia*, which had devoured the strength of Italy, crept steadily outward, carving the surface of Sicily, Africa, Spain, and Gaul into great estates cultivated by slaves or tenants. The hardy virtues born of personal independence died out, an exhaustive agriculture impoverished the soil, and wild beasts supplanted men, until at length, with a strength nurtured in equality, the barbarians broke through; Rome perished; and of a civilization once so proud nothing was left but ruins.

Thus came to pass that marvelous thing, which at the time of Rome's grandeur would have seemed as impossible as it seems now to us that the Comanches or Flatheads should conquer the United States, or the Laplanders should desolate Europe. The fundamental cause is to be sought in the tenure of land. On the one hand, the denial of the common right to land had resulted in decay; on the other, equality gave strength.

"Freedom," says M. de Laveleye ("Primitive Property," p. 116), "freedom, and, as a consequence, the ownership of an undivided share of the common property, to which the head of every family in the clan was equally entitled, were in the German village essential rights. This system of absolute equality impressed a remarkable character on the individual, which explains how small bands of barbarians made themselves masters of the Roman Empire, in spite of its skillful administration, its perfect centralization and its civil law, which has preserved the name of written reason."

It was, on the other hand, that the heart was eaten out of that great empire. "Rome perished," says Professor Seeley, "from the failure of the crop of men."

In his lectures on the "History of Civilization in Europe," and more elaborately in his lectures on the "History of Civilization in France," M. Guizot has vividly described the chaos that in Europe succeeded the fall of the Roman Empire—a chaos which, as he says, "carried all things in its bosom," and from which the structure of modern society was slowly evolved. It is a picture which cannot be compressed into a few lines, but suffice it to say that the result of this infusion of rude but vigorous life into Romanized society was a disorganization of the German, as well as the Roman structures—both a blending and an admixture of the idea of common rights in the soil with the idea of exclusive property, substantially as occurred in those provinces of the Eastern Empire subsequently overrun by the Turks. The feudal system, which was so readily adopted and so widely spread, was the result of such a blending; but underneath, and side by side with the feudal system, a more primitive organization, based on the common rights of the cultivators, took root or revived, and has left its traces all over Europe. This primitive organization, which allots equal shares of cultivated ground and the common use of uncultivated ground, and which existed in ancient Italy as in Saxon England, has maintained itself beneath absolutism and serfdom in Russia, beneath Moslem oppression in Servia, and in India has been swept, but not entirely destroyed, by wave after wave of conquest, and century after century of oppression.

The feudal system, which is not peculiar to Europe, but seems to be the natural result of the conquest of a settled country by a race among whom equality and individuality are yet strong, clearly recognized, in theory at least, that the land belongs to society at large, not to the individual. Rude outcome of an age in which might stood for right as nearly as it ever can (for the idea of right is ineradicable from the human mind, and must in some shape show itself even in the association of pirates and robbers), the feudal system yet admitted in no one the uncontrolled and exclusive right to land. A fief was essentially a trust, and to enjoyment was annexed obligation. The sovereign, theoretically the representative of the collective power and rights of the whole people, was in feudal view the only absolute owner of land. And though land was granted to individual possession, yet in its possession were involved duties, by which the enjoyer of its revenues was supposed to render back to the commonwealth an equivalent for the benefits which from the delegation of the common right he received.

In the feudal scheme the crown lands supported public expenditures which are now included in the civil list; the church lands defrayed the cost of public worship and instruction, of the care of the sick and of the destitute, and maintained a class of men who were supposed to be, and no doubt to a great extent were, devoting their lives to purposes of public good; while the military tenures provided for the public defense. In the obligation under which the military tenant lay to bring into the field such and such a force when need should be, as well as in the aid he had to give when the sovereign's eldest son was knighted, his daughter married, or the sovereign himself made prisoner of war, was a rude and inefficient recognition, but still unquestionably a recognition, of the fact, obvious to the natural perceptions of all men, that land is not individual but common property.

Nor yet was the control of the possessor of land allowed to extend beyond his own life. Although the principle of inheritance soon displaced the principle of selection, as where power is concentrated it always must, yet feudal law required that there should always be some representative of a fief, capable of discharging the duties as well as of receiving the benefits which were annexed to a landed estate, and who this should be was not left to individual caprice, but rigorously determined in advance. Hence wardship and other feudal incidents. The system of primogeniture and its outgrowth, the entail, were in their beginnings not the absurdities they afterward became.

The basis of the feudal system was the absolute ownership of the land, an idea which the barbarians readily acquired in the midst of a conquered population to whom it was familiar; but over this, feudalism threw a superior right, and the process of infeudation consisted of bringing individual dominion into subordination to the superior dominion, which represented the larger community or nation. Its units were the landowners, who by virtue of their ownership were absolute lords on their own domains, and who there performed the office of protection which M. Taine has so graphically described, though perhaps with too strong a coloring, in the opening chapter of his "Ancient Régime." The work of the feudal system was to bind together these units into nations, and to subordinate the powers and rights of the individual lords of land to the powers and rights of collective society, as represented by the suzerain or king.

Thus the feudal system, in its rise and development, was a triumph of the idea of the common right to land, changing an absolute tenure into a conditional tenure, and imposing peculiar obligations in return for the privilege of receiving rent. And during the same time, the power of landownership was trenched, as it were, from below, the tenancy at will of the cultivators of the soil very generally hardening into tenancy by custom, and the rent which the lord could exact from the peasant becoming fixed and certain.

And amid the feudal system there remained, or there grew up, communities of cultivators, more or less subject to feudal dues, who tilled the soil as common property; and although the lords, where and when they had

the power, claimed pretty much all they thought worth
claiming, yet the idea of common right was strong
enough to attach itself by custom to a considerable part
of the land. The commons, in feudal ages, must have
embraced a very large proportion of the area of most
European countries. For in France (although the ap-
propriations of these lands by the aristocracy, occasionally checked and rescinded by royal edict, had gone
on for some centuries prior to the Revolution, and during the Revolution and First Empire large distributions
and sales were made), the common or communal lands
still amount, according to M. de Laveleye, to 4,000,000
hectares, or 9,884,400 acres. The extent of the common
land of England during the feudal ages may be inferred
from the fact that though inclosures by the landed aristocracy began during the reign of Henry VII, it is stated
that no less than 7,660,413 acres of common lands
were inclosed under Acts passed between 1710 and 1843,
of which 600,000 acres have been inclosed since 1845;
and it is estimated that there still remain 2,000,000 acres
of common in England, though of course the most worthless parts of the soil.

In addition to these common lands, there existed in
France, until the Revolution, and in parts of Spain,
until our own day, a custom having all the force of
law, by which cultivated lands, after the harvest had
been gathered, became common for purposes of pas-
turage or travel, until the time had come to use the
ground again; and in some places a custom by which
any one had the right to go upon the ground which its
owner neglected to cultivate, and there to sow and reap
a crop in security. And if he chose to use manure for
the first crop, he acquired the right to sow and gather
a second crop without let or hindrance from the owner.

It is not merely the Swiss allmend, the Ditmarsh
mark, the Servian and Russian village communities;

not merely the long ridges which on English ground, now the exclusive property of individuals, still enable the antiquarian to trace out the great fields in ancient time devoted to the triennial rotation of crops, and in which each villager was annually allotted his equal plot; not merely the documentary evidence which careful students have within late years drawn from old records; but the very institutions under which modern civilization has developed, which prove the universality and long persistence of the recognition of the common right to the use of the soil.

There still remain in our legal systems survivals that have lost their meaning, that, like the still existing remains of the ancient commons of England, point to this. The doctrine of eminent domain, existing as well in Mohammedan law, which makes the sovereign theoretically the only absolute owner of land, springs from nothing but the recognition of the sovereign as the representative of the collective rights of the people; primogeniture and entail, which still exist in England, and which existed in some of the American states a hundred years ago, are but distorted forms of what was once an outgrowth of the apprehension of land as common property. The very distinction made in legal terminology between real and personal property is but the survival of a primitive distinction between what was originally looked upon as common property and what from its nature was always considered the peculiar property of the individual. And the greater care and ceremony which are yet required for the transfer of land is but a survival, now meaningless and useless, of the more general and ceremonious consent once required for the transfer of rights which were looked upon, not as belonging to any one member, but to every member of a family or tribe.

The general course of the development of modern

civilization since the feudal period has been to the subversion of these natural and primary ideas of collective
ownership in the soil. Paradoxical as it may appear,
the emergence of liberty from feudal bonds has been
accompanied by a tendency in the treatment of land to
the form of ownership which involves the enslavement
of the working classes, and which is now beginning to
be strongly felt all over the civilized world, in the pressure of an iron yoke, which cannot be relieved by any
extension of mere political power or personal liberty,
and which political economists mistake for the pressure of natural laws, and workmen for the oppressions
of capital.

This is clear—that in Great Britain today the right
of the people as a whole to the soil of their native country is much less fully acknowledged than it was in feudal
times. A much smaller proportion of the people own the
soil, and their ownership is much more absolute. The
commons, once so extensive and so largely contributing to the independence and support of the lower
classes, have, all but a small remnant of yet worthless
land, been appropriated to individual ownership and
inclosed; the great estates of the Church, which were
essentially common property devoted to a public purpose, have been diverted from that trust to enrich
individuals; the dues of the military tenants have been
shaken off, and the cost of maintaining the military
establishment and paying the interest upon an immense
debt accumulated by wars has been saddled upon the
whole people, in taxes upon the necessaries and comforts of life. The crown lands have mostly passed into
private possession, and for the support of the royal
family and all the petty princelings who marry into it,
the British workman must pay in the price of his mug
of beer and pipe of tobacco. The English yeoman—the
sturdy breed who won Crecy, and Poictiers, and Agin-

court—is as extinct as the mastodon. The Scottish clansman, whose right to the soil of his native hills was then as undisputed as that of his chieftain, has been driven out to make room for the sheep ranges or deer parks of that chieftain's descendant; the tribal right of the Irishman has been turned into a tenancy-at-will. Thirty thousand men have legal power to expel the whole population from five-sixths of the British Islands, and the vast majority of the British people have no right whatever to their native land save to walk the streets or trudge the roads. To them may be fittingly applied the words of a Tribune of the Roman People: "Men of Rome," said Tiberius Gracchus—"men of Rome, you are called the lords of the world, yet have no right to a square foot of its soil! The wild beasts have their dens, but the soldiers of Italy have only water and air!"

The result has, perhaps, been more marked in England than anywhere else, but the tendency is observable everywhere, having gone further in England owing to circumstances which have developed it with greater rapidity.

The reason, I take it, that with the extension of the idea of personal freedom has gone on an extension of the idea of private property in land, is that as in the progress of civilization the grosser forms of supremacy connected with landownership were dropped, or abolished, or became less obvious, attention was diverted from the more insidious, but really more potential forms, and the landowners were easily enabled to put property in land on the same basis as other property.

The growth of national power, either in the form of royalty or parliamentary government, stripped the great lords of individual power and importance, and of their jurisdiction and power over persons, and so repressed striking abuses, as the growth of Roman Imperialism repressed the more striking cruelties of slavery. The disintegration of the large feudal estates, which, until the tendency to concentration arising from the modern tendency to production upon a large scale is strongly felt, operated to increase the number of landowners, and the abolition of the restraints by which landowners when population was sparser endeavored to compel laborers to remain on their estates also contributed to draw away attention from the essential injustice involved in private property in land; while the steady progress of legal ideas drawn from the Roman law, which has been the great mine and storehouse of modern jurisprudence, tended to level the natural distinction between property in land and property in other things. Thus, with the extension of personal liberty, went on an extension of individual proprietorship in land.

The political power of the barons was, moreover, not broken by the revolt of the classes who could clearly feel the injustice of landownership. Such revolts took place, again and again; but again and again were they repressed with terrific cruelties. What broke the power of the barons was the growth of the artisan and trading classes, between whose wages and rent there is not the same obvious relation. These classes, too, developed under a system of close guilds and corporations, which, as I have previously explained in treating of trade combinations and monopolies, enabled them somewhat to fence themselves in from the operation of the general law of wages, and which were much more easily maintained than now, when the effect of improved methods of transportation, and the diffusion of rudimentary education and of current news, is steadily making population more mobile. These classes did not see, and do not yet see, that the tenure of land is the fundamental fact which must ultimately determine the conditions of industrial, social, and political life. And so the tendency has been to assimilate the idea of property in land with that of property in things of human production, and even steps backward have been taken, and been hailed, as steps in advance. The French Constituent Assembly, in 1789, thought it was sweeping away a relic of tyranny when it abolished tithes and imposed the support of the clergy on general taxation. The Abbé Sieyès stood alone when he told them that they were simply remitting to the proprietors a tax which was one of the conditions on which they held their lands, and reimposing it on the labor of the nation. But in vain. The Abbé Sieyès, being a priest, was looked on as defending the interests of his order, when in truth he was defending the rights of man. In those tithes, the French people might have retained a large public revenue which would not have taken one centime from the wages of labor or the earnings of capital.

And so the abolition of the military tenures in England by the Long Parliament, ratified after the accession of Charles II, though simply an appropriation of public revenues by the feudal landholders, who thus got rid of the consideration on which they held the common property of the nation, and saddled it on the people at large, in the taxation of all consumers, has long been characterized, and is still held up in the law books, as a triumph of the spirit of freedom. Yet here is the source of the immense debt and heavy taxation of England. Had the form of these feudal dues been simply changed into one better adapted to the changed times, English wars need never have occasioned the incurring of debt to the amount of a single pound, and the labor and capital of England need not have been taxed a single farthing for the maintenance of a military establishment. All this would have come from rent, which the landholders since that time have appropriated to themselves—from the tax which land-ownership levies on the earnings of labor and capital.

The landholders of England got their land on terms which required them even in the sparse population of Norman days to put in the field, upon call, sixty thousand perfectly equipped horsemen,* and on the further condition of various fines and incidents which amounted to a considerable part of the rent. It would probably be a low estimate to put the pecuniary value of these various services and dues at one-half the rental value of the land. Had the landholders been kept to this contract and no land been permitted to be inclosed except upon similar terms, the income accruing to the nation from English land would today be greater by many millions than the entire public revenues of the United Kingdom. England today might have enjoyed absolute free trade. There need not have been a customs duty, an excise, license, or income tax, yet all the present expenditures could be met, and a large surplus remain to be devoted to any purpose which would conduce to the comfort or well-being of the whole people.

Turning back, wherever there is light to guide us, we may everywhere see that in their first perceptions, all peoples have recognized the common ownership in land, and that private property in land is an usurpation, a creation of force and fraud.

As Madame de Stael said, "Liberty is ancient." Justice, if we turn to the most ancient records, will always be found to have the title of prescription.

---

* Andrew Bisset, in "The Strength of Nations," London, 1859, a suggestive work in which he calls the attention of the English people to this measure by which the landowners avoided the payment of their rent to the nation, disputes the statement of Blackstone that a knight's service was but for 40 days, and says it was during necessity.

5 OF PROPERTY IN LAND
IN THE UNITED STATES

In the earlier stages of civilization we see that land is everywhere regarded as common property. And, turning from the dim past to our own times, we may see that natural perceptions are still the same, and that when placed under circumstances in which the influence of education and habit is weakened, men instinctively recognize the equality of right to the bounty of nature.

The discovery of gold in California brought together in a new country men who had been used to look on land as the rightful subject of individual property, and of whom probably not one in a thousand had ever dreamed of drawing any distinction between property in land and property in anything else. But, for the first time in the history of the Anglo-Saxon race, these men were brought into contact with land from which gold could be obtained by the simple operation of washing it out.

Had the land with which they were thus called upon to deal been agricultural, or grazing, or forest land, of peculiar richness; had it been land which derived peculiar value from its situation for commercial purposes, or by reason of the water power which it afforded; or even had it contained rich mines of coal, iron or lead, the land system to which they had been used would have been applied, and it would have been reduced to private ownership in large tracts, as even the pueblo lands of

San Francisco, really the most valuable in the state, which by Spanish law had been set apart to furnish homes for the future residents of that city, were reduced, without any protest worth speaking of. But the novelty of the case broke through habitual ideas, and threw men back upon first principles, and it was by common consent declared that this gold-bearing land should remain common property, of which no one might take more than he could reasonably use, or hold for a longer time than he continued to use it. This perception of natural justice was acquiesced in by the General Government and the courts, and while placer mining remained of importance, no attempt was made to overrule this reversion to primitive ideas. The title to the land remained in the government, and no individual could acquire more than a possessory claim. The miners in each district fixed the amount of ground an individual could take and the amount of work that must be done to constitute use. If this work were not done, any one could relocate the ground. Thus, no one was allowed to forestall or to lock up natural resources. Labor was acknowledged as the creator of wealth, was given a free field, and secured in its reward. The device would not have assured complete equality of rights under the conditions that in most countries prevail; but under the conditions that there and then existed—a sparse population, an unexplored country, and an occupation in its nature a lottery, it secured substantial justice. One man might strike an enormously rich deposit, and others might vainly prospect for months and years, but all had an equal chance. No one was allowed to play the dog in the manger with the bounty of the Creator. The essential idea of the mining regulations was to prevent forestalling and monopoly. Upon the same principle are based the mining laws of Mexico; and the same principle was adopted in Australia, in British

Columbia, and in the diamond fields of South Africa, for it accords with natural perceptions of justice.

With the decadence of placer mining in California, the accustomed idea of private property finally pre- vailed in the passage of a law permitting the patenting of mineral lands. The only effect is to lock up oppor- tunities—to give the owner of mining ground the power of saying that no one else may use what he does not choose to use himself. And there are many cases in which mining ground is thus withheld from use for speculative purposes, just as valuable building lots and agricultural land are withheld from use. But while thus preventing use, the extension to mineral land of the same principle of private ownership which marks the tenure of other lands has done nothing for the security of improvements. The greatest expenditures of capital in opening and developing mines—expenditures that in some cases amounted to millions of dollars—were made upon possessory titles.

Had the circumstances which beset the first English settlers in North America been such as to call their attention de novo to the question of landownership, there can be no doubt that they would have reverted to first principles, just as they reverted to first principles in matters of government; and individual landowner- ship would have been rejected, just as aristocracy and monarchy were rejected. But while in the country from which they came this system had not yet fully developed itself, nor its effects been fully felt, the fact that in the new country an immense continent invited settlement prevented any question of the justice and policy of private property in land from arising. For in a new country, equality seems sufficiently assured if no one is permitted to take land to the exclusion of the rest. At first no harm seems to be done by treating this land as absolute property. There is plenty of land left for those who choose to take it, and the slavery that in a later stage of development necessarily springs from the individual ownership of land is not felt.

In Virginia and to the South, where the settlement had an aristocratic character, the natural complement of the large estates into which the land was carved was introduced in the shape of Negro slaves. But the first settlers of New England divided the land as, twelve centuries before, their ancestors had divided the land of Britain, giving to each head of a family his town lot and his seed lot, while beyond lay the free common. So far as concerned the great proprietors whom the English kings by letters patent endeavored to create, the settlers saw clearly enough the injustice of the attempted monopoly, and none of these proprietors got much from their grants; but the plentifulness of land prevented attention from being called to the monopoly which individual landownership, even when the tracts are small, must involve when land becomes scarce. And so it has come to pass that the great republic of the modern world has adopted at the beginning of its career an institution that ruined the republics of antiquity; that a people who proclaim the inalienable rights of all men to life, liberty, and the pursuit of happiness have accepted without question a principle which, in denying the equal and inalienable right to the soil, finally denies the equal right to life and liberty; that a people who at the cost of a bloody war have abolished chattel slavery, yet permit slavery in a more widespread and dangerous form to take root.

The continent has seemed so wide, the area over which population might yet pour so vast, that familiarized by habit with the idea of private property in land, we have not realized its essential injustice. For not merely has this background of unsettled land prevented the full effect of private appropriation from being felt, even in the older sections, but to permit a man to take more land than he could use, that he might compel those who afterwards needed it to pay him for the privilege of using it, has not seemed so unjust when others in their turn might do the same thing by going further on. And more than this, the very fortunes that have resulted from the appropriation of land, and that have thus really been drawn from taxes levied upon the wages of labor, have seemed, and have been heralded, as prizes held out to the laborer. In all the newer States, and even to a considerable extent in the older ones, our landed aristocracy is yet in its first generation. Those who have profited by the increase in the value of land have been largely men who began life without a cent. Their great fortunes, many of them running up high into the millions, seem to them, and to many others, as the best proofs of the justice of existing social conditions in rewarding prudence, foresight, industry, and thrift; whereas, the truth is that these fortunes are but the gains of monopoly, and are necessarily made at the expense of labor. But the fact that those thus enriched started as laborers hides this, and the same feeling which leads every ticket holder in a lottery to delight in imagination in the magnitude of the prizes has prevented even the poor from quarreling with a system which thus made many poor men rich.

In short, the American people have failed to see the essential injustice of private property in land, because as yet they have not felt its full effects. This public domain—the vast extent of land yet to be reduced to private possession, the enormous common to which the faces of the energetic were always turned, has been the great fact that, since the days when the first settlements began to fringe the Atlantic Coast, has formed our national character and colored our national thought. It is not that we have eschewed a titled aristocracy and

abolished primogeniture; that we elect all our officers
from school director up to president; that our laws
run in the name of the people, instead of in the name of
a prince; that the State knows no religion, and our
judges wear no wigs—that we have been exempted from
the ills that Fourth of July orators used to point to as
characteristic of the effete despotisms of the Old World.
The general intelligence, the general comfort, the active
invention, the power of adaptation and assimilation,
the free, independent spirit, the energy and hopefulness
that have marked our people, are not causes, but results
—they have sprung from unfenced land. This public
domain has been the transmuting force which has turned
the thriftless, unambitious European peasant into the
self-reliant Western farmer; it has given a consciousness
of freedom even to the dweller in crowded cities, and
has been a wellspring of hope even to those who have
never thought of taking refuge upon it. The child of
the people, as he grows to manhood in Europe, finds all
the best seats at the banquet of life marked "taken,"
and must struggle with his fellows for the crumbs that
fall, without one chance in a thousand of forcing or
sneaking his way to a seat. In America, whatever his
condition, there has always been the consciousness that
the public domain lay behind him; and the knowledge
of this fact, acting and reacting, has penetrated our
whole national life, giving to it generosity and independence, elasticity and ambition. All that we are
proud of in the American character; all that makes
our conditions and institutions better than those of
older countries, we may trace to the fact that land has
been cheap in the United States, because new soil has
been open to the emigrant.

But our advance has reached the Pacific. Further
west we cannot go, and increasing population can but
expand north and south and fill up what has been passed

over. North, it is already filling up the valley of the Red River, pressing into that of the Saskatchewan and pre-empting Washington Territory; south, it is covering western Texas and taking up the arable valleys of New Mexico and Arizona.

The republic has entered upon a new era, an era in which the monopoly of the land will tell with accelerating effect. The great fact which has been so potent is ceasing to be. The public domain is almost gone—a very few years will end its influence, already rapidly failing. I do not mean to say that there will be no public domain. For a long time to come there will be millions of acres of public lands carried on the books of the Land Department. But it must be remembered that the best part of the continent for agricultural purposes is already overrun, and that it is the poorest land that is left. It must be remembered that what remains comprises the great mountain ranges, the sterile deserts, the high plains fit only for grazing. And it must be remembered that much of this land which figures in the reports as open to settlement is unsurveyed land, which has been appropriated by possessory claims or locations which do not appear until the land is returned as surveyed. California figures on the books of the Land Department as the greatest land state of the Union, containing nearly 100,000,000 acres of public land—something like one-twelfth of the whole public domain. Yet so much of this is covered by railroad grants or held in the way of which I have spoken; so much consists of untillable mountains or plains which require irrigation; so much is monopolized by locations which command the water, that as a matter of fact it is difficult to point the immigrant to any part of the state where he can take up a farm on which he can settle and maintain a family, and so men, weary of the quest, end by buying land or renting it on shares. It is not that there is any real scarcity of land in California—for, an empire in herself, California will some day maintain a population as large as that of France—but appropriation has got ahead of the settler and manages to keep just ahead of him.

Some twelve or fifteen years ago the late Ben Wade of Ohio said, in a speech in the United States Senate, that by the close of this century every acre of ordinary agricultural land in the United States would be worth $50 in gold. It is already clear that if he erred at all, it was in overstating the time. In the twenty-one years that remain of the present century, if our population keep on increasing at the rate which it has maintained since the institution of the government, with the exception of the decade which included the civil war, there will be an addition to our present population of something like forty-five millions, an addition of some seven millions more than the total population of the United States as shown by the census of 1870, and nearly half as much again as the present population of Great Britain. There is no question about the ability of the United States to support such a population and many hundreds of millions more, and, under proper social adjustments, to support them in increased comfort; but in view of such an increase of population, what becomes of the unappropriated public domain? Practically there will soon cease to be any. It will be a very long time before it is all in use; but it will be a very short time, as we are going, before all that men can turn to use will have an owner.

But the evil effects of making the land of a whole people the exclusive property of some do not wait for the final appropriation of the public domain to show themselves. It is not necessary to contemplate them in the future; we may see them in the present. They have grown with our growth, and are still increasing.

We plow new fields, we open new mines, we found new

cities; we drive back the Indian and exterminate the buffalo; we girdle the land with iron roads and lace the air with telegraph wires; we add knowledge to knowledge, and utilize invention after invention; we build schools and endow colleges; yet it becomes no easier for the masses of our people to make a living. On the contrary, it is becoming harder. The wealthy class is becoming more wealthy; but the poorer class is becoming more dependent. The gulf between the employed and the employer is growing wider; social contrasts are becoming sharper; as liveried carriages appear, so do barefooted children. We are becoming used to talk of the working classes and the propertied classes; beggars are becoming so common that where it was once thought a crime little short of highway robbery to refuse food to one who asked for it, the gate is now barred and the bulldog loosed, while laws are passed against vagrants which suggest those of Henry VIII.

We call ourselves the most progressive people on earth. But what is the goal of our progress, if these are its wayside fruits?

These are the results of private property in land—the effects of a principle that must act with increasing and increasing force. It is not that laborers have increased faster than capital; it is not that population is pressing against subsistence; it is not that machinery has made "work scarce"; it is not that there is any real antagonism between labor and capital—it is simply that land is becoming more valuable; that the terms on which labor can obtain access to the natural opportunities which alone enable it to produce are becoming harder and harder. The public domain is receding and narrowing. Property in land is concentrating. The proportion of our people who have no legal right to the land on which they live is becoming steadily larger.

Says the New York *World*: "A nonresident proprietary, like that of Ireland, is getting to be the characteristic of large farming districts in New England, adding yearly to the nominal value of leasehold farms; advancing yearly the rent demanded, and steadily degrading the character of the tenantry." And the *Nation*, alluding to the same section, says: "Increased nominal value of land, higher rents, fewer farms occupied by owners; diminished product; lower wages; a more ignorant population; increasing number of women employed at hard, outdoor labor (surest sign of a declining civilization), and a steady deterioration in the style of farming—these are the conditions described by a cumulative mass of evidence that is perfectly irresistible."

The same tendency is observable in the new states, where the large scale of cultivation recalls the *latifundia* that ruined ancient Italy. In California a very large proportion of the farming land is rented from year to year, at rates varying from a fourth to even half the crop.

The harder times, the lower wages, the increasing poverty perceptible in the United States are but results of the natural laws we have traced—laws as universal and as irresistible as that of gravitation. We did not establish the republic when, in the face of principalities and powers, we flung the declaration of the inalienable rights of man; we shall never establish the republic until we practically carry out that declaration by securing to the poorest child born among us an equal right to his native soil! We did not abolish slavery when we ratified the Fourteenth Amendment; to abolish slavery we must abolish private property in land! Unless we come back to first principles, unless we recognize natural perceptions of equity, unless we acknowledge the equal right of all to land, our free institutions will be in vain; our common schools will be in vain; our discoveries and inventions will but add to the force that presses the masses down!

Why hesitate? Ye are full-bearded men,
With God-implanted will, and courage if
Ye dare but show it. Never yet was will
But found some way or means to work it out,
Nor e'er did Fortune frown on him who dared.
Shall we in presence of this grievous wrong,
In this supremest moment of all time,
Stand trembling, cowering, when with one bold stroke
These groaning millions might be ever free?—
And that one stroke so just, so greatly good,
So level with the happiness of man,
That all the angels will applaud the deed.

—E. R. TAYLOR.

CHAPTER 1

PRIVATE PROPERTY IN LAND INCONSISTENT WITH THE BEST USE OF LAND

There is a delusion resulting from the tendency to confound the accidental with the essential—a delusion which the law writers have done their best to extend, and political economists generally have acquiesced in, rather than endeavored to expose—that private property in land is necessary to the proper use of land, and that again to make land common property would be to destroy civilization and revert to barbarism.

This delusion may be likened to the idea which, according to Charles Lamb, so long prevailed among the Chinese after the savor of roast pork had been accidentally discovered by the burning down of Ho-ti's hut —that to cook a pig it was necessary to set fire to a house. But, though in Lamb's charming dissertation it was required that a sage should arise to teach people that they might roast pigs without burning down houses, it does not take a sage to see that what is required for the improvement of land is not absolute ownership of the land, but security for the improvements. This will be obvious to whoever will look around him. While there is no more necessity for making a man the absolute and exclusive owner of land, in order to induce him to improve it, than there is of burning down a house in order to cook a pig; while the making of land private property is as rude, wasteful, and uncertain a device for securing improvement, as the burning down of a house

397

is a rude, wasteful, and uncertain device for roasting a pig, we have not the excuse for persisting in the one that Lamb's Chinamen had for persisting in the other. Until the sage arose who invented the rude gridiron, which, according to Lamb, preceded the spit and oven, no one had known or heard of a pig being roasted, except by a house being burned. But, among us, nothing is more common than for land to be improved by those who do not own it. The greater part of the land of Great Britain is cultivated by tenants, the greater part of the buildings of London are built upon leased ground, and even in the United States the same system prevails everywhere to a greater or less extent. Thus it is a common matter for use to be separated from ownership.

Would not all this land be cultivated and improved just as well if the rent went to the State or municipality, as now, when it goes to private individuals? If no private ownership in land were acknowledged, but all land were held in this way, the occupier or user paying rent to the State, would not land be used and improved as well and as securely as now? There can be but one answer: Of course it would. Then would the resumption of land as common property in nowise interfere with the proper use and improvement of land.

What is necessary for the use of land is not its private ownership, but the security of improvements. It is not necessary to say to a man, "this land is yours," in order to induce him to cultivate or improve it. It is only necessary to say to him, "whatever your labor or capital produces on this land shall be yours." Give a man security that he may reap, and he will sow; assure him of the possession of the house he wants to build, and he will build it. These are the natural rewards of labor. It is for the sake of the reaping that men sow; it is for the sake of possessing houses that men build. The ownership of land has nothing to do with it.

It was for the sake of obtaining this security, that in the beginning of the feudal period so many of the smaller landholders surrendered the ownership of their lands to a military chieftain, receiving back the use of them in fief or trust, and kneeling bareheaded before the lord, with their hands between his hands, swore to serve him with life, and limb, and worldly honor. Similar instances of the giving up of ownership in land for the sake of security in its enjoyment are to be seen in Turkey, where a peculiar exemption from taxation and extortion attaches to *vakouf*, or church lands, and where it is a common thing for a landowner to sell his land to a mosque for a nominal price, with the understanding that he may remain as tenant upon it at a fixed rent.

It is not the magic of property, as Arthur Young said, that has turned Flemish sands into fruitful fields. It is the magic of security to labor. This can be secured in other ways than making land private property, just as the heat necessary to roast a pig can be secured in other ways than by burning down houses. The mere pledge of an Irish landlord that for twenty years he would not claim in rent any share in their cultivation induced Irish peasants to turn a barren mountain into gardens; on the mere security of a fixed ground rent for a term of years the most costly buildings of such cities as London and New York are erected on leased ground. If we give improvers such security, we may safely abolish private property in land.

The complete recognition of common rights to land need in no way interfere with the complete recognition of individual right to improvements or produce. Two men may own a ship without sawing her in half. The ownership of a railway may be divided into a hundred thousand shares, and yet trains be run with as much system and precision as if there were but a single owner.

In London, joint-stock companies have been formed to hold and manage real estate. Everything could go on as now, and yet the common right to land be fully recognized by appropriating rent to the common benefit. There is a lot in the center of San Francisco to which the common rights of the people of that city are yet legally recognized. This lot is not cut up into infinitesimal pieces nor yet is it an unused waste. It is covered with fine buildings, the property of private individuals, that stand there in perfect security. The only difference between this lot and those around it, is that the rent of the one goes into the common school fund, the rent of the others into private pockets. What is to prevent the land of a whole country being held by the people of the country in this way?

It would be difficult to select any portion of the territory of the United States in which the conditions commonly taken to necessitate the reduction of land to private ownership exist in higher degree than on the little islets of St. Peter and St. Paul, in the Aleutian Archipelago, acquired by the Alaska purchase from Russia. These islands are the breeding places of the fur seal, an animal so timid and wary that the slightest fright causes it to abandon its accustomed resort, never to return. To prevent the utter destruction of this fishery, without which the islands are of no use to man, it is not only necessary to avoid killing the females and young cubs, but even such noises as the discharge of a pistol or the barking of a dog. The men who do the killing must be in no hurry, but quietly walk around among the seals who line the rocky beaches, until the timid animals, so clumsy on land but so graceful in water, show no more sign of fear than lazily to waddle out of the way. Then those who can be killed without diminution of future increase are carefully separated and gently driven inland, out of sight and hearing of the herds, where they are dispatched with clubs. To throw such a fishery as this open to whoever chose to go and kill—which would make it to the interest of each party to kill as many as they could at the time without reference to the future—would be utterly to destroy it in a few seasons, as similar fisheries in other oceans have been destroyed. But it is not necessary, therefore, to make these islands private property. Though for reasons greatly less cogent, the great public domain of the American people has been made over to private ownership as fast as anybody could be got to take it, these islands have been leased at a rent of $317,500 per year,* probably not very much less than they could have been sold for at the time of the Alaska purchase. They have already yielded two millions and a half to the national treasury, and they are still, in unimpaired value (for under the careful management of the Alaska Fur Company the seals increase rather than diminish), the common property of the people of the United States.

So far from the recognition of private property in land being necessary to the proper use of land, the contrary is the case. Treating land as private property stands in the way of its proper use. Were land treated as public property it would be used and improved as soon as there was need for its use or improvement, but being treated as private property, the individual owner is permitted to prevent others from using or improving what he cannot or will not use or improve himself. When the title is in dispute, the most valuable land lies unimproved for years; in many parts of England improvement is stopped because, the estates being entailed, no security to improvers can be given; and large tracts

---

* The fixed rent under the lease to the Alaska Fur Company is $55,000 a year, with a payment of $2.62½ on each skin, which on 100,000 skins, to which the take is limited, amounts to $262,500—a total rent of $317,500.

of ground which, were they treated as public property, would be covered with buildings and crops, are kept idle to gratify the caprice of the owner. In the thickly settled parts of the United States there is enough land to maintain three or four times our present population, lying unused, because its owners are holding it for higher prices, and immigrants are forced past this unused land to seek homes where their labor will be far less productive. In every city valuable lots may be seen lying vacant for the same reason. If the best use of land be the test, then private property in land is condemned, as it is condemned by every other consideration. It is as wasteful and uncertain a mode of securing the proper use of land as the burning down of houses is of roasting pigs.

CHAPTER 2

HOW EQUAL RIGHTS TO THE LAND MAY BE ASSERTED AND SECURED

We have traced the want and suffering that everywhere prevail among the working classes, the recurring paroxysms of industrial depression, the scarcity of employment, the stagnation of capital, the tendency of wages to the starvation point, that exhibit themselves more and more strongly as material progress goes on, to the fact that the land on which and from which all must live is made the exclusive property of some.

We have seen that there is no possible remedy for these evils but the abolition of their cause; we have seen that private property in land has no warrant in justice, but stands condemned as the denial of natural right—a subversion of the law of nature that as social development goes on must condemn the masses of men to a slavery the hardest and most degrading.

We have weighed every objection, and seen that neither on the ground of equity or expediency is there anything to deter us from making land common property by confiscating rent.

But a question of method remains. How shall we do it?

We should satisfy the law of justice, we should meet all economic requirements, by at one stroke abolishing all private titles, declaring all land public property, and letting it out to the highest bidders in lots to suit, under such conditions as would sacredly guard the private right to improvements.

Thus we should secure, in a more complex state of society, the same equality of rights that in a ruder state were secured by equal partitions of the soil, and by giving the use of the land to whoever could procure the most from it, we should secure the greatest production.

Such a plan, instead of being a wild, impracticable vagary, has (with the exception that he suggests compensation to the present holders of land—undoubtedly a careless concession which he upon reflection would reconsider) been indorsed by no less eminent a thinker than Herbert Spencer, who ("Social Statics," Chap. IX, Sec. 8) says of it:

"Such a doctrine is consistent with the highest state of civilization; may be carried out without involving a community of goods, and need cause no very serious revolution in existing arrangements. The change required would simply be a change of landlords. Separate ownership would merge into the joint-stock ownership of the public. Instead of being in the possession of individuals, the country would be held by the great corporate body—society. Instead of leasing his acres from an isolated proprietor, the farmer would lease them from the nation. Instead of paying his rent to the agent of Sir John or his Grace, he would pay it to an agent or deputy agent of the community. Stewards would be public officials instead of private ones, and tenancy the only land tenure. A state of things so ordered would be in perfect harmony with the moral law. Under it all men would be equally landlords, all men would be alike free to become tenants. . . . Clearly, therefore, on such a system, the earth might be enclosed, occupied and cultivated, in entire subordination to the law of equal freedom."

But such a plan, though perfectly feasible, does not seem to me the best. Or rather I propose to accomplish the same thing in a simpler, easier, and quieter way, than that of formally confiscating all the land and formally letting it out to the highest bidders.

To do that would involve a needless shock to present customs and habits of thought—which is to be avoided.

To do that would involve a needless extension of governmental machinery—which is to be avoided.

It is an axiom of statesmanship, which the successful

founders of tyranny have understood and acted upon—
that great changes can best be brought about under old
forms. We, who would free men, should heed the same
truth. It is the natural method. When nature would
make a higher type, she takes a lower one and develops
it. This, also, is the law of social growth. Let us work
by it. With the current we may glide fast and far.
Against it, it is hard pulling and slow progress.

I do not propose either to purchase or to confiscate
private property in land. The first would be unjust;
the second, needless. Let the individuals who now hold
it still retain, if they want to, possession of what they
are pleased to call *their* land. Let them continue to
call it *their* land. Let them buy and sell, and bequeath
and devise it. We may safely leave them the shell, if we
take the kernel. *It is not necessary to confiscate land;
it is only necessary to confiscate rent.*

Nor to take rent for public uses is it necessary that
the State should bother with the letting of lands, and
assume the chances of the favoritism, collusion, and
corruption this might involve. It is not necessary that
any new machinery should be created. The machinery
already exists. Instead of extending it, all we have to
do is to simplify and reduce it. By leaving to landowners a percentage of rent which would probably be
much less than the cost and loss involved in attempting
to rent lands through State agency, and by making use
of this existing machinery, we may, without jar or shock,
assert the common right to land by taking rent for public
uses.

We already take some rent in taxation. We have
only to make some changes in our modes of taxation
to take it all.

What I, therefore, propose, as the simple yet sovereign remedy, which will raise wages, increase the earnings of capital, extirpate pauperism, abolish poverty,

give remunerative employment to whoever wishes it, afford free scope to human powers, lessen crime, elevate morals, and taste, and intelligence, purify government and carry civilization to yet nobler heights, is—*to appropriate rent by taxation.*

In this way the State may become the universal landlord without calling herself so, and without assuming a single new function. In form, the ownership of land would remain just as now. No owner of land need be dispossessed, and no restriction need be placed upon the amount of land any one could hold. For, rent being taken by the State in taxes, land, no matter in whose name it stood, or in what parcels it was held, would be really common property, and every member of the community would participate in the advantages of its ownership.

Now, insomuch as the taxation of rent, or land values, must necessarily be increased just as we abolish other taxes, we may put the proposition into practical form by proposing—

To abolish all taxation save that upon land values.

As we have seen, the value of land is at the beginning of society nothing, but as society develops by the increase of population and the advance of the arts, it becomes greater and greater. In every civilized country, even the newest, the value of the land taken as a whole is sufficient to bear the entire expenses of government. In the better developed countries it is much more than sufficient. Hence it will not be enough merely to place all taxes upon the value of land. It will be necessary, where rent exceeds the present governmental revenues, commensurately to increase the amount demanded in taxation, and to continue this increase as society progresses and rent advances. But this is so natural and easy a matter, that it may be considered as involved, or at least understood, in the proposition to put all taxes on the value of land. That is the first step upon which the practical struggle must be made. When the hare is once caught and killed, cooking him will follow as a matter of course. When the common right to land is so far appreciated that all taxes are abolished save those which fall upon rent, there is no danger of much more than is necessary to induce them to collect the public revenues being left to individual landholders.

Experience has taught me (for I have been for some years endeavoring to popularize this proposition) that wherever the idea of concentrating all taxation upon land values finds lodgment sufficient to induce consideration, it invariably makes way, but there are few of the classes most to be benefited by it, who at first, or even for a long time afterward, see its full significance and power. It is difficult for workingmen to get over the idea that there is a real antagonism between capital and labor. It is difficult for small farmers and homestead owners to get over the idea that to put all taxes on the value of land would be unduly to tax them. It is difficult for both classes to get over the idea that to exempt capital from taxation would be to make the rich richer, and the poor poorer. These ideas spring from confused thought. But behind ignorance and prejudice there is a powerful interest, which has hitherto dominated literature, education, and opinion. A great wrong always dies hard, and the great wrong which in every civilized country condemns the masses of men to poverty and want, will not die without a bitter struggle.

I do not think the ideas of which I speak can be entertained by the reader who has followed me thus far; but inasmuch as any popular discussion must deal with the concrete, rather than the abstract, let me ask him to follow me somewhat further, that we may try the remedy I have proposed by the accepted canons of taxation. In doing so, many incidental bearings may be seen that otherwise might escape notice.

CHAPTER 3

THE PROPOSITION TRIED BY THE CANONS OF TAXATION

The best tax by which public revenues can be raised is evidently that which will closest conform to the following conditions:

1. That it bear as lightly as possible upon production—so as least to check the increase of the general fund from which taxes must be paid and the community maintained.

2. That it be easily and cheaply collected, and fall as directly as may be upon the ultimate payers—so as to take from the people as little as possible in addition to what it yields the government.

3. That it be certain—so as to give the least opportunity for tyranny or corruption on the part of officials, and the least temptation to lawbreaking and evasion on the part of the taxpayers.

4. That it bear equally—so as to give no citizen an advantage or put any at a disadvantage, as compared with others.

Let us consider what form of taxation best accords with these conditions. Whatever it be, that evidently will be the best mode in which the public revenues can be raised.

I.—The Effect of Taxes upon Production

All taxes must evidently come from the produce of land and labor, since there is no other source of wealth than the union of human exertion with the material and forces of nature. But the manner in which equal amounts of taxation may be imposed may very differently affect the production of wealth. Taxation which lessens the reward of the producer necessarily lessens the incentive to production; taxation which is conditioned upon the act of production, or the use of any of the three factors of production, necessarily discourages production. Thus taxation which diminishes the earnings of the laborer or the returns of the capitalist tends to render the one less industrious and intelligent, the other less disposed to save and invest. Taxation which falls upon the processes of production interposes an artificial obstacle to the creation of wealth. Taxation which falls upon labor as it is exerted, wealth as it is used as capital, land as it is cultivated, will manifestly tend to discourage production much more powerfully than taxation to the same amount levied upon laborers, whether they work or play, upon wealth whether used productively or unproductively, or upon land whether cultivated or left waste.

The mode of taxation is, in fact, quite as important as the amount. As a small burden badly placed may distress a horse that could carry with ease a much larger one properly adjusted, so a people may be impoverished and their power of producing wealth destroyed by taxation, which, if levied in another way, could be borne with ease. A tax on date trees, imposed by Mohammed Ali, caused the Egyptian fellahs to cut down their trees; but a tax of twice the amount imposed on the land produced no such result. The tax of ten per cent. on all sales, imposed by the Duke of Alva in the Netherlands, would, had it been maintained, have all but stopped exchange while yielding but little revenue.

But we need not go abroad for illustrations. The production of wealth in the United States is largely lessened by taxation which bears upon its processes. Shipbuilding, in which we excelled, has been all but destroyed, so far as the foreign trade is concerned, and many branches of production and exchange seriously crippled, by taxes which divert industry from more to less productive forms.

This checking of production is in greater or less degree characteristic of most of the taxes by which the revenues of modern governments are raised. All taxes upon manufactures, all taxes upon commerce, all taxes upon capital, all taxes upon improvements, are of this kind. Their tendency is the same as that of Mohammed Ali's tax on date trees, though their effect may not be so clearly seen.

All such taxes have a tendency to reduce the production of wealth, and should, therefore, never be resorted to when it is possible to raise money by taxes which do not check production. This becomes possible as society develops and wealth accumulates. Taxes which fall upon ostentation would simply turn into the public treasury what otherwise would be wasted in vain show for the sake of show; and taxes upon wills and devises of the rich would probably have little effect in checking the desire for accumulation, which, after it has fairly got hold of a man, becomes a blind passion. But the great class of taxes from which revenue may be derived without interference with production are taxes upon monopolies—for the profit of monopoly is in itself a tax levied upon production, and to tax it is simply to divert into the public coffers what production must in any event pay.

There are among us various sorts of monopolies. For instance, there are the temporary monopolies created by the patent and copyright laws. These it would be extremely unjust and unwise to tax, inasmuch as they are but recognitions of the right of labor to its intangible productions, and constitute a reward held out to invention and authorship.* There are also the onerous monopolies alluded to in Chap. IV of Book III, which result from the aggregation of capital in businesses which are of the nature of monopolies. But while it would be extremely difficult, if not altogether impossible,

---

* Following the habit of confounding the exclusive right granted by a patent and that granted by a copyright as recognitions of the right of labor to its intangible productions, I in this fell into error which I subsequently acknowledged and corrected in the Standard of June 23, 1888. The two things are not alike, but essentially different. The copyright is not a right to the exclusive use of a fact, an idea, or a combination, which by the natural law of property all are free to use; but only to the labor expended in the thing itself. It does not prevent any one from using for himself the facts, the knowledge, the laws or combinations for a similar production, but only from using the identical form of the particular book or other production—the actual labor which has in short been expended in producing it. It rests therefore upon the natural, moral right of each one to enjoy the products of his own exertion, and involves no interference with the similar right of any one else to do likewise.

The patent, on the other hand, prohibits any one from doing a similar thing, and involves, usually for a specified time, an interference with the equal liberty on which the right of ownership rests. The copyright is therefore in accordance with the moral law—it gives to the man who has expended the intangible labor required to write a particular book or paint a picture security against the copying of that identical thing. The patent is in defiance of this natural right. It prohibits others from doing what has been already attempted. Every one has a moral right to think what I think, or to perceive what I perceive, or to do what I do—no matter whether he gets the hint from me or independently of me. Discovery can give no right of ownership, for whatever is discovered must have been already here to be discovered. If a man make a wheelbarrow, or a book, or a picture, he has a moral right to that particular wheelbarrow, or book, or picture, but no right to ask that others be prevented from making similar things. Such a prohibition, though given for the purpose of stimulating discovery and invention, really in the long run operates as a check upon them.

BOOK VIII   CHAPTER 3

to levy taxes by general law so that they would fall exclusively on the returns of such monopoly and not become taxes on production or exchange, it is much better that these monopolies should be abolished. In large part they spring from legislative commission or omission, as, for instance, the ultimate reason that San Francisco merchants are compelled to pay more for goods sent direct from New York to San Francisco by the Isthmus route than it costs to ship them from New York to Liverpool or Southampton and thence to San Francisco, is to be found in the "protective" laws which make it so costly to build American steamers and which forbid foreign steamers to carry goods between American ports. The reason that residents of Nevada are compelled to pay as much freight from the East as though their goods were carried to San Francisco and back again, is that the authority which prevents extortion on the part of a hack driver is not exercised in respect to a railroad company. And it may be said generally that businesses which are in their nature monopolies are properly part of the functions of the State, and should be assumed by the State. There is the same reason why Government should carry telegraphic messages as that it should carry letters; that railroads should belong to the public as that common roads should.

But all other monopolies are trivial in extent as compared with the monopoly of land. And the value of land expressing a monopoly, pure and simple, is in every respect fitted for taxation. That is to say, while the value of a railroad or telegraph line, the price of gas or of a patent medicine, may express the price of monopoly, it also expresses the exertion of labor and capital; but the value of land, or economic rent, as we have seen, is in no part made up from these factors, and expresses nothing but the advantage of appropriation. Taxes levied upon the value of land cannot check production in the slightest degree, until they exceed rent, or the value of land taken annually, for unlike taxes upon commodities, or exchange, or capital, or any of the tools or processes of production, they do not bear upon production. The value of land does not express the reward of production, as does the value of crops, of cattle, of buildings, or any of the things which are styled personal property and improvements. It expresses the exchange value of monopoly. It is not in any case the creation of the individual who owns the land; it is created by the growth of the community. Hence the community can take it all without in any way lessening the incentive to improvement or in the slightest degree lessening the production of wealth. Taxes may be imposed upon the value of land until all rent is taken by the State, without reducing the wages of labor or the reward of capital one iota; without increasing the price of a single commodity, or making production in any way more difficult.

But more than this. Taxes on the value of land not only do not check production as do most other taxes, but they tend to increase production, by destroying speculative rent. How speculative rent checks production may be seen not only in the valuable land withheld from use, but in the paroxysms of industrial depression which, originating in the speculative advance in land values, propagate themselves over the whole civilized world, everywhere paralyzing industry, and causing more waste and probably more suffering than would a general war. Taxation which would take rent for public uses would prevent all this; while if land were taxed to anything near its rental value, no one could afford to hold land that he was not using, and, consequently, land not in use would be thrown open to those who would use it. Settlement would be closer, and, consequently, labor and capital would be enabled to produce much more with the same exertion. The dog in the manger who, in this country especially, so wastes productive power, would be choked off.

There is yet an even more important way by which, through its effect upon distribution, the taking of rent to public uses by taxation would stimulate the production of wealth. But reference to that may be reserved. It is sufficiently evident that with regard to production, the tax upon the value of land is the best tax that can be imposed. Tax manufactures, and the effect is to check manufacturing; tax improvements, and the effect is to lessen improvement; tax commerce, and the effect is to prevent exchange; tax capital, and the effect is to drive it away. But the whole value of land may be taken in taxation, and the only effect will be to stimulate industry, to open new opportunities to capital, and to increase the production of wealth.

II.—As to Ease and Cheapness of Collection

With, perhaps, the exception of certain licenses and stamp duties, which may be made almost to collect themselves, but which can be relied on for only a trivial amount of revenue, a tax upon land values can, of all taxes, be most easily and cheaply collected. For land cannot be hidden or carried off; its value can be readily ascertained, and the assessment once made, nothing but a receiver is required for collection.

And as under all fiscal systems some part of the public revenues is collected from taxes on land, and the machinery for that purpose already exists and could as well be made to collect all as a part, the cost of collecting the revenue now obtained by other taxes might be entirely saved by substituting the tax on land values for all other taxes. What an enormous saving might thus be made can be inferred from the horde of officials now engaged in collecting these taxes.

This saving would largely reduce the difference between what taxation now costs the people and what it yields, but the substitution of a tax on land values for all other taxes would operate to reduce this difference in an even more important way.

A tax on land values does not add to prices, and is thus paid directly by the persons on whom it falls; whereas, all taxes upon things of unfixed quantity increase prices, and in the course of exchange are shifted from seller to buyer, increasing as they go. If we impose a tax upon money loaned, as has been often attempted, the lender will charge the tax to the borrower, and the borrower must pay it or not obtain the loan. If the borrower uses it in his business, he in his turn must get back the tax from his customers, or his business becomes unprofitable. If we impose a tax upon buildings, the users of buildings must finally pay it, for the erection of buildings will cease until building rents become high enough to pay the regular profit and the tax besides. If we impose a tax upon manufactures or imported goods, the manufacturer or importer will charge it in a higher price to the jobber, the jobber to the retailer, and the retailer to the consumer. Now, the consumer, on whom the tax thus ultimately falls, must not only pay the amount of the tax, but also a profit on this amount to every one who has thus advanced it —for profit on the capital he has advanced in paying taxes is as much required by each dealer as profit on the capital he has advanced in paying for goods. Manila cigars cost, when bought of the importer in San Francisco, $70 a thousand, of which $14 is the cost of the cigars laid down in this port and $56 is the customs duty. But the dealer who purchases these cigars to sell again must charge a profit, not on $14, the real cost of the cigars, but on $70, the cost of the cigars plus the duty. In this way all taxes which add to prices are shifted from hand to hand, increasing as they go, until they ultimately rest upon consumers, who thus pay much more than is received by the government. Now, the way taxes raise prices is by increasing the cost of production, and checking supply. But land is not a thing of human production, and taxes upon rent cannot check supply. Therefore, though a tax on rent compels the landowners to pay more, it gives them no power to obtain more for the use of their land, as it in no way tends to reduce the supply of land. On the contrary, by compelling those who hold land on speculation to sell or let for what they can get, a tax on land values tends to increase the competition between owners, and thus to reduce the price of land.

Thus in all respects a tax upon land values is the cheapest tax by which a large revenue can be raised— giving to the government the largest net revenue in proportion to the amount taken from the people.

III.—As to Certainty

Certainty is an important element in taxation, for just as the collection of a tax depends upon the diligence and faithfulness of the collectors and the public spirit and honesty of those who are to pay it, will opportunities for tyranny and corruption be opened on the one side, and for evasions and frauds on the other.

The methods by which the bulk of our revenues are collected are condemned on this ground, if on no other. The gross corruptions and fraud occasioned in the United States by the whisky and tobacco taxes are well known; the constant undervaluations of the Custom House, the ridiculous untruthfulness of income tax returns, and the absolute impossibility of getting anything like a just valuation of personal property, are matters of notoriety. The material loss which such taxes inflict —the item of cost which this uncertainty adds to the amount paid by the people but not received by the government—is very great. When, in the days of the protective system of England, her coasts were lined with an army of men endeavoring to prevent smuggling, and another army of men were engaged in evading them, it is evident that the maintenance of both armies had to come from the produce of labor and capital; that the expenses and profits of the smugglers, as well as the pay and bribes of the Custom House officers, constituted a tax upon the industry of the nation, in addition to what was received by the government. And so, all douceurs to assessors; all bribes to customs officials; all moneys expended in electing pliable officers or in procuring acts or decisions which avoid taxation; all the costly modes of bringing in goods so as to evade duties, and of manufacturing so as to evade imposts; all moieties, and expenses of detectives and spies; all expenses of legal proceedings and punishments, not only to the government, but to those prosecuted, are so much which these taxes take from the general fund of wealth, without adding to the revenue.

Yet this is the least part of the cost. Taxes which lack the element of certainty tell most fearfully upon morals. Our revenue laws as a body might well be entitled, "Acts to promote the corruption of public officials, to suppress honesty and encourage fraud, to set a premium upon perjury and the subornation of perjury, and to divorce the idea of law from the idea of justice." This is their true character, and they succeed admirably. A Custom House oath is a byword; our assessors regularly swear to assess all property at its full, true, cash value, and habitually do nothing of the kind; men who pride themselves on their personal and

commercial honor bribe officials and make false returns;
and the demoralizing spectacle is constantly presented of
the same court trying a murderer one day and a vendor
of unstamped matches the next!

So uncertain and so demoralizing are these modes of
taxation that the New York Commission, composed of
David A. Wells, Edwin Dodge and George W. Cuyler,
who investigated the subject of taxation in that State,
proposed to substitute for most of the taxes now levied,
other than that on real estate, an arbitrary tax on each
individual, estimated on the rental value of the premises
he occupied.

But there is no necessity of resorting to any arbitrary
assessment. The tax on land values, which is the least
arbitrary of taxes, possesses in the highest degree the
element of certainty. It may be assessed and collected
with a definiteness that partakes of the immovable and
unconcealable character of the land itself. Taxes levied
on land may be collected to the last cent, and though
the assessment of land is now often unequal, yet
the assessment of personal property is far more unequal,
and these inequalities in the assessment of land largely
arise from the taxation of improvements with land, and
from the demoralization that, springing from the causes
to which I have referred, affects the whole scheme of
taxation. Were all taxes placed upon land values, irrespective of improvements, the scheme of taxation would
be so simple and clear, and public attention would be
so directed to it, that the valuation of taxation could
and would be made with the same certainty that a real
estate agent can determine the price a seller can get
for a lot.

IV.—As to Equality

Adam Smith's canon is, that "The subjects of every
state ought to contribute toward the support of the gov-

ernment as nearly as possible in proportion to their respective abilities; that is, in proportion to the revenue which they respectively enjoy under the protection of the state." Every tax, he goes on to say, which falls only upon rent, or only upon wages, or only upon interest, is necessarily unequal. In accordance with this is the common idea which our systems of taxing everything vainly attempt to carry out—that every one should pay taxes in proportion to his means, or in proportion to his income.

But, waiving all the insuperable practical difficulties in the way of taxing every one according to his means, it is evident that justice cannot be thus attained.

Here, for instance, are two men of equal means, or equal incomes, one having a large family, the other having no one to support but himself. Upon these two men indirect taxes fall very unequally, as the one cannot avoid the taxes on the food, clothing, etc., consumed by his family, while the other need pay only upon the necessaries consumed by himself. But, supposing taxes levied directly, so that each pays the same amount. Still there is injustice. The income of the one is charged with the support of six, eight, or ten persons; the income of the other with that of but a single person. And unless the Malthusian doctrine be carried to the extent of regarding the rearing of a new citizen as an injury to the state, here is a gross injustice.

But it may be said that this is a difficulty which cannot be got over; that it is Nature herself that brings human beings helpless into the world and devolves their support upon the parents, providing in compensation therefor her own sweet and great rewards. Very well, then, let us turn to Nature, and read the mandates of justice in her law.

Nature gives to labor; and to labor alone. In a very Garden of Eden a man would starve but for human

exertion. Now, here are two men of equal incomes—
that of the one derived from the exertion of his labor,
that of the other from the rent of land. Is it just that
they should equally contribute to the expenses of the
State? Evidently not. The income of the one represents wealth he creates and adds to the general wealth
of the State; the income of the other represents merely
wealth that he takes from the general stock, returning
nothing. The right of the one to the enjoyment of his
income rests on the warrant of Nature, which returns
wealth to labor; the right of the other to the enjoyment
of his income is a mere fictitious right, the creation of
municipal regulation, which is unknown and unrecog-
nized by Nature. The father who is told that from his
labor he must support his children must acquiesce, for
such is the natural decree; but he may justly demand
that from the income gained by his labor not one penny
shall be taken, so long as a penny remains of incomes
which are gained by a monopoly of the natural opportunities which Nature offers impartially to all, and in
which his children have as their birthright an equal
share.

Adam Smith speaks of incomes as "enjoyed under the
protection of the state"; and this is the ground upon
which the equal taxation of all species of property is
commonly insisted upon—that it is equally protected
by the state. The basis of this idea is evidently that
the enjoyment of property is made possible by the
state—that there is a value created and maintained by
the community, which is justly called upon to meet
community expenses. Now, of what values is this true?
Only of the value of land. This is a value that does
not arise until a community is formed, and that, unlike
other values, grows with the growth of the community.
It exists only as the community exists. Scatter again
the largest community, and land, now so valuable, would

have no value at all. With every increase of population the value of land rises; with every decrease it falls. This is true of nothing else save of things which, like the ownership of land, are in their nature monopolies.

The tax upon land values is, therefore, the most just and equal of all taxes. It falls only upon those who receive from society a peculiar and valuable benefit, and upon them in proportion to the benefit they receive. It is the taking by the community, for the use of the community, of that value which is the creation of the community. It is the application of the common property to common uses. When all rent is taken by taxation for the needs of the community, then will the equality ordained by Nature be attained. No citizen will have an advantage over any other citizen save as is given by his industry, skill, and intelligence; and each will obtain what he fairly earns. Then, but not till then, will labor get its full reward, and capital its natural return.

CHAPTER **4** INDORSEMENTS AND OBJECTIONS

The grounds from which we have drawn the conclusion that the tax on land values or rent is the best method of raising public revenues have been admitted expressly or tacitly by all economists of standing, since the determination of the nature and law of rent.

Ricardo says (Chap. X): "A tax on rent would . . . fall wholly on landlords, and could not be shifted to any class of consumers," for it "would leave unaltered the difference between the produce obtained from the least productive land in cultivation and that obtained from land of every other quality. . . . A tax on rent would not discourage the cultivation of fresh land, for such land pays no rent and would be untaxed."

McCulloch (Note XXIV to "Wealth of Nations") declares that "in a practical point of view taxes on the rent of land are among the most unjust and impolitic that can be imagined," but he makes this assertion solely on the ground of his assumption that it is practically impossible to distinguish in taxation between the sum paid for the use of the soil and that paid on account of the capital expended upon it. But, supposing that this separation could be effected, he admits that the sum paid to landlords for the use of the natural powers of the soil might be entirely swept away by a tax without their having it in their power to throw any portion of the burden upon any one else, and without affecting the price of produce.

John Stuart Mill not only admits all this, but expressly declares the expediency and justice of a peculiar tax on rent, asking what right the landlords have to the accession of riches that comes to them from the general progress of society without work, risk, or economizing on their part, and although he expressly disapproves of interfering with their claim to the present value of land, he proposes to take the whole future increase as belonging to society by natural right.

Mrs. Fawcett, in the little compendium of the writings of her husband, entitled "Political Economy for Beginners," says: "The land tax, whether small or great in amount, partakes of the nature of a rent paid by the owner of land to the state. In a great part of India the land is owned by the government and therefore the land tax is rent paid direct to the state. The economic perfection of this system of tenure may be readily perceived."

In fact, that rent should, both on grounds of expediency and justice, be the peculiar subject of taxation, is involved in the accepted doctrine of rent, and may be found in embryo in the works of all economists who have accepted the law of Ricardo. That these principles have not been pushed to their necessary conclusions, as I have pushed them, evidently arises from the indisposition to endanger or offend the enormous interest involved in private ownership in land, and from the false theories in regard to wages and the cause of poverty which have dominated economic thought.

But there has been a school of economists who plainly perceived, what is clear to the natural perceptions of men when uninfluenced by habit—that the revenues of the common property, land, ought to be appropriated to the common service. The French Economists of the last century, headed by Quesnay and Turgot, proposed just what I have proposed, that all taxation should be abolished save a tax upon the value of land. As I am acquainted with the doctrines of Quesnay and his disciples only at second hand through the medium of the English writers, I am unable to say how far his peculiar ideas as to agriculture being the only productive avocation, etc., are erroneous apprehensions, or mere peculiarities of terminology. But of this I am certain from the proposition in which his theory culminated— that he saw the fundamental relation between land and labor which has since been lost sight of, and that he arrived at practical truth, though, it may be, through a course of defectively expressed reasoning. The causes which leave in the hands of the landlord a "produce net" were by the Physiocrats no better explained than the suction of a pump was explained by the assumption that nature abhors a vacuum, but the fact in its practical relations to social economy was recognized, and the benefit which would result from the perfect freedom given to industry and trade by a substitution of a tax on rent for all the impositions which hamper and distort the application of labor was doubtless as clearly seen by them as it is by me. One of the things most to be regretted about the French Revolution is that it overwhelmed the ideas of the Economists, just as they were gaining strength among the thinking classes, and were apparently about to influence fiscal legislation.

Without knowing anything of Quesnay or his doctrines, I have reached the same practical conclusion by a route which cannot be disputed, and have based it on grounds which cannot be questioned by the accepted political economy.

The only objection to the tax on rent or land values which is to be met with in standard politico-economic works is one which concedes its advantages—for it is, that from the difficulty of separation, we might, in taxing the rent of land, tax something else. McCulloch, for instance, declares taxes on the rent of land to be impolitic and unjust because the return received for the natural and inherent powers of the soil cannot be clearly distinguished from the return received from improvements and meliorations, which might thus be discouraged. Macaulay somewhere says that if the admission of the attraction of gravitation were inimical to any considerable pecuniary interest, there would not be wanting arguments against gravitation—a truth of which this objection is an illustration. For admitting that it is impossible invariably to separate the value of land from the value of improvements, is this necessity of continuing to tax *some* improvements any reason why we should continue to tax *all* improvements? If it discourage production to tax values which labor and capital have intimately combined with that of land, how much greater discouragement is involved in taxing not only these, but all the clearly distinguishable values which labor and capital create?

But, as a matter of fact, the value of land can always be readily distinguished from the value of improvements. In countries like the United States there is much valuable land that has never been improved; and in many of the States the value of the land and the value of improvements are habitually estimated separately by the assessors, though afterward reunited under the term real estate. Nor where ground has been occupied from immemorial times, is there any difficulty in getting at the value of the bare land, for frequently the land is owned by one person and the buildings by another, and when a fire occurs and improvements are destroyed, a clear and definite value remains in the land. In the oldest country in the world no difficulty whatever can attend the separation, if all that be attempted is to separate the value of the clearly distinguishable improvements, made within a moderate period, from the value of the land, should they be destroyed. This, manifestly, is all that justice or policy requires. Absolute accuracy is impossible in any system, and to attempt to separate all that the human race has done from what nature originally provided would be as absurd as impracticable. A swamp drained or a hill terraced by the Romans constitutes now as much a part of the natural advantages of the British Isles as though the work had been done by earthquake or glacier. The fact that after a certain lapse of time the value of such permanent improvements would be considered as having lapsed into that of the land, and would be taxed accordingly, could have no deterrent effect on such improvements, for such works are frequently undertaken upon leases for years. The fact is, that each generation builds and improves for itself, and not for the remote future. And the further fact is, that each generation is heir, not only to the natural powers of the earth, but to all that remains of the work of past generations.

An objection of a different kind may however be made. It may be said that where political power is diffused, it is highly desirable that taxation should fall not on one class, such as landowners, but on all; in order that all who exercise political power may feel a proper interest in economical government. Taxation and representation, it will be said, cannot safely be divorced.

But however desirable it may be to combine with political power the consciousness of public burdens, the present system certainly does not secure it. Indirect taxes are largely raised from those who pay little or nothing consciously. In the United States the class is rapidly growing who not only feel no interest in taxation, but who have no concern in good government. In our large cities elections are in great measure determined not by considerations of public interest, but by such influences as determined elections in Rome when the masses had ceased to care for anything but bread and the circus.

The effect of substituting for the manifold taxes now imposed a single tax on the value of land would hardly lessen the number of conscious taxpayers, for the division of land now held on speculation would much increase the number of landholders. But it would so equalize the distribution of wealth as to raise even the poorest above that condition of abject poverty in which public considerations have no weight; while it would at the same time cut down those overgrown fortunes which raise their possessors above concern in government. The dangerous classes politically are the very rich and very poor. It is not the taxes that he is conscious of paying that gives a man a stake in the country, an interest in its government; it is the consciousness of feeling that he is an integral part of the community; that its prosperity is his prosperity, and its disgrace his shame. Let but the citizen feel this; let him be surrounded by all the influences that spring from and cluster round a comfortable home, and the community may rely upon him, even to limb or to life. Men do not vote patriotically, any more than they fight patriotically, because of their payment of taxes. Whatever conduces to the comfortable and independent material condition of the masses will best foster public spirit, will make the ultimate governing power more intelligent and more virtuous.

But it may be asked: If the tax on land values is so advantageous a mode of raising revenue, how is it that so many other taxes are resorted to in preference by all governments?

The answer is obvious: The tax on land values is the only tax of any importance that does not distribute itself. It falls upon the owners of land, and there is no way in which they can shift the burden upon any one else. Hence, a large and powerful class are directly interested in keeping down the tax on land values and substituting, as a means for raising the required revenue, taxes on other things, just as the landowners of England, two hundred years ago, succeeded in establishing an excise, which fell on all consumers, for the dues under the feudal tenures, which fell only on them.

There is, thus, a definite and powerful interest opposed to the taxation of land values; but to the other taxes upon which modern governments so largely rely there is no special opposition. The ingenuity of statesmen has been exercised in devising schemes of taxation which drain the wages of labor and the earnings of capital as the vampire bat is said to suck the lifeblood of its victim. Nearly all of these taxes are ultimately paid by that indefinable being, the consumer; and he pays them in a way which does not call his attention to the fact that he is paying a tax—pays them in such small amounts and in such insidious modes that he does not notice it, and is not likely to take the trouble to remonstrate effectually. Those who pay the money directly to the tax collector are not only not interested in opposing a tax which they so easily shift from their own shoulders, but are very frequently interested in its imposition and maintenance, as are other powerful interests which profit, or expect to profit, by the increase of prices which such taxes bring about.

Nearly all of the manifold taxes by which the people of the United States are now burdened have been imposed rather with a view to private advantage than to the raising of revenue, and the great obstacle to the simplification of taxation is these private interests, whose representatives cluster in the lobby whenever a reduction of taxation is proposed, to see that the taxes by which they profit are not reduced. The fastening of a protective tariff upon the United States has been due to these influences, and not to the acceptance of absurd theories of protection upon their own merits. The large revenue which the civil war rendered necessary was the golden opportunity of these special interests, and taxes were piled up on every possible thing, not so much to raise revenue as to enable particular classes to participate in the advantages of tax-gathering and tax-pocketing. And, since the war, these interested parties have constituted the great obstacle to the reduction of taxation; those taxes which cost the people least having, for this reason, been found easier to abolish than those taxes which cost the people most. And, thus, even popular governments, which have for their avowed principle the securing of the greatest good to the greatest number, are, in a most important function, used to secure a questionable good to a small number, at the expense of a great evil to the many.

License taxes are generally favored by those on whom they are imposed, as they tend to keep others from entering the business; imposts upon manufactures are frequently grateful to large manufacturers for similar reasons, as was seen in the opposition of the distillers to the reduction of the whisky tax; duties on imports not only tend to give certain producers special advantages, but accrue to the benefit of importers or dealers who have large stocks on hand; and so, in the case of all such taxes, there are particular interests, capable of ready organization and concerted action, which favor the imposition of the tax, while, in the case of a tax upon the value of land, there is a solid and sensitive interest steadily and bitterly to oppose it.

But if once the truth which I am trying to make clear is understood by the masses, it is easy to see how a union of political forces strong enough to carry it into practice becomes possible.

I cannot play upon any stringed instrument; but I can tell you how of a little village to make a great and glorious city.

—THEMISTOCLES.

Instead of the thorn shall come up the fir tree, and instead of the brier shall come up the myrtle tree.

And they shall build houses and inhabit them; and they shall plant vineyards and eat the fruit of them. They shall not build and another inhabit; they shall not plant and another eat.

—ISAIAH.

CHAPTER **1** OF THE EFFECT UPON THE
PRODUCTION OF WEALTH

The elder Mirabeau, we are told, ranked the proposition of Quesnay, to substitute one single tax on rent (the *impôt unique*) for all other taxes, as a discovery equal in utility to the invention of writing or the substitution of the use of money for barter.

To whosoever will think over the matter, this saying will appear an evidence of penetration rather than of extravagance. The advantages which would be gained by substituting for the numerous taxes by which the public revenues are now raised, a single tax levied upon the value of land, will appear more and more important the more they are considered. This is the secret which would transform the little village into the great city. With all the burdens removed which now oppress industry and hamper exchange, the production of wealth would go on with a rapidity now undreamed of. This, in its turn, would lead to an increase in the value of land —a new surplus which society might take for general purposes. And released from the difficulties which attend the collection of revenue in a way that begets corruption and renders legislation the tool of special interests, society could assume functions which the increasing complexity of life makes it desirable to assume, but which the prospect of political demoralization under the present system now leads thoughtful men to shrink from.

Consider the effect upon the production of wealth.

433

To abolish the taxation which, acting and reacting, now hampers every wheel of exchange and presses upon every form of industry, would be like removing an immense weight from a powerful spring. Imbued with fresh energy, production would start into new life, and trade would receive a stimulus which would be felt to the remotest arteries. The present method of taxation operates upon exchange like artificial deserts and mountains; it costs more to get goods through a custom house than it does to carry them around the world. It operates upon energy, and industry, and skill, and thrift, like a fine upon those qualities. If I have worked harder and built myself a good house while you have been contented to live in a hovel, the taxgatherer now comes annually to make me pay a penalty for my energy and industry, by taxing me more than you. If I have saved while you wasted, I am mulct, while you are exempt. If a man build a ship we make him pay for his temerity, as though he had done an injury to the state; if a railroad be opened, down comes the tax collector upon it, as though it were a public nuisance; if a manufactory be erected we levy upon it an annual sum which would go far toward making a handsome profit. We say we want capital, but if any one accumulate it, or bring it among us, we charge him for it as though we were giving him a privilege. We punish with a tax the man who covers barren fields with ripening grain, we fine him who puts up machinery, and him who drains a swamp. How heavily these taxes burden production only those realize who have attempted to follow our system of taxation through its ramifications, for, as I have before said, the heaviest part of taxation is that which falls in increased prices. But manifestly these taxes are in their nature akin to the Egyptian Pasha's tax upon date trees. If they do not cause the trees to be cut down, they at least discourage the planting.

To abolish these taxes would be to lift the whole enormous weight of taxation from productive industry. The needle of the seamstress and the great manufactory; the cart horse and the locomotive; the fishing boat and the steamship; the farmer's plow and the merchant's stock, would be alike untaxed. All would be free to make or to save, to buy or to sell, unfined by taxes, unannoyed by the taxgatherer. Instead of saying to the producer, as it does now, "The more you add to the general wealth the more shall you be taxed!" the state would say to the producer, "Be as industrious, as thrifty, as enterprising as you choose, you shall have your full reward! You shall not be fined for making two blades of grass grow where one grew before; you shall not be taxed for adding to the aggregate wealth."

And will not the community gain by thus refusing to kill the goose that lays the golden eggs; by thus refraining from muzzling the ox that treadeth out the corn; by thus leaving to industry, and thrift, and skill, their natural reward, full and unimpaired? For there is to the community also a natural reward. The law of society is, each for all, as well as all for each. No one can keep to himself the good he may do, any more than he can keep the bad. Every productive enterprise, besides its return to those who undertake it, yields collateral advantages to others. If a man plant a fruit tree, his gain is that he gathers the fruit in its time and season. But in addition to his gain, there is a gain to the whole community. Others than the owner are benefited by the increased supply of fruit; the birds which it shelters fly far and wide; the rain which it helps to attract falls not alone on his field; and, even to the eye which rests upon it from a distance, it brings a sense of beauty. And so with everything else. The building of a house, a factory, a ship, or a railroad, benefits others besides those who get the direct profits. Nature laughs at a miser. He is like the squirrel who buries his nuts and refrains from digging them up again. Lo! they sprout and grow into trees. In fine linen, steeped in costly spices, the mummy is laid away. Thousands and thousands of years thereafter, the Bedouin cooks his food by a fire of its encasings, it generates the steam by which the traveler is whirled on his way, or it passes into far-off lands to gratify the curiosity of another race. The bee fills the hollow tree with honey, and along comes the bear or the man.

Well may the community leave to the individual producer all that prompts him to exertion; well may it let the laborer have the full reward of his labor, and the capitalist the full return of his capital. For the more that labor and capital produce, the greater grows the common wealth in which all may share. And in the value or rent of land is this general gain expressed in a definite and concrete form. Here is a fund which the state may take while leaving to labor and capital their full reward. With increased activity of production this would commensurately increase.

And to shift the burden of taxation from production and exchange to the value or rent of land would not merely be to give new stimulus to the production of wealth; it would be to open new opportunities. For under this system no one would care to hold land unless to use it, and land now withheld from use would everywhere be thrown open to improvement.

The selling price of land would fall; land speculation would receive its death blow; land monopolization would no longer pay. Millions and millions of acres from which settlers are now shut out by high prices would be abandoned by their present owners or sold to settlers upon nominal terms. And this not merely on the frontiers, but within what are now considered well settled districts. Within a hundred miles of San Francisco would be thus thrown open land enough to support, even with present modes of cultivation, an agricultural population equal to that now scattered from the Oregon boundary to the Mexican line—a distance of 800 miles. In the same degree would this be true of most of the western states, and in a great degree of the older eastern states, for even in New York and Pennsylvania is population yet sparse as compared with the capacity of the land. And even in densely populated England would such a policy throw open to cultivation many hundreds of thousands of acres now held as private parks, deer preserves, and shooting grounds.

For this simple device of placing all taxes on the value of land would be in effect putting up the land at auction to whosoever would pay the highest rent to the state. The demand for land fixes its value, and hence, if taxes were placed so as very nearly to consume that value, the man who wished to hold land without using it would have to pay very nearly what it would be worth to any one who wanted to use it.

And it must be remembered that this would apply, not merely to agricultural land, but to all land. Mineral land would be thrown open to use, just as agricultural land; and in the heart of a city no one could afford to keep land from its most profitable use, or on the outskirts to demand more for it than the use to which it could at the time be put would warrant. Everywhere that land had attained a value, taxation, instead of operating, as now, as a fine upon improvement, would operate to force improvement. Whoever planted an orchard, or sowed a field, or built a house, or erected a manufactory, no matter how costly, would have no more to pay in taxes than if he kept so much land idle. The monopolist of agricultural land would be taxed as much as though his land were covered with houses and barns, with crops and with stock. The owner of a vacant city lot would have to pay as much for the privilege of keeping other people off of it until he wanted to use it, as his neighbor who has a fine house upon his lot. It would cost as much to keep a row of tumble-down shanties upon valuable land as though it were covered with a grand hotel or a pile of great warehouses filled with costly goods.

Thus, the bonus that wherever labor is most productive must now be paid before labor can be exerted would disappear. The farmer would not have to pay out half his means, or mortgage his labor for years, in order to obtain land to cultivate; the builder of a city homestead would not have to lay out as much for a small lot as for the house he puts upon it; the company that proposed to erect a manufactory would not have to expend a great part of its capital for a site. And what would be paid from year to year to the state would be in lieu of all the taxes now levied upon improvements, machinery, and stock.

Consider the effect of such a change upon the labor market. Competition would no longer be one-sided, as now. Instead of laborers competing with each other for employment, and in their competition cutting down wages to the point of bare subsistence, employers would everywhere be competing for laborers, and wages would rise to the fair earnings of labor. For into the labor market would have entered the greatest of all competitors for the employment of labor, a competitor whose demand cannot be satisfied until want is satisfied—the demand of labor itself. The employers of labor would not have merely to bid against other employers, all feeling the stimulus of greater trade and increased profits, but against the ability of laborers to become their own employers upon the natural opportunities freely opened to them by the tax which prevented monopolization.

With natural opportunities thus free to labor; with

capital and improvements exempt from tax, and exchange released from restrictions, the spectacle of willing men unable to turn their labor into the things they are suffering for would become impossible; the recurring paroxysms which paralyze industry would cease; every wheel of production would be set in motion; demand would keep pace with supply, and supply with demand; trade would increase in every direction, and wealth augment on every hand.

CHAPTER 2

OF THE EFFECT UPON DISTRIBUTION AND THENCE UPON PRODUCTION

But great as they thus appear, the advantages of a transference of all public burdens to a tax upon the value of land cannot be fully appreciated until we consider the effect upon the distribution of wealth.

Tracing out the cause of the unequal distribution of wealth which appears in all civilized countries, with a constant tendency to greater and greater inequality as material progress goes on, we have found it in the fact that, as civilization advances, the ownership of land, now in private hands, gives a greater and greater power of appropriating the wealth produced by labor and capital.

Thus, to relieve labor and capital from all taxation, direct and indirect, and to throw the burden upon rent, would be, as far as it went, to counteract this tendency to inequality, and, if it went so far as to take in taxation the whole of rent, the cause of inequality would be totally destroyed. Rent, instead of causing inequality, as now, would then promote equality. Labor and capital would then receive the whole produce, minus that portion taken by the state in the taxation of land values, which, being applied to public purposes, would be equally distributed in public benefits.

That is to say, the wealth produced in every community would be divided into two portions. One part would be distributed in wages and interest between individual producers, according to the part each had taken in the work of production; the other part would go to the community as a whole, to be distributed in public benefits to all its members. In this all would share equally—the weak with the strong, young children and decrepit old men, the maimed, the halt, and the blind, as well as the vigorous. And justly so—for while one part represents the result of individual effort in production, the other represents the increased power with which the community as a whole aids the individual.

Thus, as material progress tends to increase rent, were rent taken by the community for common purposes the very cause which now tends to produce inequality as material progress goes on would then tend to produce greater and greater equality. Fully to understand this effect, let us revert to principles previously worked out.

We have seen that wages and interest must everywhere be fixed by the rent line or margin of cultivation —that is to say, by the reward which labor and capital can secure on land for which no rent is paid; that the aggregate amount of wealth, which the aggregate of labor and capital employed in production will receive, will be the amount of wealth produced (or rather, when we consider taxes, the net amount), minus what is taken as rent.

We have seen that with material progress, as it is at present going on, there is a twofold tendency to the advance of rent. Both are to the increase of the proportion of the wealth produced which goes as rent, and to the decrease of the proportion which goes as wages and interest. But the first, or natural tendency, which results from the laws of social development, is to the increase of rent as a quantity, without the reduction of wages and interest as quantities, or even with their quantitative increase. The other tendency, which results from the unnatural appropriation of land to private ownership, is to the increase of rent as a quantity by the reduction of wages and interest as quantities.

Now, it is evident that to take rent in taxation for public purposes, which virtually abolishes private ownership in land, would be to destroy the tendency to an absolute decrease in wages and interest, by destroying the speculative monopolization of land and the speculative increase in rent. It would be very largely to increase wages and interest, by throwing open natural opportunities now monopolized and reducing the price of land. Labor and capital would thus not merely gain what is now taken from them in taxation, but would gain by the positive decline in rent caused by the decrease in speculative land values. A new equilibrium would be established, at which the common rate of wages and interest would be much higher than now.

But this new equilibrium established, further advances in productive power, and the tendency in this direction would be greatly accelerated, would result in still increasing rent, not at the expense of wages and interest, but by new gains in production, which, as rent would be taken by the community for public uses, would accrue to the advantage of every member of the community. Thus, as material progress went on, the condition of the masses would constantly improve. Not merely one class would become richer, but all would become richer; not merely one class would have more of the necessaries, conveniences, and elegancies of life, but all would have more. For, the increasing power of production, which comes with increasing population, with every new discovery in the productive arts, with every laborsaving invention, with every extension and facilitation of exchanges, could be monopolized by none. That part of the benefit which did not go directly to increase the reward of labor and capital would go to the state—that is to say, to the whole community. With all the enormous advantages, material and mental, of a dense population, would be united the freedom and equality that can now be found only in new and sparsely settled districts.

And, then, consider how equalization in the distribution of wealth would react upon production, everywhere preventing waste, everywhere increasing power.

If it were possible to express in figures the direct pecuniary loss which society suffers from the social maladjustments which condemn large classes to poverty and vice, the estimate would be appalling. England maintains over a million paupers on official charity; the city of New York alone spends over seven million dollars a year in a similar way. But what is spent from public funds, what is spent by charitable societies and what is spent in individual charity, would, if aggregated, be but the first and smallest item in the account. The potential earnings of the labor thus going to waste, the cost of the reckless, improvident and idle habits thus generated; the pecuniary loss, to consider nothing more, suggested by the appalling statistics of mortality, and especially infant mortality, among the poorer classes; the waste indicated by the gin palaces or low groggeries which increase as poverty deepens; the damage done by the vermin of society that are bred of poverty and destitution—the thieves, prostitutes, beggars, and tramps; the cost of guarding society against them, are all items in the sum which the present unjust and unequal distribution of wealth takes from the aggregate which, with present means of production, society might enjoy. Nor yet shall we have completed the account. The ignorance and vice, the recklessness and immorality engendered by the inequality in the distribution of wealth show themselves in the imbecility and corruption of government; and the waste of public revenues, and the still greater waste involved in the ignorant and corrupt abuse of pub-

lic powers and functions, are their legitimate consequences.

But the increase in wages, and the opening of new
avenues of employment which would result from the
appropriation of rent to public purposes, would not
merely stop these wastes and relieve society of these
enormous losses; new power would be added to labor.
It is but a truism that labor is most productive where its
wages are largest. Poorly paid labor is inefficient labor,
the world over.

What is remarked between the efficiency of labor in
the agricultural districts of England where different
rates of wages prevail; what Brassey noticed as between
the work done by his better paid English navvies and
that done by the worse paid labor of the continent; what
was evident in the United States as between slave labor
and free labor; what is seen by the astonishing number
of mechanics or servants required in India or China to
get anything done, is universally true. The efficiency
of labor always increases with the habitual wages of
labor—for high wages mean increased self-respect, intelligence, hope, and energy. Man is not a machine, that
will do so much and no more; he is not an animal, whose
powers may reach thus far and no further. It is mind,
not muscle, which is the great agent of production. The
physical power evolved in the human frame is one of
the weakest of forces, but for the human intelligence the
resistless currents of nature flow, and matter becomes
plastic to the human will. To increase the comforts,
and leisure, and independence of the masses is to increase their intelligence; it is to bring the brain to the
aid of the hand; it is to engage in the common work of
life the faculty which measures the animalcule and
traces the orbits of the stars!

Who can say to what infinite powers the wealth-producing capacity of labor may not be raised by social

adjustments which will give to the producers of wealth their fair proportion of its advantages and enjoyments! With present processes the gain would be simply incalculable, but just as wages are high, so do the invention and utilization of improved processes and machinery go on with greater rapidity and ease. That the wheat crops of southern Russia are still reaped with the scythe and beaten out with the flail is simply because wages are there so low. American invention, American aptitude for laborsaving processes and machinery are the result of the comparatively high wages that have prevailed in the United States. Had our producers been condemned to the low reward of the Egyptian fellah or Chinese coolie, we would be drawing water by hand and transporting goods on the shoulders of men. The increase in the reward of labor and capital would still further stimulate invention and hasten the adoption of improved processes, and these would truly appear, what in themselves they really are—an unmixed good. The injurious effects of laborsaving machinery upon the working classes, that are now so often apparent, and that, in spite of all argument, make so many people regard machinery as an evil instead of a blessing, would disappear. Every new power engaged in the service of man would improve the condition of all. And from the general intelligence and mental activity springing from this general improvement of condition would come new developments of power of which we as yet cannot dream.

But I shall not deny, and do not wish to lose sight of the fact, that while thus preventing waste and thus adding to the efficiency of labor, the equalization in the distribution of wealth that would result from the simple plan of taxation that I propose, must lessen the intensity with which wealth is pursued. It seems to me that in a condition of society in which no one need fear poverty, no one would desire great wealth—at least, no one would take the trouble to strive and to strain for it as men do now. For, certainly, the spectacle of men who have only a few years to live, slaving away their time for the sake of dying rich, is in itself so unnatural and absurd, that in a state of society where the abolition of the fear of want had dissipated the envious admiration with which the masses of men now regard the possession of great riches, whoever would toil to acquire more than he cared to use would be looked upon as we would now look on a man who would thatch his head with half a dozen hats, or walk around in the hot sun with an overcoat on. When every one is sure of being able to get enough, no one will care to make a pack horse of himself.

And though this incentive to production be withdrawn, can we not spare it? Whatever may have been its office in an earlier stage of development, it is not needed now. The dangers that menace our civilization do not come from the weakness of the springs of production. What it suffers from, and what, if a remedy be not applied, it must die from, is unequal distribution!

Nor would the removal of this incentive, regarded only from the standpoint of production, be an unmixed loss. For, that the aggregate of production is greatly reduced by the greed with which riches are pursued, is one of the most obtrusive facts of modern society. While, were this insane desire to get rich at any cost lessened, mental activities now devoted to scraping together riches would be translated into far higher spheres of usefulness.

CHAPTER 3

OF THE EFFECT UPON INDIVIDUALS AND CLASSES

When it is first proposed to put all taxes upon the value of land, and thus confiscate rent, all landholders are likely to take the alarm, and there will not be wanting appeals to the fears of small farm and homestead owners, who will be told that this is a proposition to rob them of their hard-earned property. But a moment's reflection will show that this proposition should commend itself to all whose interests as landholders do not largely exceed their interests as laborers or capitalists, or both. And further consideration will show that though the large landholders may lose relatively, yet even in their case there will be an absolute gain. For, the increase in production will be so great that labor and capital will gain very much more than will be lost to private landownership, while in these gains, and in the greater ones involved in a more healthy social condition, the whole community, including the landowners themselves, will share.

In a preceding chapter I have gone over the question of what is due to the present landholders, and have shown that they have no claim to compensation. But there is still another ground on which we may dismiss all idea of compensation. They will not really be injured.

It is manifest, of course, that the change I propose will greatly benefit all those who live by wages, whether of hand or of head—laborers, operatives, mechanics, clerks, professional men of all sorts. It is manifest, also, that it will benefit all those who live partly by wages and partly by the earnings of their capital—storekeepers, merchants, manufacturers, employing or undertaking producers and exchangers of all sorts—from the peddler or drayman to the railroad or steamship owner—and it is likewise manifest that it will increase the incomes of those whose incomes are drawn from the earnings of capital, or from investments other than in lands, save perhaps the holders of government bonds or other securities bearing fixed rates of interest, which will probably depreciate in selling value, owing to the rise in the general rate of interest, though the income from them will remain the same.

Take, now, the case of the homestead owner—the mechanic, storekeeper, or professional man who has secured himself a house and lot, where he lives, and which he contemplates with satisfaction as a place from which his family cannot be ejected in case of his death. He will not be injured; on the contrary, he will be the gainer. The selling value of his lot will diminish—theoretically it will entirely disappear. But its usefulness to him will not disappear. It will serve his purpose as well as ever. While, as the value of all other lots will diminish or disappear in the same ratio, he retains the same security of always having a lot that he had before. That is to say, he is a loser only as the man who has bought himself a pair of boots may be said to be a loser by a subsequent fall in the price of boots. His boots will be just as useful to him, and the next pair of boots he can get cheaper. So, to the homestead owner, his lot will be as useful, and should he look forward to getting a larger lot, or having his children, as they grow up, get homesteads of their own, he will, even in the matter of lots, be the gainer. And in the present, other things considered, he will be much the gainer. For though he will have more taxes to pay upon his land, he will be released from taxes upon his house and improvements, upon his furniture and personal property, upon all that he and his family eat, drink and wear, while his earnings will be largely increased by the rise of wages, the constant employment, and the increased briskness of trade. His only loss will be, if he wants to sell his lot without getting another, and this· will be a small loss compared with the great gain.

And so with the farmer. I speak not now of the farmers who never touch the handles of a plow, who cultivate thousands of acres and enjoy incomes like those of the rich Southern planters before the war; but of the working farmers who constitute such a large class in the United States—men who own small farms, which they cultivate with the aid of their boys, and perhaps some hired help, and who in Europe would be called peasant proprietors. Paradoxical as it may appear to these men until they understand the full bearings of the proposition, of all classes above that of the mere laborer they have most to gain by placing all taxes upon the value of land. That they do not now get as good a living as their hard work ought to give them, they generally feel, though they may not be able to trace the cause. The fact is that taxation, as now levied, falls on them with peculiar severity. They are taxed on all their improvements—houses, barns, fences, crops, stock. The personal property which they have cannot be as readily concealed or undervalued as can the more valuable kinds which are concentrated in the cities. They are not only taxed on personal property and improvements, which the owners of unused land escape, but their land is generally taxed at a higher rate than land held on speculation, simply because it is improved. But further than this, all taxes imposed on commodities, and especially the taxes which, like our protective duties, are imposed with a view of raising the prices of commodities, fall on the farmer without mitigation. For in a country like the United States, which exports agricultural produce, the farmer cannot be protected. Whoever gains, he must lose. Some years ago the Free Trade League of New York published a broadside containing cuts of various articles of necessity marked with the duties imposed by the tariff, and which read something in this wise: "The farmer rises in the morning and draws on his pantaloons taxed 40 per cent. and his boots taxed 30 per cent., striking a light with a match taxed 200 per cent.," and so on, following him through the day and through life, until, killed by taxation, he is lowered into the grave with a rope taxed 45 per cent. This is but a graphic illustration of the manner in which such taxes ultimately fall. The farmer would be a great gainer by the substitution of a single tax upon the value of land for all these taxes, for the taxation of land values would fall with greatest weight, not upon the agricultural districts, where land values are comparatively small, but upon the towns and cities where land values are high; whereas taxes upon personal property and improvements fall as heavily in the country as in the city. And in sparsely settled districts there would be hardly any taxes at all for the farmer to pay. For taxes, being levied upon the value of the bare land, would fall as heavily upon unimproved as upon improved land. Acre for acre, the improved and cultivated farm, with its buildings, fences, orchard, crops, and stock, could be taxed no more than unused land of equal quality. The result would be that speculative values would be kept down, and that cultivated and improved farms would have no taxes to pay until the country around them had been well settled. In fact, paradoxical as it may at first seem to them, the effect of putting all taxation upon the value of land would be to relieve the harder working farmers of all taxation.

But the great gain of the working farmer can be seen only when the effect upon the distribution of population is considered. The destruction of speculative land values would tend to diffuse population where it is too dense and to concentrate it where it is too sparse; to substitute for the tenement house, homes surrounded by gardens, and fully to settle agricultural districts before people were driven far from neighbors to look for land. The people of the cities would thus get more of the pure air and sunshine of the country, the people of the country more of the economies and social life of the city. If, as is doubtless the case, the application of machinery tends to large fields, agricultural population will assume the primitive form and cluster in villages. The life of the average farmer is now unnecessarily dreary. He is not only compelled to work early and late, but he is cut off by the sparseness of population from the conveniences, and amusements, the educational facilities, and the social and intellectual opportunities that come with the closer contact of man with man. He would be far better off in all these respects, and his labor would be far more productive, if he and those around him held no more land than they wanted to use.* While his children, as they grew up, would neither be so impelled to seek the excitement of a city nor would they be driven so far away to seek farms of their own. Their means of living would be in their own hands, and at home.

In short, the working farmer is both a laborer and a capitalist, as well as a landowner, and it is by his

* Besides the enormous increase in the productive power of labor which would result from the better distribution of population there would be also a similar economy in the productive power of land. The concentration of population in cities fed by the exhaustive cultivation of large, sparsely populated areas, results in a literal draining into the sea of the elements of fertility. How enormous this waste is may be seen from

labor and capital that his living is made. His loss would be nominal; his gain would be real and great.

In varying degrees is this true of all landholders. Many landholders are laborers of one sort or another. And it would be hard to find a landowner not a laborer, who is not also a capitalist—while the general rule is, that the larger the landowner the greater the capitalist. So true is this that in common thought the characters are confounded. Thus to put all taxes on the value of land, while it would be largely to reduce all great fortunes, would in no case leave the rich man penniless. The Duke of Westminster, who owns a considerable part of the site of London, is probably the richest landowner in the world. To take all his ground rents by taxation would largely reduce his enormous income, but would still leave him his buildings and all the income from them, and doubtless much personal property in various other shapes. He would still have all he could by any possibility enjoy, and a much better state of society in which to enjoy it.

So would the Astors of New York remain very rich. And so, I think, it will be seen throughout—this measure would make no one poorer but such as could be made a great deal poorer without being really hurt. It would cut down great fortunes, but it would impoverish no one.

Wealth would not only be enormously increased; it would be equally distributed. I do not mean that each individual would get the same amount of wealth. That would not be equal distribution, so long as different individuals have different powers and different desires. But I mean that wealth would be distributed

the calculations that have been made as to the sewage of our cities, and its practical result is to be seen in the diminishing productiveness of agriculture in large sections. In a great part of the United States we are steadily exhausting our lands.

in accordance with the degree in which the industry, skill, knowledge, or prudence of each contributed to the common stock. The great cause which concentrates wealth in the hands of those who do not produce, and takes it from the hands of those who do, would be gone. The inequalities that continued to exist would be those of nature, not the artificial inequalities produced by the denial of natural law. The nonproducer would no longer roll in luxury while the producer got but the barest necessities of animal existence.

The monopoly of the land gone, there need be no fear of large fortunes. For then the riches of any individual must consist of wealth, properly so-called—of wealth, which is the product of labor, and which constantly tends to dissipation, for national debts, I imagine, would not long survive the abolition of the system from which they spring. All fear of great fortunes might be dismissed, for when every one gets what he fairly earns, no one can get more than he fairly earns. How many men are there who fairly earn a million dollars?

4

CHAPTER OF THE CHANGES THAT WOULD BE WROUGHT IN SOCIAL ORGANIZATION AND SOCIAL LIFE

We are dealing only with general principles. There are some matters of detail—such as those arising from the division of revenues between local and general governments—which upon application of these principles would come up, but these it is not necessary here to discuss. When once principles are settled, details will be readily adjusted.

Nor without too much elaboration is it possible to notice all the changes which would be wrought, or would become possible, by a change which would readjust the very foundation of society, but to some main features let me call attention.

Noticeable among these is the great simplicity which would become possible in government. To collect taxes, to prevent and punish evasions, to check and countercheck revenues drawn from so many distinct sources, now make up probably three-fourths, perhaps seven-eighths of the business of government, outside of the preservation of order, the maintenance of the military arm, and the administration of justice. An immense and complicated network of governmental machinery would thus be dispensed with.

In the administration of justice there would be a like saving of strain. Much of the civil business of our courts arises from disputes as to ownership of land. These would cease when the state was virtually acknowledge'd as the sole owner of land, and all occupiers became practically rent-paying tenants. The growth of morality consequent upon the cessation of want would tend to a like diminution in other civil business of the courts, which could be hastened by the adoption of the common sense proposition of Bentham to abolish all laws for the collection of debts and the enforcement of private contracts. The rise of wages, the opening of opportunities for all to make an easy and comfortable living, would at once lessen and would soon eliminate from society the thieves, swindlers, and other classes of criminals who spring from the unequal distribution of wealth. Thus the administration of the criminal law, with all its paraphernalia of policemen, detectives, prisons, and penitentiaries, would, like the administration of the civil law, cease to make such a drain upon the vital force and attention of society. We should get rid not only of many judges, bailiffs, clerks, and prison keepers, but of the great host of lawyers who are now maintained at the expense of producers; and talent now wasted in legal subtleties would be turned to higher pursuits.

The legislative, judicial, and executive functions of government would in this way be vastly simplified. Nor can I think that the public debts and the standing armies, which are historically the outgrowth of the change from feudal to allodial tenures, would long remain after the reversion to the old idea that the land of a country is the common right of the people of the country. The former could readily be paid off by a tax that would not lessen the wages of labor nor check production, and the latter the growth of intelligence and independence among the masses, aided, perhaps, by the progress of invention, which is revolutionizing the military art, must soon cause to disappear.

Society would thus approach the ideal of Jeffersonian democracy, the promised land of Herbert Spencer, the

abolition of government. But of government only as a
directing and repressive power. It would at the same
time, and in the same degree, become possible for it to
realize the dream of socialism. All this simplification
and abrogation of the present functions of government
would make possible the assumption of certain other
functions which are now pressing for recognition. Government could take upon itself the transmission of messages by telegraph, as well as by mail; of building and
operating railroads, as well as of opening and maintaining common roads. With present functions so simplified
and reduced, functions such as these could be assumed
without danger or strain, and would be under the super-
vision of public attention, which is now distracted.
There would be a great and increasing surplus revenue
from the taxation of land values, for material progress,
which would go on with greatly accelerated rapidity,
would tend constantly to increase rent. This revenue
arising from the common property could be applied to
the common benefit, as were the revenues of Sparta.
We might not establish public tables—they would be
unnecessary; but we could establish public baths, museums, libraries, gardens, lecture rooms, music and
dancing halls, theaters, universities, technical schools,
shooting galleries, play grounds, gymnasiums, etc. Heat,
light, and motive power, as well as water, might be
conducted through our streets at public expense; our
roads be lined with fruit trees; discoverers and inventors
rewarded, scientific investigations supported; and in a
thousand ways the public revenues made to foster efforts for the public benefit. We should reach the ideal
of the socialist, but not through government repression.
Government would change its character, and would
become the administration of a great co-operative society. It would become merely the agency by which the

common property was administered for the common benefit.

Does this seem impracticable? Consider for a moment the vast changes that would be wrought in social life by a change which would assure to labor its full reward; which would banish want and the fear of want; and give to the humblest freedom to develop in natural symmetry.

In thinking of the possibilities of social organization, we are apt to assume that greed is the strongest of human motives, and that systems of administration can be safely based only upon the idea that the fear of punishment is necessary to keep men honest—that selfish interests are always stronger than general interests. Nothing could be further from the truth.

From whence springs this lust for gain, to gratify which men tread everything pure and noble under their feet; to which they sacrifice all the higher possibilities of life; which converts civility into a hollow pretense, patriotism into a sham, and religion into hypocrisy; which makes so much of civilized existence an Ishmaelitish warfare, of which the weapons are cunning and fraud?

Does it not spring from the existence of want? Carlyle somewhere says that poverty is the hell of which the modern Englishman is most afraid. And he is right. Poverty is the openmouthed, relentless hell which yawns beneath civilized society. And it is hell enough. The Vedas declare no truer thing than when the wise crow Bushanda tells the eagle-bearer of Vishnu that the keenest pain is in poverty. For poverty is not merely deprivation; it means shame, degradation; the searing of the most sensitive parts of our moral and mental nature as with hot irons; the denial of the strongest impulses and the sweetest affections; the wrenching of the most vital nerves. You love your wife, you love your

children; but would it not be easier to see them die
than to see them reduced to the pinch of want in which
large classes in every highly civilized community live?
The strongest of animal passions is that with which
we cling to life, but it is an everyday occurrence in civilized societies for men to put poison to their mouths or
pistols to their heads from fear of poverty, and for
one who does this there are probably a hundred who
have the desire, but are restrained by instinctive shrink-
ing, by religious considerations, or by family ties.

From this hell of poverty, it is but natural that men
should make every effort to escape. With the impulse
to self-preservation and self-gratification combine nobler
feelings, and love as well as fear urges in the struggle.
Many a man does a mean thing, a dishonest thing, a
greedy and grasping and unjust thing, in the effort to
place above want, or the fear of want, mother or wife
or children.

And out of this condition of things arises a public
opinion which enlists, as an impelling power in the
struggle to grasp and to keep, one of the strongest—
perhaps with many men the very strongest—springs of
human action. The desire for approbation, the feeling
that urges us to win the respect, admiration, or sympathy of our fellows, is instinctive and universal. Distorted sometimes into the most abnormal manifestations,
it may yet be everywhere perceived. It is potent with
the veriest savage, as with the most highly cultivated
member of the most polished society; it shows itself
with the first gleam of intelligence, and persists to the
last breath. It triumphs over the love of ease, over the
sense of pain, over the dread of death. It dictates
the most trivial and the most important actions.

The child just beginning to toddle or to talk will make
new efforts as its cunning little tricks excite attention
and laughter; the dying master of the world gathers his

robes around him, that he may pass away as becomes a king; Chinese mothers will deform their daughters' feet by cruel stocks, European women will sacrifice their own comfort and the comfort of their families to similar dictates of fashion; the Polynesian, that he may excite admiration by his beautiful tattoo, will hold himself still while his flesh is torn by sharks' teeth; the North American Indian, tied to the stake, will bear the most fiendish tortures without a moan, and, that he may be respected and admired as a great brave, will taunt his tormentors to new cruelties. It is this that leads the forlorn hope; it is this that trims the lamp of the pale student; it is this that impels men to strive, to strain, to toil, and to die. It is this that raised the pyramids and that fired the Ephesian dome.

Now, men admire what they desire. How sweet to the storm-stricken seems the safe harbor; food to the hungry, drink to the thirsty, warmth to the shivering, rest to the weary, power to the weak, knowledge to him in whom the intellectual yearnings of the soul have been aroused. And thus the sting of want and the fear of want make men admire above all things the possession of riches, and to become wealthy is to become respected, and admired, and influential. Get money—honestly, if you can, but at any rate get money! This is the lesson that society is daily and hourly dinning in the ears of its members. Men instinctively admire virtue and truth, but the sting of want and the fear of want make them even more strongly admire the rich and sympathize with the fortunate. It is well to be honest and just, and men will commend it; but he who by fraud and injustice gets him a million dollars will have more respect, and admiration, and influence, more eye service and lip service, if not heart service, than he who refuses it. The one may have his reward in the future; he may know that his name is writ in the Book of Life, and that for him is the white robe and the palm branch of the victor against temptation; but the other has his reward in the present. His name is writ in the list of "our substantial citizens"; he has the courtship of men and the flattery of women; the best pew in the church and the personal regard of the eloquent clergyman who in the name of Christ preaches the Gospel of Dives, and tones down into a meaningless flower of Eastern speech the stern metaphor of the camel and the needle's eye. He may be a patron of arts, a Mæcenas to men of letters; may profit by the converse of the intelligent, and be polished by the attrition of the refined. His alms may feed the poor, and help the struggling, and bring sunshine into desolate places; and noble public institutions commemorate, after he is gone, his name and his fame. It is not in the guise of a hideous monster, with horns and tail, that Satan tempts the children of men, but as an angel of light. His promises are not alone of the kingdoms of the world, but of mental and moral principalities and powers. He appeals not only to the animal appetites, but to the cravings that stir in man because he is more than an animal.

Take the case of those miserable "men with muck rakes," who are to be seen in every community as plainly as Bunyan saw their type in his vision—who, long after they have accumulated wealth enough to satisfy every desire, go on working, scheming, striving to add riches to riches. It was the desire "to be something"; nay, in many cases, the desire to do noble and generous deeds, that started them on a career of money getting. And what compels them to it long after every possible need is satisfied, what urges them still with unsatisfied and ravenous greed, is not merely the force of tyrannous habit, but the subtler gratifications which the possession of riches gives—the sense of power and influence, the sense of being looked up to and respected, the sense that their wealth not merely raises them above want, but makes them men of mark in the community in which they live. It is this that makes the rich man so loath to part with his money, so anxious to get more.

Against temptations that thus appeal to the strongest impulses of our nature, the sanctions of law and the precepts of religion can effect but little; and the wonder is, not that men are so self-seeking, but that they are not much more so. That under present circumstances men are not more grasping, more unfaithful, more selfish than they are, proves the goodness and fruitfulness of human nature, the ceaseless flow of the perennial fountains from which its moral qualities are fed. All of us have mothers; most of us have children, and so faith, and purity, and unselfishness can never be utterly banished from the world, howsoever bad be social adjustments.

But whatever is potent for evil may be made potent for good. The change I have proposed would destroy the conditions that distort impulses in themselves beneficent, and would transmute the forces which now tend to disintegrate society into forces which would tend to unite and purify it.

Give labor a free field and its full earnings; take for the benefit of the whole community that fund which the growth of the community creates, and want and the fear of want would be gone. The springs of production would be set free, and the enormous increase of wealth would give the poorest ample comfort. Men would no more worry about finding employment than they worry about finding air to breathe; they need have no more care about physical necessities than do the lilies of the field. The progress of science, the march of invention, the diffusion of knowledge, would bring their benefits to all.

With this abolition of want and the fear of want, the admiration of riches would decay, and men would seek the respect and approbation of their fellows in other modes than by the acquisition and display of wealth. In this way there would be brought to the management of public affairs, and the administration of common funds, the skill, the attention, the fidelity, and integrity that can now be secured only for private interests, and a railroad or gas works might be operated on public account, not only more economically and efficiently than as at present, under joint-stock management, but as economically and efficiently as would be possible under a single ownership. The prize of the Olympian games, that called forth the most strenuous exertions of all Greece, was but a wreath of wild olive; for a bit of ribbon men have over and over again performed services no money could have bought.

Shortsighted is the philosophy which counts on selfishness as the master motive of human action. It is blind to facts of which the world is full. It sees not the present, and reads not the past aright. If you would move men to action, to what shall you appeal? Not to their pockets, but to their patriotism; not to selfishness, but to sympathy. Self-interest is, as it were, a mechanical force—potent, it is true; capable of large and wide results. But there is in human nature what may be likened to a chemical force; which melts and fuses and overwhelms; to which nothing seems impossible. "All that a man hath will he give for his life"—that is self-interest. But in loyalty to higher impulses men will give even life.

It is not selfishness that enriches the annals of every people with heroes and saints. It is not selfishness that on every page of the world's history bursts out in sudden splendor of noble deeds or sheds the soft radiance of benignant lives. It was not selfishness that turned Gautama's back to his royal home or bade the Maid of Orleans lift the sword from the altar; that held the

Three Hundred in the Pass of Thermopylæ, or gathered into Winkelried's bosom the sheaf of spears; that chained Vincent de Paul to the bench of the galley, or brought little starving children, during the Indian famine, tottering to the relief stations with yet weaker starvelings in their arms. Call it religion, patriotism, sympathy, the enthusiasm for humanity, or the love of God—give it what name you will; there is yet a force which overcomes and drives out selfishness; a force which is the electricity of the moral universe; a force beside which all others are weak. Everywhere that men have lived it has shown its power, and today, as ever, the world is full of it. To be pitied is the man who has never seen and never felt it. Look around! among common men and women, amid the care and the struggle of daily life, in the jar of the noisy street and amid the squalor where want hides—every here and there is the darkness lighted with the tremulous play of its lambent flames. He who has not seen it has walked with shut eyes. He who looks may see, as says Plutarch, that "the soul has a principle of kindness in itself, and is born to love, as well as to perceive, think, or remember."

And this force of forces—that now goes to waste or assumes perverted forms—we may use for the strengthening, and building up, and ennobling of society, if we but will, just as we now use physical forces that once seemed but powers of destruction. All we have to do is but to give it freedom and scope. The wrong that produces inequality; the wrong that in the midst of abundance tortures men with want or harries them with the fear of want; that stunts them physically, degrades them intellectually, and distorts them morally, is what alone prevents harmonious social development. For "all that is from the gods is full of providence. We are made for co-operation—like feet, like hands, like eyelids, like the rows of the upper and lower teeth."

There are people into whose heads it never enters to conceive of any better state of society than that which now exists—who imagine that the idea that there could be a state of society in which greed would be banished, prisons stand empty, individual interests be subordinated to general interests, and no one seek to rob or to oppress his neighbor, is but the dream of impracticable dreamers, for whom these practical, levelheaded men, who pride themselves on recognizing facts as they are, have a hearty contempt. But such men—though some of them write books, and some of them occupy the chairs of universities, and some of them stand in pulpits—do not think.

If they were accustomed to dine in such eating houses as are to be found in the lower quarters of London and Paris, where the knives and forks are chained to the table, they would deem it the natural, ineradicable disposition of man to carry off the knife and fork with which he has eaten.

Take a company of well-bred men and women dining together. There is no struggling for food, no attempt on the part of any one to get more than his neighbor; no attempt to gorge or to carry off. On the contrary, each one is anxious to help his neighbor before he partakes himself; to offer to others the best rather than pick it out for himself; and should any one show the slightest disposition to prefer the gratification of his own appetite to that of the others, or in any way to act the pig or pilferer, the swift and heavy penalty of social contempt and ostracism would show how such conduct is reprobated by common opinion.

All this is so common as to excite no remark, as to seem the natural state of things. Yet it is no more natural that men should not be greedy of food than that they should not be greedy of wealth. They are greedy of food when they are not assured that there will be a fair and equitable distribution which will give each enough. But when these conditions are assured, they cease to be greedy of food. And so in society, as at present constituted, men are greedy of wealth because the conditions of distribution are so unjust that instead of each being sure of enough, many are certain to be condemned to want. It is the "devil catch the hindmost" of present social adjustments that causes the race and scramble for wealth, in which all considerations of justice, mercy, religion, and sentiment are trampled under foot; in which men forget their own souls, and struggle to the very verge of the grave for what they cannot take beyond. But an equitable distribution of wealth, that would exempt all from the fear of want, would destroy the greed of wealth, just as in polite society the greed of food has been destroyed.

On the crowded steamers of the early California lines there was often a marked difference between the manners of the steerage and the cabin, which illustrates this principle of human nature. An abundance of food was provided for the steerage as for the cabin, but in the former there were no regulations which insured efficient service, and the meals became a scramble. In the cabin, on the contrary, where each was allotted his place and there was no fear that everyone would not get enough, there was no such scrambling and waste as were witnessed in the steerage. The difference was not in the character of the people, but simply in this fact. The cabin passenger transferred to the steerage would participate in the greedy rush, and the steerage passenger transferred to the cabin would at once become decorous and polite. The same difference would show itself in society in general were the present unjust distribution of wealth replaced by a just distribution.

Consider this existing fact of a cultivated and refined society, in which all the coarser passions are held in check, not by force, not by law, but by common opinion and the mutual desire of pleasing. If this is possible for a part of a community, it is possible for a whole community. There are states of society in which every one has to go armed—in which every one has to hold himself in readiness to defend person and property with the strong hand. If we have progressed beyond that, we may progress still further.

But it may be said, to banish want and the fear of want, would be to destroy the stimulus to exertion; men would become simply idlers, and such a happy state of general comfort and content would be the death of progress. This is the old slaveholders' argument, that men can be driven to labor only with the lash. Nothing is more untrue.

Want might be banished, but desire would remain. Man is the unsatisfied animal. He has but begun to explore, and the universe lies before him. Each step that he takes opens new vistas and kindles new desires. He is the constructive animal; he builds, he improves, he invents, and puts together, and the greater the thing he does, the greater the thing he wants to do. He is more than an animal. Whatever be the intelligence that breathes through nature, it is in that likeness that man is made. The steamship, driven by her throbbing engines through the sea, is in kind, though not in degree, as much a creation as the whale that swims beneath. The telescope and the microscope, what are they but added eyes, which man has made for himself; the soft webs and fair colors in which our women array themselves, do they not answer to the plumage that nature gives the bird? Man must be doing something, or fancy that he is doing something, for in him throbs the creative impulse; the mere basker in the sunshine is not a natural, but an abnormal man.

As soon as a child can command its muscles, it will

begin to make mud pies or dress a doll; its play is but the imitation of the work of its elders; its very destructiveness arises from the desire to be doing something, from the satisfaction of seeing itself accomplish something. There is no such thing as the pursuit of pleasure for the sake of pleasure. Our very amusements amuse only as they are, or simulate, the learning or the doing of something. The moment they cease to appeal either to our inquisitive or to our constructive powers, they cease to amuse. It will spoil the interest of the novel reader to be told just how the story will end; it is only the chance and the skill involved in the game that enable the card player to "kill time" by shuffling bits of pasteboard. The luxurious frivolities of Versailles were possible to human beings only because the king thought he was governing a kingdom and the courtiers were in pursuit of fresh honors and new pensions. People who lead what are called lives of fashion and pleasure must have some other object in view, or they would die of *ennui*; they support it only because they imagine that they are gaining position, making friends, or improving the chances of their children. Shut a man up, and deny him employment, and he must either die or go mad.

It is not labor in itself that is repugnant to man; it is not the natural necessity for exertion which is a curse. It is only labor which produces nothing—exertion of which he cannot see the results. To toil day after day, and yet get but the necessaries of life, this is indeed hard; it is like the infernal punishment of compelling a man to pump lest he be drowned, or to trudge on a treadmill lest he be crushed. But, released from this necessity, men would but work the harder and the better, for then they would work as their inclinations led them; then would they seem to be really doing something for themselves or for others. Was Humboldt's life an idle one? Did Franklin find no occupation when he retired from the printing business with enough to live on? Is Herbert Spencer a laggard? Did Michael Angelo paint for board and clothes?

The fact is that the work which improves the condition of mankind, the work which extends knowledge and increases power, and enriches literature, and elevates thought, is not done to secure a living. It is not the work of slaves, driven to their task either by the lash of a master or by animal necessities. It is the work of men who perform it for its own sake, and not that they may get more to eat or drink, or wear, or display. In a state of society where want was abolished, work of this sort would be enormously increased.

I am inclined to think that the result of confiscating rent in the manner I have proposed would be to cause the organization of labor, wherever large capitals were used, to assume the co-operative form, since the more equal diffusion of wealth would unite capitalist and laborer in the same person. But whether this would be so or not is of little moment. The hard toil of routine labor would disappear. Wages would be too high and opportunities too great to compel any man to stint and starve the higher qualities of his nature, and in every avocation the brain would aid the hand. Work, even of the coarser kinds, would become a lightsome thing, and the tendency of modern production to subdivision would not involve monotony or the contraction of ability in the worker; but would be relieved by short hours, by change, by the alternation of intellectual with manual occupations. There would result, not only the utilization of productive forces now going to waste; not only would our present knowledge, now so imperfectly applied, be fully used; but from the mobility of labor and the mental activity which would be generated, there would result advances in the methods of production that we now cannot imagine.

For, greatest of all the enormous wastes which the present constitution of society involves, is that of mental power. How infinitesimal are the forces that concur to the advance of civilization, as compared to the forces that lie latent! How few are the thinkers, the discoverers, the inventors, the organizers, as compared with the great mass of the people! Yet such men are born in plenty; it is the conditions that permit so few to develop. There are among men infinite diversities of aptitude and inclination, as there are such infinite diversities in physical structure that among a million there will not be two that cannot be told apart. But, both from observation and reflection, I am inclined to think that the differences of natural power are no greater than the differences of stature or of physical strength. Turn to the lives of great men, and see how easily they might never have been heard of. Had Cæsar come of a proletarian family; had Napoleon entered the world a few years earlier; had Columbus gone into the Church instead of going to sea; had Shakespeare been apprenticed to a cobbler or chimney sweep; had Sir Isaac Newton been assigned by fate the education and the toil of an agricultural laborer; had Dr. Adam Smith been born in the coal hews, or Herbert Spencer forced to get his living as a factory operative, what would their talents have availed? But there would have been, it will be said, other Cæsars or Napoleons, Columbuses or Shakespeares, Newtons, Smiths or Spencers. This is true. And it shows how prolific is our human nature. As the common worker is on need transformed into queen bee, so, when circumstances favor his development, what might otherwise pass for a common man rises into a hero or leader, discoverer or teacher, sage or saint. So widely has the sower scattered the seed, so strong is the germinative force that bids it bud and blossom. But, alas, for the stony ground, and the birds and the tares! For one who attains his full stature, how many are stunted and deformed.

The will within us is the ultimate fact of consciousness. Yet how little have the best of us, in acquirements, in position, even in character, that may be credited entirely to ourselves; how much to the influences that have molded us. Who is there, wise, learned, discreet, or strong, who might not, were he to trace the inner history of his life, turn, like the Stoic Emperor, to give thanks to the gods, that by this one and that one, and here and there, good examples have been set him, noble thoughts have reached him, and happy opportunities opened before him. Who is there, who, with his eyes about him, has reached the meridian of life, who has not sometimes echoed the thought of the pious Englishman, as the criminal passed to the gallows, "But for the grace of God, there go I." How little does heredity count as compared with conditions. This one, we say, is the result of a thousand years of European progress, and that one of a thousand years of Chinese petrifaction; yet, placed an infant in the heart of China, and but for the angle of the eye or the shade of the hair, the Caucasian would grow up as those around him, using the same speech, thinking the same thoughts, exhibiting the same tastes. Change Lady Vere de Vere in her cradle with an infant of the slums, and will the blood of a hundred earls give you a refined and cultured woman?

To remove want and the fear of want, to give to all classes leisure, and comfort, and independence, the decencies and refinements of life, the opportunities of mental and moral development, would be like turning water into a desert. The sterile waste would clothe itself with verdure, and the barren places where life seemed banned would ere long be dappled with the shade of trees and musical with the song of birds. Talents now hidden, virtues unsuspected, would come forth to make human life richer, fuller, happier, nobler. For in these round men who are stuck into three-cornered holes, and three-cornered men who are jammed into round holes; in these men who are wasting their energies in the scramble to be rich; in these who in factories are turned into machines, or are chained by necessity to bench or plow; in these children who are growing up in squalor, and vice, and ignorance, are powers of the highest order, talents the most splendid. They need but the opportunity to bring them forth.

Consider the possibilities of a state of society that gave that opportunity to all. Let imagination fill out the picture; its colors grow too bright for words to paint. Consider the moral elevation, the intellectual activity, the social life. Consider how by a thousand actions and interactions the members of every community are linked together, and how in the present condition of things even the fortunate few who stand upon the apex of the social pyramid must suffer, though they know it not, from the want, ignorance, and degradation that are underneath. Consider these things and then say whether the change I propose would not be for the benefit of every one—even the greatest landholder? Would he not be safer of the future of his children in leaving them penniless in such a state of society than in leaving them the largest fortune in this? Did such a state of society anywhere exist, would he not buy entrance to it cheaply by giving up all his possessions?

I have now traced to their source social weakness and disease. I have shown the remedy. I have covered every point and met every objection. But the problems that we have been considering, great as they are, pass into problems greater yet—into the grandest problems with which the human mind can grapple. I am about to ask the reader who has gone with me so far, to go with me further, into still higher fields. But I ask him to remember that in the little space which remains of the limits to which this book must be confined, I cannot fully treat the questions which arise. I can but suggest some thoughts, which may, perhaps, serve as hints for further thought.

What in me is dark
Illumine, what is low raise and support;
That to the height of this great argument
I may assert eternal Providence
And justify the ways of God to men.
—MILTON.

CHAPTER 1

THE CURRENT THEORY OF HUMAN PROGRESS —ITS INSUFFICIENCY

If the conclusions at which we have arrived are correct, they will fall under a larger generalization.

Let us, therefore, recommence our inquiry from a higher standpoint, whence we may survey a wider field.

What is the law of human progress?

This is a question which, were it not for what has gone before, I should hesitate to review in the brief space I can now devote to it, as it involves, directly or indirectly, some of the very highest problems with which the human mind can engage. But it is a question which naturally comes up. Are or are not the conclusions to which we have come consistent with the great law under which human development goes on?

What is that law? We must find the answer to our question; for the current philosophy, though it clearly recognizes the existence of such a law, gives no more satisfactory account of it than the current political economy does of the persistence of want amid advancing wealth.

Let us, as far as possible, keep to the firm ground of facts. Whether man was or was not gradually developed from an animal, it is not necessary to inquire. However intimate may be the connection between questions which relate to man as we know him and questions which relate to his genesis, it is only from the former upon the latter that light can be thrown. Inference cannot proceed from the unknown to the known. It is only from facts

475

of which we are cognizant that we can infer what has preceded cognizance.

However man may have originated, all we know of him is as man—just as he is now to be found. There is no record or trace of him in any lower condition than that in which savages are still to be met. By whatever bridge he may have crossed the wide chasm which now separates him from the brutes, there remain of it no vestiges. Between the lowest savages of whom we know and the highest animals, there is an irreconcilable difference—a difference not merely of degree, but of kind. Many of the characteristics, actions, and emotions of man are exhibited by the lower animals; but man, no matter how low in the scale of humanity, has never yet been found destitute of one thing of which no animal shows the slightest trace, a clearly recognizable but almost undefinable something, which gives him the power of improvement—which makes him the progressive animal.

The beaver builds a dam, and the bird a nest, and the bee a cell; but while beavers' dams, and birds' nests, and bees' cells are always constructed on the same model, the house of the man passes from the rude hut of leaves and branches to the magnificent mansion replete with modern conveniences. The dog can to a certain extent connect cause and effect, and may be taught some tricks; but his capacity in these respects has not been a whit increased during all the ages he has been the associate of improving man, and the dog of civilization is not a whit more accomplished or intelligent than the dog of the wandering savage. We know of no animal that uses clothes, that cooks its food, that makes itself tools or weapons, that breeds other animals that it wishes to eat, or that has an articulate language. But men who do not do such things have never yet been found, or heard of, except in fable. That is to say, man, wherever we know him, exhibits this power—of supplementing what nature has done for him by what he does for himself; and, in fact, so inferior is the physical endowment of man, that there is no part of the world, save perhaps some of the small islands of the Pacific, where without this faculty he could maintain an existence.

Man everywhere and at all times exhibits this faculty —everywhere and at all times of which we have knowledge he has made some use of it. But the degree in which this has been done greatly varies. Between the rude canoe and the steamship; between the boomerang and the repeating rifle; between the roughly carved wooden idol and the breathing marble of Grecian art; between savage knowledge and modern science; between the wild Indian and the white settler; between the Hottentot woman and the belle of polished society, there is an enormous difference.

The varying degrees in which this faculty is used cannot be ascribed to differences in original capacity—the most highly improved peoples of the present day were savages within historic times, and we meet with the widest differences between peoples of the same stock. Nor can they be wholly ascribed to differences in physical environment—the cradles of learning and the arts are now in many cases tenanted by barbarians, and within a few years great cities rise on the hunting grounds of wild tribes. All these differences are evidently connected with social development. Beyond perhaps the veriest rudiments, it becomes possible for man to improve only as he lives with his fellows. All these improvements, therefore, in man's powers and conditions we summarize in the term civilization. Men improve as they become civilized, or learn to co-operate in society.

What is the law of this improvement? By what common principle can we explain the·different stages of civi-

lization at which different communities have arrived?
In what consists essentially the progress of civilization,
so that we may say of varying social adjustments, this
favors it, and that does not; or explain why an institution or condition which may at one time advance it may
at another time retard it?

The prevailing belief now is, that the progress of civilization is a development or evolution, in the course of
which man's powers are increased and his qualities improved by the operation of causes similar to those which
are relied upon as explaining the genesis of species—
viz., the survival of the fittest and the hereditary transmission of acquired qualities.

That civilization is an evolution—that it is, in the
language of Herbert Spencer, a progress from an indefinite, incoherent homogeneity to a definite, coherent
heterogeneity—there is no doubt; but to say this is not
to explain or identify the causes which forward or retard
it. How far the sweeping generalizations of Spencer,
which seek to account for all phenomena under terms
of matter and force, may, properly understood, include
all these causes, I am unable to say; but, as scientifically
expounded, the development philosophy has either not
yet definitely met this question, or has given birth, or
rather coherency, to an opinion which does not accord
with the facts.

The vulgar explanation of progress is, I think, very
much like the view naturally taken by the money-maker
of the causes of the unequal distribution of wealth. His
theory, if he has one, usually is, that there is plenty of
money to be made by those who have will and ability,
and that it is ignorance, or idleness, or extravagance,
that makes the difference between the rich and the poor.
And so the common explanation of differences of civilization is of differences in capacity. The civilized races
are the superior races, and advance in civilization is ac-

cording to this superiority—just as English victories were, in common English opinion, due to the natural superiority of Englishmen to frog-eating Frenchmen; and popular government, active invention, and greater average comfort are, or were until lately, in common American opinion, due to the greater "smartness of the Yankee Nation."

Now, just as the politico-economic doctrines which in the beginning of this inquiry we met and disproved, harmonize with the common opinion of men who see capitalists paying wages and competition reducing wages; just as the Malthusian theory harmonized with existing prejudices both of the rich and the poor; so does the explanation of progress as a gradual race improvement harmonize with the vulgar opinion which accounts by race differences for differences in civilization. It has given coherence and a scientific formula to opinions which already prevailed. Its wonderful spread since the time Darwin first startled the world with his "Origin of Species" has not been so much a conquest as an assimilation.

The view which now dominates the world of thought is this: That the struggle for existence, just in proportion as it becomes intense, impels men to new efforts and inventions. That this improvement and capacity for improvement is fixed by hereditary transmission, and extended by the tendency of the best adapted individual, or most improved individual, to survive and propagate among individuals, and of the best adapted, or most improved tribe, nation, or race to survive in the struggle between social aggregates. On this theory the differences between man and the animals, and differences in the relative progress of men, are now explained as confidently, and all but as generally, as a little while ago they were explained upon the theory of special creation and divine interposition.

The practical outcome of this theory is in a sort of hopeful fatalism, of which current literature is full.* In this view, progress is the result of forces which work slowly, steadily, and remorselessly, for the elevation of man. War, slavery, tyranny, superstition, famine, and pestilence, the want and misery which fester in modern civilization, are the impelling causes which drive man on, by eliminating poorer types and extending the higher; and hereditary transmission is the power by which advances are fixed, and past advances made the footing for new advances. The individual is the result of changes thus impressed upon and perpetuated through a long series of past individuals, and the social organization takes its form from the individuals of which it is composed. Thus, while this theory is, as Herbert Spencer says†—"radical to a degree beyond anything which current radicalism conceives," inasmuch as it looks for changes in the very nature of man; it is at the same time "conservative to a degree beyond anything conceived by current conservatism," inasmuch as it holds that no change can avail save these slow changes in men's natures. Philosophers may teach that this does not lessen the duty of endeavoring to reform abuses,

---

* In semiscientific or popularized form this may perhaps be seen in best, because frankest, expression in "The Martyrdom of Man," by Winwood Reade, a writer of singular vividness and power. This book is in reality a history of progress, or, rather, a monograph upon its causes and methods, and will well repay perusal for its vivid pictures, whatever may be thought of the capacity of the author for philosophic generalization. The connection between subject and title may be seen by the conclusion: "I give to universal history a strange but true title—*The Martyrdom of Man*. In each generation the human race has been tortured that their children might profit by their woes. Our own prosperity is founded on the agonies of the past. Is it therefore unjust that we also should suffer for the benefit of those who are to come?"

† "The Study of Sociology"—Conclusion.

just as the theologians who taught predestinarianism insisted on the duty of all to struggle for salvation; but, as generally apprehended, the result is fatalism—"do what we may, the mills of the gods grind on regardless either of our aid or our hindrance." I allude to this only to illustrate what I take to be the opinion now rapidly spreading and permeating common thought; not that in the search for truth any regard for its effects should be permitted to bias the mind. But this I take to be the current view of civilization: That it is the result of forces, operating in the way indicated, which slowly change the character, and improve and elevate the powers of man; that the difference between civilized man and savage is of a long race education, which has become permanently fixed in mental organization; and that this improvement tends to go on increasingly, to a higher and higher civilization. We have reached such a point that progress seems to be natural with us, and we look forward confidently to the greater achievements of the coming race—some even holding that the progress of science will finally give men immortality and enable them to make bodily the tour not only of the planets, but of the fixed stars, and at length to manufacture suns and systems for themselves.*

But without soaring to the stars, the moment that this theory of progression, which seems so natural to us amid an advancing civilization, looks around the world, it comes against an enormous fact—the fixed, petrified civilizations. The majority of the human race today have no idea of progress; the majority of the human race today look (as until a few generations ago our own ancestors looked) upon the past as the time of human perfection. The difference between the savage and the civilized man may be explained on the theory that the

---

* Winwood Reade, "The Martyrdom of Man."

former is as yet so imperfectly developed that his progress is hardly apparent; but how, upon the theory that
human progress is the result of general and continuous
causes, shall we account for the civilizations that had
progressed so far and then stopped? It cannot be said
of the Hindoo and of the Chinaman, as it may be said of
the savage, that our superiority is the result of a longer
education; that we are, as it were, the grown men of
nature, while they are the children. The Hindoos and
the Chinese were civilized when we were savages. The
had great cities, highly organized and powerful governments, literatures, philosophies, polished manners, considerable division of labor, large commerce, and elaborate
arts, when our ancestors were wandering barbarians,
living in huts and skin tents, not a whit further advanced than the American Indians. While we have progressed from this savage state to nineteenth century
civilization, they have stood still. If progress be the
result of fixed laws, inevitable and eternal, which impel
men forward, how shall we account for this?

One of the best popular expounders of the development philosophy, Walter Bagehot ("Physics and Politics"), admits the force of this objection, and endeavors
in this way to explain it: That the first thing necessary
to civilize man is to tame him; to induce him to live in
association with his fellows in subordination to law; and
hence a body or "cake" of laws and customs grows up,
being intensified and extended by natural selection, the
tribe or nation thus bound together having an advantage
over those who are not. That this cake of custom and
law finally becomes too thick and hard to permit further
progress, which can go on only as circumstances occur
which introduce discussion, and thus permit the freedom
and mobility necessary to improvement.

This explanation, which Mr. Bagehot offers, as he
says, with some misgivings, is I think at the expense of

the general theory. But it is not worth while speaking of that, for it, manifestly, does not explain the facts.

The hardening tendency of which Mr. Bagehot speaks would show itself at a very early period of development, and his illustrations of it are nearly all drawn from savage or semisavage life. Whereas, these arrested civilizations had gone a long distance before they stopped. There must have been a time when they were very far advanced as compared with the savage state, and were yet plastic, free, and advancing. These arrested civilizations stopped at a point which was hardly in anything inferior and in many respects superior to European civilization of, say, the sixteenth or at any rate the fifteenth century. Up to that point then there must have been discussion, the hailing of what was new, and mental activity of all sorts. They had architects who carried the art of building, necessarily by a series of innovations or improvements, up to a very high point; shipbuilders who in the same way, by innovation after innovation, finally produced as good a vessel as the warships of Henry VIII; inventors who stopped only on the verge of our most important improvements, and from some of whom we can yet learn; engineers who constructed great irrigation works and navigable canals; rival schools of philosophy and conflicting ideas of religion. One great religion, in many respects resembling Christianity, rose in India, displaced the old religion, passed into China, sweeping over that country, and was displaced again in its old seats, just as Christianity was displaced in its first seats. There was life, and active life, and the innovation that begets improvement, long after men had learned to live together. And, moreover, both India and China have received the infusion of new life in conquering races, with different customs and modes of thought.

The most fixed and petrified of all civilizations of

which we know anything was that of Egypt, where even art finally assumed a conventional and inflexible form. But we know that behind this must have been a time of life and vigor—a freshly developing and expanding civilization, such as ours is now—or the arts and sciences could never have been carried to such a pitch. And recent excavations have brought to light from beneath what we before knew of Egypt an earlier Egypt still—in statues and carvings which, instead of a hard and formal type, beam with life and expression, which show art struggling, ardent, natural, and free, the sure indication of an active and expanding life. So it must have been once with all now unprogressive civilizations.

But it is not merely these arrested civilizations that the current theory of development fails to account for. It is not merely that men have gone so far on the path of progress and then stopped; it is that men have gone far on the path of progress and then gone back. It is not merely an isolated case that thus confronts the theory—*it is the universal rule*. Every civilization that the world has yet seen has had its period of vigorous growth, of arrest and stagnation; its decline and fall. Of all the civilizations that have arisen and flourished, there remain today but those that have been arrested, and our own, which is not yet as old as were the pyramids when Abraham looked upon them—while behind the pyramids were twenty centuries of recorded history.

That our own civilization has a broader base, is of a more advanced type, moves quicker and soars higher than any preceding civilization is undoubtedly true; but in these respects it is hardly more in advance of the Greco-Roman civilization than that was in advance of Asiatic civilization; and if it were, that would prove nothing as to its permanence and future advance, unless it be shown that it is superior in those things which caused the ultimate failure of its predecessors. The current theory does not assume this.

In truth, nothing could be further from explaining the facts of universal history than this theory that civilization is the result of a course of natural selection which operates to improve and elevate the powers of man. That civilization has arisen at different times in different places and has progressed at different rates, is not inconsistent with this theory; for that might result from the unequal balancing of impelling and resisting forces; but that progress everywhere commencing, for even among the lowest tribes it is held that there has been some progress, has nowhere been continuous, but has everywhere been brought to a stand or retrogression, *is* absolutely inconsistent. For if progress operated to fix an improvement in man's nature and thus to produce further progress, though there might be occasional interruption, yet the general rule would be that progress would be continuous—that advance would lead to advance, and civilization develop into higher civilization.

Not merely the general rule, but *the universal rule*, is the reverse of this. The earth is the tomb of the dead empires, no less than of dead men. Instead of progress fitting men for greater progress, every civilization that was in its own time as vigorous and advancing as ours is now, has of itself come to a stop. Over and over again, art has declined, learning sunk, power waned, population become sparse, until the people who had built great temples and mighty cities, turned rivers and pierced mountains, cultivated the earth like a garden and introduced the utmost refinement into the minute affairs of life, remained but in a remnant of squalid barbarians, who had lost even the memory of what their ancestors had done, and regarded the surviving fragments of their grandeur as the work of genii, or of the mighty race before the flood. So true is this, that when we think of the past, it seems like the inexorable law, from which we can no more hope to be exempt than the young man who "feels his life in every limb" can hope to be exempt from the dissolution which is the common fate of all. "Even this, O Rome, must one day be thy fate!" wept Scipio over the ruins of Carthage, and Macaulay's picture of the New Zealander musing upon the broken arch of London Bridge appeals to the imagination of even those who see cities rising in the wilderness and help to lay the foundations of new empire. And so, when we erect a public building we make a hollow in the largest corner stone and carefully seal within it some mementos of our day, looking forward to the time when our works shall be ruins and ourselves forgot.

Nor whether this alternate rise and fall of civilization, this retrogression that always follows progression, be, or be not, the rhythmic movement of an ascending line (and I think, though I will not open the question, that it would be much more difficult to prove the affirmative than is generally supposed) makes no difference; for the current theory is in either case disproved. Civilizations have died and made no sign, and hard-won progress has been lost to the race forever; but, even if it be admitted that each wave of progress has made possible a higher wave and each civilization passed the torch to a greater civilization, the theory that civilization advances by changes wrought in the nature of man fails to explain the facts; for in every case it is not the race that has been educated and hereditarily modified by the old civilization that begins the new, but a fresh race coming from a lower level. It is the barbarians of the one epoch who have been the civilized men of the next; to be in their turn succeeded by fresh barbarians. For it has been heretofore always the case that men under the influences of civilization, though at first improving, afterward degenerate. The civilized man of today is vastly the superior of the uncivilized; but so in the time of its vigor was the civilized man of every dead civilization. But there are such things as the vices, the corruptions, the enervations of civilization, which past a certain point have always heretofore shown themselves. Every civilization that has been overwhelmed by barbarians has really perished from internal decay.

This universal fact, the moment that it is recognized, disposes of the theory that progress is by hereditary transmission. Looking over the history of the world, the line of greatest advance does not coincide for any length of time with any line of heredity. On any particular line of heredity, retrogression seems always to follow advance.

Shall we therefore say that there is a national or race life, as there is an individual life—that every social aggregate has, as it were, a certain amount of energy, the expenditure of which necessitates decay? This is an old and widespread idea, that is yet largely held, and that may be constantly seen cropping out incongruously in the writings of the expounders of the development philosophy. Indeed, I do not see why it may not be stated in terms of matter and of motion so as to bring it clearly within the generalizations of evolution. For considering its individuals as atoms, the growth of society is "an integration of matter and concomitant dissipation of motion; during which the matter passes from an indefinite, incoherent homogeneity to a definite, coherent heterogeneity, and during which the retained motion undergoes a parallel transformation."* And thus an analogy may be drawn between the life of a society and the life of a solar system upon the nebular hypothesis. As the heat and light of the sun are produced by the

* Herbert Spencer's definition of Evolution, "First Principles," p. 396.

aggregation of atoms evolving motion, which finally ceases when the atoms at length come to a state of equilibrium or rest, and a state of immobility succeeds, which can be broken in again only by the impact of external forces, which reverse the process of evolution, integrating motion and dissipating matter in the form of gas, again to evolve motion by its condensation; so, it may be said, does the aggregation of individuals in a community evolve a force which produces the light and warmth of civilization, but when this process ceases and the individual components are brought into a state of equilibrium, assuming their fixed places, petrifaction ensues, and the breaking up and diffusion caused by an incursion of barbarians is necessary to the recommencement of the process and a new growth of civilization.

But analogies are the most dangerous modes of thought. They may connect resemblances and yet disguise or cover up the truth. And all such analogies are superficial. While its members are constantly reproduced in all the fresh vigor of childhood, a community cannot grow old, as does a man, by the decay of its powers. While its aggregate force must be the sum of the forces of its individual components, a community cannot lose vital power unless the vital powers of its components are lessened.

Yet in both the common analogy which likens the life power of a nation to that of an individual, and in the one I have supposed, lurks the recognition of an obvious truth—the truth that the obstacles which finally bring progress to a halt are raised by the course of progress; that what has destroyed all previous civilizations has been the conditions produced by the growth of civilization itself.

This is a truth which in the current philosophy is ignored; but it is a truth most pregnant. Any valid theory of human progress must account for it.

CHAPTER **2** DIFFERENCES IN CIVILIZATION
—TO WHAT DUE

In attempting to discover the law of human progress, the first step must be to determine the essential nature of these differences which we describe as differences in civilization.

That the current philosophy, which attributes social progress to changes wrought in the nature of man, does not accord with historical facts, we have already seen. And we may also see, if we consider them, that the differences between communities in different stages of civilization cannot be ascribed to innate differences in the individuals who compose these communities. That there are natural differences is true, and that there is such a thing as hereditary transmission of peculiarities is undoubtedly true; but the great differences between men in different states of society cannot be explained in this way. The influence of heredity, which it is now the fashion to rate so highly, is as nothing compared with the influences which mold the man after he comes into the world. What is more ingrained in habit than language, which becomes not merely an automatic trick of the muscles, but the medium of thought? What persists longer, or will quicker show nationality? Yet we are not born with a predisposition to any language. Our mother tongue is our mother tongue only because we learned it in infancy. Although his ancestors have thought and spoken in one language for countless generations, a child who hears from the first nothing else,

will learn with equal facility any other tongue. And so
of other national or local or class peculiarities. They
seem to be matters of education and habit, not of transmission. Cases of white children captured by Indians
in infancy and brought up in the wigwam show this.
They become thorough Indians. And so, I believe, with
children brought up by gypsies.

That this is not so true of the children of Indians or
other distinctly marked races brought up by whites is, I
think, due to the fact that they are never treated precisely as white children. A gentleman who had taught
a colored school once told me that he thought the colored
children, up to the age of ten or twelve, were really
brighter and learned more readily than white children,
but that after that age they seemed to get dull and careless. He thought this proof of innate race inferiority,
and so did I at the time. But I afterward heard a
highly intelligent Negro gentleman (Bishop Hillery) incidentally make a remark which to my mind seems a
sufficient explanation. He said: "Our children, when
they are young, are fully as bright as white children,
and learn as readily. But as soon as they get old enough
to appreciate their status—to realize that they are looked
upon as belonging to an inferior race, and can never
hope to be anything more than cooks, waiters, or something of that sort, they lose their ambition and cease
to keep up." And to this he might have added, that being the children of poor, uncultivated and unambitious
parents, home influences told against them. For, I believe it is a matter of common observation that in the
primary part of education the children of ignorant
parents are quite as receptive as the children of intelligent parents, but by and by the latter, as a general rule,
pull ahead and make the most intelligent men and
women. The reason is plain. As to the first simple
things which they learn only at school, they are on a

par, but as their studies become more complex, the child who at home is accustomed to good English, hears intelligent conversation, has access to books, can get questions answered, etc., has an advantage which tells.

The same thing may be seen later in life. Take a man who has raised himself from the ranks of common labor, and just as he is brought into contact with men of culture and men of affairs, will he become more intelligent and polished. Take two brothers, the sons of poor parents, brought up in the same home and in the same way. One is put to a rude trade, and never gets beyond the necessity of making a living by hard daily labor; the other, commencing as an errand boy, gets a start in another direction, and becomes finally a successful lawyer, merchant, or politician. At forty or fifty the contrast between them will be striking, and the unreflecting will credit it to the greater natural ability which has enabled the one to push himself ahead. But just as striking a difference in manners and intelligence will be manifested between two sisters, one of whom, married to a man who has remained poor, has her life fretted with petty cares and devoid of opportunities, and the other of whom has married a man whose subsequent position brings her into cultured society and opens to her opportunities which refine taste and expand intelligence. And so deteriorations may be seen. That "evil communications corrupt good manners" is but an expression of the general law that human character is profoundly modified by its conditions and surroundings.

I remember once seeing, in a Brazilian seaport, a Negro man dressed in what was an evident attempt at the height of fashion, but without shoes and stockings. One of the sailors with whom I was in company, and who had made some runs in the slave trade, had a theory that a Negro was not a man, but a sort of monkey, and pointed to this as evidence in proof, contending that it was not natural for a Negro to wear shoes, and that in his wild state he would wear no clothes at all. I afterward learned that it was not considered "the thing" there for slaves to wear shoes, just as in England it is not considered the thing for a faultlessly attired butler to wear jewelry, though for that matter I have since seen white men at liberty to dress as they pleased get themselves up as incongruously as the Brazilian slave. But a great many of the facts adduced as showing hereditary transmission have really no more bearing than this of our forecastle Darwinian.

That, for instance, a large number of criminals and recipients of public relief in New York have been shown to have descended from a pauper three or four generations back is extensively cited as showing hereditary transmission. But it shows nothing of the kind, inasmuch as an adequate explanation of the facts is nearer. Paupers will raise paupers, even if the children be not their own, just as familiar contact with criminals will make criminals of the children of virtuous parents. To learn to rely on charity is necessarily to lose the self-respect and independence necessary for self-reliance when the struggle is hard. So true is this that, as is well known, charity has the effect of increasing the demand for charity, and it is an open question whether public relief and private alms do not in this way do far more harm than good. And so of the disposition of children to show the same feelings, tastes, prejudices, or talents as their parents. They imbibe these dispositions just as they imbibe from their habitual associates. And the exceptions prove the rule, as dislikes or revulsions may be excited.

And there is, I think, a subtler influence which often accounts for what are looked upon as atavisms of character—the same influence that makes the boy who reads dime novels want to be a pirate. I once knew a gentleman in whose veins ran the blood of Indian chiefs. He used to tell me traditions learned from his grandfather, which illustrated what is difficult for a white man to comprehend—the Indian habit of thought, the intense but patient blood thirst of the trail, and the fortitude of the stake. From the way in which he dwelt on these, I have no doubt that under certain circumstances, highly educated, civilized man that he was, he would have shown traits which would have been looked on as due to his Indian blood; but which in reality would have been sufficiently explained by the broodings of his imagination upon the deeds of his ancestors.*

In any large community we may see, as between different classes and groups, differences of the same kind as those which exist between communities which we speak of as differing in civilization—differences of knowledge, belief, customs, tastes, and speech, which in their extremes show among people of the same race, living in the same country, differences almost as great as those between civilized and savage communities. As all stages of social development, from the stone age up, are yet to be found in contemporaneously existing communities, so in the same country and in the same city are to be found, side by side, groups which show similar diversities. In such countries as England and Germany, children of the same race, born and reared in the same place, will grow up, speaking the language differently, holding different beliefs, following different customs, and showing different tastes; and even in such a country as the

* Wordsworth, in his "Song at the Feast of Brougham Castle" has in highly poetical form alluded to this influence:

Armor rusting in his halls
On the blood of Clifford calls:
"Quell the Scot," exclaims the lance;
"Bear me to the heart of France,"
Is the longing of the shield.

BOOK X CHAPTER 2

United States differences of the same kind, though not
of the same degree, may be seen between different circles
or groups.

But these differences are certainly not innate. No
baby is born a Methodist or Catholic, to drop its h's or
to sound them. All these differences which distinguish
different groups or circles are derived from association in
these circles.

The Janissaries were made up of youths torn from
Christian parents at an early age, but they were none the
less fanatical Moslems and none the less exhibited all
the Turkish traits; the Jesuits and other orders show
distinct character, but it is certainly not perpetuated by
hereditary transmissions; and even such associations as
schools or regiments, where the components remain but
a short time and are constantly changing, exhibit general
characteristics, which are the result of mental impressions perpetuated by association.

Now, it is this body of traditions, beliefs, customs,
laws, habits, and associations, which arise in every community and which surround every individual—this
"super-organic environment," as Herbert Spencer calls
it, that, as I take it, is the great element in determining
national character. It is this, rather than hereditary
transmission, which makes the Englishman differ from
the Frenchman, the German from the Italian, the American from the Chinaman, and the civilized man from the
savage man. It is in this way that national traits are
preserved, extended, or altered.

Within certain limits, or, if you choose, without limits
in itself, hereditary transmission may develop or alter
qualities, but this is much more true of the physical
than of the mental part of a man, and much more true
of animals than it is even of the physical part of man.
Deductions from the breeding of pigeons or cattle will
not apply to man, and the reason is clear. The life of

man, even in his rudest state, is infinitely more complex. He is constantly acted on by an infinitely greater number of influences, amid which the relative influence of heredity becomes less and less. A race of men with no greater mental activity than the animals—men who only ate, drank, slept, and propagated—might, I doubt not, by careful treatment and selection in breeding, be made, in course of time, to exhibit as great diversities in bodily shape and character as similar means have produced in the domestic animals. But there are no such men; and in men as they are, mental influences, acting through the mind upon the body, would constantly interrupt the process. You cannot fatten a man whose mind is on the strain, by cooping him up and feeding him as you would fatten a pig. In all probability men have been upon the earth longer than many species of animals. They have been separated from each other under differences of climate that produce the most marked differences in animals, and yet the physical differences between the different races of men are hardly greater than the difference between white horses and black horses—they are certainly nothing like as great as between dogs of the same subspecies, as, for instance, the different varieties of the terrier or spaniel. And even these physical differences between races of men, it is held by those who account for them by natural selection and hereditary transmission, were brought out when man was much nearer the animal—that is to say, when he had less mind.

And if this be true of the physical constitution of man, in how much higher degree is it true of his mental constitution? All our physical parts we bring with us into the world; but the mind develops afterward.

There is a stage in the growth of every organism in which it cannot be told, except by the environment, whether the animal that is to be will be fish or reptile, monkey or man. And so with the newborn infant; whether the mind that is yet to awake to consciousness and power is to be English or German, American or Chinese—the mind of a civilized man or the mind of a savage—depends entirely on the social environment in which it is placed.

Take a number of infants born of the most highly civilized parents and transport them to an uninhabited country. Suppose them in some miraculous way to be sustained until they come of age to take care of themselves, and what would you have? More helpless savages than any we know of. They would have fire to discover; the rudest tools and weapons to invent; language to construct. They would, in short, have to stumble their way to the simplest knowledge which the lowest races now possess, just as a child learns to walk. That they would in time do all these things I have not the slightest doubt, for all these possibilities are latent in the human mind just as the power of walking is latent in the human frame, but I do not believe they would do them any better or worse, any slower or quicker, than the children of barbarian parents placed in the same conditions. Given the very highest mental powers that exceptional individuals have ever displayed, and what could mankind be if one generation were separated from the next by an interval of time, as are the seventeen-year locusts? One such interval would reduce mankind, not to savagery, but to a condition compared with which savagery, as we know it, would seem civilization.

And, reversely, suppose a number of savage infants could, unknown to the mothers, for even this would be necessary to make the experiment a fair one, be substituted for as many children of civilization, can we suppose that growing up they would show any difference? I think no one who has mixed much with different peoples and classes will think so. The great lesson that is thus learned is that "human nature is human nature all the world over." And this lesson, too, may be learned in the library. I speak not so much of the accounts of travelers, for the accounts given of savages by the civilized men who write books are very often just such accounts as savages would give of us did they make flying visits and then write books; but of those mementos of the life and thoughts of other times and other peoples, which, translated into our language of today, are like glimpses of our own lives and gleams of our own thought. The feeling they inspire is that of the essential similarity of men. "This," says Emanuel Deutsch—"this is the end of all investigation into history or art. *They were even as we are.*"

There is a people to be found in all parts of the world who well illustrate what peculiarities are due to hereditary transmission and what to transmission by association. The Jews have maintained the purity of their blood more scrupulously and for a far longer time than any of the European races, yet I am inclined to think that the only characteristic that can be attributed to this is that of physiognomy, and this is in reality far less marked than is conventionally supposed, as any one who will take the trouble may see on observation. Although they have constantly married among themselves, the Jews have everywhere been modified by their surroundings—the English, Russian, Polish, German, and Oriental Jews differing from each other in many respects as much as do the other people of those countries. Yet they have much in common, and have everywhere preserved their individuality. The reason is clear. It is the Hebrew religion—and certainly religion is not transmitted by generation, but by association—which has everywhere preserved the distinctiveness of the Hebrew race. This religion, which children derive, not as they derive their physical characteristics, but by precept and association, is not merely exclusive in its teachings, but has, by engendering suspicion and dislike, produced a powerful outside pressure which, even more than its precepts, has everywhere constituted of the Jews a community within a community. Thus has been built up and maintained a certain peculiar environment which gives a distinctive character. Jewish intermarriage has been the effect, not the cause of this. What persecution which stopped short of taking Jewish children from their parents and bringing them up outside of this peculiar environment could not accomplish, will be accomplished by the lessening intensity of religious belief, as is already evident in the United States, where the distinction between Jew and Gentile is fast disappearing.

And it seems to me that the influence of this social net or environment will explain what is so often taken as proof of race differences—the difficulty which less civilized races show in receiving higher civilization, and the manner in which some of them melt away before it. Just as one social environment persists, so does it render it difficult or impossible for those subject to it to accept another.

The Chinese character is fixed if that of any people is. Yet the Chinese in California acquire American modes of working, trading, the use of machinery, etc., with such facility as to prove that they have no lack of flexibility, or natural capacity. That they do not change in other respects is due to the Chinese environment that still persists and still surrounds them. Coming from China, they look forward to return to China, and live while here in a little China of their own, just as the Englishmen in India maintain a little England. It is not merely that we naturally seek association with those who share our peculiarities, and that thus language, religion and custom tend to persist where individuals are not absolutely isolated; but that these differences provoke an external pressure, which compels such association.

These obvious principles fully account for all the phenomena which are seen in the meeting of one stage or body of culture with another, without resort to the theory of ingrained differences. For instance, as comparative philology has shown, the Hindoo is of the same race as his English conqueror, and individual instances have abundantly shown that if he could be placed completely and exclusively in the English environment (which, as before stated, could be thoroughly done only by placing infants in English families in such a way that neither they, as they grow up, nor those around them, would be conscious of any distinction) one generation would be all required to thoroughly implant European civilization. But the progress of English ideas and habits in India must be necessarily very slow, because they meet there the web of ideas and habits constantly perpetuated through an immense population, and interlaced with every act of life.

Mr. Bagehot ("Physics and Politics") endeavors to explain the reason why barbarians waste away before our civilization, while they did not before that of the ancients, by assuming that the progress of civilization has given us tougher physical constitutions. After alluding to the fact that there is no lament in any classical writer for the barbarians, but that everywhere the barbarian endured the contact with the Roman and the Roman allied himself to the barbarian, he says (pp. 47–8):

"Savages in the first year of the Christian era were pretty much what they were in the eighteen hundredth; and if they stood the contact of ancient civilized men and cannot stand ours, it follows that our race is presumably tougher than the ancient; for we have to bear, and do bear, the seeds of greater diseases than the ancients carried with them. We may use, perhaps, the unvarying savage as a meter to gauge the vigor of the constitution to whose contact he is exposed."

Mr. Bagehot does not attempt to explain how it is that eighteen hundred years ago civilization did not give the like relative advantage over barbarism that it does now. But there is no use of talking about that, or of the lack of proof that the human constitution has been a whit improved. To any one who has seen how the contact of our civilization affects the inferior races, a much readier though less flattering explanation will occur.

It is not because our constitutions are naturally tougher than those of the savage, that diseases which are comparatively innocuous to us are certain death to him. It is that we know and have the means of treating those diseases, while he is destitute both of knowledge and means. The same diseases with which the scum of civilization that floats in its advance inoculates the savage would prove as destructive to civilized men, if they knew no better than to let them run, as he in his ignorance has to let them run; and as a matter of fact they were as destructive, until we found out how to treat them. And not merely this, but the effect of the impingement of civilization upon barbarism is to weaken the power of the savage without bringing him into the conditions that give power to the civilized man. While his habits and customs still tend to persist, and do persist as far as they can, the conditions to which they were adapted are forcibly changed. He is a hunter in a land stripped of game; a warrior deprived of his arms and called on to plead in legal technicalities. He is not merely placed between cultures, but, as Mr. Bagehot says of the European half-breeds in India, he is placed between moralities, and learns the vices of civilization without its virtues. He loses his accustomed means of subsistence, he loses self-respect, he loses morality; he deteriorates and dies away. The miserable creatures who may be seen hanging around frontier towns or railroad stations, ready to beg, or steal, or solicit a viler commerce, are not fair representatives of the Indian before the white man had encroached upon his hunting grounds. They have lost the strength and virtues of their former state, without gaining those of a higher. In fact, civilization, as it pushes the red man, shows no virtues. To the Anglo-Saxon of the frontier, as a rule, the aborigine has no rights which the white man is bound to respect. He is impoverished, misunderstood, cheated, and abused. He dies out, as, under similar conditions, we should die out. He disappears before civilization as the Romanized Britons disappeared before Saxon barbarism.

The true reason why there is no lament in any classic writer for the barbarian, but that the Roman civilization assimilated instead of destroying, is, I take it, to be found not only in the fact that the ancient civilization was much nearer akin to the barbarians which it met, but in the more important fact that it was not extended as ours has been. It was carried forward, not by an advancing line of colonists, but by conquest which merely reduced the new province to general subjection, leaving the social, and generally the political organization of the people to a great degree unimpaired, so that, without shattering or deterioration, the process of assimilation went on. In a somewhat similar way the civilization of Japan seems to be now assimilating itself to European civilization.

In America the Anglo-Saxon has exterminated, instead of civilizing, the Indian, simply because he has not brought the Indian into his environment, nor yet has the contact been in such a way as to induce or permit the Indian web of habitual thought and custom to be changed rapidly enough to meet the new conditions into which he has been brought by the proximity of new and powerful neighbors. That there is no innate impediment to the reception of our civilization by these uncivilized races has been shown over and over again in individual cases. And it has likewise been shown, so far as the experiments have been permitted to go, by the Jesuits in Paraguay, the Franciscans in California, and the Protestant missionaries on some of the Pacific islands.

The assumption of physical improvement in the race within any time of which we have knowledge is utterly without warrant, and within the time of which Mr. Bagehot speaks, it is absolutely disproved. We know from classic statues, from the burdens carried and the marches made by ancient soldiers, from the records of runners and the feats of gymnasts, that neither in proportions nor strength has the race improved within two thousand years. But the assumption of mental improvement, which is even more confidently and generally made, is still more preposterous. As poets, artists, architects, philosophers, rhetoricians, statesmen, or soldiers, can modern civilization show individuals of greater mental power than can the ancient? There is no use in recalling names—every schoolboy knows them. For our models and personifications of mental power we go back to the ancients, and if we can for a moment imagine the possibility of what is held by that oldest and most widespread of all beliefs—that belief which Lessing declared on this account the most probably true, though he accepted it on metaphysical grounds—and suppose Homer or Virgil, Demosthenes or Cicero, Alexander, Hannibal or Cæsar, Plato or Lucretius, Euclid or Aristotle, as re-entering this life again in the nineteenth century, can we suppose that they would show any inferiority to the men of today? Or if we take any period since the classic age, even the darkest, or any previous period of which we know anything, shall we not find men who in the conditions and degree of knowledge of their times showed mental power of as high an order as men show now? And among the less advanced races do we not today, whenever our attention is called to them, find men who in their conditions exhibit mental qualities as great as civilization can show? Did the invention of the railroad, coming when it did, prove any greater inventive power than did the invention of the wheelbarrow when wheelbarrows were not? We of modern civilization are raised far above those who have preceded us and those of the less advanced races who are our contemporaries. But it is because we stand on a pyramid, not that we are taller. What the centuries have done for us is not to increase our stature, but to build up a structure on which we may plant our feet.

Let me repeat: I do not mean to say that all men possess the same capacities, or are mentally alike, any more than I mean to say that they are physically alike. Among all the countless millions who have come and gone on this earth, there were probably never two who either physically or mentally were exact counterparts. Nor yet do I mean to say that there are not as clearly marked race differences in mind as there are clearly marked race differences in body. I do not deny the influence of heredity in transmitting peculiarities of mind in the same way, and possibly to the same degree, as bodily peculiarities are transmitted. But nevertheless, there is, it seems to me, a common standard and natural symmetry of mind, as there is of body, toward which all deviations tend to return. The conditions under which we fall may produce such distortions as the Flatheads produce by compressing the heads of their infants or the Chinese by binding their daughters' feet. But as Flathead babies continue to be born with naturally shaped heads and Chinese babies with naturally shaped feet, so does nature seem to revert to the normal mental type. A child no more inherits his father's knowledge than he inherits his father's glass eye or artificial leg; the child of the most ignorant parents may become a pioneer of science or a leader of thought.

But this is the great fact with which we are concerned: That the differences between the people of communities in different places and at different times, which we call differences of civilization, are not differences which inhere in the individuals, but differences which inhere in the society; that they are not, as Herbert Spencer holds, differences resulting from differences in the units; but that they are differences resulting from the conditions under which these units are brought in the society. In short, I take the explanation of the differences which distinguish communities to be this: That each society, small or great, necessarily weaves for itself a web of knowledge, beliefs, customs, language, tastes, institutions, and laws. Into this web, woven by each society, or rather, into these webs, for each community above the simplest is made up of minor societies, which overlap and interlace each other, the individual is received at birth and continues until his death. This is the matrix in which mind unfolds and from which it takes its stamp. This is the way in which customs, and religions, and prejudices, and tastes, and languages, grow up and are perpetuated. This is the way that skill is transmitted and knowledge is stored up, and the discoveries of one time made the common stock and stepping stone of the next. Though it is this that often offers the most serious obstacles to progress, it is this that makes progress possible. It is this that enables any schoolboy in our time to learn in a few hours more of the universe than Ptolemy knew; that places the most humdrum scientist far above the level reached by the giant mind of Aristotle. This is to the race what memory is to the individual. Our wonderful arts, our far-reaching science, our marvelous inventions—they have come through this.

Human progress goes on as the advances made by one generation are in this way secured as the common property of the next, and made the starting point for new advances.

CHAPTER **3** THE LAW OF HUMAN PROGRESS

What, then, is the law of human progress—the law under which civilization advances?

It must explain clearly and definitely, and not by vague generalities or superficial analogies, why, though mankind started presumably with the same capacities and at the same time, there now exist such wide differences in social development. It must account for the arrested civilizations and for the decayed and destroyed civilizations; for the general facts as to the rise of civilization, and for the petrifying or enervating force which the progress of civilization has heretofore always evolved. It must account for retrogression as well as for progression; for the differences in general character between Asiatic and European civilizations; for the difference between classical and modern civilizations; for the different rates at which progress goes on; and for those bursts, and starts, and halts of progress which are so marked as minor phenomena. And, thus, it must show us what are the essential conditions of progress, and what social adjustments advance and what retard it.

It is not difficult to discover such a law. We have but to look and we may see it. I do not pretend to give it scientific precision, but merely to point it out.

The incentives to progress are the desires inherent in human nature—the desire to gratify the wants of the animal nature, the wants of the intellectual nature, and the wants of the sympathetic nature; the desire to be, to know, and to do—desires that short of infinity can never be satisfied, as they grow by what they feed on.

Mind is the instrument by which man advances, and by which each advance is secured and made the vantage ground for new advances. Though he may not by taking thought add a cubit to his stature, man may by taking thought extend his knowledge of the universe and his power over it, in what, so far as we can see, is an infinite degree. The narrow span of human life allows the individual to go but a short distance, but though each generation may do but little, yet generations, succeeding to the gain of their predecessors, may gradually elevate the status of mankind, as coral polyps, building one generation upon the work of the other, gradually elevate themselves from the bottom of the sea.

Mental power is, therefore, the motor of progress, and men tend to advance in proportion to the mental power expended in progression—the mental power which is devoted to the extension of knowledge, the improvement of methods, and the betterment of social conditions.

Now mental power is a fixed quantity—that is to say, there is a limit to the work a man can do with his mind, as there is to the work he can do with his body; therefore, the mental power which can be devoted to progress is only what is left after what is required for nonprogressive purposes.

These nonprogressive purposes in which mental power is consumed may be classified as maintenance and conflict. By maintenance I mean, not only the support of existence, but the keeping up of the social condition and the holding of advances already gained. By conflict I mean not merely warfare and preparation for warfare, but all expenditure of mental power in seeking the gratification of desire at the expense of others, and in resistance to such aggression.

To compare society to a boat. Her progress through the water will not depend upon the exertion of her crew, but upon the exertion devoted to propelling her. This will be lessened by any expenditure of force required for bailing, or any expenditure of force in fighting among themselves, or in pulling in different directions.

Now, as in a separated state the whole powers of man are required to maintain existence, and mental power is set free for higher uses only by the association of men in communities, which permits the division of labor and all the economies which come with the co-operation of increased numbers, association is the first essential of progress. Improvement becomes possible as men come together in peaceful association, and the wider and closer the association, the greater the possibilities of improvement. And as the wasteful expenditure of mental power in conflict becomes greater or less as the moral law which accords to each an equality of rights is ignored or is recognized, equality (or justice) is the second essential of progress.

Thus association in equality is the law of progress. Association frees mental power for expenditure in improvement, and equality, or justice, or freedom—for the terms here signify the same thing, the recognition of the moral law—prevents the dissipation of this power in fruitless struggles.

Here is the law of progress, which will explain all diversities, all advances, all halts, and retrogressions. Men tend to progress just as they come closer together, and by co-operation with each other increase the mental power that may be devoted to improvement, but just as conflict is provoked, or association develops inequality of condition and power, this tendency to progression is lessened, checked, and finally reversed.

Given the same innate capacity, and it is evident that social development will go on faster or slower, will stop or turn back, according to the resistances it meets. In a general way these obstacles to improvement may, in relation to the society itself, be classed as external and internal—the first operating with greater force in the earlier stages of civilization, the latter becoming more important in the later stages.

Man is social in his nature. He does not require to be caught and tamed in order to induce him to live with his fellows. The utter helplessness with which he enters the world, and the long period required for the maturity of his powers, necessitate the family relation; which, as we may observe, is wider, and in its extensions stronger, among the ruder than among the more cultivated peoples. The first societies are families, expanding into tribes, still holding a mutual blood relationship, and even when they have become great nations claiming a common descent.

Given beings of this kind, placed on a globe of such diversified surface and climate as this, and it is evident that, even with equal capacity, and an equal start, social development must be very different. The first limit or resistance to association will come from the conditions of physical nature, and as these greatly vary with locality, corresponding differences in social progress must show themselves. The net rapidity of increase, and the closeness with which men, as they increase, can keep together, will, in the rude state of knowledge in which reliance for subsistence must be principally upon the spontaneous offerings of nature, very largely depend upon climate, soil, and physical conformation. Where much animal food and warm clothing are required; where the earth seems poor and niggard; where the exuberant life of tropical forests mocks barbarous man's puny efforts to control; where mountains, deserts, or arms of the sea separate and isolate men; association, and the power of improvement which it evolves, can at first go but a little way. But on the rich plains of warm climates, where human existence can be maintained with a smaller expenditure of force, and from a much smaller area, men can keep closer together, and the mental power which can at first be devoted to improvement is much greater. Hence civilization naturally first arises in the great valleys and table lands where we find its earliest monuments.

But these diversities in natural conditions, not merely thus directly produce diversities in social development, but, by producing diversities in social development, bring out in man himself an obstacle, or rather an active counterforce, to improvement. As families and tribes are separated from each other, the social feeling ceases to operate between them, and differences arise in language, custom, tradition, religion—in short, in the whole social web which each community, however small or large, constantly spins. With these differences, prejudices grow, animosities spring up, contact easily produces quarrels, aggression begets aggression, and wrong kindles revenge.* And so between these separate social aggregates arises the feeling of Ishmael and the spirit of Cain, war-

---

* How easy it is for ignorance to pass into contempt and dislike; how natural it is for us to consider any difference in manners, customs, religion, etc., as proof of the inferiority of those who differ from us, any one who has emancipated himself in any degree from prejudice, and who mixes with different classes, may see in civilized society. In religion, for instance, the spirit of the hymn—

"I'd rather be a Baptist, and wear a shining face,
    Than for to be a Methodist and always fall from grace,"

is observable in all denominations. As the English Bishop said, "Orthodoxy is my doxy, and heterodoxy is any other doxy," while the universal tendency is to classify all outside of the orthodoxies and heterodoxies of the prevailing religion as heathens or atheists. And the like tendency is observable as to all other differences.

fare becomes the chronic and seemingly natural relation of societies to each other, and the powers of men are expended in attack or defense, in mutual slaughter and mutual destruction of wealth, or in warlike preparations. How long this hostility persists, the protective tariffs and the standing armies of the civilized world today bear witness; how difficult it is to get over the idea that it is not theft to steal from a foreigner, the difficulty in procuring an international copyright act will show. Can we wonder at the perpetual hostilities of tribes and clans? Can we wonder that when each community was isolated from the others—when each, uninfluenced by the others, was spinning its separate web of social environment, which no individual can escape, that war should have been the rule and peace the exception? "They were even as we are."

Now, warfare is the negation of association. The separation of men into diverse tribes, by increasing warfare, thus checks improvement; while in the localities where a large increase in numbers is possible without much separation, civilization gains the advantage of exemption from tribal war, even when the community as a whole is carrying on warfare beyond its borders. Thus, where the resistance of nature to the close association of men is slightest, the counterforce of warfare is likely at first to be least felt; and in the rich plains where civilization first begins, it may rise to a great height while scattered tribes are yet barbarous. And thus, when small, separated communities exist in a state of chronic warfare which forbids advance, the first step to their civilization is the advent of some conquering tribe or nation that unites these smaller communities into a larger one, in which internal peace is preserved. Where this power of peaceable association is broken up, either by external assaults or internal dissensions, the advance ceases and retrogression begins.

But it is not conquest alone that has operated to promote association, and, by liberating mental power from
the necessities of warfare, to promote civilization. If
the diversities of climate, soil, and configuration of the
earth's surface operate at first to separate mankind, they
also operate to encourage exchange. And commerce,
which is in itself a form of association or co-operation,
operates to promote civilization, not only directly, but
by building up interests which are opposed to warfare,
and dispelling the ignorance which is the fertile mother
of prejudices and animosities.

And so of religion. Though the forms it has assumed
and the animosities it has aroused have often sundered
men and produced warfare, yet it has at other times been
the means of promoting association. A common worship has often, as among the Greeks, mitigated war and
furnished the basis of union, while it is from the triumph
of Christianity over the barbarians of Europe that modern civilization springs. Had not the Christian Church
existed when the Roman Empire went to pieces, Europe,
destitute of any bond of association, might have fallen
to a condition not much above that of the North American Indians or only received civilization with an Asiatic
impress from the conquering scimiters of the invading
hordes which had been welded into a mighty power by a
religion which, springing up in the deserts of Arabia,
had united tribes separated from time immemorial, and,
thence issuing, brought into the association of a common
faith a great part of the human race.

Looking over what we know of the history of the
world, we thus see civilization everywhere springing up
where men are brought into association, and everywhere
disappearing as this association is broken up. Thus the
Roman civilization, spread over Europe by the conquests
which insured internal peace, was overwhelmed by the
incursions of the northern nations that broke society

again into disconnected fragments; and the progress that now goes on in our modern civilization began as the feudal system again began to associate men in larger communities, and the spiritual supremacy of Rome to bring these communities into a common relation, as her legions had done before. As the feudal bonds grew into national autonomies, and Christianity worked the amelioration of manners, brought forth the knowledge that during the dark days she had hidden, bound the threads of peaceful union in her all-pervading organization, and taught association in her religious orders, a greater progress became possible, which, as men have been brought into closer and closer association and co-operation, has gone on with greater and greater force.

But we shall never understand the course of civilization, and the varied phenomena which its history presents, without a consideration of what I may term the internal resistances, or counter forces, which arise in the heart of advancing society, and which can alone explain how a civilization once fairly started should either come of itself to a halt or be destroyed by barbarians.

The mental power, which is the motor of social progress, is set free by association, which is, what, perhaps, it may be more properly called, an integration. Society in this process becomes more complex; its individuals more dependent upon each other. Occupations and functions are specialized. Instead of wandering, population becomes fixed. Instead of each man attempting to supply all of his wants, the various trades and industries are separated—one man acquires skill in one thing, and another in another thing. So, too, of knowledge, the body of which constantly tends to become vaster than one man can grasp, and is separated into different parts, which different individuals acquire and pursue. So, too, the performance of religious ceremonies tends to pass into the hands of a body of men specially devoted to that purpose, and the preservation of order, the administration of justice, the assignment of public duties and the distribution of awards, the conduct of war, etc., to be made the special functions of an organized government. In short, to use the language in which Herbert Spencer has defined evolution, the development of society is, in relation to its component individuals, the passing from an indefinite, incoherent homogeneity to a definite, coherent heterogeneity. The lower the stage of social development, the more society resembles one of those lowest of animal organisms which are without organs or limbs, and from which a part may be cut and yet live. The higher the stage of social development, the more society resembles those higher organisms in which functions and powers are specialized, and each member is vitally dependent on the others.

Now, this process of integration, of the specialization of functions and powers, as it goes on in society, is, by virtue of what is probably one of the deepest laws of human nature, accompanied by a constant liability to inequality. I do not mean that inequality is the necessary result of social growth, but that it is the constant tendency of social growth if unaccompanied by changes in social adjustments which, in the new conditions that growth produces, will secure equality. I mean, so to speak, that the garment of laws, customs, and political institutions, which each society weaves for itself, is constantly tending to become too tight as the society develops. I mean, so to speak, that man, as he advances, threads a labyrinth, in which, if he keeps straight ahead, he will infallibly lose his way, and through which reason and justice can alone keep him continuously in an ascending path.

For, while the integration which accompanies growth tends in itself to set free mental power to work improvement, there is, both with increase of numbers and with

increase in complexity of the social organization, a counter tendency set up to the production of a state of inequality, which wastes mental power, and, as it increases,
brings improvement to a halt.

To trace to its highest expression the law which thus
operates to evolve with progress the force which stops
progress, would be, it seems to me, to go far to the solution of a problem deeper than that of the genesis of the
material universe—the problem of the genesis of evil.
Let me content myself with pointing out the manner in
which, as society develops, there arise tendencies which
check development.

There are two qualities of human nature which it will
be well, however, first to call to mind. The one is the
power of habit—the tendency to continue to do things
in the same way; the other is the possibility of mental
and moral deterioration. The effect of the first in social
development is to continue habits, customs, laws, and
methods, long after they have lost their original usefulness, and the effect of the other is to permit the growth
of institutions and modes of thought from which the
normal perceptions of men instinctively revolt.

Now the growth and development of society not
merely tend to make each more and more dependent
upon all, and to lessen the influence of individuals, even
over their own conditions, as compared with the influence of society; but the effect of association or integration is to give rise to a collective power which is
distinguishable from the sum of individual powers.
Analogies, or, perhaps, rather illustrations of the same
law, may be found in all directions. As animal organisms increase in complexity, there arise, above the life
and power of the parts, a life and power of the integrated
whole; above the capability of involuntary movements,
the capability of voluntary movements. The actions
and impulses of bodies of men are, as has often been

observed, different from those which, under the same circumstances, would be called forth in individuals. The fighting qualities of a regiment may be very different from those of the individual soldiers. But there is no need of illustrations. In our inquiries into the nature and rise of rent, we traced the very thing to which I allude. Where population is sparse, land has no value; just as men congregate together, the value of land appears and rises—a clearly distinguishable thing from the values produced by individual effort; a value which springs from association, which increases as association grows greater, and disappears as association is broken up. And the same thing is true of power in other forms than those generally expressed in terms of wealth.

Now, as society grows, the disposition to continue previous social adjustments tends to lodge this collective power, as it arises, in the hands of a portion of the community; and this unequal distribution of the wealth and power gained as society advances tends to produce greater inequality, since aggression grows by what it feeds on, and the idea of justice is blurred by the habitual toleration of injustice.

In this way the patriarchal organization of society can easily grow into hereditary monarchy, in which the king is as a god on earth, and the masses of the people mere slaves of his caprice. It is natural that the father should be the directing head of the family, and that at his death the eldest son, as the oldest and most experienced member of the little community, should succeed to the headship. But to continue this arrangement as the family expands, is to lodge power in a particular line, and the power thus lodged necessarily continues to increase, as the common stock becomes larger and larger, and the power of the community grows. The head of the family passes into the hereditary king, who comes to look upon himself and to be looked upon by others

as a being of superior rights. With the growth of the
collective power as compared with the power of the individual, his power to reward and to punish increases,
and so increase the inducements to flatter and to fear
him; until finally, if the process be not disturbed, a nation grovels at the foot of a throne, and a hundred
thousand men toil for fifty years to prepare a tomb for
one of their own mortal kind.

So the war chief of a little band of savages is but one
of their number, whom they follow as their bravest and
most wary. But when large bodies come to act together,
personal selection becomes more difficult, a blinder
obedience becomes necessary and can be enforced, and
from the very necessities of warfare when conducted on
a large scale absolute power arises.

And so of the specialization of function. There is a
manifest gain in productive power when social growth
has gone so far that instead of every producer being
summoned from his work for fighting purposes, a regular military force can be specialized; but this inevitably
tends to the concentration of power in the hands of the
military class or their chiefs. The preservation of internal order, the administration of justice, the construction and care of public works, and, notably, the
observances of religion, all tend in similar manner to
pass into the hands of special classes, whose disposition it is to magnify their function and extend their
power.

But the great cause of inequality is in the natural
monopoly which is given by the possession of land. The
first perceptions of men seem always to be that land is
common property; but the rude devices by which this is
at first recognized—such as annual partitions or cultivation in common—are consistent with only a low stage of
development. The idea of property, which naturally
arises with reference to things of human production, is

easily transferred to land, and an institution which when
population is sparse merely secures to the improver and
user the due reward of his labor, finally, as population
becomes dense and rent arises, operates to strip the producer of his wages. Not merely this, but the appropriation of rent for public purposes, which is the only way
in which, with anything like a high development, land
can be readily retained as common property, becomes,
when political and religious power passes into the hands
of a class, the ownership of the land by that class, and
the rest of the community become merely tenants. And
wars and conquests, which tend to the concentration of
political power and to the institution of slavery, naturally result, where social growth has given land a value,
in the appropriation of the soil. A dominant class, who
concentrate power in their hands, will likewise soon concentrate ownership of the land. To them will fall large
partitions of conquered land, which the former inhabitants will till as tenants or serfs, and the public domain,
or common lands, which in the natural course of social
growth are left for awhile in every country, and in which
state the primitive system of village culture leaves pasture and woodland, are readily acquired, as we see by
modern instances. And inequality once established, the
ownership of land tends to concentrate as development
goes on.

I am merely attempting to set forth the general fact
that as a social development goes on, inequality tends
to establish itself, and not to point out the particular
sequence, which must necessarily vary with different conditions. But this main fact makes intelligible all the
phenomena of petrifaction and retrogression. The unequal distribution of the power and wealth gained by the
integration of men in society tends to check, and finally
to counterbalance, the force by which improvements are
made and society advances. On the one side, the masses
of the community are compelled to expend their mental

powers in merely maintaining existence. On the other side, mental power is expended in keeping up and intensifying the system of inequality, in ostentation, luxury, and warfare. A community divided into a class that rules and a class that is ruled—into the very rich and the very poor, may "build like giants and finish like jewelers"; but it will be monuments of ruthless pride and barren vanity, or of a religion turned from its office of elevating man into an instrument for keeping him down. Invention may for awhile to some degree go on; but it will be the invention of refinements in luxury, not the inventions that relieve toil and increase power. In the arcana of temples or in the chambers of court physicians knowledge may still be sought; but it will be hidden as a secret thing, or if it dares come out to elevate common thought or brighten common life, it will be trodden down as a dangerous innovator. For as it tends to lessen the mental power devoted to improvement, so does inequality tend to render men adverse to improvement. How strong is the disposition to adhere to old methods among the classes who are kept in ignorance by being compelled to toil for a mere existence, is too well known to require illustration; and on the other hand the conservatism of the classes to whom the existing social adjustment gives special advantages is equally apparent. This tendency to resist innovation, even though it be improvement, is observable in every special organization —in religion, in law, in medicine, in science, in trade guilds; and it becomes intense just as the organization is close. A close corporation has always an instinctive dislike of innovation and innovators, which is but the expression of an instinctive fear that change may tend to throw down the barriers which hedge it in from the common herd, and so rob it of importance and power; and it is always disposed to guard carefully its special knowledge or skill.

It is in this way that petrifaction succeeds progress.

The advance of inequality necessarily brings improvement to a halt, and as it still persists or provokes unavailing reactions, draws even upon the mental power necessary for maintenance, and retrogression begins.

These principles make intelligible the history of civilization.

In the localities where climate, soil, and physical conformation tended least to separate men as they increased, and where, accordingly, the first civilizations grew up, the internal resistances to progress would naturally develop in a more regular and thorough manner than where smaller communities, which in their separation had developed diversities, were afterward brought together into a closer association. It is this, it seems to me, which accounts for the general characteristics of the earlier civilizations as compared with the later civilizations of Europe. Such homogeneous communities, developing from the first without the jar of conflict between different customs, laws, religions, etc., would show a much greater uniformity. The concentrating and conservative forces would all, so to speak, pull together. Rival chieftains would not counterbalance each other, nor diversities of belief hold the growth of priestly influence in check. Political and religious power, wealth and knowledge, would thus tend to concentrate in the same centers. The same causes which tended to produce the hereditary king and hereditary priest would tend to produce the hereditary artisan and laborer, and to separate society into castes. The power which association sets free for progress would thus be wasted, and barriers to further progress be gradually raised. The surplus energies of the masses would be devoted to the construction of temples, palaces, and pyramids; to ministering to the pride and pampering the luxury of their rulers; and should any disposition to improvement arise among the classes of leisure it would at once be

checked by the dread of innovation. Society developing in this way must at length stop in a conservatism
which permits no further progress.

How long such a state of complete petrifaction, when
once reached, will continue, seems to depend upon external causes, for the iron bonds of the social environment which grows up repress disintegrating forces as
well as improvement. Such a community can be most
easily conquered, for the masses of the people are trained
to a passive acquiescence in a life of hopeless labor. If
the conquerors merely take the place of the ruling class,
as the Hyksos did in Egypt and the Tartars in China,
everything will go on as before. If they ravage and destroy, the glory of palace and temple remains but in
ruins, population becomes sparse, and knowledge and
art are lost.

European civilization differs in character from civilizations of the Egyptian type because it springs not from
the association of a homogeneous people developing
from the beginning, or at least for a long time, under
the same conditions, but from the association of peoples
who in separation had acquired distinctive social characteristics, and whose smaller organizations longer prevented the concentration of power and wealth in one
center. The physical conformation of the Grecian peninsula is such as to separate the people at first into a
number of small communities. As those petty republics
and nominal kingdoms ceased to waste their energies in
warfare, and the peaceable co-operation of commerce
extended, the light of civilization blazed up. But the
principle of association was never strong enough to save
Greece from intertribal war, and when this was put an
end to by conquest, the tendency to inequality, which
had been combated with various devices by Grecian
sages and statesmen, worked its result, and Grecian
valor, art, and literature became things of the past.

And so in the rise and extension, the decline and fall, of Roman civilization, may be seen the working of these two principles of association and equality, from the combination of which springs progress.

Springing from the association of the independent husbandmen and free citizens of Italy, and gaining fresh strength from conquests which brought hostile nations into common relations, the Roman power hushed the world in peace. But the tendency to inequality, checking real progress from the first, increased as the Roman civilization extended. The Roman civilization did not petrify as did the homogeneous civilizations where the strong bonds of custom and superstition that held the people in subjection probably also protected them, or at any rate kept the peace between rulers and ruled; it rotted, declined and fell. Long before Goth or Vandal had broken through the cordon of the legions, even while her frontiers were advancing, Rome was dead at the heart. Great estates had ruined Italy. Inequality had dried up the strength and destroyed the vigor of the Roman world. Government became despotism, which even assassination could not temper; patriotism became servility; vices the most foul flouted themselves in public; literature sank to puerilities; learning was forgotten; fertile districts became waste without the ravages of war —everywhere inequality produced decay, political, mental, moral, and material. The barbarism which overwhelmed Rome came not from without, but from within. It was the necessary product of the system which had substituted slaves and coloni for the independent husbandmen of Italy, and carved the provinces into estates of senatorial families.

Modern civilization owes its superiority to the growth of equality with the growth of association. Two great causes contributed to this—the splitting up of concentrated power into innumerable little centers by the influx of the Northern nations, and the influence of Christianity. Without the first there would have been the petrifaction and slow decay of the Eastern Empire, where church and state were closely married and loss of external power brought no relief of internal tyranny. And but for the other there would have been barbarism, without principle of association or amelioration. The petty chiefs and allodial lords who everywhere grasped local sovereignty held each other in check. Italian cities recovered their ancient liberty, free towns were founded, village communities took root, and serfs acquired rights in the soil they tilled. The leaven of Teutonic ideas of equality worked through the disorganized and disjointed fabric of society. And although society was split up into an innumerable number of separated fragments, yet the idea of closer association was always present—it existed in the recollections of a universal empire; it existed in the claims of a universal church.

Though Christianity became distorted and alloyed in percolating through a rotting civilization; though pagan gods were taken into her pantheon, and pagan forms into her ritual, and pagan ideas into her creed; yet her essential idea of the equality of men was never wholly destroyed. And two things happened of the utmost moment to incipient civilization—the establishment of the papacy and the celibacy of the clergy. The first prevented the spiritual power from concentrating in the same lines as the temporal power; and the latter prevented the establishment of a priestly caste, during a time when all power tended to hereditary form.

In her efforts for the abolition of slavery; in her Truce of God; in her monastic orders; in her councils which united nations, and her edicts which ran without regard to political boundaries; in the lowborn hands in which she placed a sign before which the proudest knelt; in her

bishops who by consecration became the peers of the
greatest nobles; in her "Servant of Servants," for so
his official title ran, who, by virtue of the ring of a
simple fisherman, claimed the right to arbitrate between
nations, and whose stirrup was held by kings; the
Church, in spite of everything, was yet a promoter of
association, a witness for the natural equality of men;
and by the Church herself was nurtured a spirit that,
when her early work of association and emancipation
was well-nigh done—when the ties she had knit had
become strong, and the learning she had preserved had
been given to the world—broke the chains with which
she would have fettered the human mind, and in a great
part of Europe rent her organization.

The rise and growth of European civilization is too
vast and complex a subject to be thrown into proper
perspective and relation in a few paragraphs; but in all
its details, as in its main features, it illustrates the
truth that progress goes on just as society tends toward
closer association and greater equality. Civilization is
co-operation. Union and liberty are its factors. The
great extension of association—not alone in the growth
of larger and denser communities, but in the increase of
commerce and the manifold exchanges which knit each
community together and link them with other though
widely separated communities; the growth of international and municipal law; the advances in security of
property and of person, in individual liberty, and towards democratic government—advances, in short, towards the recognition of the equal rights to life, liberty,
and the pursuit of happiness—it is these that make our
modern civilization so much greater, so much higher,
than any that has gone before. It is these that have set
free the mental power which has rolled back the veil of
ignorance which hid all but a small portion of the globe
from men's knowledge; which has measured the orbits of
the circling spheres and bids us see moving, pulsing life

in a drop of water; which has opened to us the ante-chamber of nature's mysteries and read the secrets of a long-buried past; which has harnessed in our service physical forces beside which man's efforts are puny; and increased productive power by a thousand great inventions.

In that spirit of fatalism to which I have alluded as pervading current literature, it is the fashion to speak even of war and slavery as means of human progress. But war, which is the opposite of association, can aid progress only when it prevents further war or breaks down antisocial barriers which are themselves passive war.

As for slavery, I cannot see how it could ever have aided in establishing freedom, and freedom, the synonym of equality, is, from the very rudest state in which man can be imagined, the stimulus and condition of progress. Auguste Comte's idea that the institution of slavery destroyed cannibalism is as fanciful as Elia's humorous notion of the way mankind acquired a taste for roast pig. It assumes that a propensity that has never been found developed in man save as the result of the most unnatural conditions—the direst want or the most brutalizing superstitions*—is an original impulse, and that he, even in his lowest state the highest of all animals, has natural appetites which the nobler brutes do not show. And so of the idea that slavery began civilization by giving slaveowners leisure for improvement.

Slavery never did and never could aid improvement. Whether the community consist of a single master and a single slave, or of thousands of masters and millions of slaves, slavery necessarily involves a waste of human

---

* The Sandwich Islanders did honor to their good chiefs by eating their bodies. Their bad and tyrannical chiefs they would not touch. The New Zealanders had a notion that by eating their enemies they acquired their strength and valor. And this seems to be the general origin of eating prisoners of war.

power; for not only is slave labor less productive than
free labor, but the power of masters is likewise wasted
in holding and watching their slaves, and is called away
from directions in which real improvement lies. From
first to last, slavery, like every other denial of the natural equality of men, has hampered and prevented progress. Just in proportion as slavery plays an important
part in the social organization does improvement cease.
That in the classical world slavery was so universal, is
undoubtedly the reason why the mental activity which
so polished literature and refined art never hit on any
of the great discoveries and inventions which distinguish
modern civilization. No slaveholding people ever were
an inventive people. In a slaveholding community the
upper classes may become luxurious and polished; but
never inventive. Whatever degrades the laborer and
robs him of the fruits of his toil stifles the spirit of
invention and forbids the utilization of inventions and
discoveries even when made. To freedom alone is given
the spell of power which summons the genii in whose
keeping are the treasures of earth and the viewless
forces of the air.

The law of human progress, what is it but the moral
law? Just as social adjustments promote justice, just
as they acknowledge the equality of right between man
and man, just as they insure to each the perfect liberty
which is bounded only by the equal liberty of every
other, must civilization advance. Just as they fail in
this, must advancing civilization come to a halt and
recede. Political economy and social science cannot
teach any lessons that are not embraced in the simple
truths that were taught to poor fishermen and Jewish
peasants by One who eighteen hundred years ago was
crucified—the simple truths which, beneath the warpings
of selfishness and the distortions of superstition, seem to
underlie every religion that has ever striven to formulate the spiritual yearnings of man.

CHAPTER **4** HOW MODERN CIVILIZATION
MAY DECLINE

The conclusion we have thus reached harmonizes completely with our previous conclusions.

This consideration of the law of human progress not only brings the politico-economic laws, which in this inquiry we have worked out, within the scope of a higher law—perhaps the very highest law our minds can grasp —but it proves that the making of land common property in the way I have proposed would give an enormous impetus to civilization, while the refusal to do so must entail retrogression. A civilization like ours must either advance or go back; it cannot stand still. It is not like those homogeneous civilizations, such as that of the Nile Valley, which molded men for their places and put them in it like bricks into a pyramid. It much more resembles that civilization whose rise and fall is within historic times, and from which it sprung.

There is just now a disposition to scoff at any implication that we are not in all respects progressing, and the spirit of our times is that of the edict which the flattering premier proposed to the Chinese Emperor who burned the ancient books—"that all who may dare to speak together about the She and the Shoo be put to death; that those who make mention of the past so as to blame the present be put to death along with their relatives."

Yet it is evident that there have been times of decline, just as there have been times of advance; and it is further evident that these epochs of decline could not at first have been generally recognized.

He would have been a rash man who, when Augustus was changing the Rome of brick to the Rome of marble, when wealth was augmenting and magnificence increasing, when victorious legions were extending the frontier, when manners were becoming more refined, language more polished, and literature rising to higher splendors —he would have been a rash man who then would have said that Rome was entering her decline. Yet such was the case.

And whoever will look may see that though our civilization is apparently advancing with greater rapidity than ever, the same cause which turned Roman progress into retrogression is operating now.

What has destroyed every previous civilization has been the tendency to the unequal distribution of wealth and power. This same tendency, operating with increasing force, is observable in our civilization today, showing itself in every progressive community, and with greater intensity the more progressive the community. Wages and interest tend constantly to fall, rent to rise, the rich to become very much richer, the poor to become more helpless and hopeless, and the middle class to be swept away.

I have traced this tendency to its cause. I have shown by what simple means this cause may be removed. I now wish to point out how, if this is not done, progress must turn to decadence, and modern civilization decline to barbarism, as have all previous civilizations. It is worth while to point out how this may occur, as many people, being unable to see how progress may pass into retrogression, conceive such a thing impossible. Gibbon, for instance, thought that modern civilization could never be destroyed because there remained no barbarians to overrun it, and it is a common idea that the invention of printing by so multiplying books has prevented the possibility of knowledge ever again being lost.

The conditions of social progress, as we have traced the law, are association and equality. The general tendency of modern development, since the time when we can first discern the gleams of civilization in the darkness which followed the fall of the Western Empire, has been toward political and legal equality—to the abolition of slavery; to the abrogation of status; to the sweeping away of hereditary privileges; to the substitution of parliamentary for arbitrary government; to the right of private judgment in matters of religion; to the more equal security in person and property of high and low, weak and strong; to the greater freedom of movement and occupation, of speech and of the press. The history of modern civilization is the history of advances in this direction—of the struggles and triumphs of personal, political, and religious freedom. And the general law is shown by the fact that just as this tendency has asserted itself civilization has advanced, while just as it has been repressed or forced back civilization has been checked.

This tendency has reached its full expression in the American Republic, where political and legal rights are absolutely equal, and, owing to the system of rotation in office, even the growth of a bureaucracy is prevented; where every religious belief or non-belief stands on the same footing; where every boy may hope to be President, every man has an equal voice in public affairs, and every official is mediately or immediately dependent for the short lease of his place upon a popular vote. This tendency has yet some triumphs to win in England, in extending the suffrage, and sweeping away the vestiges of monarchy, aristocracy, and prelacy; while in such countries as Germany and Russia, where divine right is yet a good deal more than a legal fiction, it has a con-

siderable distance to go. But it is the prevailing tendency, and how soon Europe will be completely republican
is only a matter of time, or rather of accident. The
United States are therefore in this respect, the most advanced of all the great nations, in a direction in which
all are advancing, and in the United States we see just
how much this tendency to personal and political freedom can of itself accomplish.

Now, the first effect of the tendency to political equality was to the more equal distribution of wealth and
power; for, while population is comparatively sparse,
inequality in the distribution of wealth is principally due
to the inequality of personal rights, and it is only as
material progress goes on that the tendency to inequality
involved in the reduction of land to private ownership
strongly appears. But it is now manifest that absolute
political equality does not in itself prevent the tendency
to inequality involved in the private ownership of land,
and it is further evident that political equality, co-
existing with an increasing tendency to the unequal
distribution of wealth, must ultimately beget either the
despotism of organized tyranny or the worse despotism
of anarchy.

To turn a republican government into a despotism the
basest and most brutal, it is not necessary formally to
change its constitution or abandon popular elections.
It was centuries after Cæsar before the absolute master
of the Roman world pretended to rule other than by
authority of a Senate that trembled before him.

But forms are nothing when substance has gone, and
the forms of popular government are those from which
the substance of freedom may most easily go. Extremes
meet, and a government of universal suffrage and theoretical equality may, under conditions which impel the
change, most readily become a despotism. For there
despotism advances in the name and with the might

of the people. The single source of power once secured, everything is secured. There is no unfranchised class to whom appeal may be made, no privileged orders who in defending their own rights may defend those of all. No bulwark remains to stay the flood, no eminence to rise above it. They were belted barons led by a mitered archbishop who curbed the Plantagenet with Magna Charta; it was the middle classes who broke the pride of the Stuarts; but a mere aristocracy of wealth will never struggle while it can hope to bribe a tyrant.

And when the disparity of condition increases, so does universal suffrage make it easy to seize the source of power, for the greater is the proportion of power in the hands of those who feel no direct interest in the conduct of government; who, tortured by want and embruted by poverty, are ready to sell their votes to the highest bidder or follow the lead of the most blatant demagogue; or who, made bitter by hardships, may even look upon profligate and tyrannous government with the satisfaction we may imagine the proletarians and slaves of Rome to have felt, as they saw a Caligula or Nero raging among the rich patricians. Given a community with republican institutions, in which one class is too rich to be shorn of its luxuries, no matter how public affairs are administered, and another so poor that a few dollars on election day will seem more than any abstract consideration; in which the few roll in wealth and the many seethe with discontent at a condition of things they know not how to remedy, and power must pass into the hands of jobbers who will buy and sell it as the Prætorians sold the Roman purple, or into the hands of demagogues who will seize and wield it for a time, only to be displaced by worse demagogues.

Where there is anything like an equal distribution of wealth—that is to say, where there is general patriotism, virtue, and intelligence—the more democratic the gov-

ernment the better it will be; but where there is gross
inequality in the distribution of wealth, the more democratic the government the worse it will be; for, while
rotten democracy may not in itself be worse than rotten
autocracy, its effects upon national character will be
worse. To give the suffrage to tramps, to paupers, to
men to whom the chance to labor is a boon, to men who
must beg, or steal, or starve, is to invoke destruction.
To put political power in the hands of men embittered
and degraded by poverty is to tie firebrands to foxes and
turn them loose amid the standing corn; it is to put out
the eyes of a Samson and to twine his arms around the
pillars of national life.

Even the accidents of hereditary succession or of selection by lot, the plan of some of the ancient republics,
may sometimes place the wise and just in power; but in
a corrupt democracy the tendency is always to give
power to the worst. Honesty and patriotism are
weighted, and unscrupulousness commands success. The
best gravitate to the bottom, the worst float to the top,
and the vile will only be ousted by the viler. While as
national character must gradually assimilate to the
qualities that win power, and consequently respect, that
demoralization of opinion goes on which in the long
panorama of history we may see over and over again
transmuting races of freemen into races of slaves.

As in England in the last century, when Parliament
was but a close corporation of the aristocracy, a corrupt
oligarchy clearly fenced off from the masses may exist
without much effect on national character, because in
that case power is associated in the popular mind with
other things than corruption. But where there are no
hereditary distinctions, and men are habitually seen to
raise themselves by corrupt qualities from the lowest
places to wealth and power, tolerance of these qualities
finally becomes admiration. A corrupt democratic gov-

ernment must finally corrupt the people, and when a people become corrupt there is no resurrection. The life is gone, only the carcass remains; and it is left but for the plowshares of fate to bury it out of sight.

Now this transformation of popular government into despotism of the vilest and most degrading kind, which must inevitably result from the unequal distribution of wealth, is not a thing of the far future. It has already begun in the United States, and is rapidly going on under our eyes. That our legislative bodies are steadily deteriorating in standard; that men of the highest ability and character are compelled to eschew politics, and the arts of the jobber count for more than the reputation of the statesman; that voting is done more recklessly and the power of money is increasing; that it is harder to arouse the people to the necessity of reforms and more difficult to carry them out; that political differences are ceasing to be differences of principle, and abstract ideas are losing their power; that parties are passing into the control of what in general government would be oligarchies and dictatorships; are all evidences of political decline.

The type of modern growth is the great city. Here are to be found the greatest wealth and the deepest poverty. And it is here that popular government has most clearly broken down. In all the great American cities there is today as clearly defined a ruling class as in the most aristocratic countries of the world. Its members carry wards in their pockets, make up the slates for nominating conventions, distribute offices as they bargain together, and—though they toil not, neither do they spin—wear the best of raiment and spend money lavishly. They are men of power, whose favor the ambitious must court and whose vengeance he must avoid. Who are these men? The wise, the good, the learned—men who have earned the confidence of their fellow-citizens by the purity of their lives, the splendor of their talents, their probity in public trusts, their deep study of the problems of government? No; they are gamblers, saloon keepers, pugilists, or worse, who have made a trade of controlling votes and of buying and selling offices and official acts. They stand to the government of these cities as the Prætorian Guards did to that of declining Rome. He who would wear the purple, fill the curule chair, or have the fasces carried before him, must go or send his messengers to their camps, give them donatives and make them promises. It is through these men that the rich corporations and powerful pecuniary interests can pack the Senate and the bench with their creatures. It is these men who make school directors, supervisors, assessors, members of the legislature, congressmen. Why, there are many election districts in the United States in which a George Washington, a Benjamin Franklin or a Thomas Jefferson could no more go to the lower house of a state legislature than under the Ancient Régime a baseborn peasant could become a Marshal of France. Their very character would be an insuperable disqualification.

In theory we are intense democrats. The proposal to sacrifice swine in the temple would hardly have excited greater horror and indignation in Jerusalem of old than would among us that of conferring a distinction of rank upon our most eminent citizen. But is there not growing up among us a class who have all the power without any of the virtues of aristocracy? We have simple citizens who control thousands of miles of railroad, millions of acres of land, the means of livelihood of great numbers of men; who name the governors of sovereign states as they name their clerks, choose senators as they choose attorneys, and whose will is as supreme with legislatures as that of a French king sitting in bed of justice. The undercurrents of the times seem to sweep us back again to the old conditions from which we dreamed we had escaped. The development of the artisan and commercial classes gradually broke down feudalism after it had become so complete that men thought of heaven as organized on a feudal basis, and ranked the first and second persons of the Trinity as suzerain and tenant-in-chief. But now the development of manufactures and exchange, acting in a social organization in which land is made private property, threatens to compel every worker to seek a master, as the insecurity which followed the final break-up of the Roman Empire compelled every freeman to seek a lord. Nothing seems exempt from this tendency. Industry everywhere tends to assume a form in which one is master and many serve. And when one is master and the others serve, the one will control the others, even in such matters as votes. Just as the English landlord votes his tenants, so does the New England mill owner vote his operatives.

There is no mistaking it—the very foundations of society are being sapped before our eyes, while we ask, *how* is it possible that such a civilization as this, with its railroads, and daily newspapers, and electric telegraphs, should ever be destroyed? While literature breathes but the belief that we have been, are, and for the future must be, leaving the savage state further and further behind us, there are indications that we are actually turning back again toward barbarism. Let me illustrate: One of the characteristics of barbarism is the low regard for the rights of person and of property. That the laws of our Anglo-Saxon ancestors imposed as penalty for murder a fine proportioned to the rank of the victim, while our law knows no distinction of rank, and protects the lowest from the highest, the poorest from the richest, by the uniform penalty of death, is looked upon as evidence of their barbarism and our civilization. And so, that piracy, and robbery, and slave trading, and blackmailing, were once regarded as legitimate occupations, is conclusive proof of the rude state of development from which we have so far progressed.

But it is a matter of fact that, in spite of our laws, any one who has money enough and wants to kill another may go into any one of our great centers of population and business, and gratify his desire, and then surrender himself to justice, with the chances as a hundred to one that he will suffer no greater penalty than a temporary imprisonment and the loss of a sum proportioned partly to his own wealth and partly to the wealth and standing of the man he kills. His money will be paid, not to the family of the murdered man, who have lost their protector; not to the State, which has lost a citizen; but to lawyers who understand how to secure delays, to find witnesses, and get juries to disagree.

And so, if a man steal enough, he may be sure that his punishment will practically amount but to the loss of a part of the proceeds of his theft; and if he steal enough to get off with a fortune, he will be greeted by his acquaintances as a viking might have been greeted after a successful cruise. Even though he robbed those who trusted him; even though he robbed the widow and the fatherless; he has only to get enough, and he may safely flaunt his wealth in the eyes of day.

Now, the tendency in this direction is an increasing one. It is shown in greatest force where the inequalities in the distribution of wealth are greatest, and it shows itself as they increase. If it be not a return to barbarism, what is it? The failures of justice to which I have alluded are only illustrative of the increasing debility of our legal machinery in every department. It is becoming common to hear men say that it would be better to revert to first principles and abolish law, for then in self-defense the people would form vigilance committees and take justice into their own hands. Is this indicative of advance or retrogression?

All this is matter of common observation. Though we may not speak it openly, the general faith in republican institutions is, where they have reached their fullest development, narrowing and weakening. It is no longer that confident belief in republicanism as the source of national blessings that it once was. Thoughtful men are beginning to see its dangers, without seeing how to escape them; are beginning to accept the view of Macaulay and distrust that of Jefferson.* And the people at large are becoming used to the growing corruption. The most ominous political sign in the United States today is the growth of a sentiment which either doubts the existence of an honest man in public office or looks on him as a fool for not seizing his opportunities. That is to say, the people themselves are becoming corrupted. Thus in the United States today is republican government running the course it must inevitably follow under conditions which cause the unequal distribution of wealth.

Where that course leads is clear to whoever will think. As corruption becomes chronic; as public spirit is lost; as traditions of honor, virtue, and patriotism are weakened; as law is brought into contempt and reforms become hopeless; then in the festering mass will be generated volcanic forces, which shatter and rend when seeming accident gives them vent. Strong, unscrupulous men, rising up upon occasion, will become the exponents of blind popular desires or fierce popular passions, and dash aside forms that have lost their vitality. The sword will again be mightier than the pen, and in carnivals of destruction brute force and wild frenzy will

---

* See Macaulay's letter to Randall, the biographer of Jefferson.

alternate with the lethargy of a declining civilization.

I speak of the United States only because the United States is the most advanced of all the great nations. What shall we say of Europe, where dams of ancient law and custom pen up the swelling waters and standing armies weigh down the safety valves, though year by year the fires grow hotter underneath? Europe tends to republicanism under conditions that will not admit of true republicanism—under conditions that substitute for the calm and august figure of Liberty the petroleuse and the guillotine!

Whence shall come the new barbarians? Go through the squalid quarters of great cities, and you may see, even now, their gathering hordes! How shall learning perish? Men will cease to read, and books will kindle fires and be turned into cartridges!

It is startling to think how slight the traces that would be left of our civilization did it pass through the throes which have accompanied the decline of every previous civilization. Paper will not last like parchment, nor are our most massive buildings and monuments to be compared in solidity with the rock-hewn temples and titanic edifices of the old civilizations.* And invention has given us, not merely the steam engine and the printing press, but petroleum, nitroglycerine, and dynamite.

Yet to hint, today, that our civilization may possibly be tending to decline, seems like the wildness of pessimism. The special tendencies to which I have alluded are obvious to thinking men, but with the majority of thinking men, as with the great masses, the belief in substantial progress is yet deep and strong—a fundamental belief which admits not the shadow of a doubt.

---

* It is also, it seems to me, instructive to note how inadequate and utterly misleading would be the idea of our civilization which could be gained from the religious and funereal monuments of our time, which are all we have from which to gain our ideas of the buried civilizations.

But any one who will think over the matter will see that this must necessarily be the case where advance gradually passes into retrogression. For in social development, as in everything else, motion tends to persist in straight lines, and therefore, where there has been a previous advance, it is extremely difficult to recognize decline, even when it has fully commenced; there is an almost irresistible tendency to believe that the forward movement which has been advance, and is still going on, is still advance. The web of beliefs, customs, laws, institutions, and habits of thought, which each community is constantly spinning, and which produces in the individual environed by it all the differences of national character, is never unraveled. That is to say, in the decline of civilization, communities do not go down by the same paths that they came up. For instance, the decline of civilization as manifested in government would not take us back from republicanism to constitutional monarchy, and thence to the feudal system; it would take us to imperatorship and anarchy. As manifested in religion, it would not take us back into the faiths of our forefathers, into Protestantism or Catholicity, but into new forms of superstition, of which possibly Mormonism and other even grosser "isms" may give some vague idea. As manifested in knowledge, it would not take us toward Bacon, but toward the literati of China.

And how the retrogression of civilization, following a period of advance, may be so gradual as to attract no attention at the time; nay, how that decline must necessarily, by the great majority of men, be mistaken for advance, is easily seen. For instance, there is an enormous difference between Grecian art of the classic period and that of the lower empire; yet the change was accompanied, or rather caused, by a change of taste. The artists who most quickly followed this change of taste were in their day regarded as the superior artists. And so of literature. As it became more vapid, puerile, and stilted, it would be in obedience to an altered taste, which would regard its increasing weakness as increasing strength and beauty. The really good writer would not find readers; he would be regarded as rude, dry, or dull. And so would the drama decline; not because there was a lack of good plays, but because the prevailing taste became more and more that of a less cultured class, who, of course, regard that which they most admire as the best of its kind. And so, too, of religion; the superstitions which a superstitious people will add to it will be regarded by them as improvements. While, as the decline goes on, the return to barbarism, where it is not in itself regarded as an advance, will seem necessary to meet the exigencies of the times.

For instance, flogging, as a punishment for certain offenses, has been recently restored to the penal code of England, and has been strongly advocated on this side of the Atlantic. I express no opinion as to whether this is or is not a better punishment for crime than imprisonment. I only point to the fact as illustrating how an increasing amount of crime and an increasing embarrassment as to the maintenance of prisoners, both obvious tendencies at present, might lead to a fuller return to the physical cruelty of barbarous codes. The use of torture in judicial investigations, which steadily grew with the decline of Roman civilization, it is thus easy to see, might, as manners brutalized and crime increased, be demanded as a necessary improvement of the criminal law.

Whether in the present drifts of opinion and taste there are as yet any indications of retrogression, it is not necessary to inquire; but there are many things about which there can be no dispute, which go to show that our civilization has reached a critical period, and that unless a new start is made in the direction of social equality, the nineteenth century may to the future mark its climax. These industrial depressions, which cause as much waste and suffering as famines or wars, are like the twinges and shocks which precede paralysis. Everywhere is it evident that the tendency to inequality, which is the necessary result of material progress where land is monopolized, cannot go much further without carrying our civilization into that downward path which is so easy to enter and so hard to abandon. Everywhere the increasing intensity of the struggle to live, the increasing necessity for straining every nerve to prevent being thrown down and trodden under foot in the scramble for wealth, is draining the forces which gain and maintain improvements. In every civilized country pauperism, crime, insanity, and suicides are increasing. In every civilized country the diseases are increasing which come from overstrained nerves, from insufficient nourishment, from squalid lodgings, from unwholesome and monotonous occupations, from premature labor of children, from the tasks and crimes which poverty imposes upon women. In every highly civilized country the expectation of life, which gradually rose for several centuries, and which seems to have culminated about the first quarter of this century, appears to be now diminishing.*

It is not an advancing civilization that such figures show. It is a civilization which in its undercurrents has already begun to recede. When the tide turns in bay or river from flood to ebb, it is not all at once; but here it still runs on, though there it has begun to recede.

* Statistics which show these things are collected in convenient form in a volume entitled "Deterioration and Race Education," by Samuel Royce, which has been largely distributed by the venerable Peter Cooper of New York. Strangely enough, the only remedy proposed by Mr. Royce is the establishment of kindergarten schools.

When the sun passes the meridian, it can be told only
by the way the short shadows fall; for the heat of the
day yet increases. But as sure as the turning tide must
soon run full ebb; as sure as the declining sun must
bring darkness, so sure is it, that though knowledge yet
increases and invention marches on, and new states are
being settled, and cities still expand, yet civilization has
begun to wane when, in proportion to population, we
must build more and more prisons, more and more
almshouses, more and more insane asylums. It is not
from top to bottom that societies die; it is from bottom
to top.

But there are evidences far more palpable than any
that can be given by statistics, of tendencies to the ebb
of civilization. There is a vague but general feeling of
disappointment; an increased bitterness among the working classes; a widespread feeling of unrest and brooding
revolution. If this were accompanied by a definite idea
of how relief is to be obtained, it would be a hopeful
sign; but it is not. Though the schoolmaster has been
abroad some time, the general power of tracing effect
to cause does not seem a whit improved. The reaction
toward protectionism, as the reaction toward other exploded fallacies of government, shows this.* And even
the philosophic freethinker cannot look upon that vast
change in religious ideas that is now sweeping over the
civilized world without feeling that this tremendous fact
may have most momentous relations, which only the
future can develop. For what is going on is not a
change in the form of religion, but the negation and

* In point of constructive statesmanship—the recognition of fundamental principles and the adaptation of means to ends, the Constitution
of the United States, adopted a century ago, is greatly superior to the
latest State Constitutions, the most recent of which is that of California
—a piece of utter botchwork.

destruction of the ideas from which religion springs. Christianity is not simply clearing itself of superstitions, but in the popular mind it is dying at the root, as the old paganisms were dying when Christianity entered the world. And nothing arises to take its place. The fundamental ideas of an intelligent Creator and of a future life are in the general mind rapidly weakening. Now, whether this may or may not be in itself an advance, the importance of the part which religion has played in the world's history shows the importance of the change that is now going on. Unless human nature has suddenly altered in what the universal history of the race shows to be its deepest characteristics, the mightiest actions and reactions are thus preparing. Such stages of thought have heretofore always marked periods of transition. On a smaller scale and to a less depth (for I think any one who will notice the drift of our literature, and talk upon such subjects with the men he meets, will see that it is subsoil and not surface plowing that materialistic ideas are now doing), such a state of thought preceded the French Revolution. But the closest parallel to the wreck of religious ideas now going on is to be found in that period in which ancient civilization began to pass from splendor to decline. What change may come, no mortal man can tell, but that some great change must come, thoughtful men begin to feel. The civilized world is trembling on the verge of a great movement. Either it must be a leap upward, which will open the way to advances yet undreamed of, or it must be a plunge downward which will carry us back toward barbarism.

CHAPTER 5 THE CENTRAL TRUTH

In the short space to which this latter part of our inquiry is necessarily confined, I have been obliged to omit much that I would like to say, and to touch briefly where an exhaustive consideration would not be out of place.

Nevertheless, this, at least, is evident, that the truth to which we were led in the politico-economic branch of our inquiry is as clearly apparent in the rise and fall of nations and the growth and decay of civilizations, and that it accords with those deep-seated recognitions of relation and sequence that we denominate moral perceptions. Thus have been given to our conclusions the greatest certitude and highest sanction.

This truth involves both a menace and a promise. It shows that the evils arising from the unjust and unequal distribution of wealth, which are becoming more and more apparent as modern civilization goes on, are not incidents of progress, but tendencies which must bring progress to a halt; that they will not cure themselves, but, on the contrary, must, unless their cause is removed, grow greater and greater, until they sweep us back into barbarism by the road every previous civilization has trod. But it also shows that these evils are not imposed by natural laws; that they spring solely from social maladjustments which ignore natural laws, and that in removing their cause we shall be giving an enormous impetus to progress.

544

The poverty which in the midst of abundance pinches and embrutes men, and all the manifold evils which flow from it, spring from a denial of justice. In permitting the monopolization of the opportunities which nature freely offers to all, we have ignored the fundamental law of justice—for, so far as we can see, when we view things upon a large scale, justice seems to be the supreme law of the universe. But by sweeping away this injustice and asserting the rights of all men to natural opportunities, we shall conform ourselves to the law —we shall remove the great cause of unnatural inequality in the distribution of wealth and power; we shall abolish poverty; tame the ruthless passions of greed; dry up the springs of vice and misery; light in dark places the lamp of knowledge; give new vigor to invention and a fresh impulse to discovery; substitute political strength for political weakness; and make tyranny and anarchy impossible.

The reform I have proposed accords with all that is politically, socially, or morally desirable. It has the qualities of a true reform, for it will make all other reforms easier. What is it but the carrying out in letter and spirit of the truth enunciated in the Declaration of Independence—the "self-evident" truth that is the heart and soul of the Declaration—*"That all men are created equal; that they are endowed by their Creator with certain unalienable rights; that among these are life, liberty, and the pursuit of happiness!"*

These rights are denied when the equal right to land —on which and by which men alone can live—is denied. Equality of political rights will not compensate for the denial of the equal right to the bounty of nature. Political liberty, when the equal right to land is denied, becomes, as population increases and invention goes on, merely the liberty to compete for employment at starvation wages. This is the truth that we have ignored.

And so there come beggars in our streets and tramps on our roads; and poverty enslaves men who we boast are political sovereigns; and want breeds ignorance that our schools cannot enlighten; and citizens vote as their masters dictate; and the demagogue usurps the part of the statesman; and gold weighs in the scales of justice; and in high places sit those who do not pay to civic virtue even the compliment of hypocrisy; and the pillars of the republic that we thought so strong already bend under an increasing strain.

We honor Liberty in name and in form. We set up her statues and sound her praises. But we have not fully trusted her. And with our growth so grow her demands. She will have no half service!

Liberty! it is a word to conjure with, not to vex the ear in empty boastings. For Liberty means Justice, and Justice is the natural law—the law of health and symmetry and strength, of fraternity and co-operation.

They who look upon Liberty as having accomplished her mission when she has abolished hereditary privileges and given men the ballot, who think of her as having no further relations to the everyday affairs of life, have not seen her real grandeur—to them the poets who have sung of her must seem rhapsodists, and her martyrs fools! As the sun is the lord of life, as well as of light; as his beams not merely pierce the clouds, but support all growth, supply all motion, and call forth from what would otherwise be a cold and inert mass all the infinite diversities of being and beauty, so is liberty to mankind. It is not for an abstraction that men have toiled and died; that in every age the witnesses of Liberty have stood forth, and the martyrs of Liberty have suffered.

We speak of Liberty as one thing, and of virtue, wealth, knowledge, invention, national strength and national independence as other things. But, of all these, Liberty is the source, the mother, the necessary condition. She is to virtue what light is to color; to wealth what sunshine is to grain; to knowledge what eyes are to sight. She is the genius of invention, the brawn of national strength, the spirit of national independence. Where Liberty rises, there virtue grows, wealth increases, knowledge expands, invention multiplies human powers, and in strength and spirit the freer nation rises among her neighbors as Saul amid his brethren —taller and fairer. Where Liberty sinks, there virtue fades, wealth diminishes, knowledge is forgotten, invention ceases, and empires once mighty in arms and arts become a helpless prey to freer barbarians!

Only in broken gleams and partial light has the sun of Liberty yet beamed among men, but all progress hath she called forth.

Liberty came to a race of slaves crouching under Egyptian whips, and led them forth from the House of Bondage. She hardened them in the desert and made of them a race of conquerors. The free spirit of the Mosaic law took their thinkers up to heights where they beheld the unity of God, and inspired their poets with strains that yet phrase the highest exaltations of thought. Liberty dawned on the Phœnician coast, and ships passed the Pillars of Hercules to plow the unknown sea. She shed a partial light on Greece, and marble grew to shapes of ideal beauty, words became the instruments of subtlest thought, and against the scanty militia of free cities the countless hosts of the Great King broke like surges against a rock. She cast her beams on the four-acre farms of Italian husbandmen, and born of her strength a power came forth that conquered the world. They glinted from shields of German warriors, and Augustus wept his legions. Out of the night that followed her eclipse, her slanting rays fell again on free cities, and a lost learning revived, modern civilization began, a new world was unveiled; and as

Liberty grew, so grew art, wealth, power, knowledge, and refinement. In the history of every nation we may read the same truth. It was the strength born of Magna Charta that won Crecy and Agincourt. It was the revival of Liberty from the despotism of the Tudors that glorified the Elizabethan age. It was the spirit that brought a crowned tyrant to the block that planted here the seed of a mighty tree. It was the energy of ancient freedom that, the moment it had gained unity, made Spain the mightiest power of the world, only to fall to the lowest depth of weakness when tyranny succeeded liberty. See, in France, all intellectual vigor dying under the tyranny of the seventeenth century to revive in splendor as Liberty awoke in the eighteenth, and on the enfranchisement of French peasants in the Great Revolution, basing the wonderful strength that has in our time defied defeat.

Shall we not trust her?

In our time, as in times before, creep on the insidious forces that, producing inequality, destroy Liberty. On the horizon the clouds begin to lower. Liberty calls to us again. We must follow her further; we must trust her fully. Either we must wholly accept her or she will not stay. It is not enough that men should vote; it is not enough that they should be theoretically equal before the law. They must have liberty to avail themselves of the opportunities and means of life; they must stand on equal terms with reference to the bounty of nature. Either this, or Liberty withdraws her light! Either this, or darkness comes on, and the very forces that progress has evolved turn to powers that work destruction. This is the universal law. This is the lesson of the centuries. Unless its foundations be laid in justice the social structure cannot stand.

Our primary social adjustment is a denial of justice. In allowing one man to own the land on which and from

which other men must live, we have made them his
bondsmen in a degree which increases as material progress goes on. This is the subtle alchemy that in ways
they do not realize is extracting from the masses in
every civilized country the fruits of their weary toil;
that is instituting a harder and more hopeless slavery in
place of that which has been destroyed; that is bringing
political despotism out of political freedom, and must
soon transmute democratic institutions into anarchy.

It is this that turns the blessings of material progress
into a curse. It is this that crowds human beings into
noisome cellars and squalid tenement houses; that fills
prisons and brothels; that goads men with want and
consumes them with greed; that robs women of the
grace and beauty of perfect womanhood; that takes
from little children the joy and innocence of life's
morning.

Civilization so based cannot continue. The eternal
laws of the universe forbid it. Ruins of dead empires
testify, and the witness that is in every soul answers,
that it cannot be. It is something grander than Benevo-
lence, something more august than Charity—it is Justice
herself that demands of us to right this wrong. Justice that will not be denied; that cannot be put off—
Justice that with the scales carries the sword. Shall
we ward the stroke with liturgies and prayers? Shall we
avert the decrees of immutable law by raising churches
when hungry infants moan and weary mothers weep?

Though it may take the language of prayer, it is blas-
phemy that attributes to the inscrutable decrees of
Providence the suffering and brutishness that come of
poverty; that turns with folded hands to the All-Father
and lays on Him the responsibility for the want and
crime of our great cities. We degrade the Everlasting.
We slander the Just One. A merciful man would have
better ordered the world; a just man would crush with

his foot such an ulcerous ant hill! It is not the Almighty, but we who are responsible for the vice and
misery that fester amid our civilization. The Creator
showers upon us his gifts—more than enough for all.
But like swine scrambling for food, we tread them in the
mire—tread them in the mire, while we tear and rend
each other!

In the very centers of our civilization today are want
and suffering enough to make sick at heart whoever does
not close his eyes and steel his nerves. Dare we turn
to the Creator and ask Him to relieve it? Supposing
the prayer were heard, and at the behest with which the
universe sprang into being there should glow in the sun
a greater power; new virtue fill the air; fresh vigor the
soil; that for every blade of grass that now grows two
should spring up, and the seed that now increases fifty-
fold should increase a hundredfold! Would poverty
be abated or want relieved? Manifestly no! Whatever
benefit would accrue would be but temporary. The new
powers streaming through the material universe could
be utilized only through land. And land, being private
property, the classes that now monopolize the bounty of
the Creator would monopolize all the new bounty. Landowners would alone be benefited. Rents would increase,
but wages would still tend to the starvation point!

This is not merely a deduction of political economy;
it is a fact of experience. We know it because we have
seen it. Within our own times, under our very eyes,
that Power which is above all, and in all, and through
all; that Power of which the whole universe is but the
manifestation; that Power which maketh all things, and
without which is not anything made that is made, has
increased the bounty which men may enjoy, as truly as
though the fertility of nature had been increased. Into
the mind of one came the thought that harnessed steam
for the service of mankind. To the inner ear of another

was whispered the secret that compels the lightning to bear a message round the globe. In every direction have the laws of matter been revealed; in every department of industry have arisen arms of iron and fingers of steel, whose effect upon the production of wealth has been precisely the same as an increase in the fertility of nature. What has been the result? Simply that landowners get all the gain. The wonderful discoveries and inventions of our century have neither increased wages nor lightened toil. The effect has simply been to make the few richer; the many more helpless!

Can it be that the gifts of the Creator may be thus misappropriated with impunity? Is it a light thing that labor should be robbed of its earnings while greed rolls in wealth—that the many should want while the few are surfeited? Turn to history, and on every page may be read the lesson that such wrong never goes unpunished; that the Nemesis that follows injustice never falters nor sleeps! Look around today. Can this state of things continue? May we even say, "After us the deluge!" Nay; the pillars of the State are trembling even now, and the very foundations of society begin to quiver with pent-up forces that glow underneath. The struggle that must either revivify, or convulse in ruin, is near at hand, if it be not already begun.

The fiat has gone forth! With steam and electricity, and the new powers born of progress, forces have entered the world that will either compel us to a higher plane or overwhelm us, as nation after nation, as civilization after civilization, have been overwhelmed before. It is the delusion which precedes destruction that sees in the popular unrest with which the civilized world is feverishly pulsing only the passing effect of ephemeral causes. Between democratic ideas and the aristocratic adjustments of society there is an irreconcilable conflict. Here in the United States, as there in Europe, it may be seen arising. We cannot go on permitting men to vote and forcing them to tramp. We cannot go on educating boys and girls in our public schools and then refusing them the right to earn an honest living. We cannot go on prating of the inalienable rights of man and then denying the inalienable right to the bounty of the Creator. Even now, in old bottles the new wine begins to ferment, and elemental forces gather for the strife!

But if, while there is yet time, we turn to Justice and obey her, if we trust Liberty and follow her, the dangers that now threaten must disappear, the forces that now menace will turn to agencies of elevation. Think of the powers now wasted; of the infinite fields of knowledge yet to be explored; of the possibilities of which the wondrous inventions of this century give us but a hint. With want destroyed; with greed changed to noble passions; with the fraternity that is born of equality taking the place of the jealousy and fear that now array men against each other; with mental power loosed by conditions that give to the humblest comfort and leisure; and who shall measure the heights to which our civilization may soar? Words fail the thought! It is the Golden Age of which poets have sung and highraised seers have told in metaphor! It is the glorious vision which has always haunted man with gleams of fitful splendor. It is what he saw whose eyes at Patmos were closed in a trance. It is the culmination of Christianity—the City of God on earth, with its walls of jasper and its gates of pearl! It is the reign of the Prince of Peace!

The days of the nations bear no trace
  Of all the sunshine so far foretold;
The cannon speaks in the teacher's place—
  The age is weary with work and gold,
And high hopes wither, and memories wane;
  On hearths and altars the fires are dead;
But that brave faith hath not lived in vain—
  And this is all that our watcher said.

—FRANCES BROWN.

CONCLUSION
THE PROBLEM OF INDIVIDUAL LIFE

My task is done.

Yet the thought still mounts. The problems we have been considering lead into a problem higher and deeper still. Behind the problems of social life lies the problem of individual life. I have found it impossible to think of the one without thinking of the other, and so, I imagine, will it be with those who, reading this book, go with me in thought. For, as says Guizot, "when the history of civilization is completed, when there is nothing more to say as to our present existence, man inevitably asks himself whether all is exhausted, whether he has reached the end of all things?"

This problem I cannot now discuss. I speak of it only because the thought which, while writing this book, has come with inexpressible cheer to me, may also be of cheer to some who read it; for, whatever be its fate, it will be read by some who in their heart of hearts have taken the cross of a new crusade. This thought will come to them without my suggestion; but we are surer that we see a star when we know that others also see it.

The truth that I have tried to make clear will not find easy acceptance. If that could be, it would have been accepted long ago. If that could be, it would never have been obscured. But it will find friends—those who will toil for it; suffer for it; if need be, die for it. This is the power of Truth.

Will it at length prevail? Ultimately, yes. But in
our own times, or in times of which any memory of us
remains, who shall say?

For the man who, seeing the want and misery, the
ignorance and brutishness caused by unjust social institutions, sets himself, in so far as he has strength, to
right them, there is disappointment and bitterness. So
it has been of old time. So is it even now. But the
bitterest thought—and it sometimes comes to the best
and bravest—is that of the hopelessness of the effort,
the futility of the sacrifice. To how few of those who
sow the seed is it given to see it grow, or even with certainty to know that it will grow.

Let us not disguise it. Over and over again has the
standard of Truth and Justice been raised in this world.
Over and over again has it been trampled down—often-
times in blood. If they are weak forces that are opposed to Truth, how should Error so long prevail? If
Justice has but to raise her head to have Injustice flee
before her, how should the wail of the oppressed so long
go up?

But for those who see Truth and would follow her;
for those who recognize Justice and would stand for her,
success is not the only thing. Success! Why, False-
hood has often that to give; and Injustice often has that
to give. Must not Truth and Justice have something to
give that is their own by proper right—theirs in essence,
and not by accident?

That they have, and that here and now, every one
who has felt their exaltation knows. But sometimes the
clouds sweep down. It is sad, sad reading, the lives of
the men who would have done something for their fellows. To Socrates they gave the hemlock; Gracchus
they killed with sticks and stones; and One, greatest
and purest of all, they crucified. These seem but types.
Today Russian prisons are full, and in long proces-

sions, men and women, who, but for high-minded patriotism, might have lived in ease and luxury, move in chains towards the death-in-life of Siberia. And in penury and want, in neglect and contempt, destitute even of the sympathy that would have been so sweet, how many in every country have closed their eyes? This we see.

But do we see it all?

In writing I have picked up a newspaper. In it is a short account, evidently translated from a semiofficial report, of the execution of three Nihilists at Kieff—the Prussian subject Brandtner, the unknown man calling himself Antonoff, and the nobleman Ossinsky. At the foot of the gallows they were permitted to kiss one another. "Then the hangman cut the rope, the surgeons pronounced the victims dead, the bodies were buried at the foot of the scaffold, and the Nihilists were given up to eternal oblivion." Thus says the account. I do not believe it. No; not to oblivion!

I have in this inquiry followed the course of my own thought. When, in mind, I set out on it I had no theory to support, no conclusions to prove. Only, when I first realized the squalid misery of a great city, it appalled and tormented me, and would not let me rest, for thinking of what caused it and how it could be cured.

But out of this inquiry has come to me something I did not think to find, and a faith that was dead revives.

The yearning for a further life is natural and deep. It grows with intellectual growth, and perhaps none really feel it more than those who have begun to see how great is the universe and how infinite are the vistas which every advance in knowledge opens before us—vistas which would require nothing short of eternity to explore. But in the mental atmosphere of our times, to the great majority of men on whom mere creeds have lost their hold, it seems impossible to look on this yearning save as a vain and childish hope, arising from man's egotism, and for which there is not the slightest ground or warrant, but which, on the contrary, seems inconsistent with positive knowledge.

Now, when we come to analyze and trace up the ideas that thus destroy the hope of a future life, we shall find them, I think, to have their source, not in any revelations of physical science, but in certain teachings of political and social science which have deeply permeated thought in all directions. They have their root in the doctrines, that there is a tendency to the production of more human beings than can be provided for; that vice and misery are the result of natural laws, and the means by which advance goes on; and that human progress is by a slow race development. These doctrines, which have been generally accepted as approved truth, do what, except as scientific interpretations have been colored by them, the extensions of physical science do not do--they reduce the individual to insignificance; they destroy the idea that there can be in the ordering of the universe any regard for his existence, or any recognition of what we call moral qualities.

It is difficult to reconcile the idea of human immortality with the idea that nature wastes men by constantly bringing them into being where there is no room for them. It is impossible to reconcile the idea of an intelligent and beneficent Creator with the belief that the wretchedness and degradation which are the lot of such a large proportion of human kind result from his enactments; while the idea that man mentally and physically is the result of slow modifications perpetuated by heredity, irresistibly suggests the idea that it is the race life, not the individual life, which is the object of human existence. Thus has vanished with many of us, and is still vanishing with more of us, that belief which in the battles and ills of life affords the strongest support and deepest consolation.

Now, in the inquiry through which we have passed, we have met these doctrines and seen their fallacy. We have seen that population does not tend to outrun subsistence; we have seen that the waste of human powers and the prodigality of human suffering do not spring from natural laws, but from the ignorance and selfishness of men in refusing to conform to natural laws. We have seen that human progress is not by altering the nature of men; but that, on the contrary, the nature of men seems, generally speaking, always the same.

Thus the nightmare which is banishing from the modern world the belief in a future life is destroyed. Not that all difficulties are removed—for turn which way we may, we come to what we cannot comprehend; but that difficulties are removed which seem conclusive and insuperable. And, thus, hope springs up.

But this is not all.

Political Economy has been called the dismal science, and as currently taught, is hopeless and despairing. But this, as we have seen, is solely because she has been degraded and shackled; her truths dislocated; her harmonies ignored; the word she would utter gagged in her mouth, and her protest against wrong turned into an indorsement of injustice. Freed, as I have tried to free her—in her own proper symmetry, Political Economy is radiant with hope.

For properly understood, the laws which govern the production and distribution of wealth show that the want and injustice of the present social state are not necessary; but that, on the contrary, a social state is possible in which poverty would be unknown, and all the better qualities and higher powers of human nature would have opportunity for full development.

And, further than this, when we see that social development is governed neither by a Special Providence nor by a merciless fate, but by law, at once unchangeable and beneficent; when we see that human will is the great factor, and that taking men in the aggregate, their condition is as they make it; when we see that economic law and moral law are essentially one, and that the truth which the intellect grasps after toilsome effort is but that which the moral sense reaches by a quick intuition, a flood of light breaks in upon the problem of individual life. These countless millions like ourselves, who on this earth of ours have passed and still are passing, with their joys and sorrows, their toil and their striving, their aspirations and their fears, their strong perceptions of things deeper than sense, their common feelings which form the basis even of the most divergent creeds—their little lives do not seem so much like meaningless waste.

The great fact which Science in all her branches shows is the universality of law. Wherever he can trace it, whether in the fall of an apple or in the revolution of binary suns, the astronomer sees the working of the same law, which operates in the minutest divisions in which we may distinguish space, as it does in the immeasurable distances with which his science deals. Out of that which lies beyond his telescope comes a moving body and again it disappears. So far as he can trace its course the law is ignored. Does he say that this is an exception? On the contrary, he says that this is merely a part of its orbit that he has seen; that beyond the reach of his telescope the law holds good. He makes his calculations, and after centuries they are proved.

Now, if we trace out the laws which govern human life in society, we find that in the largest as in the smallest community, they are the same. We find that what seem at first sight like divergences and exceptions are but manifestations of the same principles. And we find that everywhere we can trace it, the social law runs into and conforms with the moral law; that in the life of a community, justice infallibly brings its reward and injustice its punishment. But this we cannot see in individual life. If we look merely at individual life we cannot see that the laws of the universe have the slightest relation to good or bad, to right or wrong, to just or unjust.* Shall we then say that the law which is manifest in social life is not true of individual life? It is not scientific to say so. We would not say so in reference to anything else. Shall we not rather say this simply proves that we do not see the whole of individual life?

The laws which Political Economy discovers, like the facts and relations of physical nature, harmonize with what seems to be the law of mental development—not a necessary and involuntary progress, but a progress in which the human will is an initiatory force. But in life, as we are cognizant of it, mental development can go but a little way. The mind hardly begins to awake ere the bodily powers decline—it but becomes dimly conscious of the vast fields before it, but begins to learn and use its strength, to recognize relations and extend

* Let us not delude our children. If for no other reason than for that which Plato gives, that when they come to discard that which we told them as pious fable they will also discard that which we told them as truth. The virtues which relate to self do generally bring their reward. Either a merchant or a thief will be more successful if he be sober, prudent, and faithful to his promises; but as to the virtues which do not relate to self—

"It seems a story from the world of spirits,
When any one obtains that which he merits,
Or any merits that which he obtains."

its sympathies, when, with the death of the body, it passes away. Unless there is something more, there seems here a break, a failure. Whether it be a Humboldt or a Herschel, a Moses who looks from Pisgah, a Joshua who leads the host, or one of those sweet and patient souls who in narrow circles live radiant lives, there seems, if mind and character here developed can go no further, a purposelessness inconsistent with what we can see of the linked sequence of the universe.

By a fundamental law of our minds—the law, in fact, upon which Political Economy relies in all her deductions—we cannot conceive of a means without an end; a contrivance without an object. Now, to all nature, so far as we come in contact with it in this world, the support and employment of the intelligence that is in man furnishes such an end and object. But unless man himself may rise to or bring forth something higher, his existence is unintelligible. So strong is this metaphysical necessity that those who deny to the individual anything more than this life are compelled to transfer the idea of perfectibility to the race. But as we have seen, and the argument could have been made much more complete, there is nothing whatever to show any essential race improvement. Human progress is not the improvement of human nature. The advances in which civilization consists are not secured in the constitution of man, but in the constitution of society. They are thus not fixed and permanent, but may at any time be lost—nay, are constantly tending to be lost. And further than this, if human life does not continue beyond what we see of it here, then we are confronted, with regard to the race, with the same difficulty as with the individual! For it is as certain that the race must die as it is that the individual must die. We know that there have been geologic conditions under which human life was impossible on this earth. We know that they must return again. Even now, as the earth circles on her appointed orbit, the northern ice cap slowly thickens, and the time gradually approaches, when its glaciers will flow again, and austral seas, sweeping northward, bury the seats of present civilization under ocean wastes, as it may be they now bury what was once as high a civilization as our own. And beyond these periods, science discerns a dead earth, an exhausted sun—a time when, clashing together, the solar system shall resolve itself into a gaseous form, again to begin immeasurable mutations.

What then is the meaning of life—of life absolutely and inevitably bounded by death? To me it seems intelligible only as the avenue and vestibule to another life. And its facts seem explainable only upon a theory which cannot be expressed but in myth and symbol, and which, everywhere and at all times, the myths and symbols in which men have tried to portray their deepest perceptions do in some form express.

The scriptures of the men who have been and gone—the Bibles, the Zend Avestas, the Vedas, the Dhammapadas, and the Korans; the esoteric doctrines of old philosophies, the inner meaning of grotesque religions, the dogmatic constitutions of Ecumenical Councils, the preachings of Foxes, and Wesleys, and Savonarolas, the traditions of red Indians, and beliefs of black savages, have a heart and core in which they agree—a something which seems like the variously distorted apprehensions of a primary truth. And out of the chain of thought we have been following there seems vaguely to rise a glimpse of what they vaguely saw—a shadowy gleam of ultimate relations, the endeavor to express which inevitably falls into type and allegory. A garden in which are set the trees of good and evil. A vineyard in which there is the Master's work to do. A passage—from life behind to life beyond. A trial and a struggle, of which we cannot see the end.

Look around today.

Lo! here, now, in our civilized society, the old allegories yet have a meaning, the old myths are still true. Into the Valley of the Shadow of Death yet often leads the path of duty, through the streets of Vanity Fair walk Christian and Faithful, and on Greatheart's armor ring the clanging blows. Ormuzd still fights with Ahriman—the Prince of Light with the Powers of Darkness. He who will hear, to him the clarions of the battle call.

How they call, and call, and call, till the heart swells that hears them! Strong soul and high endeavor, the world needs them now. Beauty still lies imprisoned, and iron wheels go over the good and true and beautiful that might spring from human lives.

And they who fight with Ormuzd, though they may not know each other—somewhere, sometime, will the muster roll be called.

Though Truth and Right seem often overborne, we may not see it all. How can we see it all? All that is passing, even here, we cannot tell. The vibrations of matter which give the sensations of light and color become to us indistinguishable when they pass a certain point. It is only within a like range that we have cognizance of sounds. Even animals have senses which we have not. And, here? Compared with the solar system our earth is but an indistinguishable speck; and the solar system itself shrivels into nothingness when gauged with the star depths. Shall we say that what passes from our sight passes into oblivion? No; not into oblivion. Far, far beyond our ken the eternal laws must hold their sway.

The hope that rises is the heart of all religions! The

poets have sung it, the seers have told it, and in its deepest pulses the heart of man throbs responsive to its truth. This, that Plutarch said, is what in all times and in all tongues has been said by the pure hearted and strong sighted, who, standing as it were, on the mountain tops of thought and looking over the shadowy ocean, have beheld the loom of land:

"*Men's souls, encompassed here with bodies and passions, have no communication with God, except what they can reach to in conception only, by means of philosophy, as by a kind of an obscure dream. But when they are loosed from the body, and removed into the unseen, invisible, impassable, and pure region, this God is then their leader and king; they there, as it were, hanging on him wholly, and beholding without weariness and passionately affecting that beauty which cannot be expressed or uttered by men.*"

GLOSSARY

GLOSSARY

Agassiz, Louis John Rudolph (1807–1873). Swiss naturalist and teacher in America.

Agincourt. Village in France; scene of the battle of 1415 in which the English, under Henry V, though greatly outnumbered, vanquished the French.

Ahriman. The Spirit of Evil. *See* Ormuzd.

Allmend, Swiss. Common lands. A portion of them served to cover the expenses of public services, schools, churches and welfare. The arable portions, situated near the villages, were distributed in parcels for which lots were drawn every ten or twenty years, with right of use for life.

Allodial (alodial) tenures. Land held in unlimited ownership.

Alva (Alba), Duke of (1508–1582). Spanish general who was sent as governor to the Netherlands in 1567; notorious for his cruelty.

Anderson, Dr. James (1662–1728). Scottish genealogist, antiquarian and historian.

Antæus. According to Greek mythology, a wrestler who renewed his strength every time he touched the earth. He was lifted from the ground and strangled by Hercules.

Apples of Sodom. A fruit described by ancient writers as externally of fair appearance, but which dissolved into smoke and ashes when plucked.

Astors. An American family founded by John Jacob Astor (1763–1848), a German-born merchant who emigrated to America in 1783. First through fur trading, then through shrewd investments in New York real estate, he amassed the largest fortune of any American up to that time.

"Augustus wept his legions." Refers to the defeat of the Roman army under Varus by the German tribes who refused to submit to Roman tyranny. When news of the disaster reached him, Augustus (the first Roman Emperor) paced his palace crying, "O Varus! Varus! Give me back my legions!"

Bacon, Sir Francis (1561–1626). English philosopher, statesman and author.

Bagehot, Walter (1826–1877). English economist and author. His *Physics and Politics* is a description of the evolution of communities.

Bancroft, Hubert Howe (1832–1918). American historian.

Bastiat, Frédéric (1801–1850). French economist, famous for his wit and 'logic; author of *Harmonies Economiques* and many brilliant and effective pamphlets and essays opposing government interference with natural economic laws.

Behm, Ernst (1830–1884). German geographer and statistician.

Bentham, Jeremy (1748–1833). English jurist and utilitarian philosopher. "The greatest happiness of the greatest number," was his criterion of moral goodness.

Besant, Annie (1847–1933). British theosophist, once an ardent freethinker; later a leader in a Hindu political movement.

Black Death. Pestilences which destroyed the great reservoir of cheap labor in England in the fourteenth century.

Blackheath Field. An open common in southeast London; famous rallying ground in English history.

Blackstone, Sir William (1723–1780). Most famous of the English jurists; author, *Commentaries on the Laws of England*.

Brassey, Earl (1836–1918). Civil lord of the Admiralty who carried out important inquiries into wages, conditions of labor and administration in the English dockyards.

Brehon, Irish. A class of lawyers in ancient Ireland. Brehon Law derived from precedents, commentaries of brehons, decrees of the national assemblies, and custom, and was in effect over most of Ireland until the end of the sixteenth century.

Buckingham, George Villiers, first Duke of (1592–1628). Recipient of many royal favors.

Buckle, Henry Thomas (1821–1862). English historian; author, *History of Civilization in England.*

"Build like giants and finish like jewelers." The boast of the Mogul shahs, referring to themselves as architects and builders.

Bunyan, John (1628–1688). English writer; author, *Pilgrim's Progress.*

Burke, Edmund (1729–1797). British statesman and political writer; favored emancipation of the House of Commons from royal control, the freeing of the American colonies and of Ireland and India.

"But for the grace of God, there go I." From *Writings*, by John Bradford (Vol. II). On seeing a criminal passing by he expressed his emotions in the words, "There, but for the grace of God, goes John Bradford."

Bute, Marquises of. Members of a famous British peerage who were the recipients of many royal favors.

Butler, Joseph (1692–1752). English bishop; author, *Analogy of Religion, Natural and Revealed, to the Constitution and Course of Nature.*

Cadmus. The legendary founder of Thebes. According to Greek mythology, he slew a dragon and sowed its teeth. Armed men sprang up who fought one another until five remained; these became the ancestors of the Theban families.

Cairnes, Prof. John Elliott (1823–1875). British political economist of the classical school.

Caligula ("Little Boot"). Nickname of Caius Caesar (A.D. 12–41). His savage and voluptuous nature revealed itself in cruelty and licentiousness.

"Camel and the needle's eye." "It is easier for a camel to go through the eye of a needle than for a rich man to enter into the kingdom of God." (Matt. XIX:24.)

Carey, Prof. Henry Charles (1793–1879). American economist, advocate of the protective tariff. He rejected the classical rent theory, contending that cultivation progresses from the poor to better lands and yields increasing rather than diminishing returns.

Carlyle, Thomas (1795–1881). British essayist, historian and philosopher.

Carnatic (Karnatik). A region and old division between the Eastern Ghats and the Coromandel coast in southern India.

Cato the Censor, Marcus Porcius (234–149 B.C.). Roman patriot, remarkable for the austerity of his life and manners.

Chateaubriand, François René, Vicomte de (1768–1848). French author; a brilliant representative of the reaction against the ideas of the French Revolution.

Chinchas. Islands in the Pacific Ocean, off Peru.

Christian. *See* Greatheart.

Clive, Lord Robert (1725–1774). British statesman and general who led in the conquest of India.

Cobbett, William (1762–1835). English political writer.

Cobden Club. Founded by seven Manchester merchants to promote a movement for the abolition of the Corn Laws. Out of this grew the Anti-Corn Law League, a national association, which laid the foundation for Britain's great era of free trade. The guiding mind was that of Richard Cobden (1804–1865).

Coloni. Husbandmen or farmers. Under the later Roman Empire, serfs or tenant farmers bound to the soil and required to pay a fixed rent.

Commons. Uninclosed land, especially in England, belonging or pertaining to the community at large and subject to the rights of common use.

Comstock. A celebrated gold and silver lode with many bonanzas; discovered in 1859 in Nevada where Virginia City now stands.

Comte, Isidore Auguste Marie François Xavier (1798–1857). French philosopher; founder of "positivism," a system of philosophy.

Cooper, Peter (1791–1883). American inventor and philanthropist.

Cooper, Thomas (1759–1840). American educator and political philosopher.

Copernican theory. A theory of astronomy founded by the Pole, Nicholaus Copernicus (Koppernigk) (1473–1543).

Crécy. Village in northern France where the English defeated the French in 1346, against tremendous odds.

Cuban slave. Slaves were used in Cuba largely on sugar and tobacco plantations. Cuban slavery was abolished in 1880.

Curule chair. In Roman history, the chair of state in which only those of highest rank were allowed to sit.

Darwin, Charles Robert (1809–1882). British naturalist; author, *On the Origin of Species by Means of Natural Selection,* which maintains that the process of natural selection tends to favor the survival of individuals whose peculiarities render them best adapted to their environment.

"Deluge, after us the." Ascribed to Madame de Pompadour and also to Louis XV of France.

Demonetization of silver. *See* Silver.

Deutsch, Emmanuel Oscar Menahem (1829–1873). German Orientalist of Hebrew descent; assistant in the British Museum library.

Dhammapada. A portion of the Buddhist scriptures.

Ditmarsh mark. A tract of wild land outside the villages in Ditmarschen, a region in southwestern Schleswig-

Holstein, over which certain rights were exercised in common.

Dives. The rich man in the parable of the rich man and Lazarus (Luke XVl: 19–31).

Ecumenical Council. A council convoked from the entire church throughout the world; especially the Roman Catholic Church.

Elia. *See* Lamb, Charles.

Entail. A law limiting the inheritance of lands to the lineally descendant heirs of persons to whom it is granted.

"Ephesian dome, fired the." The Temple of Artemis, at Ephesus, destroyed in 356 B.C. by Herostratus, who, desiring to acquire eternal fame if only by a great crime, set it ablaze.

Erasmus, Desiderius (c 1466–1536). Dutch scholar.

Faithful. A character in Bunyan's *Pilgrim's Progress*. He is put to death at Vanity Fair.

Fasces. In ancient Rome, a bundle of rods containing an ax, carried before the high magistrate as a symbol of his authority.

Fawcett, Henry (1833–1884). English politician and economist; loyal follower of Mill, whose economic theory he popularized and demonstrated by concrete examples.

Fawcett, Dame Millicent Garrett (1847–1929). Author of an elementary manual on political economy; leader of the constitutional movement for women's suffrage in England. Wife of Henry Fawcett.

Fee simple. A condition of landownership which imposes no restrictions regarding those who may inherit.

Feudal system. The political system which prevailed in Europe in the Middle Ages. It bound the vassal to the land owned by the lord.

Fief. A feudal estate.

Flatheads. American Indian tribes who allowed their heads to grow in the natural way. Other tribes compressed their skulls in order to give the head a pointed shape.

Floods. An American family founded by James Clair Flood (1826–1889), who formed a successful mining partnership to exploit the Comstock Lode.

Fourteenth Amendment. An amendment to the Constitution of the United States, adopted in 1868, establishing the citizenship of Negroes.

Fox, George (1624–1691). English founder of the Society of Friends, or Quakers.

Garonne. A river flowing through Spain and France.

Gautama (Buddha). Indian mystic; founder of Buddhism.

Genghis Khan (c 1162–1227). Mongol conqueror of many parts of Asia and Europe.

Godoonof (Godunov), Boris Feodorovich (c 1552–1605). Tsar of Muscovy; later tsar of all Russia. His ukase of 1587 forbade the peasantry to transfer themselves from one landowner to another, and led to the institution of serfdom in its most grinding form.

Godwin, William (1756–1836). English political and miscellaneous writer, opponent of Malthus, whose *Inquirer* provoked Malthus' exposition of his population theory.

Goulds. An American family founded by Jay Gould (1836–1892), who, through manipulation of various railroad combinations, etc., amassed a tremendous fortune.

Gracchus, Tiberius Sempronius (c 162–133 B.C.) Roman statesman who, with his brother Caius Sempronius (c 153–121 B.C.), sought to bring about a class of independent farmers by reviving, with modifications, the Licinian Laws. The brothers, often referred to as the "Gracchi," were murdered by those who feared the results of the reforms they tried to institute.

Great Eastern. A famous British steamship which sailed the seas from 1859 to 1887; for many years the largest vessel afloat.

Greatheart. In Bunyan's *Pilgrim's Progress*, the guide of Christian's wife and children upon their journey to the Celestial City.

Great King. Darius I (c 558–c 486 B.C.), the Persian emperor who tried to conquer Greece.

Guizot, François Pierre Guillaume (1787–1874). French historian and statesman.

Hallam, Henry (1777–1859). English historian generally described as a "philosophical historian" because he fixed his attention on results rather than on persons.

Hastings, Warren (1732–1818). First governor-general of British India who planned the system of civil administration.

Helotism. A state of serfdom among the ancient Spartans. The helots paid their masters a fixed portion of the products of the ground they cultivated.

Herschel, Sir William (1738–1822). English astronomer; discoverer of the planet Uranus.

Horse leech, he [man] is the daughter of the. "The horseleach hath two daughters, crying, Give, give." (Prov. XXX:15.)

House of Bondage. Mentioned in the first of the ten commandments. (Exod. XX:2.)

House of Have and House of Want. Probably inspired by Cervantes' *Don Quixote.* "There were but two families in the world, Have-much and Have-little."

Humboldt, Alexander von (1769–1859). German naturalist and traveler who laid the foundation of the sciences of physical geography and meteorology.

Hyder Ali (*c* 1722–1782). Mohammedan ruler and commander, Maharaja of Mysore; the most formidable Asiatic rival the British ever encountered in India.

Hyksos (Shepherd Kings). Early invaders of Egypt.

Hyndman, H. M. (1842–1921). A founder of British Socialism. On the outbreak of World War I he became a strong nationalist and, later on, an equally vehement anti-Bolshevik.

Inclosure of commons. The Statute of Merton, which became law in 1235, began the inclosure of the common lands of England. During the reigns of Henry VIII and Edward VI the inclosure was largely completed.

Ishmael. Son of Abraham and Hagar. He and his mother were cast out by Abraham and wandered in the desert. The boy grew up, as had been prophesied, a "wild man; his hand will be against every man, and every man's hand against him." (Gen. XVI:12.)

Jacob. Son of Isaac and Rebekah who bound himself to Laban in order to win the hand of Laban's daughter, Rachel. (Gen. XXV:26.)

Janissaries. A military force of the Ottoman Empire organized in the fourteenth century and suppressed in 1826 because of its unruliness. It was made up largely of children conscripted from Christian families and reared to be fierce warriors.

Koran. The sacred scripture of Islam.

Kubla Khan, sunny dome of. In an unfinished poem by Coleridge, reference is made to "A stately pleasure dome" built "Where Alph, the sacred river ran, Down to a sunless sea." Kubla (Kublai) Khan (1216–1294) founded the Mongol dynasty in China and was the first of his race to rise above the innate barbarism of the Mongols. He built and beautified Peking as his capital city.

Laban. *See* Jacob.

Lacs, forty. Lac is a Hindu word meaning mark or sign and refers to one hundred thousand, or, broadly, a very large amount.

Lamb, Charles (1775–1834). Pseudonym, "Elia." English essayist and critic.

Land Department, United States. A term growing out of an unsuccessful movement started in the 1870's for the formation of an independent Department of Public Lands. A Land Office was started in 1785 as part of the federal treasury and handled the survey, classification and alienation of a billion or more acres of the public domain. Renamed the General Land Office in 1812 it was, in 1849, transferred to the Department of the Interior, where it has remained.

La Plata pampa. A treeless, grassy plain in Argentina.

Latimer, Hugh (*c* 1485–1555). Bishop and martyr who died at the stake in Oxford in 1555. One of the chief promoters of the Reformation in England. *See also,* "Play the man, Master Ridley!"

Laveleye, Emile Louis Victor de (1822–1892). Belgian political economist and political writer.

Lazarus. *See* Dives.

Lazzaroni of Naples. Homeless idlers who live by chance work and begging. Leperos of Mexico. Similar to lazzaroni of Naples.

Lessing, Gotthold Ephraim (1729–1781). German dramatist and critic who in his last years engaged in bitter theological controversies against Pastor Goeze of Hamburg and others.

Licinian Law. A body of laws proposed by the Roman tribunes, Licinius Calvus Stolo and Lucius Sextius, and passed in 367 B.C. after a long, obstructive contest. These laws curbed the exploitation of the plebeians, limited the use of slave labor on large estates and defined the area of public land which any individual might use.

Lucullus, Lucius Licinius (*c* 110–57 B.C.). Roman naval and military commander who retired as the wealthiest Roman of his time. Famous for his banquets. According to Plutarch, on an occasion when no guests were present, he demanded that the best of everything be served because "Tonight Lucullus dines with Lucullus."

Lycurgus (*c* 9th century B.C.). A Spartan legislator; the traditional author of the laws and institutions of Sparta.

Macaulay, Lord Thomas Babington (1800–1859). English historian, essayist and politician. In a letter to Henry S. Randall, the biographer of Jefferson, written in 1857, he predicted that after her fertile and unoccupied land had been pre-empted, the laborers of the United States would know conditions of poverty such as then prevailed in England and that the nation would at such time destroy itself through its own democratic institutions. "The Huns and Vandals who ravaged the Roman empire came from without; your Huns and Vandals will have been engendered within your own country by your own institutions [because] . . . There is nothing to stop you. Your constitution is all sail and no anchor."

Maccabees. A revolutionary group led by Mattathias and his five sons, dominant in Jerusalem in the second century B.C. They fought against the tyranny of the Syrian king, Antiochus Esiphanes, were victorious, and then established a dynasty which ruled more or less tyrannically until Herod (40 B.C.).

Mæcenas, Caius Cilnius (*c* 73–8 B.C.). Roman patron of letters; friend and patron of Horace and Virgil.

Magna Charta (Carta). Issued at Runnymede by King John in 1215, under compulsion from his barons. It laid a foundation for the security of English political and personal liberty.

Maine, Sir Henry James Sumner (1822–1888). English jurist and historian; author, *Ancient Law*, the object of which was "to indicate some of the earliest ideas of mankind as they are reflected in ancient law, and to point out the relation of those ideas to modern thought."

Malthus, Thomas Robert (1766–1834). English economist. His work, *An Essay on the Principle of Population as It Affects the Future Improvement of Society, with Remarks on the Speculations of Mr. Godwin, M. Condorcet and Other Writers*, published in 1798, influenced opinion in the first half of the nineteenth century. He believed that the realization of a happy society will always be hindered by the miseries consequent on the tendency of population to increase faster than the means of subsistence. A chance reading of Malthus' essay stimulated Charles Darwin to seek the key to biological change in the process of natural selection brought about by the struggle for existence.

McCulloch, John Ramsey (1789–1864). British economist and statistician.

"Men with muckrakes." The text refers to a character in *Pilgrim's Progress* who spends his time raking muck and never sees the crown above his head.

Metayer (metayage) system. The cultivation of land for a proprietor by one who receives a proportion of the produce. While it never existed in England, in certain provinces of Italy and France it was once almost universal and is still common. It is also practiced in the United States, Portugal, Greece and countries bordering on the Danube.

Mill, John Stuart (1806–1873). English philosopher, economist and author. He showed consistently that any despotism, however benevolent, must in fact cramp and destroy the development of any people. He was torn all his life between his passion for individual liberty and initiative and his sense of the benefits of social control.

Mirabeau (the elder), Victor Riqueti, Marquis de (1715–1789). French author and economist; one of the Physiocrats. He believed that the means of subsistence are the limit of population.

Mohammed (Mehemet) Ali (1769–1849). Military commander; later Pasha or Viceroy of Egypt. Under his rule, in 1808, most of the land belonging to private individuals was confiscated in return for small pensions to the owners. By this revolutionary method of land "naturalization," Mehemet Ali became proprietor of nearly all the soil of Egypt. He also created for himself a monopoly in the chief products of the country, including dates. Using forced labor, and at the sacrifice of 20,000 lives, he built the Mahmudiya canal between Alexandria and the Nile and then developed the cultivation of cotton in the Delta. He restored the port of Alexandria to a place of importance and re-established the overland transit of goods from Europe to India via Egypt.

Montesquieu, Charles Louis de Secondat, Baron de la Brède et de (1689–1755). French philosophical historian who satirized the French social, political, ecclesiastical and literary follies of his day.

More, Sir Thomas (1478–1535). English lord chancellor; author of *Utopia*, and defender of the Roman Catholic faith. He was put to death for his refusal to renounce papal authority and to sanction Henry VIII's divorce from Catherine. Later canonized.

"Mud-sills" of society. Persons of low social state or condition, so called because the mud sill is the foundation timber of a structure, placed directly on the ground.

Nasse, Prof. Erwin (1829–1890). German economist; one of the early professorial Socialists, who insisted on the insufficiency of affording a free field to individual interests and on the necessity for the application of moral ideas.

Nightingale, Florence (1820–1910). English hospital reformer; heroine of the Crimean War.

Ormuzd (Ormazd, Ahura-Mazda). A symbolic figure in the religion taught by Zoroaster. The supreme deity, the principle of good, creator of the world and guardian of mankind; opponent of Ahriman, the spirit of evil.

Patenting of mineral land. A grant conveying the right to extract from a piece of land, the surface of which may or may not be owned by the patentee, such metals as gold, silver, copper, lead, zinc, antimony and tin. Along the Atlantic seaboard, the original land grants included mineral as well as all other rights. Elsewhere, chiefly in the Rocky Mountains and the Pacific states, mineral rights are granted only after certain conditions affecting the exploration of the deposits have been fulfilled .

Patmos. The island on which St. John lived as an exile and where he saw the visions of the Apocalypse.

Perry. Prof. Arthur Latham (1830–?). American political economist.

Petroleuse. A woman who, during the fighting of 1871, took part in setting afire with kerosene many of the most magnificent buildings in Paris.

Physiocrats. *See* Quesnay.

Pickwick's stone. In Dickens' *Pickwick Papers* it is related that Mr. Pickwick finds a stone marker on which some letters are carved. He believes the letters to be part of an inscription of great antiquity. Then follows an amusing description of the reactions of learned societies, the ingenious and erudite speculations of their members, of rival controversies springing up as to the meaning of the inscription, without anyone solving the question; then, finally, of how they unite in reviling Mr. Blotton after he discovers that it has no historical significance but is simply the idle carvings of the cottager before whose home the stone was found.

Pillars of Hercules. Two promontories at the eastern end of the Strait of Gibraltar. It is fabled that Hercules set them there during his travels to find the oxen of Geryon.

Pisgah. The mountain, or mountaintop, east of the north end of the Dead Sea, from which Moses viewed the Land of Promise.

Pitcairn Island. The island in the south Pacific settled by the mutineers from the *Bounty* in 1790.

Plantagenet, the. King John, who was of the House of Plantagenet. *See also* Magna Charta.

"Play the man, Master Ridley!" The words of Hugh Latimer to Nicholas Ridley as they walked toward the stake in Oxford where they were burned to death. "Be of good comfort, Master Ridley, and play the man; we shall this day light such a candle by God's grace in England as (I trust) shall never be put out."

Pliny (the younger), Caius Plinius Cæcilias Secundus (*c* A.D. 61–113). Latin prose author.

Plutarch (*c* A.D. 46–120). Greek biographer and moralist; author, *Parallel Lives.*

Poictiers (Poitiers). A village in France where, in 1356, the English, under the Black Prince, defeated the much greater forces of the French who were led by King John.

Pons asinorum (Lat.) "Bridge of asses." A term given to the fifth proposition of the first book of Euclid because students have so much trouble getting over it. A critical test of ability imposed upon the inexperienced or ignorant.

Prætorian Guard. The Roman emperor's bodyguard, instituted by Augustus and consisting at first of nine and later of ten cohorts. This body came to have great power, making and unmaking emperors.

Price, Richard (1723–1791). English moral and political philosopher.

Priestley, Joseph (1733–1804). English chemist and nonconformist minister; author of many political tracts attacking his government's policy toward the American colonies.

Primogeniture, system of. The right of the eldest son, or eldest male relative, to take all the real estate of which the ancestor died seized and intestate, to the exclusion of all female and younger male descendants of equal degree. In England it is common for estates to be entailed so that the owner cannot, by will, change the line of succession.

Ptolemy, Claudius Ptolemæus, of Alexandria. Celebrated mathematician, geographer and astronomer of the second century A.D.; author of the ancient doctrine that the sun, planets and stars revolve around the earth.

Public domain. As regards land, that held in the name of the people by the United States Government, which it may sell or otherwise dispose of.

Quarter section. In the United States and Canada, a tract of land containing 160 acres.

Quesnay, François (1694–1774). French economist, once physician to the king. About 1750 he became acquainted with C. M. deGournay, and around these two men was formed the philosophic sect of the *Economistes* or *Physiocrates.* Its object was to exhibit by means of certain formulae the way in which the products of agriculture, considered to be the only source of wealth, would, in a state of perfect liberty, be distributed among the several classes of the community, and also to represent by other formulae the modes of distribution which take place under systems of governmental restraint and regulation, with the evil results arising from such violations of the natural order.

Rack-rent. An excessive or unreasonably high rent.

Ramayana. One of the two great epics of India which details the life and adventures of the hero, Ramachandra.

Reductio ad absurdum (Lat.). Reducing to the absurd. A method of proving a proposition by showing the absurdity of all of its alternatives, or of disproving it by showing the absurdity of its implications.

Ricardo, David (1772–1823). English economist who formulated the rent theory contributed earlier by Anderson and Petty. He was expert on the subjects of currency and banking. His chief work is *Principles of Political Economy.*

Rogers, Prof. James Edwin Thorold (1823–1890). English economist; author, *History of Agriculture and Prices in England, Six Centuries of Work and Wages,* etc.

Rohillas. A tribe of Afghan marauders who, in the early eighteenth century, conquered a district of Hindustan, giving it the name of Rohilkhand.

Roman peace. A peace imposed by the conqueror upon the conquered.

Rothschilds. A family of bankers who acquired an unexampled position from the magnitude of their financial transactions.

Rousseau, Jean Jacques (1712–1778). French philosopher; known for his views on education, tyranny and equality. His most famous work is *Social Contract;* his masterpiece, *Confessions.*

Ryot. In India, a peasant or cultivator of the soil.

Saer and daer stock tenancy. Two forms of tenancy under early Irish law. Under the saer (free tenant) form, the tenant might hire stock animals from the "flaith" (chief or noble) without surety and without impairing his status in the community. Under the daer (bond tenant) form, stock was borrowed under onerous conditions which degraded the tenant.

St. Gothard (Gotthard) tunnel. A famous railway tunnel, nine miles long, under an Alpine pass.

Savonarola, Girolamo (1452–1498). Famous Italian monk and reformer who was excommunicated, tortured and hanged.

Seeley, Sir John Robert (1834–1895). English essayist and historian.

She and the Shoo. A reference to the two most ancient books of China, the Shu Ching *(Canon of History)* and the Shih Ching *(Canon of Odes).* The Chinese emperor referred to is Shih Huang Ti (246 B.C.), by whose order the ancient books of China were burned.

Sievès, Emmanuel-Joseph (1748–1836). French abbé and statesman; one of the chief theorists of the revolutionary and Napoleonic eras.

Silver, demonetization of. With a number of other nations, the United States for a time endeavored to maintain convertible currency based on both gold and silver specie, with the relative value of the two metals established by statute. The system had created difficulties and had in effect been suspended in the United States as early as the first half of the nineteenth century. During the Civil War, the federal government had issued large amounts of paper currency not redeemable in either gold or silver. Between 1873 and 1879, a number of acts were passed looking to the resumption of specie payments; that is to say, to the restoration of the right to receive from the treasury a fixed amount of a specified metal in exchange for a paper bill. Earlier moves away from the free coinage of silver and the use of silver coins as legal tender were confirmed and strengthened by this series of acts, and by 1879 currency was again redeemable in gold. Members of Congress from the silver-producing states and states with heavily mortgaged farms dubbed this policy the "Crime of 1873," and the phrase was used by them to explain each of the economic depressions that followed.

Smith, Adam (1723–1790). Famous British economist. He taught logic and moral philosophy at Glasgow University and later took up the study of the science of political economy. His *Wealth of Nations* established the Classical School in the English-speaking world.

Social Statics. See Spencer, Herbert.

Solon ("*Lawgiver*") (c 638–c 588 B.C.). Athenian statesman whose law encouraging trade and manufacture laid the foundation of the commercial greatness of Athens.

Spencer, Herbert (1820–1903). English philosopher, founder of the system to which he gave the name "synthetic philosophy." Author of many works, including *Social Statics.*

Sphinx of Fate, riddle of the. According to legend, the Sphinx of Thebes proposed to all passers-by this riddle: What animal walks on four legs in the morning, two legs in the afternoon, three legs at night? Upon their failure to answer the riddle correctly, the Sphinx devoured them. Finally, Oedipus answered correctly, upon which the Sphinx destroyed itself.

Staël, Anne Louise Germaine de Holstein, Baronne de (1766–1817). French authoress and leader in society; famous for her coterie.

Stanfords. A wealthy American family. Leland Stanford, capitalist and politician, was the first president of the Central Pacific Railroad. He gave the Leland Stanford Junior University to California, with an endowment of about $20,000,000.

Stewart. Text reference is probably to Alexander Turney Stewart (1803–1876), an Irish-born American drygoods merchant and capitalist who amassed great wealth.

Stoic Emperor. Marcus Aurelius. The quotation is from his *Meditations.*

Stuarts (Stewart, Steuart). Members of the royal family of Scotland, some of whom ascended the throne of England.

Surajah Dowlah (Siraj-ud-Daula). Nawab of Bengal who ordered 146 English prisoners thrown into the Black Hole of Calcutta in 1756. Heat and lack of air killed 123 of them within a few hours. He was defeated by Clive at Plassey in 1757.

Sutro tunnel. A tunnel, named for its promoter, Adolph Sutro, built at Virginia City, connecting with and draining the mines of the Comstock Lode.

Suzerain. A feudal lord.

Swetchine, Madame Anne Sophie Soymonof (1782–1857). Russian mystic who settled in Paris after 1815 and there maintained a salon famous for its high courtesy, intellectual brilliance and religious atmosphere.

Swift, Jonathan (1667–1745). British satirist. Author of many works, including *Gulliver's Travels* and *A Modest Proposal for Preventing the Children of Poor People from being a Burden to their Parents or the Country.*

Taine, Hippolyte Adolphe (1828–1893). French critic and historian.

Tamerlane's (Timur) pyramid of skulls. Two pyramidal towers constructed by Tamerlane (1336–1405) with the skulls of his enemies slain during the battle of Takrit, cemented together with clay from the River Tigris. Upon the foundation stones he inscribed, "Behold the fate of lawless men and evildoers."

Tenancy-at-will. A tenancy which either landlord or tenant may terminate at any moment by the mere expression of the wish.

Teutonic mark. Common land. *See* Ditmarsh mark for one example.

Thermopylæ, Pass of. A Greek pass leading from Locris into Thessaly; famous for its heroic defense by the Spartan king, Leonidas, and his 300 soldiers, against the Persian army of Xerxes advancing on Greece in 480 B.C.

Third Estate. The common people. Clergy comprised the First Estate; nobles, the Second. A turning point in French history was reached when the Third Estate one day failed to remain bareheaded in the presence of the king.

Thornton, William Thomas (1813–1880). British writer. Secretary for public works in the India Office; author, *Overpopulation and its Remedy,* etc.

Titus, Flavius Sabinus Vespasianus (A.D. 40–81). Roman emperor who besieged Jerusalem and then captured it by attacking from the north, where the wall had not been completed.

Tocqueville, Alexis Charles Henri Maurice Clérel, Comte de (1805–1859). French statesman and political writer, famous for his report on his travels through the new United States.

Townsend, Rev. Joseph (1739–1816). Popular preacher, traveler and author, best known for his *Dissertation on the Poor Laws,* an important pamphlet in the poor law controversy of the eighteenth century.

Truce of God. An attempt of the church in the Middle Ages to alleviate the evils of private warfare.

Turgot, Anne Robert Jacques, Baron de Laune (1727–1781). French statesman, political economist and financier; student of Quesnay and one of the Physiocratic school. As the intendant of Limoges and controller-general of finance, he planned many beneficial reforms aimed toward abolishing feudal privileges, shifting taxes to fall on all classes equitably, securing liberty of trade and establishing a comprehensive system of public instruction. However, he was so bitterly opposed by the clergy and nobility that he was dismissed by the king in May, 1776.

Tweed, William Marcy (1823–1878). American politician; leader of the infamous "Tweed Ring," a group of politicians who robbed the city of New York of many millions. Tweed held several public offices; died in prison.

Ulster tenant right. A check, imposed by custom in Ulster and elsewhere in Ireland upon the arbitrary raising of rent when the tenant's term had expired.

Vanderbilt. An American family founded by Cornelius Vanderbilt (1794–1877). He amassed a great fortune by acquiring the controlling interests in many railroads and consolidating them into a single line, New York to Buffalo.

Vanity Fair. In Bunyan's *Pilgrim's Progress,* a year-long fair held in the town of Vanity. Hence, the world as a place where vanity and ostentation prevail.

Veda. The most ancient sacred literature of the Hindus.

Vere de Vere, Lady Clara. The typical cold, haughty aristocrat who is the subject of a poem by Tennyson.

Vested rights. Those rights which have become complete and consummated.

Villeinage (villenage). A condition of serfdom among the peasantry during the Middle Ages. The serf was his lord's slave, but was free in his legal relations with all others. Villeins appear to have had no rights as regards the lord except the right to his protection against their being maimed or killed. They could be sold or removed from the land at his will.

Vincent de Paul (1576–1660). French Roman Catholic reformer; later canonized. Founder of the Sisters of Charity.

Vishnu. The second god of the Hindu Trimurti.

Voltaire, François Marie Arouet de (1694–1778). French philosopher and author.

Wade, Benjamin Franklin (1800–1878). American statesman; member of the Senate from 1851 to 1869, first as an antislavery Whig and later as a Republican.

Wagner. The text reference is probably to Moritz Wagner (1813–1887), German traveler, naturalist and geographer, who wrote on evolution.

Walker, Prof. Amasa (1799–1875). American economist; author of a popular textbook, *The Science of Wealth;* father of Francis Amasa Walker.

Walker, Francis Amasa (1840–1897). American soldier, economist and author. He so effectively combated the old theory of the "wage fund" as to lead to its abandonment or material modification by American students. He was also an advocate of international bimetallism.

Wallace, Alfred Russel (1823–1913). British naturalist and author.

Wayland, Francis (1796–1865). American educator; advocate of temperance and of the abolition of slavery.

Wesley, John (1703–1791). English divine; founder of Methodism.

West, Sir Edward (1783–1828). English writer on economics; author, *Essay on the Application of Capital to Land*.

Westminster, Dukes of. The title was bestowed in 1831 upon Robert Grosvenor. Their lands include, today, some of the most fashionable sections of the West End of London.

Winkelried's bosom. Arnold von Winkelried, Swiss patriot, is said to have decided the Swiss victory at Sempach in 1386 by rushing toward the Austrians and grasping all the spears he could reach, burying them in his breast, thus making an opening in the enemy ranks into which the Swiss rushed, over his dead body.

Young, Arthur (1741–1820). English agriculturist and writer on agricultural economy.

Zemindars (zamindars). In countries under Mohammedan rule they were collectors of land taxes. Through extortions they became landowners.

Zend Avesta. The sacred Zoroastrian writings of ancient Persia.

INDEX